'So you want to be a writer? This guide is a fine p[...] is virtually nothing that is not covered—from reas[...] writing tips for the longhand practitioners and computer whiz-kids, right through to getting published, promoting your work, the rigours of writing and full lists of Australian publishers and agents.'
—Matt Condon, novelist and *Sun-Herald* Literary Editor

'This would have to be about the best aid for writers in Australia that I have come across in the past few years.'
—Fifty-Plus News

'The book is chock-full of useful info, from how to set out a nag letter to a magazine which has not yet printed an article as promised, to lists of literary websites. It's a very democratic and all-encompassing book, covering everything from self-publishing and writing family histories, to how to get hold of an agent to negotiate the best deal for your potential blockbuster.'
—Tracy Sorenson, *The City Hub*

'Throughout, Dunn writes in a jargon-free, easily understood manner that guarantees easy acceptance. This work will be a godsend for both writers' groups and writers' centres.'
—Elizabeth Dean, *Australian Book Review*

'*The Writer's Guide* is the book I've been looking for for months! Thanks for writing it.'
—Sylva MLR Cornejo (New Zealand)

'This is one of the most informative, well-presented guides I have ever used and very importantly it is giving Australian writers the vital information that is so necessary to their progress along the angst-ridden path to their final goal of being published.'
—Heather Yates, creative writing tutor

'I have set your excellent book, *The Writer's Guide*, as required reading in two units here at QUT [Queensland University of Technology].'
—Donna Lee Brien

'I enjoyed your book *The Writer's Guide* and I suspect it helped me get my book accepted by Wiley.'
—Rob Aalders

'As a writer and writing tutor I have found *The Writer's Guide* to be the best resource currently available in Australia ... it is a practical, reliable and essential resource for any writer.'
—Sharon Rundle, author

'Irina Dunn has left no stone unturned to make this guide as comprehensive as possible ... she is a realist, very well acquainted with her subject, and does not lead amateur writers into thinking they have an easy road to success ... she has managed to teach even this old dog some invaluable new tricks.'
—MCH, anonymous assessor for Writespot Publisher

'I have been recommending your book *The Writer's Guide* to many students and customers at Gleebooks. *The Writer's Guide* is one of the clearest and most commonsensical compendiums around.'
—Christopher Cyrill, author and bookseller

'You'll be happy to know that *The Writer's Guide* is one of the three books always by my side, overused. Your book is not only easy to understand and full of relevant information, it has added much value to a newbie in the writing and publishing industry like me. True, I have lots of other similar books, but I keep coming back to yours all the time.'
—Tellern Asiado

'Throughout my communications with the magazine editor, I kept referring to Irina's informative guidelines to stay focused on my goal—getting published. As a result, the story was accepted as the feature article.'
—Marie-Agnes Lo Cascio

'Your book is an encyclopaedia of information for writers! I'm finding it invaluable, and much better than the other books I have on the same subject.'
—Alice Hawkins

'*The Writer's Guide* was a huge help, a wonderful guide.'
—Tanya Dallas

IRINA DUNN has been the Executive Director of the NSW Writers' Centre since 1992. After obtaining an English Honours Degree at the University of Sydney, she worked variously as a tutor in the English Department at the University of Sydney, as a journalist, editor, film-maker, school and TAFE teacher, university lecturer, writer and arts administrator. She won a prize for the text *A Natural Legacy: Ecology in Australia*, which she co-wrote and co-edited with Harry Recher and Daniel Lunney, and received an international documentary prize for her film *Fighting for Peace*. She represented New South Wales as an independent senator from 1988 to 1990. In 1999, she received a Graduate Diploma in Russian from Macquarie University.

Irina was born in Shanghai, China, and is of Russian, Irish, Portuguese and Chinese background.

Being a writer is a vocation.
It's not about money or dreams . . .
it's like wanting to be a painter or a poet
— *Carmel Bird*

the writer's guide

a companion
  to writing for
pleasure or
  publication

IRINA DUNN

ALLEN&UNWIN

This edition published in 2002
First published in 1999

Copyright © Irina Dunn, 1999, 2002

All rights reserved. No part of this book may be reproduced or transmitted in any form or by any means, electronic or mechanical, including photocopying, recording or by any information storage and retrieval system, without prior permission in writing from the publisher. The *Australian Copyright Act 1968* (the Act) allows a maximum of one chapter or 10 per cent of this book, whichever is the greater, to be photocopied by any educational institution for its educational purposes provided that the educational institution (or body that administers it) has given a remuneration notice to Copyright Agency Limited (CAL) under the Act.

Allen & Unwin
83 Alexander Street
Crows Nest NSW 2065, Australia
Phone: (61 2) 8425 0100
Fax: (61 2) 9906 2218
Email: info@allenandunwin.com
Web: www.allenandunwin.com

National Library of Australia
Cataloguing-in-Publication entry:

Dunn, Irina.
   The writer's guide: a companion to writing for pleasure or publication.

   2nd ed.
   Bibliography.
   Includes index.
   ISBN 1 86508 832 3.

   1. Authorship—Australia—Handbooks, manuals, etc.
   2. English language—Writing. 3. Creative writing.
   4. Business writing. 5. Speechwriting. I. Title.

808.066

Front cover quote: From an interview with Kate Grenville in *Rooms of Their Own* by Jennifer Ellison, Penguin, 1986.
Internal design by Nada Backovic
Illustration on p. xvi by Michael Leunig is courtesy Leunig/*The Age*
Set in 11/13.5 pt Fairfield by DOCUPRO, Canberra
Printed in Australia by McPherson's Printing Group

10 9 8 7 6 5 4 3 2 1

CONTENTS

Preface to Second Edition xiii
Acknowledgments xiv
Introduction xvii

PART ONE   GETTING STARTED 1
1.1   Why write? 3
1.2   Write what? 5
    1.2.1   Functional, technical or creative writing 6
    1.2.2   Writing fact or fiction? 7
1.3   Writing for whom? 8
    1.3.1   Your ideal reader 8
    1.3.2   Writing for yourself 8
    1.3.3   Writing for others 9
1.4   The writing and publishing scene 10
    1.4.1   The impact of the internet 13
    1.4.2   The local book market 13

PART TWO   KINDS OF WRITING 17
2.1   Writing for the page 19
    2.1.1   Functional writing 19
        Reports, public relations material, copywriting, newsletters, commissioned publishing
    2.1.2   Non-fiction 23
        Journals and diaries, letters, community writing, family history, autobiography, memoirs, journalism and reportage, essays, reviews, biography
    2.1.3   Adult fiction 38
        Poetry, short stories, fiction (novels and novellas), tips for budding novelists
2.2   Writing for performance 47
    2.2.1   Writing for television and film 47
        Helpful organisations, screenwriting software

	2.2.2	Writing for the stage	50
	2.2.3	Writing radio drama	50
	2.2.4	Performance poetry and storytelling	52
2.3	Writing for children		52
	2.3.1	Shaping your project	53
	2.3.2	Getting to know the field	54
	2.3.3	Children's book illustration	56
2.4	Children and young writers		56
2.5	Internet and multimedia writing		57
	2.5.1	Zines	57
	2.5.2	Hyperfiction	58
	2.5.3	Multimedia	59

PART THREE   GETTING DOWN TO WRITING   61

Advice for beginners   63

3.1	Writing habits		64
	3.1.1	Tips for writers who use longhand	65
	3.1.2	Tips for writers who use typewriters	65
	3.1.3	Tips for writers who use word processors	65
3.2	Reading habits		66
3.3	Getting equipped		68
	3.3.1	The basic tools	68
	3.3.2	Why you need a computer	68
	3.3.3	What kind of computer?	70
	3.3.4	Computer printers	71
	3.3.5	Software	72
	3.3.6	Computer courses	74
	3.3.7	CD-ROMs and CD burners	75
	3.3.8	Internet	75
		Email, the World Wide Web (WWW)	
	3.3.9	The writer's library	78
	3.3.10	The green office	80
		The good old-fashioned fountain pen, paper, envelopes, postage, lighting and ventilation, exercise	
3.4	Gathering material		83
	3.4.1	Interview techniques	84
		Types of interview, interview tools, interview tips	
	3.4.2	Researching	86
3.5	Drafting and editing		88
	3.5.1	Self-editing	89

Structure, style, content, copy editing
	3.5.2	Getting editing practice	94
	3.5.3	Redrafting	94
	3.5.4	Editorial services	95
	3.5.5	Manuscript assessment services	96
3.6	Support and skill development		97
	3.6.1	Writers' centres	97
	3.6.2	Professional writing organisations	99
	3.6.3	Other writing organisations	99
	3.6.4	Writers' groups	100
	3.6.5	The Regional Writers' Network	102
	3.6.6	Starting your own reading group	103
	3.6.7	Courses and workshops	104

Courses at tertiary institutions, continuing and open education programs, workshops, seminars and short courses

	3.6.8	Mentorships	106
3.7	Performance skills		107
3.8	Translation skills		108
	3.8.1	Australian Institute of Interpreters and Translators (AUSIT)	109
	3.8.2	National Accreditation Authority for Translators and Interpreters (NAATI)	109
	3.8.3	Australian Literary Translators' Association (ALiTrA)	109
	3.8.4	Translation grants	110

PART FOUR   GETTING PUBLISHED   113

4.1	Researching your readers/audience/market		115
4.2	Finding suitable avenues for publication		116
	4.2.1	Periodicals	117

Choosing the right periodical, submitting material to periodicals

	4.2.2	Literary competitions	120
	4.2.3	Submitting book-length manuscripts	122

Finding the right publisher, international publishers

	4.2.4	Internet publishing	125

Internet publishing services, software, payment, marketing

4.3	The business of book publishing		128
	4.3.1	An overview of the industry	129
	4.3.2	The stages of publication	130
		Selecting material, the role of publishers' editors, design, pre-press, production, marketing, distribution and promotion	
4.4	Presenting your work		135
	4.4.1	Covering letter	135
	4.4.2	Title page or cover sheet	137
	4.4.3	Typing and formatting	139
	4.4.4	Binding and pagination	140
	4.4.5	Synopsis and contents page (for book-length manuscripts)	140
	4.4.6	Sample chapters and chapter outline (for book-length manuscripts)	140
	4.4.7	Return postage	141
	4.4.8	Records	141
	4.4.9	Multiple submissions	141
4.5	Children's book markets		142
	4.5.1	Trade or general publishers	142
	4.5.2	Educational publishers	143
	4.5.3	Tips for aspiring illustrators of children's books	144
4.6	Dealing with a magazine editor		145
	4.6.1	Reminder letter	146
4.7	Dealing with a book publisher		147
	4.7.1	Contracts	149
	4.7.2	Beware unscrupulous publishers!	150
	4.7.3	Rights	151
	4.7.4	Responsibilities	152
	4.7.5	Royalties and advances	152
	4.7.6	Copyright	153
	4.7.7	Protecting electronic rights	157
	4.7.8	Moral rights	158
	4.7.9	Plagiarism	160
	4.7.10	Permission fees	160
	4.7.11	Defamation and obscenity	162
4.8	The role of agents		162
	4.8.1	What can agents do for you?	163
	4.8.2	Are agents necessary?	164
	4.8.3	Looking for an agent?	165

		4.8.4	What does an agent charge?	166
		4.8.5	Finding an international agent	167
	4.9	DIY publishing or self-publishing		167
		4.9.1	Editing	169
		4.9.2	Parts of a book	169
			Half-title page, title page, imprint page, Cataloguing-in-Publication information, ISBN, ISSN	
		4.9.3	Design and layout	174
		4.9.4	Costing your book	174
		4.9.5	The cover	175
		4.9.6	Printers	176
		4.9.7	An unusual twist to self-publishing	177
		4.9.8	Distribution	177
		4.9.9	Legal deposit requirements	178
		4.9.10	Publicity and promotion	179
	4.10	Getting your script produced		180
		4.10.1	Film and television	180
			Professional help	
		4.10.2	Opportunities for playwrights	182
		4.10.3	Radio markets	184
			ABC Radio, community radio, approaching New Zealand radio producers	
	4.11	Surviving rejection		187

PART FIVE   PROMOTING YOUR BOOK — **189**

5.1	Working with a publicist	191
5.2	Your personal promotion strategy	192
5.3	Preparing for interviews	194
5.4	Your book launch	195
5.5	Your own website	195
5.6	On getting reviews and being reviewed	196
	5.6.1 Major review publications	198
	5.6.2 Reviews of self-published works	198
	5.6.3 Is a bad review better than no review?	199

PART SIX   WRITING AS A CAREER, OR 'DON'T GIVE UP YOUR DAY JOB' — **203**

6.1	Sources of income	205

	6.1.1	Income from books	205
		Royalties, advances, Public Lending Right Scheme, New Zealand Authors' Fund, Educational Lending Right Scheme, Copyright Agency Limited, Copyright Licensing Limited (NZ), backlists, options	
	6.1.2	Income from stage productions	215
	6.1.3	Income for screenwriters	215
	6.1.4	Payment to writers for writing-related work	215
	6.1.5	Employment opportunities	216
	6.1.6	Government literary grants and prizes	217
		The Australia Council for the Arts, State Government funding for literature, Creative New Zealand	
	6.1.7	Other prizes, grants and awards	220
	6.1.8	Residencies	224
	6.1.9	Awards, competitions, residencies and festivals for scriptwriters	225
6.2	Tax deductions and keeping records		226
	6.2.1	Writers' income	226
	6.2.2	Writers' expenses	227
	6.2.3	Averaging income	229
	6.2.4	Seeking help	230

POSTSCRIPT   **231**

PART SEVEN   RESOURCES   **235**

Agents	239
Assessment	243
Bibliography	255
Children and youth	271
Children's book publishers	285
Festivals and events	294
Legal deposit libraries	303
Literary websites	307
Search engines	315
Magazines and journals	316
Organisations	331
Poetry publishers	353
Publicity questionnaire (Allen & Unwin)	358
Recommended rates for writers	361
Index	366

PREFACE TO SECOND EDITION

I am delighted that the first edition of *The Writer's Guide* has proven to be so useful to its 4000 readers, as the testimonials on pages i–ii show. Thank you for your interest and feedback.

This edition has been revised to take into account recent developments in e-publishing and computer software, while the reference section has been completely updated. I have also added the contact details of many short-film festivals around Australia because they considerably expand the opportunities for new screenwriters and their production teams to submit their works for consideration either in competition or just for exposure to an audience.

Let me stress here my firm belief that you cannot become a good writer unless you are a good reader. Other writers, both living and dead, will show you ways of using words you have not thought of, and, if you are attentive to their style, tone, voice and other characteristics while you read you will learn much and your own writing will inevitably improve as you experiment with your craft.

Once again, I offer this second edition as a practical guide to developing your writing skills in whatever field of writing you wish to pursue. Although writing and reading skills seem to be under threat in the internet age, the book is far from dead. There is a unique pleasure and stimulation to be had from the printed page as you read the words of a good writer or communicate your own thoughts to your readers. No other human activity can leap the barriers of time and space as writing and reading can to bring you into contact with other cultures and other worlds.

Irina Dunn
July 2002

ACKNOWLEDGMENTS

Producing such a book as this, especially when it attempts to cover both Australia and New Zealand, requires the assistance of many people with research, advice, editing and data entry.

For their editorial comments on the manuscript I would like to acknowledge: Jackie Yowell (Allen & Unwin), Michael Wilding (Chair, NSW Writers' Centre), Lynne Spender (former Executive Director, Australian Society of Authors), Laurel Cohn (former Office Manager, NSW Writers' Centre), Graham Bassett (former Management Committee member, NSW Writers' Centre), Libby Gleeson (children's book author), Patti Miller (author), Marisa Cano (community writing tutor), Barbara Mobbs (literary agent), Robin Appleton (freelance editor and trainer), Frank Moorhouse (author), Pat Woolley (Fast Books) and Brenda Lee (Romance Writers' Association). For research and data entry I would like to thank Therese Waters, Glenn Phillips and Karolina Ristevski.

Thanks for encouragement and support are due to my colleagues, some of whom have now moved on: Marian Devitt (Northern Territory Writers' Centre), Chris McKenzie (Victorian Writers' Centre), Barbara McFadyen (South Australian Writers' Centre), Susan Hayes (State Literature Officer, Western Australia), Hilary Beaton (Queensland Writers' Centre) and Anne-Maree Britton (ACT Writers' Centre).

Many individuals and organisations in both Australia and New Zealand were very patient with my numerous requests for information: they include Rosemary Wildblood, Lavina Monteiro and Katie Abbott (Creative New Zealand), Margaret Brookes (Department of Communications and the Arts), Jenny Jones and Diane Brown (New Zealand Society of Authors), Sally Gallagher (Children's Literature Association of New Zealand), Ian McDonald (Australian Copyright

Acknowledgments

Council), Frances Kinnaird (New Zealand Books in Print), Lee-Anne Donnolley (Australian National Playwrights' Centre), Amanda Lawrence (Asialink), Judith Rodriguez and Barbara McGilvray (Australian Literary Translators' Association), Louise Gough (Playlab), Priscilla Yates (Australian Writers' Guild), Dan Byrnes and other members of the New England Writers' Centre, Heather Murray (Association of New Zealand Literature), Barbara Murison (Wellington Children's Book Association), Fergus Barrowman (Sport Literary Magazine), Bill Sewell (New Zealand Books), Elizabeth Alley (Radio New Zealand), Jim Beatson (Community Broadcasting Association of Australia), Chris Gallagher (Australian Script Centre), Nicola Bryden (Australian Institute of Interpreters and Translators), Kathryn Burnett (New Zealand Writers' Guild), Louise Easter and Philip Tew (Canterbury Public Library), Kerry Buchan (Wordstruck Festival), Wendy Harrex (Book Publishers' Association of New Zealand), Karen Ross (New Zealand Book Council), Sylvia Carr (National Library of Australia), Jenny Keestra (New Zealand Children's Book Foundation), Bob Hoffman (Australian Online Bookshop), John Barr (Booksellers New Zealand), Fiona Winning (Playworks), Lauris Edmond (Peppercorn Press), David Bateman (publisher), Keith Binnington (Writer's Bookcase), Barbara Brooks (biographer), John McDavitt (Playmarket), Michael McGennan (internet writer), Ron Burton (freelance copywriter) and Chris Price (Landfall). Also, a very special thanks to Professor Craig Peterson of Xyber Computing Services.

Every effort has been made to ensure the accuracy of the contents at the time of printing. If you have any comments on the book, any corrections of this edition, or suggestions for the next edition, I would be very glad to hear from you. Please send amendments, suggestions and/or additions to:

Irina Dunn
Executive Director
NSW Writers' Centre
PO Box 1056
Rozelle NSW 2039 Australia
Phone: (02) 9555 9757
Fax: (02) 9818 1327
Email: nswwc@ozemail.com.au
Website: www.nswwriterscentre.org.au

INTRODUCTION

If you wish to take up writing it is probably because you have a passionate yearning to use the medium of words to express your personal thoughts and feelings, or to record your impressions and observations of the world around you.

Once you experience a strong desire to write, it is a simple matter to begin. All you need do is pick up a pen and write down on a sheet of paper what is on your mind or in your heart. The rewards are there almost immediately. You can look at the page and read what you have written. You may be delighted with what you see, you may not, but at least you have started down the road in pursuit of an activity that is one of the most worthwhile and interesting that human beings can engage in.

Why? Because words can create something meaningful and real out of the human repository of intangible feelings and thoughts.

It is a thrilling and liberating experience to realise that you have the power to fashion a whole imaginary world from the building blocks of language, a world which you can enjoy in solitude or share with others.

Many people take great pleasure in creating a written work which they intend never to show anyone else because this gives them an outlet for their creative impulse, or acts as a therapeutic remedy for an unhappy or hectic life. As Socrates said, the unexamined life is not worth living, and so, through language and words, people have the means to analyse their own lives and the lives of those around them. This is an exercise in self-expression or, as T.S. Eliot put it so aptly, 'a raid on the inarticulate', which can help writers understand not only their society and the world in which they live but also their own response to it which, until expressed in words, was embryonic, unformed, inchoate.

> 'I often feel that I find everything is so senseless, and I think that's why I write. You write to find out what you think about things.'
>
> Helen Hodgman interviewed by Nikki Barrowclough, *Good Weekend, Sydney Morning Herald*, 4 May 1996.

Staring at a piece of blank paper wondering what to say and how to say it can be a discomfiting experience, but an even more frustrating experience is to read your own words and realise that they don't adequately capture what you really want to express. This should not be a cause for despair but the stimulus to develop the craft of writing to a stage where you are pleased with the result. The urge to write, coupled with an active imagination, an inquiring mind and a willingness to persevere, will bring great satisfaction to those who wish to pursue any kind of writing, whether fiction or non-fiction.

Developing your skills as a writer will certainly require discipline to practise your craft regularly, but you can also seek feedback from fellow writers; attend courses, workshops and seminars; participate in readings; study and analyse the works of other writers; and discover and understand how the world of publishing operates. Constructive criticism of your writing will help you hone your skills, and the assurance you gain from this, together with the development of your own distinctive voice, will make it easier for you to improve your written expression and find your particular readers.

> 'Writing has been my saviour. It makes me use my hand, my brain. It calms my nerves. I love to be among papers and pencils and books, it makes me happy and healthy.'
>
> Elisa Tabernaberri quoted in 'The Therapeutical Benefits of Writing', *Ambitious Friends*, vol. 4, no. 1, Autumn 1997.

To survive, you will need determination and persistence to pursue your craft, especially if you want to see your work published. Try to be realistic about what you can achieve, develop a thick skin when it comes to rejections, and don't take such setbacks personally. Remember that rejection is rarely based on quality alone, but is as much a factor of market trends and other arbitrary matters over which the individual writer has no control.

The establishment of writers' centres in every state has been a boon for both aspiring and established writers. New South Wales is also blessed with eight regional writers' centres catering for local writers and readers. As resource and information organisations, writers' centres are a one-stop shop for writers wishing to find out about the whole enterprise of writing. All produce regular newsletters and magazines packed with useful information and conduct a range of fascinating courses and workshops, as well as holding literary events such as readings and book launches. The NSW Writers' Centre also holds four literary festivals each year: the Autumn Writing Festival in early March, the Popular Writing Festival in early July, and the Carnivale Literary Festival in mid-October, which is held in conjunction with the centre's annual Australian Publishers' Book Show. Writers' centre staff can advise you on any and every aspect of writing and publishing, from information about seminars, festivals, literary competitions, editors, manuscript assessors and literary agents to the most suitable publishing outlets for your particular kind of writing.

Aspiring writers who join writers' centres can avoid many of the mistakes likely to be made when they work in isolation. In my ten years as Director of the NSW Writers' Centre I have watched many hopeful writers tentatively commence their writing careers full of trepidation and timidity only to find that within months, after sustained efforts at improving their craft, they have developed the confidence to read their work in front of others, to submit material to journals and newspapers, and even to self-publish their own books. Moreover, they discover in writers' centres a community of like-minded people who understand their passion for writing and can support them in their efforts. Writers come from all walks of life and from many different backgrounds, and at writers' centres you will have the opportunity to exchange ideas with people you would not usually meet in your normal circle of friends and acquaintances. Discussion, dialogue and debate are part of a writer's life and can lead to fresh ways of viewing, and writing about, the world as well as introducing you to new and stimulating friends.

Let me encourage you to make use of the great opportunities that writers' centres provide and to offer you a warm welcome to the wonderful world of writing.

PART ONE
GETTING STARTED

1.1 WHY WRITE?

'Why do you want to write?' This is a fitting question with which to begin a book whose aim is to encourage and excite you to write, because your first task as a writer is to look inwards and to clarify your reasons for writing. Ask yourself the following questions as an introductory exercise, and see what you come up with in your own mind. Your answers will help you find a purpose, and to understand your own motivation, for writing.

> 'Writers, actors and artists
> youse call yerselfs
> actors, writers and artists
> I know youse for what youse are
> prostitutes, pimps and pooftahs
> and the police has been called for.'
>
> From the poem 'Miss Porteous Stops the Party', Barrett Reid.

Do you want to write

- to understand yourself/others/the world around you?
- to tell stories?
- to inform and instruct?
- to record?
- to create a new world with all the powers of language?
- to rally readers to a cause?
- to express yourself in a way that can't otherwise be satisfied except by words on the page or screen?

Are you writing

- for personal pleasure?
- as a form of relaxation or amusement, a way of passing the time equivalent to doing a crossword?
- because it is a professional requirement of your job?
- for the pleasure of appearing in print?
- to communicate your thoughts to a reader?
- perhaps even to earn money?

Or do you want to write, as Danish writer Karen Blixen (aka Isak Dinesen) did, because she didn't know what else to do?

Most writers pursue writing for some or all of the reasons given above, while others simply say, without explanation, 'I write because I have to write'. Such writers have a compulsion, a deep need that must be gratified irrespective of whether the outcome is published or not, although most would prefer to be published in some form because they want to share their thoughts with other human beings.

Whether or not your work is intended for publication, there are many good reasons to write.

Writing is an inexpensive pastime, requiring no more than pen and paper to begin with. With these tools, you can do it anywhere. It stimulates your imagination and keeps your brain active. It allows you to articulate your thoughts and to express your ideas, wishes and fears. It helps you to understand how humans communicate and to be more aware of the abuse of language in advertising and politics and other areas where words are deliberately manipulated to deceive, dupe or cajole their audience or readers.

Writing offers as its tools the entire lexicon of the English (or indeed any other) language, an extraordinary range of old and new words, expressions, phrases, slang, colloquialisms and neologisms out of which to construct an article, a short story, a poem, a novel, a script, a biography or a memoir.

Having opened this book, you most likely enjoy writing, the act of creating a sequence of words to describe a personal experience or a character you've met, to argue a point, or even to fashion an entire fictional world. You may, when you were young, have written short stories or poems for your classmates or siblings to delight in, and you probably did well in class compositions on those topics all children are asked to write about — the family holidays at Christmas, a trip to the beach, the person you most admire.

You may keep a journal or write short stories or poems. Perhaps you practise your skills by writing letters to the editors of newspapers. You could even have finished the first draft of the great Australian or New Zealand novel which is tucked away in the bottom drawer awaiting the light of day.

> 'To write passably well is, in general, to say with simplicity what one has to say, being able to read it over a week later, a year later, and still find it valid.'
>
> Nettie Palmer, *Talking it Over*, Sydney, 1932, p. 146.

You may be a young person looking for avenues to express your thoughts and feelings about the world. Perhaps you are already working in the communications field and dream of moving across to creative writing. You may be a writing tutor who wishes to improve both your teaching and your writing skills, or you could be at home wanting a creative outlet while caring for young children, or retired and looking for an interesting pursuit. Whatever your situation, writing offers a pleasurable, stimulating and inexpensive occupation that can be carried out solo in your own time, in your own home, and at your own pace.

Women who have retired from work and been relieved of their family responsibilities often take to writing like ducks to water. They join writers' centres, enter literary competitions and submit poems and short stories to magazines and journals and have considerable success, judging by the congratulations pages of writers' centre newsletters. Australian novelists Elizabeth Jolley and Patricia Shaw both commenced their publishing careers in their 50s.

Perhaps you now want to take the next step and are ready to devote considerable time to honing your skills in preparation for publication of some sort. This is a courageous decision, because surrendering your writing to the gaze of others can be an act of exposure of your most intimate thoughts and feelings. It may open you to criticism, it may cause you embarrassment, and it is a lonely occupation spending hours in front of a computer, but if you're determined to begin, this book will help you on your way.

> 'I'm not a girl — I'm a woman. I want things. Shall I ever have them? To write all the morning and then to get lunch over quickly and to write again in the afternoon & have supper and one cigarette together and then to be alone again until bedtime...'
>
> Katherine Mansfield, (eds. Vincent O'Sullivan and Margaret Scott), *The Collected Letters of Katherine Mansfield, 1903–1917*, vol. 1, Oxford, 1984, p. 177.

Like all artforms, writing is a craft and takes practice. The sooner you start, the sooner you will become more proficient in choosing your words and arranging them on the page in a way that best expresses what you have to say. It's not easy, but the effort is immensely rewarding.

1.2   WRITE WHAT?

Having answered the question 'Why do I want to write?' to your own satisfaction, your next question may be 'What do I want to write?' Do you want to write functional material such as newsletters or reports, or are you more interested in what is called 'creative writing', that is, poems, short stories or even a novel? Do you wish to write fact or fiction, or some hybrid form combining both?

1.2.1 Functional, technical or creative writing

All writing is creative to some degree. The organisation of words on the page, for whatever purpose, requires skill and creative effort to be successful. This applies to every kind of writing, whether functional (reports, assessments), technical (manuals, scientific papers), reference (handbooks, field guides), or pure fantasy. The need to order material appropriately, decide on the correct language for the subject, and make choices about what to emphasise, are creative techniques that apply to all forms of writing, so categories such as 'functional' and 'creative' are not necessarily mutually exclusive.

Journalists know well that a string of facts is not enough in itself to make an article. They need to interpret, explain or put a 'spin' on the raw material by isolating the most dramatic or quirky detail, even if it is trivial in relation to the entire story, and placing that in the lead paragraph to catch the attention of their readers. Similarly, a travel article in which you provide information as well as colour about a destination requires both functional writing in the presentation of essential information as well as a creative effort in your selection of material and your description of locations. You will inevitably include practical information for travellers, such as different kinds of accommodation, restaurants to visit, or tourist traps to avoid, but you can also use your creativity in describing historical and cultural sites of significance and other items that may interest your readers.

Writing to a strict brief and for a particular purpose can also be a creative exercise, as in the case of copywriting, which is aimed at selling particular products and services. Freelance copywriter Ron Burton emphasises the creative aspects of the genre when he says: 'Advertising copywriters are the writers who conjure up and manip-

> 'It's a queer thing how craft comes into writing. I mean down to details. Par example. In Miss Brill I chose not only the length of every sentence, but even the sound of every sentence. I chose the rise and fall of every paragraph to fit her, and to fit her on that day at that very moment. After I'd written it I read it aloud — numbers of times — just as one would play over a musical composition — trying to get nearer and nearer and nearer to the expression of Miss Brill — until it fitted her.'
>
> Katherine Mansfield, *The Letters of Katherine Mansfield*, vol. 2, London, 1928, p. 88.

ulate words, thoughts and images in order to create persuasive advertising. With the right words and images, a good copywriter can make even a boring bathroom cleanser appear to be the most exciting and desirable product in the world!' ('Copywriting', brochure, Qld, 1998.)

In the same way, a good novelist can, with the right words and images, enliven even the most boring character in the world. Remember the ingratiating Uriah Heep, a very tedious sort of character but nonetheless one of Charles Dickens' great creations?

1.2.2   Writing fact or fiction?

The delineation between fact and fiction is not always clear-cut. Much of what passes as factual writing, such as scientific papers or journalism, actually requires a fair amount of interpretation, synthesis, analysis, and projection or prediction. While some might argue that interpretation and the like are not qualities of fiction, they do exercise a writer's experience, intellect and imagination, all of which fiction writers also draw on for their work.

Some writers, such as Helen Garner, now write in a hybrid form of journalism using the techniques of both fact and fiction promoted by such practitioners of the 'New' or 'gonzo' Journalism as Tom Wolfe, Truman Capote, Norman Mailer, Hunter S. Thompson and other American writers of the 1960s and 1970s. This technique allows the journalist to skilfully blend straight reportage with some of the techniques of fiction to create an interesting new genre which has now found great popularity with the reading public.

Conversely, fiction writers often research factual material as a basis for their imaginary creation. Thomas Keneally's novel about the Jewish Holocaust, *Schindler's List*, is based on interviews with Jewish survivors sheltered by a German industrialist in Nazi Germany. The chairman of the Booker Prize Committee, which awarded the prize to Keneally in 1982, commented on the work: 'It seemed to me that the artistic and literary element lies in the structure of the book — in the way in which the author has put together the testimony and evidence he collected *and the sequence in which he chooses to release the facts*' [my emphasis]. In this respect, the novelist's enterprise is the same as the journalist's —

the selective release of information in an order intended to achieve the maximum impact for that piece of writing.

1.3 WRITING FOR WHOM?

1.3.1 Your ideal reader

Who is your ideal reader? It may be family or friends, your business colleagues, the members of your organisation, a particular section of the general reading public such as gardeners, anonymous surfers on the net, or the novel-consuming public. Whoever they are, your work will be better received by your readers if, while you are writing, you keep in mind their needs, interests, level of sophistication and expectations. And, with your readership in mind, you will be much better prepared to tackle the task of writing.

> 'If there was no-one left in the world, I'd keep writing and painting — for the ghosts, for whoever comes next.'
>
> Keri Hulme, *New Zealand Herstory 1984*, Auckland, 1983, p. 4.

1.3.2 Writing for yourself

If you are a beginner you may, at least initially, wish to write only for yourself until you develop some confidence in the medium. Even if you are writing for yourself alone you may also begin to realise that you need help in structuring your work, in polishing and refining it, in developing it to a point where you are satisfied that its form and content truly reflect what you are trying to achieve.

See Part 3.5 for information on 'Drafting and editing'

Your personal writing can take any form you choose in your desire to experiment with the medium. Whether you decide to jot down your impressions of people or incidents in a diary or journal, or write letters to imaginary figures, you will get a buzz from seeing the results of your first efforts on the page.

See Part 2.1.2 for information on writing journals, diaries and letters

It is always a good idea to take care in recording details likely to be forgotten in the future. You may find when reading your own writing in years to come that the offhand reference, the initials you used instead of a name, the unsourced quote you thought you'd always remember, may come to haunt you with their unfamiliarity.

1.3.3 Writing for others

Writing for a readership imposes certain disciplines on the writer, such as the need to be intelligible and interesting, the need to order your material in a cogent and consistent way, and the need for clarity of expression in your choice of words and phrases. With practice, this discipline helps you learn how to craft your writing to suit your target audience.

Your audience may not always be strangers. You may have family, friends, professional colleagues or a community group in mind when writing your family history, a memoir, a report or newsletter, or a piece to be read at a community gathering. On the other hand, you may want to write for as broad a readership as possible, as is the case if you aim to publish your work commercially, whether it be as journalism, fiction, biography, reviews or a reference work.

If you are writing with a particular readership in mind, even for a small circle of family and friends, there are certain things you will have to take into account such as your readers' interests, the background knowledge you can safely assume in your intended audience, the content of your material, the 'spin' you put on it, the tone of your voice, the length of the piece, and the way in which it is presented. There is plenty of assistance available, from writing manuals to correspondence courses, from writers' centres to workshop groups. All are there to provide structured or

> 'The idea that you can just write for yourself and not worry about getting it out there is a myth. Writing is a public, not a private act, even if what's being talked about is private. The Pre-Raphaelite image of a young woman writing at a desk with a pencil in her lips and her eyes pointing skywards tells us, that even in her most private, and innermost personal thoughts, there is an "Addressed" even if only that to which it is addressed is the fleeting "flight-of-fancy" of a young woman. A writer always addresses the addressed even if it is done with the lips-shut and the eyes bleeding-out mountains of tears in the manner of a Roy Liechtenstein.'
>
> Π.O., 'Private or public writing', Write On, vol. 10, no. 2, March 1999.

See Part 3.6 for information on 'Support and skill development'

informal support, guidance and advice for the developing writer.

1.4 THE WRITING AND PUBLISHING SCENE

It is said that everyone has at least one book in them, at least one story to tell, at least one important piece of information or advice to impart. Anyone with basic literacy skills can write and be taught to improve their writing, and almost everyone will derive satisfaction from this activity.

Certainly, it is clear from the burgeoning of writers' centres and literary organisations, festivals, competitions, awards and readings in recent years that there is an increasing interest in both writing and reading.

Some bestselling writers are fêted the world over and are making handsome earnings from sales of their books and associated products, while the advent of desktop publishing programs has dramatically expanded the number of small publications taking contributions from aspiring writers as well as the number of books being self-published.

Never before have so many books been published and, oddly enough in this context, never before have so many been pulped. On 7 July 1997, the *New York Times* reported: 'In a watershed year for the business of books the publishing industry is struggling with record-breaking returns of unsold copies, a steady decline in adult trade sales and a shelf-life for new titles that has compressed to somewhere between radicchio and active culture yoghurt.' In the rush to capture readers who can now select from a wide range of entertainment options, international publishers are gambling on making huge returns from selected authors in the high-risk world of book production — and often failing.

In the late 1990s mergers transformed the world of publishing. The takeover, in mid-1998, of Random House by the world's largest English-language publisher, the German company Bertelsmann, sent shivers down the spines of many smaller publishers who feared they would be pushed out of the main game by the trend toward global, commercial and homogenised publishing. In Australia, this resulted in the Bertelsmann-owned Transworld merging with Random House to become Random House Australia.

In January 2002, the *Weekly Book Newsletter*, which services the Australian book trade, announced that Pearson PLC's two publishing companies in Australia, Pearson Education Australia and Penguin Books Australia, were merging into a single company to be known as Pearson Australia, which would have more than 600 staff and annual sales of more than $250 million. The former CEO of Penguin, Peter Field, who was appointed to head the newly formed company, stressed that the new enlarged company would 'offer more together to colleagues, authors and customers than we could as separate units within Pearson'. He commented that the 'combined company will be one that prizes the strengths of Penguin and Pearson Education; its people, its brands, reputations and styles. Customers and authors, our most important partners, will benefit from the increased reach in service, support and creativity of the combined talents of Penguin and Pearson people'. Anticipating concern in the industry, he noted that 'we will be using scale where it makes sense, and thinking small where we should individualise'.

In contrast to the Pearson/Penguin merger, a large company may retain the name and the disposition of a smaller company it acquires, which then becomes an 'imprint' of the larger publishing company. For example, Picador, which specialises in adult fiction, is an imprint of Pan Macmillan. Some of the larger publishing houses have a multitude of imprints. For example, Viking, McPhee Gribble, Puffin, Ladybird Books, Signet and Hamish Hamilton are just some of the publishing imprints owned by Penguin.

> 'Multinationals like Pearsons paid large sums of money for small publishers run in the traditional style by bespectacled boffins who knew their business and ran them well. They were swamped by corporate culture and were expected to deliver unrealistic profit levels. More and more books were published to feed the beast and generate more cash.'
>
> Former Reed publisher Jennifer Byrne quoted by Sally Loane in 'Publish and be drowned', *Sydney Morning Herald*, 22 November 1997.

Authors are concerned that in the new globalised market they will find fewer avenues for publication since many publishers have become concentrated under fewer roofs. In Australia and New

Zealand the decline in the number of major independent publishers compounds the perennial difficulty of getting international attention for local authors in a competitive international scene. As *Sydney Morning Herald* journalist Susan Wyndham noted (13–14 April 2002), 'But in a tightening market, there are more authors, especially those whose books are likely to sell only a few thousand copies, who won't be published, at least by the major houses . . . the push is clearly towards further concentration: big publishers, big books.'

Responses are not all negative, however, and some of the smaller independent publishers, such as the American company Grove Atlantic, are welcoming the opportunities presented by the new publishing environment. Grove Atlantic's Morgan Entrekin says that, 'As the world becomes increasingly globalised, the more the world will need people with different kinds of stories to tell and different kinds of voices to tell them'. Director of Britain's Fourth Estate, Christopher Potter, says that the idea of an Australian genre of writing is not relevant and that 'It is the literariness that counts, whether you are writing about Australian themes or not' ('Independents' day' by Angela Bennie, Spectrum Books, *Sydney Morning Herald*, 4 July 1998). By contrast, Michael Heyward of Melbourne's Text Publishing believes that 'the internationalisation and mainstreaming' of the big publishers will prove to be a blessing for independent Australian publishers by helping to 'define the Australocentric nature of our publishing'.

The explosion of electronic communication has also had its impact on the book trade. In 1997 the international publishing industry was in crisis. In the United States, book sales were down 10 per cent on the previous year, their traditional market taken over by music, television and software companies, whose profits were up 20 per cent. When the profits of HarperCollins, the publishing arm of News Corporation, dived by more than 80 per cent, the company reduced its list of US and UK authors by two-thirds. Nonetheless, there were more than 25 000 publishers operating in the United States in the mid-1990s. Many were publishing small-run, niche market books, and were supported by a well-developed network of distributors experienced in promoting and selling such titles.

A similar situation has arisen in Australia, where there has been a considerable growth in smaller book and electronic publishers. The NSW Writers' Centre has run an Australian Publishers' Book Show since 1999 specifically for the smaller independent

Getting Started

Australian-owned publishers, some of whom have only a few titles on their lists. Others are specialist publishers, such as theatre publisher Currency Press, poetry publisher Five Islands Press, Aboriginal books publisher Magabala Books, feminist books publisher Spinifex, and companies like Brandl & Schlesinger and Indra with lists of quality fiction and non-fiction, as well as the university presses. The NSW Writers' Centre now has a list of about 350 such publishers on its database.

1.4.1 The impact of the internet

The arrival of the internet has exponentially enlarged potential readerships with easy access to global electronic bookstores such as the US-based Amazon online bookstore, whose sales in 1997 rose by 87 per cent to reveal the huge number of readers using the net. Mind you, it was not until late 2001 that it first posted a profit. Another site helps you locate the book you want at the best possible price by searching 25 net bookshops for you. For readers of classical literature, the Project Gutenberg site now offers 5000 electronic texts for readers to download or read on the screen. The Australian Project Gutenberg site offers both Australian and international texts.

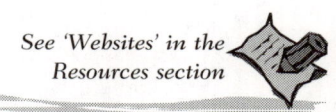

See 'Websites' in the Resources section

At the same time, public writing sites have made it possible for anybody to be read on the net at one of the many net addresses dedicated to this purpose. For example, the websites www.geocities.com and www.communicationgame.com allow you to create your own website gratis and post your own writing to that site.

See Part 2.5 'Internet and multimedia writing' for a discussion of writing for digital media, and Part 4.2.4 'Internet publishing'

Although the net will open up many new opportunities for writers, this new medium also carries its own problems, especially those relating to copyright protection and remuneration for writers.

1.4.2 The local book market

The Australian and New Zealand publishing industries have been affected by competition from the new technologies, and some

13

companies have lost book sales and market share. Nonetheless, a study conducted into the Australian publishing industry in 1999–2000 by the Australian Bureau of Statistics reveals a healthy local market. The industry published 9755 new Australian titles, of which 8669 were originated by Australian publishers. Australian titles comprised 61 per cent of total book sales and 65 per cent of educational book sales. In all, 77.3 million Australian books sold for $684.9 million for an overall average price of $8.90 per book. The total number of books sold in 1999–2000 represents an increase of 13 per cent on figures released in 1997–1998. Combined with a 2 per cent increase in the average price of books (owing in part to the introduction of the GST), this means that the total value of book sales by publishers was 16 per cent above that of 1997–1998. Export sales of books rose 46 per cent between 1997–1998 and 1999–2000, almost double the sales reached in 1995–1996.

Similar figures are not available for New Zealand.

The book market has become much tighter and publishers are now less likely to take risks. Increasingly they are conducting market research to see what kinds of titles are popular with their readers and which ones are most profitable, dropping those which the bookshops return unsold, even if the writer is well-known.

Publishers receive hundreds and sometimes thousands of manuscripts each year for consideration. By far the majority of these are unsolicited, that is, they are works which the publisher has not asked for and which have been sent by authors on the off-chance that they will interest the publisher. Although most publishers are loath to deal with these unsolicited manuscripts, they are, nonetheless, always on the look-out for work of quality and work which will fill a niche in the publishing market.

> 'It's true to say that the rate of publication has decreased in recent years but if a work has sufficient worth it will be taken up. That has always been the case. It is largely a case of finding the right publisher for a particular work.'
>
> Scholastic publisher Alf Mappin interviewed in *New Writers' News*, February 1998.

> 'Language, talk to me, language
> teach me what to say
> in the face of disaster,
> in the height of hope,
> as things fall away.
> Mother-tongue, lingua franca,
> all that anyone knows,
> bring me, kindly bring me
> to a perfect close.'
>
> From 'Language talk to me', Evan Lloyd Jones.

Sending an unsolicited manuscript to a publisher will be the first attempt by many writers to get their work between the covers of a book. The percentage of such manuscripts that reach publication, however, is tiny. This is for many reasons, but perhaps the main consideration of the publisher is whether the work will fit into that company's 'list', the range of titles that the publisher specialises in. Thus even a manuscript of high quality may be rejected because it is unsuitable for that publisher's list. Although receiving a rejection letter is a painful experience for any writer, it should be regarded as just one step in the process. Swallow the hurt and send the manuscript out again, or put it aside for a while and then have another look at it to see if you can improve it.

> 'There are no good books or bad ones, only ones that sell and those that don't.'
>
> Brian Clouston quoted by Don Drummond in 'A logistical triumph,' *Australian Bookseller and Publisher* Jan/Feb 2002.

See Part 4.11 'Surviving rejection'

Prospective authors will be more favourably considered if they have some kind of publishing record, usually a history of publication of short fiction and non-fiction pieces in magazines, newspapers and other periodicals, and perhaps even a record of success in writing competitions. This indicates a serious intention to write on the part of new authors, and gives publishers some confidence that novice writers have a professional approach to their craft.

See Part 4.2.1 for further information about periodicals and Part 4.2.2 for information about literary competitions

15

PART TWO
KINDS OF WRITING

2.1 WRITING FOR THE PAGE

If you know what you want to write about, but not how you want to express it, consider the various forms of writing in deciding which is most suitable for you, whether it's stage or radio plays, essays or articles, biography, reviews, short stories, poetry or travel writing.

Although you may write well in a number of genres, you will probably eventually start specialising in a particular form of writing as the one you do best. A close study of different kinds of writing will help you discover which is most appropriate for what you want to say, and experimenting with different forms will help you determine which one most suits your style of writing.

Many of the traditional categories have become hybrids to produce new or resuscitated forms such as the fact-based novel, the fictional memoir and the verse novel. Feel free to experiment in your writing style — who knows, you may be the inventor of a new hybrid which takes the literary world by storm!

The following categories are only a selection of some of the forms of writing available to you. To get an idea of how writers have tackled each of these, consult your local library for examples of writing in the various genres.

2.1.1 Functional writing

Few people in any kind of job can escape the necessity of occasionally having to produce pieces of 'functional' writing, that is, writing which has a direct purpose, usually to inform or instruct or report on something. This kind of writing creates its own rules for the writer to adhere to, rules based on the purpose of the writing and the most effective way to communicate that purpose.

Reports

Report writing is taught as part of communications courses at colleges and universities for good reasons. Most of us will have to write at least one report in our lifetime, and some people spend many if not most of their working hours collecting material for reports, then writing and editing them, and perhaps even desktop-publishing them.

Because reports are written primarily to convey particular information about a subject, their contents should be presented as logically and clearly as possible, with a structure that usually includes some or all of the following:

- title
- abstract or synopsis
- executive summary
- introduction
- statement of aims or purpose
- data analysis or examination of material
- discussion
- conclusion(s)
- proposals for action, recommendations
- bibliography or references.

Reports are generally written in an objective way, in the third person, with the analysis presented in unambiguous language. The content is best organised into a hierarchy of headings and sub-headings. The use of section and paragraph numbering and other formatting devices will assist in clarifying the 'argument' of the report and conveying its message.

There are many different kinds of reports and each has its own format and content. For example, annual reports are intended to convey information about the financial and operational progress of an organisation or company over a specified period, usually the preceding financial year. They generally include reports from key personnel in the organisation, usually the Chair, the Treasurer and the Executive Officer, as well as presenting financial information as tables or pie-charts. There are also progress reports, minutes (reports of a meeting), research reports, marketing reports, academic essays, and so on. There are many useful publications that describe the format of different kinds of reports and suggest examples of the types of layout of each report.

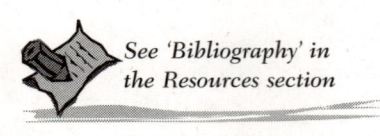

See 'Bibliography' in the Resources section

Try drafting an outline of your report in point form before you start writing it. This will help you arrange your material in the best order for your subject. Although report writers have a practical purpose in writing a report, they are as much responsible for the sequence in which they choose to release the facts as Thomas Keneally was when he wrote his novel *Schindler's List*.

Public relations material

Writing public relations material is something you may be required to do as part of your job, and it can be a daunting task when you face it for the first time. You may be asked to write about a product or your company's services, or to promote a particular campaign, or to raise money for your organisation.

The most common form of public relations material is the press release. Like a good news story, a press release will grab the reader's attention if written with an imaginative opening. Eye-catching headings, a clever turn of phrase and a succinct style will help convey your message. Think of the most important things you want to say and try arranging them in order of importance as headings. If you can think of a single word which encapsulates the content of a point, so much the better and, during this process, always keep in mind your intended audience and how they will respond to your material.

Copywriting

For writers who wish to make money out of their craft, advertising copywriting is probably the most lucrative of all the commercial genres.

Copywriting is highly paid and, on a word-for-word basis, probably exceeds even the highest rates paid to writers producing text to order, which in 2002 was about $1000 per 1000 words. Certainly income earned from this source exceeds the earnings of even top-selling authors, unless you are Bryce Courtenay, who has, by the way, a copywriting background.

See 'Bibliography' in the Resources section for the Copywriter's Companion

Copywriters in a major capital-city advertising agency may earn between $40 000 and $200 000 per annum and possibly more if they are very good at their work, while freelance copywriters could earn between $20 and $100 per hour and even $150 if they are talented.

In this consumer world there is always a need for advertisers to sell products, and so there will always be a need for copywriters. It is a specialised form of writing and, although there is some training available for those who wish to develop their skills in this area, the courses are often expensive. Charles Sturt University in Bathurst offers a Bachelor of Arts in Communications that includes modules on advertising, commercial radio, journalism (print and broadcast), public relations and organisational communication, and theatre media or online media production. The Academy of Photogenic Arts provides a course with a large component of television commercial production, and the Macleay College offers a public relations course. The APM Training Institute also offers courses in advertising, while the Australian College of Journalism has a correspondence course in Australian Public Relations, Publicity and Promotions.

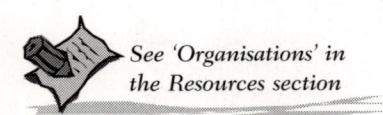

See 'Organisations' in the Resources section

Newsletters

Tens of thousands of newsletters circulate in societies such as Australia and New Zealand where freedom of communication is valued and utilised.

The principal purpose of a newsletter is to convey information to readers with a common interest, whether that be a childcare group, a bowling association, a particular place of employment, or a community organisation. As such, newsletters provide good training for writers learning to craft their work to appeal to a particular readership.

If you are contributing a piece to a newsletter, familiarise yourself with the style of the publication and the tone of other articles. Always check with the editor about word limits and whether illustrative or photographic material is desired.

The success of a newsletter depends largely on its editor, who also usually contributes written pieces. The difference between a newsletter which remains unopened in the recipient's in-tray or on the kitchen table of its intended reader and one which is eagerly opened on receipt lies in the presentation of material that is relevant, interesting and accessible.

If you are faced with the responsibility of producing a newsletter, take a critical look at the newsletters which pass across your desk and examine them for their style, content, layout and so on. Isolate which features you find attractive or useful and try to use these in your next publication.

Most newsletter editors have desktop-publishing skills and some training in layout and design as well as a natural flair for presenting information in an attractive way. If you want to brush up on your skills, some colleges offer short courses on editing small publications which provide tips on layout, design, editing, use of typefaces and other features of newsletters and small publications.

Commissioned publishing

Professional authors are sometimes commissioned by government bodies or private organisations to produce a book or other publication, such as a history, for that particular organisation. In these cases, the organisation provides a fairly specific brief, pays the author a fee to write the text according to the brief, and makes use of its own sales and distribution channels to promote and sell the work.

You may be required to surrender your copyright under such an arrangement, and this may not be such a bad thing since the commissioned piece may be too specific to the job to be published elsewhere. Ensure that the terms of your commission are clearly stated in a contract and do not rely on verbal agreements.

2.1.2 Non-fiction

Although fiction is the most popular form of writing for recreation, don't forget that, if your intention is to publish your work, adult non-fiction is by far the larger market of the two, with many more outlets for good non-fiction writing. Some of the more popular non-fiction genres are dealt with in this section.

Journals and diaries

Whether you intend to write for your own pleasure and satisfaction or to be published, keeping a diary or journal can be an exciting and practical way of kickstarting your writing career.

The great advantage of a journal is that you can carry it wherever you go. In it you can record new words and phrases you hear, ideas that cross your mind, snatches of overheard conversation, an outline of the next article you want to write, your impressions of an incident or character, an account of the day's events — in fact, anything at all. Later, in the solitude of your work space, you can consult your journal to remind yourself of what you wanted to write about, how you wanted to express it, and so on.

The diaries and journals of many writers have been published as books in their own right. One of my favourites is Annie Dillard's *Pilgrim at Tinker Creek*, which won her the Pulitzer Prize. In Australia, Kate Llewellyn has successfully published journals of her time living in the Blue Mountains, including *Waterlily: Blue Mountains Journal*, while in New Zealand, Neva Clarke McKenna published *Angel in God's Office — My Wartime Diaries*. A study of these and other books in the genre will introduce you to the possibilities of the journal or diary as a valuable method of developing your powers of observation and reflection.

Letters

How can you be guaranteed of at least one reader? Write a letter. Letters can amuse and instruct your family, friends and colleagues. Expressing yourself in this way can be a satisfying experience for both you and your reader if the content is well phrased and imaginatively conveys an incident, experience or mood.

When you are on the road (or in the air or on the sea) letters are an excellent way to start practising for travel articles or, indeed, even for fiction. Observations, incidents, reflections and historical notes are all components of both kinds of writing. Don't forget to keep copies of your letters to other people. You may find this useful when you are trying to piece together a correspondence later on.

The internet has opened up a whole new style of letter writing by email (electronic mail). No longer do your friends and family have to wait for your long-distance letters through the post, termed 'snailmail' by email users. They can read your letters within seconds of your writing them, and respond just as quickly. The same letter can even be emailed to many recipients, with or without a few adjustments to personalise it for individual readers. And email letters can be filed on computer disk, a handy saving on storage space and paper.

Community writing

Community writing is so called because it emerges from community groups which do not normally have opportunities to express their views in writing.

Community writing programs are generally aimed at specific sectors of the community — young people, migrants, the elderly — who may not consider themselves as writers but nonetheless have something to say.

If you are from a minority or marginal group in society, you may find a community organisation supporting a writing program to encourage you and your compatriots to develop your own voices and to express in words something of your experiences and impressions. Even if it is not published, the material produced by the group can be presented to an audience at readings, or displayed as an exhibition of writings hanging on the wall.

If you are a writing tutor or are interested in leading a community writing program, there are some important issues you should be aware of. As community writing groups are generally made up of people of different ages, backgrounds, levels of education, interests and needs, you must consider these differences when preparing the overall program and individual sessions.

If you are running a general writing workshop (as opposed to a workshop on a specific form such as articles, short story or autobiography), it is likely that participants will be interested in different genres. A program that touches on all types of writing will not only keep everybody happy, but may also encourage participants to have a go at genres they had never considered before. Thus community writing workshops often take on a multifaceted structure in order to cater for the needs of all the participants.

Furthermore, each session may combine tuition, practical exercises, a reading of participants' work and information sharing (on writing courses, organisations, literary events, etc.). In this way, both

> 'I want to tell you that this course offered me lots of fun and pleasure, and specially gave me more confidence to write in English. I felt so good, better than ever. It was like a new adventure for me. I was busy looking for rhyme and rhythm: poems eased the pain in my little soul, poems softened the lump in my throat, poems took the burden off my shoulders as my pen ran to catch up with my thoughts.'
>
> Elisa Tabernaberri quoted in 'The Therapeutical Benefits of Writing', *Ambitious Friends*, vol. 4, no. 1, Autumn 1997.

> 'I have seen people walk into my workshops like the world had lost its meaning to them, only to see them leave with a smile on their face and the signs of a load off their back. I have witnessed people coming in the first day and nervously telling me they could not write "a word" and would just stay "to listen if you don't mind", only to see them leave the last day with a portfolio crammed with writings and an anxious "when are the next workshops happening?" on their lips.'
>
> Marisa Cano, 'The Therapeutical Benefits of Writing', *Ambitious Friends*, vol. 4, no. 1, Autumn 1997.

> 'A few years ago I was going through a bad stage in my life, emotionally speaking. I felt depressed and afraid of everything. Then I took up writing, and my whole life and lifestyle changed. Today my best therapy is to write a poem. It is my way of coping with headaches and feelings of loneliness and longing for my family overseas, specially during the Christmas season.'
>
> Elisa Tabernaberri quoted in 'The Therapeutical Benefits of Writing', *Ambitious Friends*, vol. 4, no. 1, Autumn 1997.

beginners and more experienced writers have a chance to learn, practise their skills, receive public acknowledgment, get feedback on their work, and obtain useful information that may further their progress as writers.

As a community writing tutor, you will often find yourself trying to persuade people without much education or without skills in the dominant language that they can learn to express themselves in a new tongue. The results can be gratifying when an enthusiastic budding writer emerges from the process.

Writing as therapy

Community writing contains, as a significant sub-category, the literature of survivors and survival, stories of courage, endurance and perseverance under the most difficult conditions of migration, domestic violence, economic disadvantage, urban poverty and rural hardship, political oppression and censorship.

Such writings fulfil several distinct purposes. A major one is therapy, whereby the very act of writing, of expressing profound suffering, serves as a means of discharging anger and grief and of externalising painful experiences and converting them into a meaningful and coherent expression on the page (or screen).

Another purpose is to share the personal experiences, the stories omitted by the official histories, the stories that bind people to one another as they discover and take comfort in the fact that others are genuinely interested in finding out about their lives.

Family history

It may well be that your first introduction to writing is through your interest in the lives and experiences of your family and forebears. All families are interesting because all of them, to a greater or lesser extent, reflect the broader history of a country. Indeed, pioneering stories of early settlers have long been of historical value in countries like Australia and New Zealand, especially when the lives of particular families have influenced the development of the country. The details of their lives — what they wore, their homes and habits — provide wonderful insights into the social history of the times.

There are many useful guides on how to write a family history — what material to collect, where to go for genealogical research and how to conduct a good interview, among other things.

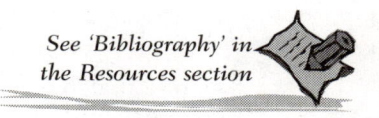

See 'Bibliography' in the Resources section

The most logical way to start your family history is to draw up your family tree, showing in graphic form as many relatives as you can remember from previous generations and the present members of your family and their relationships to one another. With this in hand, approach your family members to fill in the blanks and to derive further names and dates. This is a good time to have a reliable tape recorder handy as your relatives reminisce on family members long departed or not heard from for years.

Interviewing

Although it may seem odd to interview a family member, you could well be surprised at the material you're able to uncover in the more formal setting of a question-and-answer session. Before the interview, prepare some questions to elicit basic information that will provide the framework of your family history. Be prepared to listen (and record) with patience, even when your subject strays from the topic. This may lead to a revelation of some aspect of your family history long buried in the memory of your relative. Even if you are familiar with the material, it will help your interviewee to relax if you are an attentive listener.

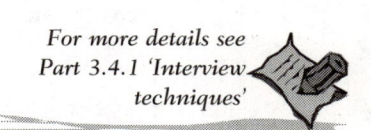

For more details see Part 3.4.1 'Interview techniques'

The Writer's Guide

Tapes

A word of advice about those cassette tapes. Don't leave them lying around for too long because they may get damaged. Although it is an arduous task, transcribe the tapes yourself as soon as possible after an interview (and this will help you remember what was said) or give them to a professional transcription service. Make sure the transcription is set out clearly on one side of the page only, with one and a half or double spacing and wide margins to allow you room to make notations and raise queries. You may wish to add your own notes at the end of a transcription to help jog your memory of the interview when you are ready to begin writing.

Research

It is rare that you will be able to fill in all the pieces of the puzzle of your family history just from talking to relatives and family friends. You will probably need to conduct further research by visiting libraries or writing to institutions overseas for copies of documents such as birth, wedding or migration certificates.

See Part 3.3.8 for further information on the internet and Part 3.4.2 for more information on researching

Most public libraries offer internet access, a useful tool for those researching their family history. There is much interesting genealogical material on the internet, such as information on how to begin your family history, deciphering old handwriting, old disease names and their modern definitions, emigration statistics, and a raft of sites relating to particular countries. Remember to label your notes accurately with the source and date of your material.

At this point you may wish to revisit some of your interviewees to clarify matters they raised in their interview or to elicit further details on some point which puzzles you.

Shaping your material

Shaping your material into an interesting piece of work is the greatest challenge facing any writer, whether of fiction or non-fiction. With family histories, this may depend on whether you want to tell the story in simple historical terms, sticking to the facts in chronological order and writing in the third person, or whether you want to have a narrative presence in the story — that is, make your own voice heard as a narrator speaking from your individual perspective. If you are writing only for family members, you may allow yourself some private jokes, but if you are thinking of publication these will have to be explained to a general reader.

Family histories often begin with the oldest known generation and travel through time chronologically. For many people, this time span extends only to grandparents or great-grandparents. Although this is a useful way, at least initially, of ordering your material, don't feel you must stick with it if you think your family's story may be better recounted by beginning with another generation — say, the youngest — and working back in time. When you start writing, don't worry too much about the missing details but instead imagine you are filling in a jigsaw puzzle with pieces constructed from the anecdotes, dates and other known facts you have accumulated from your research and interviews.

If you really have command of your material, you may wish to switch back and forth, drawing parallels between family members from different generations to create a sort of mosaic effect, but remember that your reader must make sense of your story and may be confused by sudden jumps in time.

Writing a family history can be an exciting enterprise shared with your relatives and friends. With cheap desktop publishing now available, the production of a book of your family's history is a wonderful legacy to leave to your successors. Your local historical society or library may also be interested in retaining a copy for their records. Not only have you created a valuable personal and historical document, but you may also find you are stimulated to test your writing talents in other genres as a result of your first efforts in writing.

Autobiography

Many people begin their writing with autobiographical material, for obvious reasons: your own life is what you know best. Your memories and impressions, the characters you've met, family members, incidents, all these provide the substance of directly autobiographical work and they can also be woven into fictional material.

To get an idea of the possibilities of the genre, read as many autobiographies as you can to discover the many ways in which the

> 'Autobiography is one way of making sense in the maelstrom, a form that feeds the desire to know and say, and seems almost as natural as speech.'
>
> Morag Fraser, 'Our master's voice', *The Australian's Review of Books*, May 1998.

subject can be presented to readers. A fascinating life does not necessarily make fascinating reading, although it probably helps in maintaining reader interest. The crucial quality in autobiographical writing is the voice of the narrator. What holds reader interest in an autobiography is not so much the content, or even an elegant command of language, but the strength, individuality and character of the voice. Even a writer who uses language simply, such as Albert Facey (*A Fortunate Life*, Penguin 1985), has wide appeal because of his forthright, lively and often humorous voice.

> 'Autobiographical writing is not family history although it will almost certainly include some family history. Neither is it a litany of well-researched facts or a straightforward historical account; it is a personal journal of exploration, exciting and sometimes confronting.'
>
> Patti Miller, *Writing Your Life: A Journey of Discovery*, Allen & Unwin, Sydney 2001.

Vivid impressions, memories that tug on the heart, colourful characters, turning points in your life, family tensions — all these provide the material for your personal story, and it is how *you* arrange and describe it that will make it interesting for your readers. Don't feel constrained to organise your material chronologically. You could arrange it thematically, or begin in the present with flashbacks, or use some other technique such as highlighting major incidents in your life.

Many people write autobiography to heal a trauma in the family, or to provide a family record, or for social history, but if you are considering publishing your work, consider whether your story has wider appeal. Publishers are generally interested in an autobiography only if you are famous, or if you deal with a particular issue in an inspirational way, such as overcoming a handicap, or if you have an unusual or exciting story to tell.

See 'Bibliography' in the Resources section for D.W. Thorpe's *Australian Literary Awards and Fellowships* and Parts 6.1.6 and 6.1.7 for information about prizes, grants, fellowships and awards

Australians and New Zealanders are great readers of autobiography, especially tales of heroism and overcoming adversity, such as the first volume of successful farmer Sara Henderson's autobiography

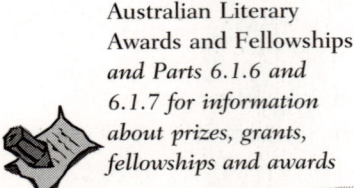

From Strength to Strength or Heather Heberley's *Weather Permitting*. Only one Australian literary award, the National Biography Award, is provided for biographical and autobiographical writing. The only designated prize for biography in New Zealand is the Montana New Zealand Book Award for Biography. The winner receives $5000 prize money and is eligible for the Montana Medal for an outstanding book of non-fiction and a further award of $10 000. There are no other awards specifically for biography, but most of the awards, particularly the National Library Fellowship, the University writers in residence and the Creative New Zealand Writers' Residency in Berlin (valued at up to $60 000) are open to biographers.

Memoirs

Memoirs have become a popular form of writing in the late twentieth century, with many celebrity authors rushing into print to reveal intimate aspects of their personal lives. Generally less complete than an autobiography, memoirs offer you the freedom to blend descriptions of your unique lived experience, social commentary, reflection, description, anecdotes, and observations about a particular period or aspect of your life and times. Thus personal revelation provides an insight into contemporary culture as well as presenting the mind of a unique and interesting individual.

Although the confessional memoir has a seedy past in its association with tabloid journalism, and literary critics may raise their eyebrows over the quality of much confessional writing, it is becoming increasingly acceptable in literary circles as a genre in its own right. Its popularity in the marketplace speaks for itself: readers are curious about the intimate details of other people's lives and will pay to read about them.

The scope of the memoir has been expanded by experiments in the use of fictional techniques. Practitioners of such

> 'We live in a culture where almost everyone has gone into tell-all overdrive, from Stuart Diver [the sole survivor of the Thredbo ski resort disaster] to the Duchess of York and her recent appearance with Oprah Winfrey. The distinction between the public and private spheres or the quality media and the tabloids is no longer sharp. Confession is a growth industry — but whether its products are as empty as its critics say is open to dispute.'
>
> Catharine Lumby, in 'Written Confessions', *Sydney Morning Herald*, 3 January 1998.

'creative non-fiction' transform the truth by using fictional techniques to present a greater truth. One example is Mandy Sayer's *Dreamtime Alice*, which carries a disclaimer that states 'fictional names and descriptive details have sometimes been used as literary devices'. This links her memoir to the 'creative non-fiction' literary movement in the United States.

The classification of a memoir as fiction or non-fiction can become a challenge for literary judges if it crosses certain clear-cut boundaries. Roger McDonald wrote a fictionalised account of his travels as a shearer's cook in *Shearers' Motel* (1992), which was entered in both the Miles Franklin Award for fiction and the Banjo Award for non-fiction. He was forced to withdraw it from the former, but it won the latter.

Similarly, literary judges could not find a niche for Bob Ellis's book *Goodbye Jerusalem*:

> I howled petulance when I heard my dusklit memoir of the Labor Party *Goodbye Jerusalem* had been entered as fiction in the Premier's Awards — and, even under that label, rightly rejected. Even thus, I suspect, *Schindler's List* would fail if entered under golfing nostalgia . . . I got very snaky at this. 'Why is there not a category,' I growled at a passing female judge, 'called radiated memoir? or autobiographical turbulence or annotated albums or tinted perspectives? One where Robert's [Dessaix's] book, [*Night Letters*] and mine . . . would fit,' he complained (*Sydney Morning Herald*, 23 August 1997).

Above all, memoirs must carry a strong sense of an individual voice to engage their readers. If you are inclined to tell all, and can do it with panache, verve, and a dash of literary imagination, then this could be the genre for you.

Journalism and reportage

If you want to work as a full-time newspaper journalist, and be paid for it, you will

---

'The power of well written English is tremendous, something that appears to be overlooked by many of those who are paid to write . . . the best writing will keep readers interested, by changing pace and voice, introducing new information and insights, providing aids to comprehension. The best writing will not leave the reader feeling that the information has been squeezed through a mincer removing shades of meaning and nuances, along with the fat and gristle.'

Julianne Schultz on journalism, 'Writing hinges on training', *Courier-Mail*, 10 April 1996.

probably need to demonstrate a deep interest in and knowledge of news and current events by presenting prospective employers with a substantial *curriculum vitae* listing published articles, reviews, interviews, and so on. If you are a university student, take the opportunity to write as much as you can for the student newspaper as this will later prove your long-standing commitment to the pursuit of journalism. You will also need to demonstrate highly developed communication skills, both oral and written. Although a degree is not essential, it helps to have a university qualification in economics, politics, communications or media studies.

One advertisement for trainee journalists for the *Sydney Morning Herald* stated: 'Ideal candidates must demonstrate excellence in all their work and be extremely well organised and energetic. They should be self-starters, be able to generate good story ideas and be able to work under pressure on several assignments within tight deadlines.' Applicants were required to submit 'a body of published work' with their application. This is a tall order, but if you have the right qualities, qualifications and experience, this could be a very rewarding and satisfying profession for you.

Numerous free local newspapers, entertainment magazines and gig guides welcome new writers and are prepared to give them a chance. The discipline of writing for a periodical is great practice for any writer, new or experienced. Although you may not be adequately remunerated (if at all) take the opportunity to contribute to such papers just to get the practice of meeting deadlines, writing copy to a word limit, and finding out about the process of newspaper and magazine production.

You have your choice of writing articles on topical subjects of your own choosing, or as the editor directs you, and if a paid journalist position becomes available on the publication, you may be first in line for consideration by the editor.

The NSW Writers' Centre offers brochures on both degree and non-degree courses in writing and journalism.

Feature articles

If your penchant is for non-fiction and you are not a full-time journalist, feature articles are a challenging and interesting way of developing your writing skills and having fun at the same time.

If you have expertise in a particular area of knowledge, there is likely to be a demand for what you have to say.

Articles can be instructional, informational ('how-to'), polemical, humorous, descriptive or observational. The potential topics are endless: current affairs, gardening, pets, computers, entertainment, political comment, social critique, interviews with interesting people, whatever takes your fancy. Keep in mind the requirements of the newspaper or magazine you are writing for when choosing your subject and style.

Articles are generally about 500 to 1500 words long, depending on the specifications of the particular publication. In popular publications, articles are written in a conversational style, usually on a topical theme. Specialist publications such as computer magazines require a different language, style and tone if you are addressing yourself to experts. Again, depending on the subject, you may choose to write an objective, factual article, or be more subjective and express a particular point of view. Pay some attention to the opening paragraph of your article: make it exciting enough to capture the reader's interest and hold it to the end of your piece.

There is a large market for well-written articles, because periodicals such as newspapers, journals and magazines need copy to fill their pages week after week, month after month. Articles suitable for celebrations — St Valentine's Day, Anzac Day, Mardi Gras — or other current events are sometimes sought by local press or magazines, so keep your eyes peeled.

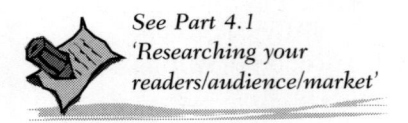

See Part 4.1 'Researching your readers/audience/market'

Travel writing

Newspaper offers of 'How to Make $35 000 a Year as a Freelance Travel Writer' attract the eye of those who have romantic (and probably unrealistic) ideas about combining work and travel. Of course, you will discover that before you can become a well-paid travel writer you must first learn the tricks of the trade. You can invest in a course or textbook that teaches the essentials, but one of the best preparations for becoming a good travel writer is to read widely from magazines, newspapers and books and analyse for yourself what makes an interesting travel article or book.

Keeping a notebook while travelling is, of course, essential if you want to remind yourself later of vivid sights and impressions. In it you can record your observations and notes about landscape, weather, interesting characters, local customs and dialects, food, hotels and shopping, signs, scraps of conversation, weather reports, shopping lists, quotes from local newspapers and other written material, phone numbers, and anything else you may be able to use for your article. These details will not in themselves make an interesting article, but they are the material from which you will draw when it comes to writing your first draft.

Some travel writers advise you not to get bogged down in the quotidian detail of your travels as these may not retain your reader's interest. Nor should you indulge in long purple passages of descriptive writing at the expense of interesting and useful facts. However, it is also true to say that the personal observations of the writer are sometimes exactly what makes the article interesting to the reader.

Essays

The essay flourished in England and America in the more leisurely period of the eighteenth and nineteenth centuries, and some readers will remember from their student days studying collections by masters of the form — Francis Bacon, Joseph Addison, Charles Lamb, William Hazlitt and Matthew Arnold, as well as twentieth-century writers such as Virginia Woolf and Katherine Mansfield.

> 'It is precisely within the accommodating confines of the essay that such latitude is available: ungoverned by formula, narrative or other protocol, the essay is a sort of living literary heresy and the cheerful vehicle of any and all heresy.'
>
> Brian Matthews, 'Red Herrings Inc.', *The Australian's Review of Books*, November 1997.

Essay writing is often associated with a literary period before the advent of television and other communications channels brought the world instantaneously into our living-rooms. With its reflective and thoughtful tone emanating from a personal voice, the essay allows its author to muse on any particular subject matter, to range across historical times, to develop a theme, or to meander along the byways of thought.

For many years, the essay was neglected in the face of increasing challenges from fiction. There has never been a major government award for essay writing in Australia and New Zealand, although there are competitions for essay writing which are listed in the newsletters of writers' centres when they occur.

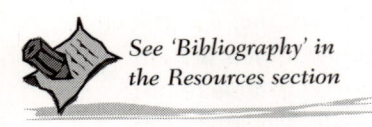

See 'Bibliography' in the Resources section

The form seems to be making a comeback with the publication of various collections, including Imre Salusinszky's *The Oxford Book of Australian Essays*, an historical selection which contains a range of nineteenth- and twentieth-century Australian essays, and Morag Fraser's *Seams of Light: Best Antipodean Essays*.

Interesting new directions in the essay allow the writer to experiment with a variety of genres: journalism, political and social analyses, autobiographical reflections, and literary and cultural criticism, among others.

If the essay form appeals to you and you would like to try your hand at it, read as many contemporary and historical collections as you can find to see how the form has been used by different writers and is currently developing.

Reviews

Writing reviews of plays, books and films, and other forms of entertainment is a practical way of developing your critical analysis and writing skills. The exercise of assessing a particular work, whether written or performed, in terms of its genre, dialogue, treatment of subject, characterisation, and so on will help you develop your own writing expertise as you learn to identify the common problems faced by novelists, poets, scriptwriters and writers of other forms.

There are many opportunities to publish your reviews if they are well-written, interesting to read, the right length, and they suit the style of a particular publication. Try give-away newspapers like *The City Hub* in Sydney or *Beat Magazine* in Melbourne or, if you are a student, the campus newspapers.

Not all publications can afford to pay reviewers, but you will probably receive free books or free tickets, and these offer at least some compensation for your efforts, not to mention the thrill of seeing your name in print in the by-line. This will also look good on your CV.

Biography

Writing the life story of another person is a great responsibility and requires hard work, discretion and analytical judgment. But above all, it requires the capacity to excite the reader with the quality of your writing and the way you treat your raw material. It is an ambitious project, one that could take several years of researching and interviewing, and many drafts of a manuscript.

> 'Translating a life into words is one of the most creative acts you can engage in — a virtual act of magic.'
>
> Patti Miller, *Writing Your Life: A Journey of Discovery*, Allen & Unwin, Sydney, 1994, p. 21.

Many of the comments made about family history also apply to biography, but there is one obvious major difference: because there is only one subject of a biography, the biographer is required to give considerably more detail in order to flesh out the story and give it some substance.

Your first question as a biographer is 'Am I sufficiently interested in or fascinated by my subject to "live" with her or him for several years?' If your answer is yes, then consider whether sufficient information is available about your subject to provide a good meaty biography. For this you may have to do some preliminary research.

If your subject is still living, you can, after asking permission to write the biography, ask him or her what material is available and get some idea of the people you could interview for additional information on, and impressions of, the subject. Of course, if your subject is opposed to your enterprise, as Germaine Greer was to that of her unauthorised biographer Christine Wallace, then your task becomes much more difficult. Greer was so hostile to Wallace's efforts that she denied her access to her papers and vilified her in the press, calling her a 'flesh-eating bacterium' among other names. The co-operation of your subject will make your task much easier, but the acquaintance of your subject may also make it more difficult for you to write a dispassionate account of their life.

> 'The writer of fiction knows, or at least can know, everything about his or her created characters. It is different for the biographer, who has in much the same way to make a person out of words, but who is bound by a contract with readers; the biographer's narrative must be about the facts of a life. It can't be made up. That is, it must not seem to be.'
>
> Chris Wallace-Crabbe 'The facts of a life', *The Australian's Review of Books*, September 1997.

If your subject is dead, you may have to get permission from surviving relatives to access papers held privately or in libraries. Be prepared to spend many hours sifting through documents, correspondence, newspaper articles and other material in your search to find the information you need to construct your biography.

Part of your research will be to read all kinds of biographies to determine what structure to give your work, what themes to emphasise, what material to use, and what to discard. You could also contact published biographers whose books you admire and ask them how they approached their work, the difficulties they faced and how they overcame them.

Biography and related genres are becoming increasingly popular on the bookshelves. Of the 200 titles published by Allen & Unwin in 2001, 7–8 per cent were in this category, while they made up 10 per cent of Pan Macmillan's 2001 list. The biennial National Biography Award, with prize money in 2002 of $12 500, has done much to focus attention on this interesting genre.

2.1.3 Adult fiction

The most popular form of writing is adult fiction, which embraces poetry, short stories and novels. These three forms offer writers an opportunity to exercise their creative imagination and produce a work entirely of their own making, a world of words in which every image, character, incident and impression is fashioned by the writer. Although a fictional world may have little or no relationship to the real world, the writer wants, by fictional means, to express some deeper truth about the world that he or she feels intuitively.

Poetry

People write poetry because they enjoy using words to create something that is unique and individual and expresses their thoughts, feelings and impressions. A poem is a more manageable size than, say, a novel, and there is a huge range of forms to experiment with, from the traditional 14-line sonnet to bush verse to contempo-

> 'Poetry [is] the artistically controlled expression of feelings, the embodiment of a truth, created for its own sake . . .'
>
> Poet Robert Gray, 'Chronicle of a death', *The Australian's Review of Books*, August 1997.

Kinds of Writing

rary blank verse (without a rhyme), from humorous forms such as the limerick to the lengthy epic. Just for practice, try your hand at writing in one of the established forms such as the sonnet — you may be surprised at the results.

As you will discover, poetry not only offers considerable scope for imaginative self-expression but also provides a discipline in the use of rhyme, rhythm, conciseness of expression, and imagery. It can be rewarding to compose a poem for a loved one on the occasion of a special event or recite one of your own amusing verses at a gathering of family or friends. A well-crafted poem may even win you a heart on St Valentine's Day!

One of the best ways of developing your poetic craft is to read, read, read, as many poets as you can, both contemporary and classic, from Australia, New Zealand, and abroad. Read aloud the poetry of others in the quiet of your study or office: this is a marvellous way of really hearing what they have to say, and how they say it. In university and public libraries, as well as on the internet, you can find recordings of great poets, such as T.S. Eliot, reading their own works, as well as videotaped interviews with poets discussing their poetry. Poets usually feature at writers' festivals, too, and are pleased to answer questions about their writing methods, sources of inspiration, and the intricacies of their craft.

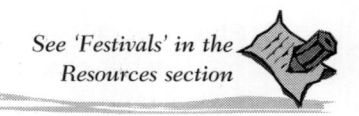

See 'Websites' in the Resources section for poetry websites

See 'Festivals' in the Resources section

Poetry intended for publication may well be a finely reworked draft of poems you wrote for yourself and now wish to share with the world. Before submitting your work to a publisher, show your poems to friends, relatives and colleagues, and get their comments. This could give you some ideas of what to change to make your poetry more accessible, more interesting, better structured and better expressed.

See Part 3.6.4 'Writers' groups'

A.J. Rochester, a Sydney performance poet who asked her colleagues to critique one of her poems, went on to win a performance competition with the amended version of her poem which had been 'worked over' by the group.

Although poetry is more difficult to edit than prose, try your hand at it by playing around with words, rhythm, line lengths and different images to see whether you can improve what you have written. If you have a friend who also writes poetry, try editing your friend's work and offer yours for the same scrutiny. This can be a productive exercise.

Poetry outlets

Few book publishers in Australia and New Zealand are interested in publishing poetry. Despite the large numbers of people writing poetry, the market for poetry books is tiny and so the competition to publish a volume of poems is fierce. To achieve this, a poet must first have published many individual poems in periodicals or won prizes in literary competitions.

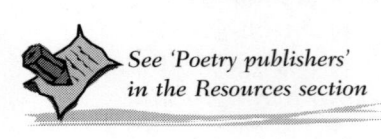

See 'Poetry publishers' in the Resources section

Numerous literary competitions are run each year in both Australia and New Zealand and are advertised in the magazines of writers' centres. Some of these offer publication of the winning and commended entries as part of the prize. By writing on a particular theme with a specified word length, as well as to a deadline, you will achieve the discipline you need to improve your craft. Although the prize money is usually small, the satisfaction of receiving a place or a commendation with a certificate will boost your morale and encourage you in your work. It is important to follow the rules of entry; if you don't, your entry may well be disqualified before it is even read.

See Part 4.2.2 'Literary competitions'

Most literary magazines accept poetry, but remember that they are of varying quality and reputation. Many do not pay cash for contributions but instead offer copies of the publication. Such magazines are not usually available in newsagents, but writers' centres offer members access to their libraries where you can view a variety of literary magazines to see if your material suits their style and content before you submit it to the editor. Some non-literary magazines and newspapers also publish poetry.

See 'Magazines and journals' in the Resources section and the marketing guides listed in the 'Bibliography'

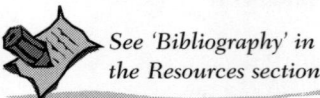

A useful reference is the *2000 Australian Poetry Catalogue*. This contains the names of Australian poetry publishers and

See 'Bibliography' in the Resources section

Kinds of Writing

their current poetry lists, as well as information about poetry magazines and journals, poetry organisations and prizes. The NSW Writers' Centre publishes the *Journals Directory*, which lists many Australian poetry outlets.

There are poets' organisations you can join, including the Sydney-based Poets Union, the Melbourne Poets, the New Zealand Poetry Society and the Australian Bush Poets Association, all of which produce newsletters with material of specific interest to poets, including information about readings, competitions and poetry publishers.

See 'Organisations' in the Resources section

Readings

From the earliest pioneering days, poetry recitals have been popular pastimes, engaging the interest of audiences around the campfire to the more contemporary venues of pubs, clubs, bookshops and art galleries.

A great way of testing your poems to see if they 'work' is to find one of the many reading venues springing up in both metropolitan and regional cities. These offer the opportunity to read your work in front of an audience and get instantaneous feedback from their responses. Many venues welcome new poets and, if you are shy at first, you will quickly overcome your timidity with practice and perseverance. And even if at first you don't want to read, just attending such venues and listening to other poets will not only be entertaining and instructive but may result in valuable friendships and contacts with whom you can discuss matters poetic. Writers' centres list upcoming readings in their newsletters.

> 'Poetry does everything better than prose . . . There are great prose writers, but a superb poet can make language sing and scrape along your nerves. And hit you between the eyes or between the legs. There's nothing a great poet can't do . . . The irony of poetry, and perhaps its revenge, is that it has a much longer shelf life than prose. Prose dates very, very quickly. A good poem can have a shelf life of thousands of years. You'll get more out of poetry.'
>
> Dorothy Porter, 'Pop goes the poet', *Sydney Morning Herald*, 23 March 1996.

See Part 2.2.4 'Performance poetry' and Part 3.7 'Performance skills'

41

Short stories

Short stories are an excellent way to begin writing fiction. Selfcontained, they are a manageable length for the novice. They allow a wide range of possibilities, from the straight yarn of a Henry Lawson, to a tale with a twist in the ending, to a mood piece or a character sketch.

Short story writers face the same difficulties as poets in finding a publisher. Although the large commercial publishers are not keen to publish collections of short stories except by well-known writers, or on topical themes they think will sell to a general market, there are other outlets for short story writers.

Many literary and popular magazines publish short fiction and regularly call for submissions. Some even pay! Take note, however, that a literary quarterly which publishes three stories per issue can publish only about twelve stories per annum. Some magazines even run competitions for their readers as a way of choosing submissions. Study these publications for their style before forwarding your work.

Other outlets for short stories are the many competitions run by writing groups and other organisations. Often the competitions are on a particular theme and request entries of a particular length. The discipline of following these conditions and meeting a deadline gives you a specific goal to work towards and, of course, the thrill of winning a place or being commended will spur you on to better efforts. It will also add to your publishing résumé — a must if you want to be taken seriously as a writer. The best way of finding out about competitions is to join a writers' centre to receive a regular

---

> 'You can do practically anything in a short story. You can write stories that are like poems, with the emphasis on mood, on meditation, on perception — like Anna Kavan or Katherine Mansfield. Or you can write stories that are all narrative, all plot — like the classics of O. Henry. And the Argentinian writer Jorge Luis Borges showed that you could write stories that were like Encyclopaedia entries . . . It is this potential for variety, this utter plasticity or flexibility of form, that makes the story so attractive. You can do so many things with it.'
>
> Michael Wilding, 'Writing Short Stories', address to the Society of Women Writers at the NSW Writers' Centre, March 1997.

See 'Magazines' in the Resources section and the 'Bibliography' for Australian Writer's Marketplace, the NSW Writers' Centre's Journals Directory and other marketing guides

See 'Organisations' in the Resources section

newsletter with details of the many competitions run throughout Australia, New Zealand and, occasionally, internationally.

When book publishers produce anthologies of short stories, it is usually on a particular theme, such as *The Picador Book of the Beach* (edited by Robert Drewe) and *Sisters* (edited by Drusilla Modjeska). For your story to be included in an anthology, either it will have been previously published in a journal or magazine or you will be invited by the editor to contribute.

Fiction (novels and novellas)

The production of a well-crafted novel remains the enduring aim of writers who want to take on the ultimate challenge of producing an entire fictional world of their own creation, its characters, settings, action, psychology, values and philosophy all originating in the imagination of the author, whether or not the book is based on real events. This is truly a noble enterprise, one which requires heroic stamina to see it through numerous drafts to eventual publication.

Often new writers commence their writing life by producing a novel or novella (a short novel) using the subject matter they know best — their own life experiences. So it is not surprising that the first novels of many fiction writers are loosely autobiographical in the sense that the authors have used their personal experience as a basis for fiction. James Joyce produced such a work, termed *bildungsroman*, in *A Portrait of the Artist as a Young Man*.

However, there are many other genres of fiction open to you, such as crime, romance, historical, popular, fantasy and science fiction. Read widely in your chosen genre and study its characteristics to gain proficiency.

Certain novel forms do not require the sustained effort of a lengthy, traditional type of novel. Some contemporary novels

> 'What I convince myself of through the marathon of writing a book, what impels me to slog through that lonely odyssey, is a belief that what I'm writing is necessary. As Thomas Keneally said in an interview: "The great thing, if you're a writer, is that you are perpetually taken by a concept which you believe the world needs — against all the evidence." You know that the world needs a solution for the ozone problem, the famine cycles, the Grand Uniting Theory in physics. And the world also needs the way your novel sees it . . .'
>
> 'Being a loser, as it were, an open memo from Sue Woolfe to Jane Palfreyman, Publisher Random House', 'Australian Writers World', *The Australian's Review of Books*, July 1997.

> 'You need a skin as thin as a cigarette paper to write a novel and the hide of an elephant to publish it.'
>
> Frank Dalby Davidson quoted in letter from Marie Davison to Stephen Murray-Smith, 23 June 1982.

consist of a series of shorter pieces of writing linked by a theme or a loose set of characters (and sometimes a set of loose characters!), or by some incidents which, taken together, constitute a narrative. This could be an easier form to tackle than the traditional form because it is like a series of connected short stories. An early exponent of this model in Australia, Frank Moorhouse, gave it the name of 'discontinuous narrative' in works such as *Futility and Other Animals*.

If you have begun your writing career in a big way with a novel, good for you. It is a mammoth task. It is important to remember, however, that very few first novels are published. The manuscript that may become your first published work is more likely to be your second or third attempt at a full-length novel. There are several reasons for this.

> 'I'm an incredibly slow and torturous writer, so nothing's easy for me to write. It nearly killed me. I found it very difficult, because when you are writing a first novel, you are working out how to write a novel.'
>
> Delia Falconer, quoted by Jane Freeman in the *Sydney Morning Herald*, 25 October 1997.

Firstly, many new writers underestimate the craft involved in writing a successful novel. The production of a readable and interesting novel, in all its complexity, is achievable usually only after years of writing practice, and requires not only a great command of the material but also an understanding of the possibilities of the genre. It is probably wise to begin with shorter forms of fiction until you have developed the skills to produce an extended work such as a novel. By all means start (and finish) that novel, but don't forget that in writing short pieces you can experiment with form and content and develop the craft of writing in other ways. Your novel will probably go through many revisions; only after you have mastered certain techniques should you feel ready to submit it to the critical eye of a publisher.

Secondly, publishers receive literally thousands of unsolicited novel manuscripts each year. They may not read them at all before returning them with a rejection letter, so a brilliant piece of work among these rejected manuscripts could easily go unnoticed. One

Kinds of Writing

publisher regularly employs a journalist to go through large piles of such manuscripts and, after years of such work, he has not yet found any that he thinks are of publishable standard. I can see him now, surrounded on the huge table by untidy heaps of manuscripts of which he reads just the first few pages before throwing them on the reject pile. Your manuscript is likely to be lost in this jumble unless your work is exceptionally good, or you are recommended by someone such as a literary agent, whose judgment the publisher trusts, or you have a very good publishing record and/or have won literary competitions.

See Part 4.8 'The role of agents' for further information about how an agent can help you

Thirdly, even if a publisher commends your manuscript you may still have difficulty getting it published because its subject, treatment and style are not what publishers are looking for. Australian and New Zealand publishers together release hundreds of new novels each year by established and developing writers. Their decisions are largely based on what they think the market wants — in other words, what they think will sell. They are now as subject to the same fads and fashions as any consumer industry; an example was the mid-1990s 'grunge' novel phase which shot several young Australian writers to prominence in a very short time. If your novel is not in the currently fashionable genre, it may have to wait until such time as the trend changes, or until your reputation is firmly established in other fields or forms of writing.

> 'It is the quality of a man's imagination, his sense of values and his powers of observation that make him a good writer, and he must have an adequate command of words to express himself. But the most brilliant ability to arrange words in new patterns, without these three things, will not make him good. The greatness of a novel depends on its content of humanity.'
>
> Martin a'Beckett Boyd, *Day of My Delight*, Melbourne, 1965.

There is a way of side-stepping these difficulties. There is only one major competition for unpublished novels in Australia (regrettably none in New Zealand) which guarantees publication for the winner. Often one or two of the shortlisted manuscripts from this competition, the Vogel Award for writers under thirty-five, are also published. But winning is not easy.

See Parts 6.1.6 and 6.1.7 for information about prizes, grants, fellowships and awards

The competition is ferocious and the winners will inevitably reflect the personal preferences of the judges.

Tips for budding novelists

> 'The art of the novel is to encapsulate a complete world which, by evoking subconscious sympathies, touches off the reader's deepest involvement — even while remaining plainly unreachable . . . The invented world is what allows the novel freedom to live as a work of art. And the checked facts are what induce the reader to believe in it . . . But one thing remains as true today as ever: a novel requires two creators — writer and reader — who together, as God-supplanters, collaborate in making a complete, imagined world.'
>
> Rodney Hall, 'New world order', *The Australian's Review of Books*, May 1997.

- Write about what you know, about something you have experienced — an interesting character, an amusing incident, an overheard conversation, a breathtaking scene. This way your written voice is likely to sound more genuine, more authentic.
- Make your story plausible, follow actions through and resolve transitory issues.
- Decide on the point of view — who's telling the story, which character is central?
- Become familiar with your characters and keep their names the same throughout your drafts.
- Maintain colour, mood and tension.
- Listen to how people use language and then practise writing dialogue.
- Choose language that suits the characters and the circumstances.
- Be sure that your descriptive passages do not overshadow the story.
- Read your work aloud, preferably into a tape recorder so that you can appreciate how your readers might respond. Mark passages to rework, and when the reworking is done record the reading again and see how your writing has improved.
- Keep notes and records of the sources of your information.
- Undertake adequate research if you are writing about people, things and places you know little about.

Make sure you don't . . .

- name characters and then misname them later in the work or change the spelling;

- clothe the characters in different outfits in the same scene;
- get vital details incorrect, such as where the shadow would fall at the time of the crime;
- leave the washing on the line for three months!

You wouldn't do that, would you?

2.2 WRITING FOR PERFORMANCE

Performance writing embraces many mediums: stage, film, television, radio. It is generally a collaborative effort in which the writer interacts with producer, director, editor and actor. If you are overly protective of your script then you may find this process quite unnerving as your colleagues make adjustments, cut or add dialogue, and in other ways change your precious original script. You will discover that your script is not sacrosanct, that others involved in the project want to have their say on what works and what doesn't. Be prepared for this and be a willing listener. Scriptwriting is a co-operative process and you must be flexible to survive script meetings.

A script is generally a more difficult form of writing for a beginner than, say, a short story, because certain well-defined conventions must be followed. These apply not only to the presentation of the work — that is, in script format — but also to continuity of action, dramatisation, dialogue, interaction between characters, and structural development of the storyline or plot. The scriptwriter needs to be aware of the possibilities and limitations of the medium, whether stage, screen, television or radio, and write accordingly.

2.2.1 Writing for television and film

It is hard to break into screen writing without extensive education and training, considerable practical experience, a great deal of luck, and sheer hard work and persistence. Because screen production is so expensive, commercial television and film producers usually employ only tried and tested writers so novice screenwriters have few opportunities to test their work in a full screen production.

Commercial television imposes enormous demands on the writer because the ratings govern whether a particular drama succeeds or fails, and networks are ruthless in disposing of productions that do not win the time slot. Even government-owned television stations chase ratings and look for material that will capture mass audience interest.

There are many genres of screenwriting. You will need to decide whether your script is for a feature film, telemovie, miniseries, serial, documentary, docudrama, animation, short film, or some other form. Watch as many examples of your chosen genre as possible to learn about its scope and limitations.

Your next task is to produce your work in several stages. These are:

> 'For at the end of the day, it's not the concept or the writing or the timing or the funding or the production or the casting or the music or the direction, let alone the awards or the critical acclaim or huge traffic on the web site that matters.
>
> It's the ratings, baby. It's the ratings.'
>
> Roger Simpson on commercial television productions, 'Ratings, reason and television drama', *Between the Sheets*, vol. 1, no. 1, 19 November 1997.

- An outline: usually a one-page description of your proposal to use in approaching potentially interested parties such as producers or directors.
- A treatment: a more detailed version, usually of about a dozen pages, which describes the action in narrative form and is written with the visual medium in mind.
- The script: written in appropriate screenplay format, it provides producer, director, technicians and actors with a complete version of the work exactly as it is to be performed.

Screenwriters probably spend most of their time writing treatments and rewriting scripts for films that never get off the ground. This work can bring in good money and, indeed, many Hollywood screenwriters make most of their money writing scripts that are never realised on the screen. However, this can be a demoralising enterprise.

Helpful organisations

If you are determined to pursue screenwriting, there are several organisations that provide training. These include some universities and private colleges, the Australian Film, Television and Radio School, the Australian Writers' Guild, the New Zealand Writers' Guild and other writing organisations such as the writers' centres.

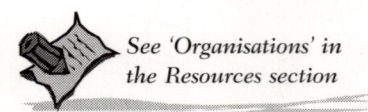

See 'Organisations' in the Resources section

The demand for training increased with the growth of film festivals showcasing new short films, and private outfits, such as Embryo Films and Prolific Productions, now offer writing and directing courses for beginners at reasonable prices. The establishment of Fox Studios in Sydney has provided an appropriate venue for many for such training. Your nearest writers' centre can provide details of where screenwriting courses are held.

Some of these organisations also have libraries of scripts in all performance mediums. Try to get hold of as many film and television scripts as you can to look at their layout and best of all, if possible, follow them as they are being performed to see how the script is interpreted in the medium.

Perhaps the best introduction to undertake as a beginner is to watch a lot of film and television productions, taking note of the techniques used by writers to convey their story and to present their characters.

Screenwriting software

Software packages can help you develop plot and character for a screenplay by showing you the alternatives and allowing you as the writer to select the details. Software is constantly being upgraded and improved, with many new products entering the market, but it is worth mentioning some that were available in 2002 to give you an idea of what screenwriting software is about.

Embryo Films offers several software packages for screenwriters. They are Screenwriter 2000, which allows you to write in standard screenplay format, and provides many useful features. For example, Simple Interface enables you to jump between different elements of the screenplay, Internet Collaboration permits you to write with a partner over the internet, and the text-to-speech feature allows you to assign male or female voices to your characters and let Screenwriter's text-to-speech engine read them back to you. Another software package, StoryView, allows you to create a visual timeline, design a well-paced story and track character changes, sub-plots and themes to see how they play over time. Another package, Dramatica, allows writers to build a story from first concept through to a solid story with 'powerful themes, intriguing plots and great characters'. The Dramatica package

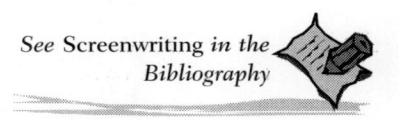

See **Screenwriting** *in the Bibliography*

offers brainstorming ideas, character naming and casting features to help you visualise your characters and build a story that works.

2.2.2 Writing for the stage

Writing for the stage is a specialised area requiring a great deal of training and practice, and it helps if you have seen and read as many plays as possible in all genres, from Shakespearean tragedies and comedies to contemporary performance works. Take note of the way the dialogue is constructed, how the personalities of the characters are revealed, how the plot is developed, and special devices used by the playwright for dramatic effect. Also pay attention to the stage directions and understand their purpose.

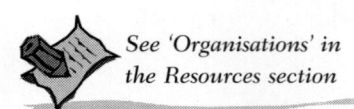

See 'Organisations' in the Resources section

In both Australia and New Zealand, there are organisations to help you develop your playwriting skills, including the Australian National Playwrights Centre, the Melbourne Writers Theatre, the National Institute of Dramatic Art, Playlab, Playworks and, in New Zealand, Playmarket. Many of these organisations conduct courses or play readings with established playwrights, or offer a mentoring scheme to help see your play through from original idea to first reading and, possibly, production. Many also provide script assessment services.

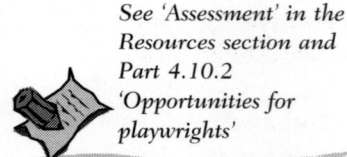

See 'Assessment' in the Resources section and Part 4.10.2 'Opportunities for playwrights'

The Australian Script Centre collects unpublished scripts for use by drama teachers, students, theatre companies and playwrights. For a play to be accepted you must be a member of the Australian Writers' Guild, the Australian Society of Authors or the Australian National Playwrights Centre, or your play must have been produced or commissioned.

2.2.3 Writing radio drama

The writing of radio drama requires great subtlety because the writer must rely on sound alone to evoke the characters, action, plot development, environment, mood and atmosphere. The radio writer creates visual or mental images of the scene, an impression of the characters, and an understanding of the action entirely from the dialogue and the sound effects, and must be very skilful in establishing an appropriate balance between the two.

Radio drama is an intimate medium because it speaks to one listener directly in a personal way, usually in a domestic environment. It also demands active participation by its audience members since their only engagement with the medium is through the faculty of hearing. For these reasons, the medium of radio is also easy to disengage from as a result of a telephone call, a knock at the door, the cry of a baby, or any other distraction.

> 'The challenge for the scriptwriter [of radio drama] is to ensure the listener's free association with sound doesn't subvert the drama — this is achieved by the development of dramatic logic: a logic of situation and of character, and the probable outcomes of their inter-relation.'
>
> Christopher Williams, Script Editor, ABC Radio Drama, 'Notes for Radio Dramatists', March 1995, ABC Audio Arts, GPO Box 9994, Sydney 2001.

Unlike a stage production where the audience is captive in a darkened theatre, has negligible distractions from the action on stage and has paid money to attend the performance, radio drama will lose its listeners if it is unclear, uninteresting, or too disturbing. The listener can simply turn off the radio or switch to another station.

The human voice is the main ingredient of radio drama, and character and emotion are conveyed through diction, tonal range, word usage, pitch and speech rhythms. The dialogue alone must reveal the personalities of the *dramatis personae* and carry the action of the play, usually without assistance from a narrator. Any utterance or sound effect must advance the drama in some way. If not, it is dispensable.

The intimacy of radio drama allows the writer to alternate between differing points of view in a way that could be confusing on stage or screen. However, it is important not to bewilder or overwhelm the listener with too many voices unless this is intentional.

One of the best ways of developing the art of radio drama writing is to listen attentively to as much drama as possible and note how the writer works to create dramatic interest through the use of certain techniques. Some writers' organisations offer radio writing workshops with professionals in the medium.

2.2.4 Performance poetry and storytelling

> 'What's so fascinating about Performance Poetry is that you can't really define it . . . There's a sense of the connectedness between the performance and the audience, a sense of occasion where something is created because of the presence of everyone.'
>
> Jeltje, 'Writer and Reader', *Southerly*, Summer 1997–98, vol. 57, no. 4.

In its revival of the oral traditions of poetry, storytelling and performance poetry have become popular forms of entertainment in many venues in Australia and New Zealand since the 1980s. These genres attract writers with singing or acting skills who use their literary craft as one component of their performance.

The Poetry Grand Slam or Poetry Sprint, in which poets present work within a fixed time limit (such as one minute), has become a regular feature of writers' festivals and attracts large crowds to performances which have all the excitement of sporting events.

There are many venues, such as pubs and clubs, that host regular performance poetry nights where the brave and the bold, the experienced and the novice, can strut their stuff before a vocal audience that has grown rapidly in response to this exciting new poetic medium. Like the emergence of 'rap' music, this new medium makes poetry relevant to the lives of its audience, touching as it does on the everyday subjects of ordinary life. Its practitioners don't need a degree; they can be street kids with a well-developed sense of rhyme and rhythm.

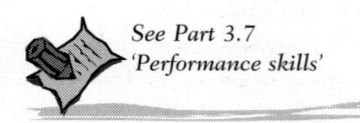

See Part 3.7 'Performance skills'

2.3 WRITING FOR CHILDREN

Children's book publishing, whether picture books or longer texts of fiction or non-fiction, is a highly specialised field requiring a great deal of passion, research and commitment.

Some new writers mistakenly believe that writing for children will be easier than writing for adults, so they start with a children's book as an attempt to break into publishing. It may seem easy enough to produce a simple text with illustrations that will appeal to children but, in reality, it is a great challenge to create a work that will engage young readers. An insincere attempt at children's writing rarely succeeds.

Although it is not difficult to have an idea for a children's book, it is as hard as any other kind of writing to make it work; authors are surprised to discover that writing a children's book takes as much time and craft as it takes to write for adults. Most writers will do many drafts of a manuscript before they (and their publisher) are happy with the result.

> 'Writing a 400-word children's book is as hard as writing a 40 000 word novel.'
>
> Author of the classic children's picture book *Possum Magic* Mem Fox, quoted in Candida Baker, 'A minor's masterpiece', *The Australian Magazine*, 29–30 November 1997, p. 35.

2.3.1 Shaping your project

The children of today live in a very different world from the one you grew up in, so beware of writing in a time warp. Your story should be appropriate for a contemporary child and not an echo of something from a bygone era. (Of course, historical subject matter is fine but outdated writing isn't!)

Write about what you know rather than trying to invent the kind of story you think a children's book should be. If your proposed story is about talking inanimate objects, then you may have a struggle finding a publisher today. Qualities such as a good narrative, a lively style, humour, insight and feeling are just as important in books for children as they are in adult fiction. Acknowledging the sophistication of their young readers, the best children's authors don't pull their punches, and don't flinch from tough subject matter such as parental conflict, racism, sexual matters and bodily functions, fear, drugs and other previously taboo topics.

Spelling, punctuation and grammar are important in any children's work, which is not to say that colloquial forms of speech must not be used, or even that 'bad language' has no place in children's books. However, children's book writers should know the rules of language: if you break them in the text it must be for a particular purpose, and not because you are ignorant of them.

Children's books refer to anything from picture books to be read

> 'I do believe we've impoverished language a lot through the advent of television and the fast pace of life. We've encouraged a short span of attention in children. I think an elegantly written book, a book that has style, a book that is rich in adjectives, has a place alongside the fast-paced story. I know there's a fashion with short sentences, but short sentences can still be rich. We're impoverishing children's lives by offering them only the bland, the facile and the easy.'
>
> Libby Hathorn quoted in 'Truth and consequence', 'Good Weekend', *Sydney Morning Herald*, 25 July 1998.

aloud to pre-schoolers to young adult fiction of up to about 70 000 words. Publishers provide guidelines on word counts, or how many words they require, for different types of children's books. Have a look at lots of books to get a feel for what length, language levels and illustrations are appropriate at any particular age.

Picture books are almost invariably of a fixed page extent, usually 32 pages long. Of this, 26–28 pages are text, and they are carefully designed to integrate with the illustrations. Many new children's authors make the mistake of writing too much and not leaving enough to the imagination of the child. The attention span of a child is shorter than that of an adult. Page after page of rhyming couplets is rarely acceptable, but if you are determined to write in this style, be sure of the scansion. Read your work aloud to yourself and listen for clumsy rhythms.

2.3.2 Getting to know the field

See 'Children's book publishers' in the Resources section for publishers of children's books in Australia and New Zealand

Before you can expect to write a publishable book for children, see which books are being successfully published and carefully study their plots, characterisation and themes to find out why they are popular with their young readers. It is important to look at the work of contemporary children's book authors and not just those books you enjoyed as a child if you want to avoid producing outdated material.

Cultivate a relationship with your local children's librarian or specialist children's bookseller. Take their advice on what's best and read it. Ask the librarian why she or he recommends particular books.

Kinds of Writing

To find out more about the field and to become familiar with the recipients of children's book awards, join organisations such as the Children's Book Council in Australia, and in New Zealand the New Zealand Children's Book Foundation, the Children's Literature Association of New Zealand or the Wellington Children's Book Association. Read the books which win awards as well as those which are popular with young readers yet never rate a mention in the prize lists. Compare their stylistic qualities, content, illustrations and themes, and determine how these individually contribute to the whole book.

See 'Organisations' in the Resources section

Subscribe to specialist review journals such as the Australian journals *Magpies*, about books for young children (which has a New Zealand section), and *Viewpoint*, which covers books for children aged eleven and up, or the New Zealand journals *Well Read* and *Talespinner* (journal of reviews of children's books) as well as other magazines for children.

See 'Bibliography' and 'Children and Youth' in the Resources section

Seminars, workshops and talks by children's book authors held by writers' centres, libraries or community organisations will give you access to professional specialists in their field who are usually delighted to answer questions from aspiring children's book writers.

It is useful to test your story on a child or children you know. Remember, though, that few children feel comfortable telling adults 'not to give up their day job'. Their appreciation of your story might also be augmented by the special attention you pay to children by reading to them. Alternatively, ask a teacher friend to try it out in the classroom — kids, like adults, are franker if they don't face the author.

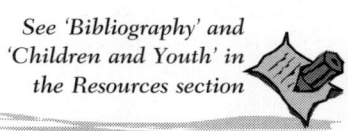

> 'In the kids' lit world, the CBC [Children's Book Council's] Book of the Year awards are the Oscars, the Nobel prize, Lotto and the Higher School Certificate combined. With one difference. First prize in this particular contest is nowhere near as important as getting on the short list.
>
> The short list. Oh, how that phrase reverberates through the kids' books biz. Authors have nightmares about it. Publishers rate it up there with "lunch". Kids view it with puzzled suspicion because so often their favourite books don't appear on it.'
>
> Morris Gleitzman in *The Australian's Review of Books*, August 1997.

55

2.3.3 Children's book illustration

There are few formal courses available in children's book illustration. Some courses are available in Continuing Education programs, and some graphic design colleges offer children's book illustration as a component of longer design courses. However, most published illustrators have not studied the craft formally, so practice in the field is often the only training available to a new illustrator.

New illustrators will gain much by joining the organisations listed in Part 2.3.2. These will put you in touch with other illustrators and voluntary professional groups which can advise you. There are also two organisations specifically established for children's book illustrators: the Society of Book Illustrators and the Society of Children's Book Writers and Illustrators, both of which publish regular newsletters and offer professional advice and assistance to aspiring children's book illustrators.

See 'Organisations' in the Resources section and Part 4.5.3 'Tips for aspiring illustrators of children's books'

2.4 CHILDREN AND YOUNG WRITERS

Children and youth who show a talent for writing can be assisted to develop their skills in all kinds of ways. Several magazines such as *Voiceworks* offer writing opportunities for school-age and young adult writers. Most magazines have small staffs, so contributors may have a long wait before hearing from a particular publication. Lack of funds also drives many small magazines out of business. Young writers can help them to survive by taking out subscriptions to their favourite magazines.

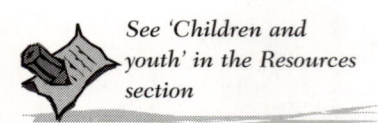

See 'Children and youth' in the Resources section

Major competitions are organised for young writers, including many by the Fellowship of Australian Writers. The Judah Waten Story Writing Competition (administered by the Whitehorse Manningham Regional Library Corporation) is an annual short story competition awarded in three age categories — open, fourteen to eighteen years, and ten to thirteen years — with first, second and third prizes offered in all categories.

There are organisations which hold writing workshops for children of primary, junior secondary and upper secondary levels, as well as writers who visit schools to give workshops and talks.

Commercial book publication is harder for young writers than for adults, but there are still opportunities around. Young writers could try submitting manuscripts to selected publishers with a publishing program that solicits material from this age group.

See 'Organisations' and 'Children and youth' in the Resources section

2.5 INTERNET AND MULTIMEDIA WRITING

Internet writing is an exciting new avenue for writers because it allows anyone to place their work on the screen and find readers from all over the world.

Check out the e-zines listed in the Resources section under 'Websites'

There are literally thousands of sites where you can participate by adding your own writing, whether short stories, poems, or a novel.

For further information on internet publishing see Part 4.2.4

Alternatively, you can create a personal website specifically for your own work, which you can change and develop at any time. Such sites active in 2002 included www.geocities.com and www.communicationgame.com.

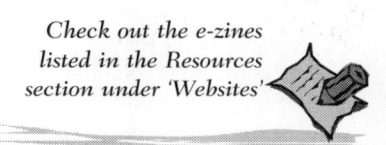

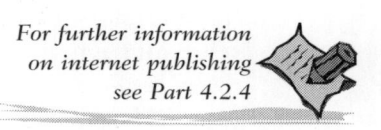

2.5.1 Zines

Zines is the word coined to describe internet magazines that appear on the web and solicit contributions from readers. These began proliferating with the development of the internet, and now cover every subject imaginable, from surfing hints to literature to entertainment reviews to pets, sport, gardening and self-help.

The Writer's Guide

The quality of the material on these sites depends on the amount of time the manager of the site spends on ensuring the work is carefully edited, kept up to date and well presented. To find out which sites will interest you, read the information technology section of your newspaper carefully, or subscribe to specialist magazines for information and advice about the latest sites, how to access them, and what they offer. Remember that many zines come into and go out of existence as quickly as shooting stars across the electronic airwaves, depending on the commitment and finances of the editor, so it is best to do a bit of research and not waste precious time online trying to find a site that has sunk without a trace.

Sydney poet John Tranter, who edits an online literary magazine called *Jacket*, comments on internet writing: 'But among the mass of forgettable material I suppose there must be a half dozen geniuses.' More optimistic is fellow writer Alan Gold, who says there are some fine literary journals with experimental writing on the net: 'Yes, it's unedited. But it's raw and it's full of guts and some of it's just wonderful and some of it is just awful.' ('Writers put their pens to cyberspace', Suzy Freeman-Greene, *The Age*, 17 October 1998.)

The electronic journal of the Australian Association of Writing Programs, called *Text*, receives all submissions electronically via email and publishes only on the web. Free subscription to the journal is available on receipt of your email address. Simply send your email address to the editors and they will email you direct access to the website for the latest issue of *Text* and include you on their automatic electronic mailout of further issues.

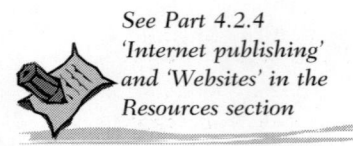

See Part 4.2.4 'Internet publishing' and 'Websites' in the Resources section

You can have a great deal of fun surfing the net to find other interesting sites and see your work not only appear on them, but also attract comment from other contributors and readers.

2.5.2 Hyperfiction

Hyperfiction is an emerging genre in which writers produce a non-linear work of fiction with alternative pathways that allow the reader to choose which direction to take at each stage of the plot.

This form of writing can be done only on a computer as it requires hotlinks, highlighted words, phrases or pictures in the text that allow the reader to select which path to follow in the story.

For example, in the hyperfiction *Victory Garden* created by American writer Stuart Moulthrop, a soldier writes home from the Gulf War: 'Tell *Thea* she's a jerk for *not writing* . . . She will probably ask you to help her out, but this time please *just say no*.' The words 'Thea', 'not writing' and 'just say no' are highlighted on the screen and present the reader with a choice of clicking on one of these three options. If 'Thea' is selected, the reader is presented with another screen which describes Thea's shock at the impending war. The 'not writing' option takes the reader to an angry letter from the soldier to Thea, while clicking on 'just say no' gives the reader a description of a bar at the soldier's college. In all, *Victory Garden* comprises 993 short writing 'spaces' or hypertext pages, with a total of 2804 links.

This form of writing is a challenge for the writer used to producing linear text. Rather than creating a single sequential flow of words as in a book, the hyperfiction writer has to produce a kind of web of incidents and characters and make sure that all the links make sense. This kind of writing can evolve beyond the creation of a story to become a multimedia production with graphics, sound and film or video.

2.5.3 Multimedia

The development of multimedia is a whole new potentially lucrative market for writers.

Just as screen technology did not produce an artform that reached a wider audience until the storytellers — the screenwriters — created compelling stories for films, so the content of web technology will remain insubstantial until writers specialised in the artform begin to make their contribution and create an audience for the medium.

Multimedia writing is a collaborative enterprise in which writers (or, as they are sometimes disparagingly called, 'text providers') collaborate with graphic artists, video-clip makers, cartoonists and others. Together they produce a work which does not have a linear format like a book but whose structure is more like a maze with alternative paths which can be followed at any point along the way. This structure will inevitably affect the kind of writing produced for multimedia.

In contrast to a book, which is a linear presentation of material mostly designed to be read from beginning to end, the multimedia product allows the user any point of entry and any point of departure, with a range of conclusions and even, sometimes, no conclusion at all.

Multimedia writers must learn to write for discrete screens, the basic 'page' of a multimedia work. Because these screens are not intended to be read sequentially it is important for multimedia writers to bear in mind the potential departure points (or hotlinks) where the reader may want to digress, possibly never to return. Although this has most implications for non-fiction writing, especially educational texts such as encyclopaedias that lend themselves to such electronic browsing, the medium also suits fiction: the author can produce a multistranded narrative with various pathways for the plot to take and alternative endings which are selected by the reader. This is already being done in book form for young readers, and easily translates to the screen with the addition of interactive audio-visuals, graphics and animation.

Developments in interactive software have pushed the technology towards products which allow the user to play an active role in the process of consumption. All these products require writers to become part of the process of creating a complex package involving many creators. The challenge for the writer is to contribute to the integration of the cross-disciplinary genres into a form that maximises the potential of the medium.

> 'Poets, documentary makers, short fiction writers, biographers, all will make their own electronic products. This will not be a virtual reality, but a new reality of publication and distribution, of disseminating ideas, of access to information. Narratives will be constructed to conform to the possibilities, and limitations, of electronic publishing. Our sense of genre will be altered by these developments, perhaps even more than film and television have altered it.'
>
> Paul Hetherington, 'Re-inventing the Storyteller: Multimedia as a Creative Tool', paper delivered at the National Book Council's 2nd National Book Summit, 1996.

PART THREE
GETTING DOWN TO WRITING

ADVICE FOR BEGINNERS

Writing is, on the whole, a solitary enterprise, and you will undoubtedly experience the full gamut of emotions from elation to doubt, from inspiration to writer's block, from frustration to satisfaction. But you needn't feel alone. Whether new or experienced, most writers suffer the same sensitivities about their work. Before you rush into print, explore the many ways of improving your writing, develop your editing skills and take advantage of the services offered by writers' centres.

Enrolling in a writing course brings you into a circle of other people who understand your endeavour. Your writers' centre can give you details of its own writing courses as well as those held at universities, community colleges, private colleges and by correspondence. It also offers advice on a wide range of writing subjects, holds seminars, readings and book launches, and provides rooms for its members to hold meetings and discussions.

There are useful and interesting books on the subject of writing to help you on your way and many literary festivals to attend in both metropolitan and regional areas. As well, many venues such as pubs, cafés, bookshops and art galleries hold public readings where you can try out a new poem or short story in front of a sympathetic audience of fellow writers who know what it's like to read in public for the first time and will certainly not boo and hiss you off the stage!

> 'That's always my biggest problem. The blank page. Once you've got it [the words], you can play with it — even if playing with it involves deleting it line by line and replacing it, it's still not as hard as writing it the first time.'
>
> Deborah Wilton interviewed by Niki Caro, *Write Up*, the New Zealand Writers' Guild Newsletter, August 1998.

> 'Getting your stories read, entering competitions, being a member of a Writers' Centre — they're all ways of accessing information and garnering a level of respect and support for your work. And of learning your craft.'
>
> Sophie Cunningham, Trade Publisher, Allen & Unwin, in 'Agents, Publishers and Writers', *Write On*, vol. 9, no. 4, May 1998.

See 'Bibliography' and 'Festivals' in the Resources section

3.1 WRITING HABITS

It is important that you establish a place where you can sit and write comfortably: either at home, in front of a computer at your desk or with a pen and notebook at the kitchen table, or somewhere else, such as a rented studio in a writers' centre or a small office in a suburban shopping centre. Choose your writing place where distractions can be minimised, where housework, telephone calls, television and radio, family demands, gardening and other diversions will not break into your writing.

It is also useful to get into the habit of establishing a particular time of the day for writing, and even of allocating a certain number of hours to this activity. Some writers work best in the mornings, others prefer to burn the midnight oil, while some claim they work only when inspiration strikes. It all depends on your lifestyle and the amount of time you are prepared and able to give it.

Some well-known writers, such as the novelists Sue Woolfe and Kate Grenville, and the journalist Adele Horin, have been able to raise young children while pursuing successful writing careers. It is a matter of self-discipline and, above all, practice. Some authors, such as Marele Day, get as much down on paper as they possibly can before they begin the arduous task of shaping and editing their work, while others, such as Delia Falconer, spend hours pacing out the rhythm of their sentences before setting down a single word. Whichever way you work, establish a special place where you can be alone with your thoughts and allow those creative juices to flow.

'I write whenever I can find the time — which is usually late at night. I like setting deadlines for myself in order to stay motivated. The more I write, the more it seems each piece of work has its own timeframe. Some things you can rattle off, others take longer to gestate, each page is like squeezing blood. My solution to this is to have several projects going at once. That way, if you go stale on one thing you can work on something else, then come back to it when the juices are running again.'

Novelist/filmmaker Keith Hill interviewed in *Write Up*, April 1998.

'Frank Sargeson works in the mornings. Do you?'

A notice on Frank Sargeson's front door, c.1940, recorded by Kendrick Smithyman, 'A Sort of Poet Too', *Islands*, vol. 21, Auckland, 1978.

3.1.1 Tips for writers who use longhand

- Avoid making notes on envelopes and serviettes.
- Use exercise books in preference to note pads that can fall apart.
- Number and date your exercise books for each draft.
- Number your pages and add the letter (a) after the number for pages added later.
- As you finish reading your work, use different coloured highlighters to mark sentences or paragraphs to be rewritten, deleted or moved.
- If you are doing research create a scrapbook with cuttings and photographs for reference.

> 'Once I actually start on the writing, I am very disciplined. I think you have to be. I don't stop until I've completed a story or a chapter . . . You shouldn't give up if you feel strongly that your work is publishable. Enter as many competitions as you can — you can learn a great deal that way. If you ask yourself why you write and the answer is because you love writing, then you should keep on doing it.'
>
> Children's author Moya Simons interviewed in *New Writers' News*, February 1998.

3.1.2 Tips for writers who use typewriters

- Make sure your ribbons are always clean and the typing clear.
- Avoid retyping by using different coloured pens for your various draft reworkings on the one copy.
- Retype only when you are satisfied that you have polished the writing.
- Always keep a copy of the draft.

3.1.3 Tips for writers who use word processors

- Work on your hard disk and always make a second copy of the original there. Use the 'save' command on your word

processor frequently, and program your computer to save your work automatically every few minutes.
- Don't forget to back up your files regularly to an external disk or cartridge — preferably after each session of writing. Label the disk or cartridge and note which draft it is or the date on which you last worked on it. This caution cannot be overemphasised: too many writers (including the writer of this book!) have lost hours of work owing to a sudden blackout or power surge, and it is a dreary and disheartening business to recreate what you have lost.
  Every writer has a tragic story to tell about words which have disappeared into the ether because of a failure to save or to back up. Retrieving files from a hard disk is expensive and, even with expert assistance, success cannot be guaranteed.
- Inquire about the layout of the typescript that publishers expect and follow those requirements.
- Avoid using tabs, hard returns and other formatting commands; these add to the cost of typesetting. The typeface and design for your work are decided by the designer.
- If italics are needed, underline those words on the printout and write 'italics' in the margin.
- Avoid using bold.
- Use matching opening and closing quotation marks in dialogue.

All these tips make the designer's and typesetter's work much faster.

3.2   READING HABITS

One of the best ways of learning the techniques of writing is through studying the language and methods of other writers. For this, you must become a voracious reader if you are not already, and a regular habitué of libraries and bookshops. Second-hand bookshops are a great place to pick up wonderful literary treasures for a bargain price. There you can bury your head in books which expose you to new ideas and experiences, and sample the styles and idiosyncrasies of a host of writers from around the world.

Getting Down to Writing

An American study showed that the human brain emits very little activity in front of a television — even less than in sleep — and a great deal of activity in the act of reading. But there are different ways of reading, and here I'm not talking of that purely escapist kind of reading that has you racing through the pages to get to the resolution of the plot.

In order to discover the practices of other authors, you have to read consciously and carefully, noting the use of language, the construction of the sentences, the creation of character and plot, the author's manipulation of voice, the selection of particular words, the syntax, word order, and so on. As you read, think about what you like, about what seems to work, and what makes that piece of writing successful or not. It takes a great deal of skill and patience to become a good reader, but the effort is worth it in the insight it yields to dedicated followers of the written word. And don't forget, the use of libraries, CDs and the internet makes it affordable to bring the world's literature into your living-room or your writer's study.

Don't be discouraged by the talent and skills of writers more advanced than you, nor overwhelmed by the difficulties facing your own attempts to express yourself through language. Like all trades and crafts, writing can be taught, and learned, and improves with constant application.

When you come to do your own writing, be conscious of maintaining your distinctive voice and not losing sight of your own ideas. Try to ensure that your admiration for certain writers does not lead to an overly derivative style in your work.

> 'You start by imitating writers you admire. Then you go on to other writers, and imitate them. There is nothing wrong in this. What is wrong is when would-be writers refuse to read other writers . . . Often people claim, I have my unique voice, it will be contaminated by the influence of other writers. I don't think this is true. I suspect it is utter nonsense. Nobody starts off with a unique voice. Our literary voice is learned. We may think the things we first write are original, but they are not: they are the product of what we were given to read at school . . . I don't know of any significant writer who does not read other writing . . . I don't think we can expect other people to read what we write unless we read what other people write too.'
>
> Michael Wilding, Address to the Society of Women Writers, NSW Writers' Centre, March 1997.

> 'What I found particularly gratifying was when people said they read [The Monkey's Mask] quickly for the story and then read it again slowly for the poetry.'
>
> Dorothy Porter, 'Pop goes the poet', *Sydney Morning Herald*, 23 March 1996.

3.3 GETTING EQUIPPED

3.3.1 The basic tools

The basic tools of any writer are pen and paper or, more likely, a ballpoint pen and a notebook. Carry a notebook with you wherever you go to make a note of things that strike you as interesting, to write down your observations, a new word, a sudden thought about a work in progress, or some interesting detail you want to follow up. Those inexpensive but handsome Chinese blank-lined notebooks, which are readily available from newsagents, are suitable and come in different sizes to fit your bag and your pocket. Alternatively, you can make your 'notes' directly onto tape and write them up later. A small tape recorder can be slipped easily into your pocket or bag when you are leaving home.

Some writers claim that the tools they use for writing affect their style. In particular, they point to different styles resulting from the use of a pen on the page compared to words produced on a screen. Some writers always begin their first drafts with words written with a fountain pen on alternating lines of a blank page: this method is portable, allows for instant editing between the lines, and is a sensuous experience in itself with a smoothly flowing nib. But it has its pitfalls. When a fire consumed Lily Brett's home she warned: 'What wasn't burnt was drenched by the fire brigade. I have a real tip for anyone who writes diaries: use biro. I've always written in fountain pen and everything was one mass of ink.' (Interviewed by Jenny Tabakoff in 'The Apple of Her Eye', Spectrum Books, *Sydney Morning Herald*, 30 August 1997.)

3.3.2 Why you need a computer

Once you get past the initial phase of writing down your first thoughts, you will discover that a computer is the most efficient way of dealing with a large volume of words on your road to publication. Although some writers are still shy of such technology, they will welcome it once they realise that the costs of getting someone else to type their manuscripts are quite prohibitive, especially if the manuscript needs to go through several drafts, as most do.

Getting Down to Writing

If you have never used a computer before, if you are a technophobe, if you are sceptical of what computers can do for your writing, if you are sick of asking friends to type out your material or of paying for a typist, you are in for a treat. A computer will make your writing life much easier and slash the time spent on editing and rewriting.

You may not be aware of some of the wonderful software programs that will not only make your work easier for you as a writer, but will also give you an edge in presentation on the page.

Research is also easier with the use of a computer. You can, for example:

- create a multitude of separate files for different subjects and organise them logically under different headings in your computer files
- use email to access people across the globe
- download material directly from the web onto your computer and use the material without having to retype it.

Try as you may, you can't avoid using a computer if you want to produce material for publication because typescript is no longer acceptable to book publishers or to magazines and journals. Handwriting, of course, is completely out of the question. Once you get the hang of using a computer you will wonder why it took you so long to get one and how you ever managed without this essential piece of equipment and its companion, the desktop printer.

> 'In spite of their obvious lack of technological sophistication, the humble writer's notebook provides one of the most simple and reliable devices for recording a vast range of potential literary treasures. Quotations and other fragments from the works of Henry Miller, Jean Genet, Blaise Cendrars, Albert Camus and Antoine de Saint-Exupery, as well as poems, scribbled notes, reflections, postcards and other objets d'art are just a few examples of the sorts of literary flotsam and jetsam that can be found in my much-treasured notebooks.
>
> The beauty and importance of the notebook undoubtedly lies not so much in what is recorded, but in the fact that there is so much that can be recorded. Unlike the journal, notebooks are by their very nature random and spontaneous: the golden rule is that there are no firm rules about form or structure. Record what you like where and whenever you like. Notebooks are the ideal way of recording overheard conversations, observations, random thoughts and streams of consciousness — all of which may provide some inspiring and intriguing material to use either as a departure point for writing or as material in an existing writing project.'
>
> Marcus D. Niski, 'On keeping a writer's notebook', *The Australian Writer*, no. 313, February/March 1999.

3.3.3 What kind of computer?

In effect, there are only two types of computers to choose from — Apple Macintosh computers (commonly called Macs), and IBM or IBM-compatible computers (commonly called PCs). If all you need is a simple word processor, that is, a computer to be used solely for the purpose of producing text, you have the choice of a range of fairly inexpensive PCs or early Macintosh models. Because computers are replaced by newer models so quickly, you can probably pick up a recent second-hand model for half the cost of a new computer.

> 'As soon as I could, I bought a computer, and immediately found it natural to work with as far as novels, short stories and essays were concerned. Somehow the transmission of thought to screen follows the workings of my mind — I get a huge, unconscious slab down, then later, when it is all saved, my rational mind can go into play and methodically revise it, with no boring retyping.'
>
> Sophie Masson, 'One author's view', *The Weekend Australian*, 30–31 May 1998.

The laptop computer

If you want a light portable computer, known as a notebook or laptop, you can expect to pay more because you are paying for the technology that goes into reducing its weight. It is said that the latest-model notebooks perform about half as well as the latest desktop computers and cost about twice as much. There are three categories of notebooks: budget (under $3500 in 2002), performance (between $3500 and $6000) and ultra-light (above $6000).

If you're determined to buy a notebook computer, choose a well-known brand and never pay the retail price as you can always find a cheaper one by shopping around. In 2002, you could buy a notebook for as little as $2500 and as much as $10 000 or more, depending on what you want it to do for you. Those at the lower end of the market should be perfectly adequate for your writing needs and for surfing the net. It is not worthwhile to pay a lot for a laptop as a new model is released every few months. Ensure that your laptop has built-in drives for floppy disks and CDs, as well as a modem option.

The advantage of a laptop is obvious: it can travel with you wherever you go and be available whenever inspiration strikes, whether you are on holidays, on a business trip, or visiting friends or relatives. One of the difficulties of a laptop is the location of the mouse trackball or touchpad in an awkward position on the keyboard, but you can attach an external mouse which will speed your navigation around the screen.

3.3.4 Computer printers

You will also need a printer that is compatible with your computer. The most expensive, because of their reproduction quality, are laser printers. If you want a simple printer just for printing out black text, a dot-matrix or an inkjet (or bubble-jet) printer will serve your purposes — and your pocket — very well.

The dot-matrix printer is the cheapest. Because these printers pound the paper they are able to make carbon impressions, but they make a lot of noise, which can be distracting. If you are going for this type, choose the one with the highest number of pins as this will give the greatest definition. The 9-pin is the lowest quality but is fast, while the 24-pin is slower but the quality is better.

Inkjets are also inexpensive (anywhere from $100 in 2002) and can print high-quality text and images. This will probably be your choice if you want a printer which can produce good-looking text. Inkjet cartridges will produce about 500 pages of text and cost about $50.

The laser printer is expensive (in 2002 they were at least $1000), but the quality of the print is suitable for publication, so if you are thinking of self-publishing and doing it all yourself, this is definitely the choice for you.

The quality of both the inkjet and laser printer is determined by the number of dots per inch, or dpi. The higher the dpi, the better the resolution. The top-of-the-range inkjets have 1440 dpi and in 2002 they cost about $700. The better personal laser printers have a resolution of 1200 dpi, and one cartridge, at a cost of about $160, can produce about 5000 pages.

If you intend to do a great deal of printing then the laser printer will, in the long run, be the most cost-effective and give you the best quality.

Perhaps the best source of advice is friends who have had their own computers and printers for a while and can show you exactly how they use their hardware (computer and printer) and what software (applications or programs) they are using. Before you make that important purchase, research the computers available on the market, talk to the salespeople in computer stores about your needs, and get comparative quotes.

Remember, computing is a fiercely competitive market and prices can vary significantly between sales outlets for the same model.

3.3.5 Software

Word-processing programs

Many computers are sold with software which includes a word-processing program and several other basic applications such as a spreadsheet and a desktop-publishing program. The type of word-processing program you need will depend on what kind of work you are doing. For example, this book was commenced on Microsoft Word 6 for a Mac but the program had great difficulty coping with the book's size and could not update fields for the contents list and index. In the end I was forced to purchase a later version which could better manage large documents, but even this was not entirely successful. I was told that Word was not suitable for the production of large documents whereas another, quite expensive, program called Framemaker should have been my choice. Ask the salesperson to show you some of the software range available and make sure you describe your writing needs so that you purchase the program that is best for you.

Certain kinds of editing, such as copy editing, are easily done on a computer with a word-processing program. On-screen editing is much faster than manual editing with a pen because it allows you to rearrange sentences and cut and paste whole paragraphs with a few keystrokes.

Word-processing programs have many useful features, including the following:

- Editorial changes and revisions can be shown on the screen, so that you can see at a glance what has been changed, moved, added or deleted.
- Editorial changes can also be turned off and made invisible, so that you can look at a clean text without viewing the editorial changes.

Getting Down to Writing

- Different versions of the text can be saved and later compared, and if you want to restore parts of the text they are easily accessible.
- On large-screen (17" plus) computers the two versions of a text can be displayed side by side, or one on top of the other, for easy comparison.
- If you think you are using a particular word too often, you can locate the word easily and then replace it with a different word each time.
- Spellcheck facilities allow you to pick up most spelling mistakes and unusual words, but relying on this alone is risky as a mistake can sometimes be read as a 'reel' word.
- With word-counting commands you can check the length of your work when you are writing to a word limit, such as for competitions or for a publisher who has asked for a manuscript of a particular number of words.
- You can use commands for establishing different levels of headings and dot points to give your text a better visual structure.
- Pagination and repagination is done automatically as you type.
- With a simple command you can view or print your entire manuscript with the spacing you choose — single, one and a half, double or more.
- the contents list and index are easily prepared on such programs and their pagination can be automatically updated with a single command.

If you buy a computer without software included, take the advice of many computer experts who recommend that you spend the same amount on software as on hardware — that is, the same amount on the programs you want to use as on the equipment that will run them.

Desktop-publishing programs

If you are producing newsletters, publicity material and other text which requires a certain amount of graphic design, then you may need to consider purchasing a desktop-publishing (DTP) program. Such programs may require a more expensive computer with a larger screen and a greater capacity than one used only for word-processing. DTP programs such as Adobe Pagemaker and

QuarkXPress, which are used by printers, are expensive, but there are cheaper alternatives which will give your work a professional look, make it more legible, and impress your readers.

Indeed, many word-processing programs have a number of DTP features which allow you to present your text with graphics, place sections of text in shaded boxes with borders of different widths, include graphs and tables in your text, and give you a good range of other features such as automatic repagination and presentation of text in columns.

Software packages are constantly being updated, so discuss your DTP needs with a reputable software seller to make sure that you buy a package that is able to cope with your requirements but you don't end up paying for a range of functions that are unnecessary in your work.

Creative writing programs

An increasing number of software packages are available for fiction writers and scriptwriters. These lead you through the writing process step by step; for example, they introduce characters and conflict situations and invite you to write in details specific to your own story. Such programs make plot development easy and could help you overcome writer's block.

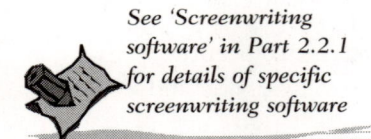

See 'Screenwriting software' in Part 2.2.1 for details of specific screenwriting software

3.3.6   Computer courses

Many courses on word-processing, desktop publishing and other computer programs are offered by community colleges, TAFE colleges and community centres. Before you select a course, first make a choice about which computer you need for your purposes so that you can attend the appropriate course, that is, for either IBM or Macintosh users. Most programs have been designed for both IBM and Macintosh, but they operate slightly differently depending on the type of computer.

Private colleges charge much higher rates than public colleges and community centres for similar courses. More personal attention at a private college might not be sufficient compensation for paying up to three or four times the price. Most courses are offered at introductory, intermediate and advanced levels.

3.3.7 CD-ROMs and CD burners

CD-ROMs are compact disks which contain a huge amount of information in text, graphic and photographic form, and may include moving images and sound. One CD-ROM can contain the whole of the *Encyclopaedia Britannica,* and indeed such a disk is sold in computer shops. If you want to use this resource in your research, or even to keep children engrossed for hours in front of their computer either researching their essays or playing games while you're writing on yours, you must purchase a computer which has a CD-ROM drive. The faster the CD-ROM drive, the quicker you will be able to read the information. ROM stands for 'read only memory', which means you can read (or hear or see) what is on the disk, but you cannot record anything onto it.

The range of CD-ROMs is increasing daily, and includes a big selection of practical subjects such as gardening and a good choice of research material, such as collections of classic novels, the whole of Shakespeare's works, and various dictionaries and thesauruses. Many bibliographies and indexes are held in libraries on CD-ROM, so even if you do not use them at home, you may find yourself searching through one in your local public or university library.

The more recently developed CD burners allow you to record a huge amount of print, visual and aural information on the one CD. This technology is superceding disks and cartridges as the favoured form of storage and backup.

3.3.8 Internet

The internet is a global network of government, university, corporate and private computers which allows the rapid exchange of information via such services as email and the World Wide Web. As such, it offers writers a fantastic new research facility which can be conducted at home from your computer.

To connect to the net and receive all the services it provides, you will need a modem. Most computers sold now have a built-in modem. An external modem plugs into your computer at one end and into a telephone line at the other end, as well as into a source of power. Make sure your modem is fast enough to read complex graphics as well as text if you want to surf the net regularly. (If you don't want to view the graphics, which can take a lot of time to download, you can switch them off for faster downloading. However, so much material nowadays is integrated with the graphics on websites that you may miss important information if you turn off the graphics function.)

Once you have your modem, you will need to subscribe to an internet service provider (ISP). You dial the provider to connect to the internet and access email and the web. This is called 'logging on'. Many local providers will supply a modem and a CD with the appropriate software and set you up on the net for a modest charge, as well as throwing in free use of the net for a specified period of time. In this period you should be able to learn how to use it quickly and efficiently. Check that your provider has a local access point so that you can log on at local, rather than long-distance, rates.

Much of the software you need to access the World Wide Web is freely available on the net, but internet service providers usually supply most of what you need in their package. There are hundreds of providers in Australia and New Zealand. The largest providers in Australia are Ozemail, Big Pond and AOL (America On Line) Australia. Some operating systems, such as Windows XP, also include an internet connection and offer a choice of three providers — Connect.com, Big Pond and Ozemail, all of which have national networks that offer local-call access to major centres.

The best advice you can take is not to sign up with an internet service provider for more than two or three months until you have tested its service and costs. Telephone technical support is often required until you get used to using the net, and providers who do not offer their customers such assistance will not retain their business for long.

If you are sick of sitting at your computer waiting for large amounts of information to download, try the new DSL (digital subscriber line) broadband technology. Although more expensive this will save you hours of thumb-twiddling frustration.

Email

One recent electronic development can make writing, researching and editing much easier for the writer. It is the simple email (or electronic mail), which allows you to receive and send text across the world in a matter of seconds, either as an email message, or as a document attached to the email. And all for the price of a local phone-call.

Email allows editors of books or periodicals an easy method of collecting material for their publications; there is no need either to transfer a file from disk to computer or, much more time-consuming, to type in the material from hard copy, that is, from a page. Text sent as part of an email message may lose its formatting and require reformatting if it is to be used for publication. However, with a simple cut-and-paste technique on the computer, you can take text off the email screen and insert it as text in an ordinary word file and then format it in the text size and style you want. Alternatively, a document sent to you as an attachment to an email allows you to receive the original document as a separate file on your computer with the layout intact, provided you have the appropriate software to open the document.

Email is also an excellent way of obtaining responses from, say, research institutions abroad in a much shorter period than it takes to send a letter through the post, and it can be a much more immediate, and indeed personal, way to communicate with your colleagues or fellow writers. An email message sent from another country will be in your computer 'letterbox' within a few seconds from the time it was sent, and your reply can be returned within the same length of time. It may not be as personal as the telephone, but it is certainly cheaper.

The World Wide Web (WWW)

The World Wide Web, or simply 'the web', is a great facility that allows you to 'surf' the world's resources for information of all kinds. Although it may seem complicated to a novice, with practice you will be able to comb the information available on the net for your own particular needs without having to move from your desk.

For search engines which specialise in Australian sites see 'Websites' in the Resources section

When you surf the web you can either go to a particular web address by entering it in the computer in a designated field and pressing the return key, or you can use what is called a search engine

See 'Search engines' in the Resources section

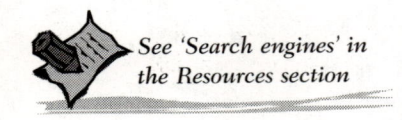

to find sites related to your particular interest. A search engine is a free service which scans the web for information about your topic. With practice you will discover which are the best search engines for your particular needs.

The internet allows you, among other things, to join writers' groups on the web, or participate in international discussions, or read any of the huge range of electronic zines published only on the net. You can search the web for the many literary sites available from around the world, get information about authors, read literary works published on the net, access specific sites which contain, for example, works from the Beat poets, and find out about upcoming literary events. You can publish your own work, either in a dedicated site with its own unique address, or as part of someone else's site. The Australian Society of Authors (ASA) offers its members, for a small fee, an opportunity to place a bibliography of their works and a sample of writing on their own web page on the ASA's OzAuthors site.

Internet references

One of the questions that has been puzzling contemporary researchers is the validity of internet references. As many sites on the net are placed there by individuals or groups merely expressing an opinion, the content is just that — opinion — and has little validity as such and so is not particularly useful as a citation. In contrast, most academic journals and periodicals are refereed — that is, articles and papers submitted to such publications are checked by at least one or two referees for their content, methodology and conclusions, and so have stood the test of close scrutiny.

When quoting internet references in a bibliography, include the web address and, if it is shown, the date of the material, but do not expect to include the exact equivalents of citations of printed material such as page number, publisher and place of publication.

3.3.9   The writer's library

Most writers, whether of fiction or non-fiction, require a fairly good collection of reference works if they don't want to be traipsing off to the library every time they want to look up a basic reference. The

Getting Down to Writing

following works are proposed because they provide the basis of a literary reference collection. Keep these books handy to your writing place where you can easily consult them.

You will certainly need at least one comprehensive style dictionary, such as the *Oxford Australian Writers' Dictionary* by Shirley Purchase. This provides an authoritative guide on numerous issues of style and usage, such as:

- spelling dilemmas
- names of people and places
- foreign words and phrases
- to italicise or not to italicise
- abbreviations and acronyms
- capitalisation and punctuation.

Another essential reference is a general dictionary, such as the *Macquarie Australian Dictionary*, which contains many entries taken from the works of Australian writers, as well as a host of new terms in specialist fields such as computing and from popular culture. New Zealand writers will find *The Dictionary of New Zealand English: New Zealand Words and their Origins* a fascinating literary resource.

If you have a particular interest in the historical development of English words you will need an etymological dictionary such as the *Shorter Oxford Dictionary*; this gives examples of historical and archaic usage from writers who have used such words or who have coined their own, the dates of first usage and obsolescence. The *Collins Cobuild English Dictionary* and others in the series (*Idioms, Phrasal Verbs*) provide comprehensive lists of words based on current usage. If Aboriginal words are your interest, *Macquarie Aboriginal Words* offers a diverse selection from Aboriginal and Torres Strait Islander languages with background notes on the history and culture behind the words. For a well-researched book on colloquial contemporary speech, have a look at the *Macquarie Book of Slang: Australian Slang in the 90s*.

Other books you will find useful for your writing include:

- a thesaurus, such as *The Macquarie Thesaurus*, which provides lists of the antonyms and synonyms of words;
- a dictionary of literary terms, such as M.H. Abrams' *A Glossary of Literary Terms*, which will assist you in

- identifying figures of speech, genres, types of poems, different rhyming schemes, and so on;
- various guides to writing in your chosen area (such as business writing or novel writing);
- *Style Manual for Authors, Editors and Printers* by the Australian Government Publishing Service, or *Write Edit Print: Style Manual for Aotearoa New Zealand,* which give the nationally accepted ways of writing and presenting certain words, phrases and names of things on the page;
- a handy grammar reference, such as *The Cambridge Grammar of the English Language,* Cambridge University Press, Cambridge, 2002;
- for faulty spelling, obtain a copy of *Spelling Made Easy* by Barbara Dykes and Constance Thomas.

Even if you don't wish to purchase them, *The ALS Guide to Australian Writers: A Bibliography, 1963–1995* and the *Who's Who of Australian Writers* are handy library references if you want to find out about Australian writers. In addition to the bibliographic listing, the former work also provides critical articles and selected reviews from a wide range of journals and newspapers.

You should also have on hand a good atlas, a comprehensive encyclopaedia (available on CD-ROM), a world almanac, various dictionaries of mythology and quotations. You will need a good edition of the Bible and a concordance to go with it if you are researching biblical references.

A comprehensive 'Bibliography' in the Resources section at the back of this book gives a wide selection of reference works, both new and classic, with which to begin or enhance your writer's library collection.

3.3.10 The green office

Although writing is relatively inexpensive as an occupation, there are ways in which you can save yourself money as well as contribute to the conservation of the environment and safeguard your health. Once you have established your work space, you may like to consider some of the following suggestions.

The good old-fashioned fountain pen

Considered by many writers to be the most important tool in the initial stages of creation, the good old-fashioned fountain pen will save you a lot of expense on the purchase of disposable pens over the years. You can have your choice of a range of coloured inks in bottles, or, a little less environmentally friendly, you can purchase disposable ink cartridges. Remember, though, that ink may run with exposure to moisture and humidity.

Paper

Paper is one of the most expensive items in the writer's budget. You can save on these costs by shopping around for the most competitive prices. Per-ream costs vary greatly depending on quality and whether it is recycled or not. If you buy in bulk it is considerably cheaper and you may be able to make a joint purchase with friends to get a discount rate.

You can also save paper by using the reverse side of used paper for your drafts. Take care to identify each draft by a header or footer in case the pages become mixed up or reversed and you are left trying to figure out which side belongs to your current draft. Any paper typed on one side can be reused. One of your local businesses may be prepared to donate used paper providing that it is for your personal consumption only and does not leave your office. Try ringing them to see if you can occasionally pick up a box of paper. They may be happy to see it put to use rather than thrown out. A word of caution, though. Some papers which have been photocopied on one side with dense images (rather than typescript) may damage or soil the cartridges on your printer or photocopier, so it is better to try one out before sending lots of pages through your equipment.

Good-quality recycled papers are compatible with most equipment and will not damage it. If you buy these you will be helping to develop a market which does not rely on the felling of more forests for paper products.

When you have used both sides of the paper and no longer need it, it can be picked up for recycling by your local council or by a private company. If these services are not available to you, the paper can be used as layers in your compost bin to separate vegetable matter, or as mulch in the garden.

The use of a computer may considerably reduce your dependence on retaining hard copies of letters and other documents since they can simply be stored as files on your computer.

If you don't need a full A4-sized sheet of paper for writing a letter or note, use A5 (half A4) stationery. You can set up your computer to print on A5 paper when necessary.

Envelopes

Have you ever thought of dispensing with envelopes entirely for certain kinds of mail? A letter folded over and fastened with sticky tape can be stamped, addressed and posted through the mail, while used envelopes can be recycled by pasting a sheet of paper over the address. You may not wish to use recycled envelopes for recipients you want to impress, but consider it for other material you send through the mail. Local businesses and some organisations may be prepared to give you their used envelopes and jiffy bags rather than throwing them away.

Postage

Postage is generally an unavoidable, and often big, expense for writers sending bulky manuscripts. The best way to avoid large postage costs is to send query letters first and wait for an expression of interest before mailing a large manuscript. If you are prepared for a lengthy wait, send letters and manuscripts to overseas destinations by surface mail, which is considerably cheaper than airmail.

If you are producing a periodical which you send out regularly, you may be eligible for a bulk postage rate. Inquire about discounts at your local post office. Periodicals sent through the post do not require envelopes, plastic wrapping, or even a sheet of paper for the mailing address if you leave room on the back page for address labels. The magazine or journal can then simply be folded and fastened with sticky tape with space for the mailing label on the outside.

Lighting and ventilation

A room flooded with natural light will save on power bills during the day (as well as being easier on your eyes), while fluorescent tubes provide cheaper night lighting than incandescent globes. Long-life globes, although initially more expensive to purchase than ordinary globes, will also save you money in the long run.

Unventilated offices can become very stuffy with machines emitting certain kinds of radiation and papers collecting dust. Good ventilation will keep your head clearer for work. To reduce dust, store papers in filing cabinets or filing boxes. Books should, ideally, be contained in bookshelves with glass doors, but if you cannot afford such a luxury, try dusting (or vacuuming) them regularly, to control both those dust mites which may affect your breathing, and the silverfish which will happily eat their way into your precious library.

Exercise

If you spend hours of each day staring into your computer screen, take a regular ten-minute break to exercise your body and your eyes. Get up and walk around, stretch your arms and back and legs. Shrug your shoulders, draw in your chin towards your neck, and roll your eyes around and stare into the distance to help relax strained muscles. You may look weird to an onlooker, but who cares? Your muscles will be more relaxed, you will feel refreshed and you will be able to continue with your work. Ergonomically designed chairs, screens, keyboards and mice are a boon for writers spending long hours at their computer.

3.4 GATHERING MATERIAL

All writers need to develop their interview, research and note-taking skills, irrespective of whether you write fiction or non-fiction. Even if you are writing poetry you may want to consult another poet, read something about poetic language, revise your knowledge of a particular school of poetry, or even interview a poet.

3.4.1 Interview techniques

Almost inevitably, you will interview someone during the course of your occupation or career as a writer. And why? Because a personal account in the subject's own words breathes life into an article, a story, a biography or an anecdote. It can provide you with personal information and insights that could not easily be gleaned from other sources. Thus interviewing is a skill you can use irrespective of what kind of writing you are pursuing. Even for fiction, for example, you may need to talk to a specialist in some field to get material on which to base a character.

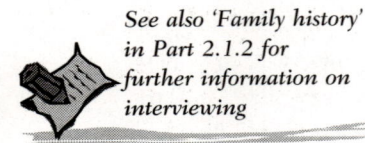

See also 'Family history' in Part 2.1.2 for further information on interviewing

To conduct successful interviews, develop your listening skills, and in particular, an empathic method of questioning that elicits the material you are interested in, as well as an analytical ability to separate worthwhile from worthless material.

A good interviewer makes his or her subject feel at ease, encourages them to speak frankly, and is flexible enough within the prepared framework of the interview to divert from prepared questions to follow an interesting deviation during the conversation.

Types of interview

There are two kinds of interviews: the background interview and the subject interview.

The background interview is conducted for the purpose of gaining information about a particular topic other than the interviewee, and is often used by reporters researching an article. It can take place over the telephone, and often has to if your interviewee is a long distance away or if you have limited time and many people to contact.

The subject interview is conducted with a person who is the topic of the interview itself and from whom you are seeking certain information about his or her life, such as his or her experiences and opinions. This kind of interview is best conducted in person rather than by phone or, for example, in written form such as a letter.

Interview tools

An A5-sized spiral-bound notebook which you can pop into your bag or pocket is your first interview tool. Although you may be recording your interview, it is always wise to take the precaution of backing up your tape with a written record, jotting down notes and phrases used by the subject and other things you want to remind yourself of later.

In addition to your interviewer's notebook, another essential tool for recording interviews is a reliable and unobtrusive voice recorder with an inbuilt microphone, which can be purchased for very little from electronics shops. Test it in the shop to make sure it gives you the sound quality you need for your work. Remember always to check, before the meeting, that your subject agrees to the interview being recorded. If he or she is uncomfortable with the idea of everything being recorded, reassure your subject that you will turn the tape off at any time on request.

Before your interview, double-check that the microphone works, and carry spare batteries. Be sure to know how to use the recorder: it is embarrassing to have to go back to your subject for another interview because you didn't know how to operate your equipment. Sometimes it is impossible to get a second chance if your subject has moved away or died.

Inexpensive microphones for recording phone interviews are available from electronics shops. It is crucial that you get permission from your subject before recording phone interviews or conversations, as there are legal implications if you use information or quotes from an interview recorded without consent.

Interview tips

Here is a checklist of the things you should do in preparing for an interview and conducting it.

- Research your topic. This may involve some library work, consulting a dictionary of biography, or asking another person some questions about your topic or subject.
- Prepare a list of questions you wish to ask.
- Arrange an appointment with your subject and state clearly what you wish to interview him or her about and, if relevant, which publication you are intending to publish the interview in.

The Writer's Guide

- If you intend to record the interview, obtain your subject's consent when you arrange the appointment.
- Arrive at the interview on time with all your necessary equipment in good working order, and any material you may wish to show your subject. If the interview is to be conducted in your office or home, make sure that your subject is made welcome and put at ease.
- Begin your interview with some general questions to establish rapport and help your subject to relax.
- Be prepared to deviate from your prepared questions if you find your subject starts to reveal something interesting and more relevant for your purpose. On the other hand, if you find your interview straying from the topic, gently lead your subject back to the theme without appearing to be rude or aggressive.
- If you find your subject raises some interesting points that you wish to follow up while he or she is speaking, and you don't want to interrupt, jot down any matters you want to raise later.
- If your interview is for publication, don't embarrass your subject by reproducing grammatical errors or other idiosyncrasies of speech which show your subject to be uneducated.
- Don't rely entirely on your tape recorder, even though the temptation to do so is great. It is useful to develop a kind of shorthand while taking notes, but make sure you can understand it later.
- Transcribe your interview as soon as possible after the event before you forget what was said and how it was said.
- You may need to telephone your subject after the interview to check on some details, but be careful not to leave this too long in case your subject forgets what he or she said or for some reason is not contactable.

3.4.2   Researching

Research is an integral part of your work as a writer, no matter which genre you work in. Although novelists are creating a fictional world, their work is more compelling if they get the details right. Readers complain if writers misspell place-names, if they get historical details wrong, or are guilty of an anachronism such as referring to a household gadget before it came into use.

The first skill in good research is to take clear notes, with full details of source material, including name of author, publisher, name of journal, issue number, page number, date of publication, and so on. You may also wish to record the date on which you made your notes because this may become important if additional material, dated later than your research, comes to hand.

Keep your notes in good order, and either type them up immediately or file them in manila folders, an expanding cardboard file, a document box, plastic pockets, or a filing cabinet. Label them with appropriate headings so that you will not have difficulty finding them later. If you organise your paper and computer files properly, you will always be able to retrieve the material you need at a moment's notice. This becomes especially important if you are working on more than one project at a time or when you must meet a deadline. Carefully and systematically record the names, addresses and phone numbers of useful contacts in an address book or on the computer.

Librarians are always prepared to help interested readers. If you don't know how to use a library's computer system to search for a subject, ask your librarian. Once you've got the hang of it, you will be able to generate a comprehensive list of references on your chosen topic. University libraries in both metropolitan and regional areas have excellent collections of all kinds of material, including newspapers on microfilm, and have access to large databases belonging to their own and other universities. Don't forget that university libraries are not only for the use of academics and students; members of the public can access their resources, although there are usually restrictions on borrowing.

One website will give you access to the wealth of information held in Australian libraries. At the Australian Libraries Gateway you can locate all the libraries in Australia and find out their contact details and services offered and the resources they hold, search their catalogues, and access on-line exhibitions, events, image collections and oral histories.

These days, much research is conducted on the World Wide Web and it is a real art to be able to navigate your way to

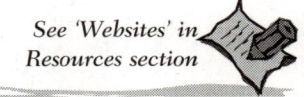

See 'Websites' in Resources section

See 'The World Wide Web' in Part 3.3.8 for more information on search engines, as well as 'Websites' in the Resources section for a list of search engines

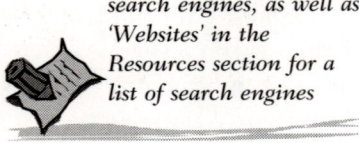

sites that are useful for your purposes. Again, librarians are usually very willing to help you find your way around the web. There are also helpful introductory courses which will give you a start in your virtual explorations, but there is nothing like the actual practice of sitting in front of your computer and using various search engines to obtain the information you are seeking. Keep a notebook handy next to the computer for jotting down comments about the sites you visit. Those you wish to revisit can be marked (as 'bookmarks' or 'favourites') by an instruction in the menu bar at the top of the screen. This will allow you to go straight to the site when next you're on the web without retyping the long web address.

Remember, though, that a great deal of material is not yet available on the web, including private collections of personal papers, rare books, and other records deposited in libraries by individuals or organisations. You will, however, generally be able to find the whereabouts of such collections through the web by accessing the catalogues of libraries and other institutions.

Of course, not all your research will be conducted by computer or at libraries. Research takes writers to the most interesting and even weird places in their search for facts and authenticity. Crime writers Marele Day and Gabrielle Lord have both visited police departments to obtain information on police procedures, the appearance and decomposition rates of dead bodies, and other forensic details. Other writers need to contact land titles offices, coroners' courts, newspaper offices, factories, scientific laboratories, observatories, and so on in the course of their research. If you're doing such research, make a note of the date of your contact, your sources of information, and important details, and record any observations you made at the time. These can be valuable *aides-mémoirs* when you revisit your notes later on.

3.5   DRAFTING AND EDITING

Very few people can write a piece of work that is immediately lucid, concise and well-expressed: that is why editing plays such an important role in the process of writing. It is vital to producing a polished piece of work that is professional and readable, whether a short story, article, report, family history or, in fact, anything that you wish other people to read.

There are several stages of editing work for publication. First is the editing you do yourself on your own manuscript before showing it to anyone else. After you have polished your manuscript to the best of your ability, consider joining a writers' group that will give you feedback on you work (gratis), and only then seek the services of a professional manuscript assessor or editor to give your work that extra polish that an expert eye will bring to it. This will improve the quality of your manuscript and thus increase its chance of being favourably regarded by a periodicals editor, literary agent or book publisher.

See Part 3.5.4 'Editorial services' and Part 3.5.5 'Manuscript assessment services' later in this section

If you have a contract with a publisher, your manuscript will be edited by an editor appointed by the publisher. The kind of editing you do as a writer on your own work is different from the kind of editing done by a publisher's editor although there is some overlap.

See 'The role of publishers' editors' in Part 4.3.2

3.5.1 Self-editing

The essence of good editing is in refining your work to the point where it is as good as it can possibly be: where the voice, tone and pace are right for the subject; where every word is necessary, appropriate and precise and in exactly the right place in the sentence; where every sentence has its logic in relation to those before and after; where each paragraph develops the plot or idea, and the structure of the entire work has a satisfying completeness about it.

Editing acts as a kind of quality control on your writing, a checkpoint where your work is evaluated in terms of its impact on your readers. Editing will be more effective if you leave some time between the writing and the editing process since this will allow you to look at your work with fresh eyes.

Whether you are writing fiction or non-fiction, the following kinds of editing will help you improve your manuscript by providing a different editorial focus at each stage of the process:

The Writer's Guide

> "'I learned how to be a better writer by learning how to be a better editor,' he says. 'We had the novelist Robert Stone for one semester and he really tore my early efforts apart. As well as teaching me how to put the right words in the right places to make a sentence, he taught me to test the thought behind each sentence. I realised how derivative, cliched and dishonest I was being.'
>
> 'Those lessons have remained: "Now I rewrite as I go, forever scrubbing and rescanning sentences and muttering 'wanker' to myself."'
>
> Garry Disher interviewed by Murray Waldren, 'Making crime pay', *The Weekend Australian*, 27–28 March 1999.

- Structural editing requires you to stand back from the minutiae of your work and examine the logical sequence of the work as well as its overall structure and the way the parts are arranged to form a whole.
- Editing for style and content requires you to check for inconsistencies in style and expression and to make sure that any factual material you use is correct, not defamatory and does not breach copyright.
- Copy editing involves line-by-line attention to spelling, grammar and punctuation.

If you are editing a work of fiction, make sure you check, for example:

- that the spelling of the characters' names and place-names is correct
- that the punctuation is consistent in narrative and dialogue
- that the dialogue is strong, convincing and has a purpose
- that the plot is plausible and the author has provided clues for the reader
- that the narrative has a clear progression
- that the pace and tone of the writing are appropriate
- that the sequence of events, dates and times is correct
- that issues are resolved
- that each chapter is equally strong
- that the opening sentence of each chapter is compelling.

Structure

Before you begin any detailed copy editing, analyse the structure of your work. Structural editing is perhaps the most intellectually demanding of the editing processes because you have to look at how your piece holds together — its logical development; its continuity; the progression of ideas; the development of characters and the evolution of plot if it is a work of fiction; and the revelation of information in the most appropriate, interesting, or dramatic sequence whether it is fiction or non-fiction.

Some writers prefer to draft an outline of their work so as to get the structure right from the beginning. If you have not done this, you might find it useful to sketch the structure of your first draft. With a non-fiction work you could do this in a series of headings and sub-headings, but if your work is fiction, you might have to draw a diagram with radiating links between characters, incidents and chapters.

Style

When you are satisfied with the overall structure of your work, turn your attention to its stylistic qualities. During the process of writing you might not have been able to spot the stylistic inconsistencies in your writing, but when you can view it as a whole, the process of editing for style can begin. At this stage, questions such as the following will help you polish your manuscript:

- Are the language and tone appropriate for the subject and readership?
- Are there unintentional changes in the style of expression through the manuscript?
- Is any chapter or section weaker, less developed than another?
- Are you using the same verbs, nouns or phrases too often?
- Do too many sentences open with repeated words or expressions?
- Are your sentences or paragraphs lacking variation, tone, length, rhythm?
- Does the piece flow smoothly?
- Are you using the passive voice when an active voice could give your writing more vigour?
- Are you using difficult vocabulary for effect or because it is necessary for your purpose?

> 'I'm ecstatic if I write more than a half a page in a day. Often that comes from walking around repeating a sentence over and over and over, playing around until I get it right. Probably when I come home after a full day of walking and talking to myself, I have two good sentences.'
>
> Delia Falconer quoted by Jane Freeman, *Sydney Morning Herald*, 25 October 1997.

The Writer's Guide

- Can you think of better words or phrases to replace those you're not happy with?

Eventually you will develop your own list of questions depending on which features of your work you think need special attention. It is useful to keep a list of these questions handy for all your work, irrespective of what you are writing.

Some writers edit their work on screen, some prefer to work on a printed draft, and others spend much time structuring and editing their work in their heads before they put anything down on paper or screen. It seems that, whichever way you do it, it takes time to produce the style you are aiming for. Even the most talented writers spend years perfecting their craft.

Content

Whether you are writing fiction or non-fiction, you need to check your manuscript for factual errors in place-names, historical references, dates, geographical locations, and so on. Uncorrected errors could be detected by readers and reviewers and not only cause embarrassment but also lead to the book being dismissed as inaccurate. Such errors, when obvious to a reader, are distracting and undermine the integrity of the text.

When checking for content, also ask yourself if any information needs to be added, whether you have too much information, whether it is presented in the right order, and whether it is presented in the best possible way for the reader.

See Part 4.7.10 'Permission fees'

If you have used quotations from other writers, you may have to get permission to use them and possibly even pay a fee.

See Part 4.7.11 'Defamation'

Check your text for any statement that could possibly be defamatory. Your editor may pick it up, but you cannot leave such scrutiny to the publisher's editor alone as it is the writer who is presumed to understand the details, context and potential impact of what has been written. Don't forget that usually the author is jointly responsible for defamation with the publisher, as set out in the contract. If you are

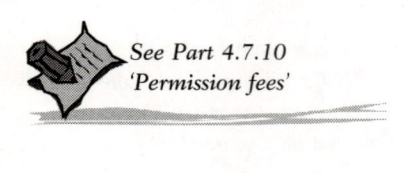

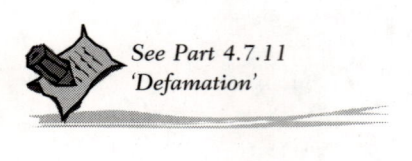

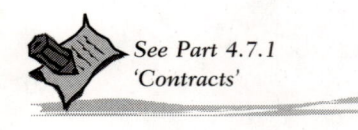

See Part 4.7.1 'Contracts'

in any doubt whether some statement you want to publish is defamatory, mark it for discussion with your editor or publisher.

If you are self-publishing you could be taking a risk if you write anything likely to harm a person's reputation, even if it might be true. Both you and the printer would be named in any defamation suit.

Sexist and racist language

Our use of particular words has been a concern to women and other disadvantaged groups in society who have tried to draw attention to the inherent sexism and racism in language and to provide an alternative vocabulary which is inclusive and does not carry pejorative connotations.

In the early stages of the women's movement there was an attempt to replace words such as 'chairman' with neutral words such as 'chair'. However, feminists such as Dale Spender have pointed out that we will lose the feminine forms of such words if we do not restore their use, and so they advocate forms such as 'chairwoman', and even 'matron' as the equivalent of 'patron'.

Language is dynamic and changes with each generation of speakers, who develop a new vocabulary and styles of expression as a reflection of the society in which they live. Thus the word 'motel' seemed strange when it was first introduced to describe a hotel with parking for its guests; now no-one blinks an eye at it. In the same way, we invent and habituate ourselves to new forms of words and work out new ways of expressing new ideas. Now certain expressions, such as the use of 'man' to describe humanity, seem not only sexist but also somewhat old-fashioned.

In the introduction to his book on *The Conscious Brain*, Dr Stephen Rose (Penguin 1978), a notable brain surgeon and author, commented that in order to examine afresh the established concepts of the brain, he would also have to re-examine the language in which those concepts were expressed. For him, that meant throwing out sexist terms because of their intrinsic linguistic bias and writing in a way that accurately reflected the reality of people's lives. In this he joins other writers conscious of the subliminal effects of language and the way our ideas are shaped by the words we use.

Copy editing

The most meticulous form of editing is copy editing — that is, editing for correct and consistent grammar, spelling and punctuation as well as consistency of presentation, for example, in punctuation marks, in titles, and in the types of headings used. Editing is done either on screen or by hand on a hard (paper) copy of the manuscript.

After you have finished your on-screen editing, check the hard copy of your text as you can usually spot errors or inconsistencies on the page that you do not pick up on the screen. At the same time, check the layout to see if it could be improved and made clearer for the reader.

See WiP Directory of Education and Training for the Publishing Industry *listed in 'Bibliography' in the Resources section*

Some writers' organisations, such as the NSW Writers' Centre, certain universities and some private colleges, such as the Macleay College in Sydney, hold editing courses which cover everything from the structure of a publishing house to copyright, permissions, style editing, indexing, and proof-reading. The cost of these courses may be tax deductible if you receive any income from your writing.

See Part 6.2 'Tax deductions and keeping records'

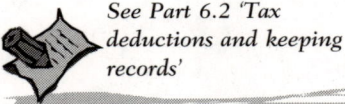

3.5.2 Getting editing practice

One of the best ways of learning how to edit your own work is to have a go at editing someone else's work and let them have a go at editing yours. You have much to learn as you view your own work through another person's eyes and see their work through yours. This is a valuable and instructive process to undertake before you begin the process of redrafting your own work. The great advantage of this form of co-operation is that it can be conducted in person or by mail, email, telephone or fax.

3.5.3 Redrafting

It has been said that there is no such thing as good writing, only good rewriting or, in other words, good redrafting.

Once you have edited your manuscript and received some feedback on your work from others, you will, almost inevitably, need to go back and redraft it extensively. This could include changing the structure radically or altering the content of whole sections, or even changing an entire character in a work of fiction. Don't be disappointed if this is the case. The sometimes tedious process of rewriting will lead to an improvement in your work, and the more you practise the more skilled you will become at it. Many writers produce multiple drafts of their work and are not satisfied until they have worked it over at least several times, if not several dozen times. Just as sculptors and painters use their chisels and brushes to fashion, in stages, a shape out of a block of marble or a painted image on a canvas, so dedicated writers must polish their words through successive drafts with the same painstaking effort their fellow artists exercise in their respective crafts.

> 'Everybody writes crappy first drafts. I'd write things and I'd think this is terrible, I'll never be a writer, and I learnt that everybody goes from a first draft to an 18th draft or a fifth draft; nobody starts with a fantastic first draft.'
>
> Mary-Rose MacColl quoted in 'Creative Masters', *Courier-Mail*, 27 April 1996.

When you are ready for the redrafting process, look at the hard copy of your manuscript and correct it by hand. You can flip easily through the manuscript to find the sections you want to alter, and place certain pages alongside others to make a comparison. This process is difficult to carry out on the computer unless you use a split-screen format, and even then you get only a limited view of each piece of text.

Some writers recommend leaving a piece for six months or so before redrafting. After such a break you can approach it afresh to see if it has achieved what you would like and whether it requires further editing or redrafting. Most likely it will.

3.5.4 Editorial services

After you have polished your work as well as you can, you may wish to get advice from a professional editor before submitting your manuscript for publication. Although this may increase your chances of success, you will need to weigh up for yourself whether it is worth paying for a professional editorial service. For those able to afford it, working with a professional editor can be a great way of improving your writing skills and obtaining constructive comments on your work.

Editorial services are widely available in Australia and New Zealand and you can find out about them from your local writers' centre.

The Society of Editors, established in several states in Australia, and the New Zealand Book Editors Association, are professional organisations which publish newsletters and offer workshops, seminars and lectures on different aspects of editing and publishing throughout the year. The Society of Editors (NSW and Victoria branches) publish registers of editors along with their experience, qualifications and editing specialities. Whether you are interested in editing your own work, or even pursuing a career as an editor, membership of an editors' group gives you access to professional editorial development programs and contacts in the publishing industry.

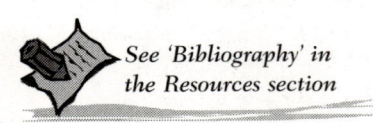

See 'Bibliography' in the Resources section

If you decide to have your manuscript edited, choose your editor carefully, depending on what you have written and the editor's own experience with that particular form of writing. Remember that editors are professionals and charge as such: if you want a reasonable job done, you will have to pay for it. You can save yourself money if you make sure that you have conducted all the steps outlined above in editing your own manuscript before handing your text across to a professional editor. You don't need to waste money on paying an editor to correct mistakes you could have picked up yourself from reading the text carefully or using a spellcheck on your computer.

If you want to reduce editorial costs, you might choose to give only a part of your manuscript to an editor for comment, and then finish the job yourself along the lines suggested by your editor. Some organisations, such as the Fellowship of Australian Writers in Sydney, offer a reduced editorial service on part of a manuscript and charge per hour; in 2002 this was $50 per hour (or $40 for FAW members). This could be a useful service for you if you want comment on a portion of your work to help you on your way with the rest. Alternatively, you might wish to give the whole manuscript to an editor either for detailed comment or for broader structural editing.

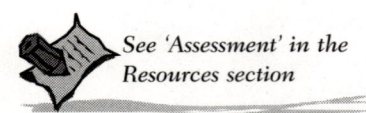

See 'Assessment' in the Resources section

3.5.5 Manuscript assessment services

Manuscript assessment services offer to examine your manuscript for its weaknesses and strengths, the quality of its writing and its publishing potential.

A professional manuscript assessment agency should understand the current publishing scene and be able to make some general recommendations about your potential market. Such agencies do not usually provide editing, agenting or publishing services, but offer an evaluation of the manuscript and advise you on how to get the manuscript to a publishable standard. In 2002, a standard manuscript evaluation cost between $250 and $750. Usually assessment is provided in the form of a written report of two or three pages, which contains comments on style, content and, with some agencies, comment on the commercial viability of the project.

By the time you are ready to use a full assessment service (and to pay for it), you will have already redrafted your piece of work several times and improved it as much as you can on your own or with the help of a professional editor. Manuscript assessment services are available through various agencies in both Australia and New Zealand, with individuals and businesses offering services for all kinds of writing: fiction, non-fiction, children's books, poetry, film scripts, television scripts and plays.

The quality of the assessment varies greatly from agency to agency, so inquire about what kind of service is provided and what you will get for your money.

Script assessments are also offered by film and playwriting bodies to assist writers before they submit their script to a producer or director or funding body.

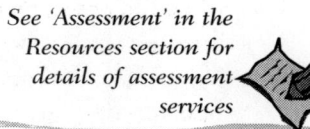

See 'Assessment' in the Resources section for details of assessment services

3.6 SUPPORT AND SKILL DEVELOPMENT

3.6.1 Writers' centres

Writers' centres should be the first port of call for emerging and aspiring writers wishing to develop their skills, knowledge and literary contacts. They offer a focus for writing activity and work with a wide range of literary organisations and publishing companies to promote writing and writers in our society. In Australia there is a writers' centre in each state, and New South Wales is blessed with eight regional writers' centres (Armidale, Blue Mountains, Broken Hill, Byron Bay, Newcastle, Orange, Wagga Wagga, Wollongong) in addition to the NSW Writers' Centre based in Sydney.

See 'Organisations' in Resources section for a full listing of writers' centres

Growing interest in writing as well as the hunger for guidance and information has resulted in steep increases in membership of writers' centres all over Australia. For example, the NSW Writers' Centre grew from a few dozen members in 1991, when it was established, to more than 2500 in just ten years. In 2002, the combined memberships of all the writers' centres in Australia came to about 12 000, while the professional organisations (the Australian Society of Authors and the Australian Writers' Guild) accounted for a further 6000 writers.

Each of the writers' centres was specifically established as a resource and information organisation to assist new, developing and professional writers on every aspect of writing and publishing, from questions about copyright and where to get published, to information about self-publishing and how to approach a literary agent. The centres run a continuing program of workshops, seminars, forums and readings catering to all ages and all types of writing, and to those in the cities as well as in regional areas. They have a range of information available in the form of brochures, booklets and books, and offer advice to members in person, by email, mail and over the phone.

All centres produce regular newsletters or magazines which publish the latest information about literary competitions, festivals, seminars, forums and readings, as well as articles of interest to writers. The publication of comprehensive lists of current literary competitions is of special interest to emerging writers wishing to test their skills and find avenues for their writing. Publishing opportunities are also listed regularly in writers' centre newsletters.

3.6.2 Professional writing organisations

There are also professional bodies for writers whose works have been published, broadcast or performed. These are the Australian Society of Authors and New Zealand Society of Authors, both for published writers, and the Australian Writers' Guild and New Zealand Writers' Guild for professional screenwriters (film, television and video), dramatists and multimedia writers. These organisations also offer associate memberships for writers whose work has not yet been published or produced.

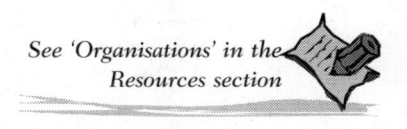

See 'Organisations' in the Resources section

For creative writing teachers, there is the Australian Association of Writing Programs (AAWP), formed in 1996 to enable teachers of creative writing in tertiary institutions across the country to meet and exchange thoughts and ideas on the teaching of creative writing. It has an annual conference at which refereed papers are given, keynote speakers address appropriate topics, and much informal contact is made.

3.6.3 Other writing organisations

Australia's oldest and largest writing organisation, the Fellowship of Australian Writers, has numerous branches across the country which hold regular workshops, discussions and seminars. Unlike the professional bodies, membership is open to anyone interested in writing.

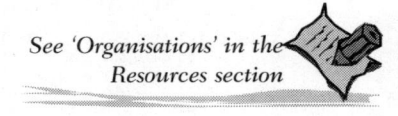

See 'Organisations' in the Resources section

There are also many other writing organisations catering to specific communities of writers such as the Poets Union, the Children's Book Council and the Society of Women Writers.

3.6.4 Writers' groups

> 'The formal and informal feedback, the workshops and writers' clubs, the poetry readings, and the magazines themselves — perform [a] most important role by providing real opportunities, at every level, for writers to assess their own and others' work.'
>
> Claire Murdoch, 'One degree of separation', *New Zealand Books*, August 1998.

A useful, interesting (and cheap) way of getting feedback on your writing is to join a writers' group that meets regularly to comment on the work of its members. Such groups are often associated with writers' centres and meet in premises provided gratis by their centre. Although this is not the same as formal training at a university or college, it provides participants with the opportunity to hone their skills in analysing the work of other writers while at the same time receiving considered opinions on their own work.

Some writing groups meet for a particular interest. For example, in Sydney there is an AIDS Council writing group specifically formed to offer its members, all of whom are HIV positive, a way of expressing themselves and getting their voice heard in the community through newsletters and other publications. The support offered by other writers in the same situation is a useful therapeutic tool as well as a creative outlet. Similarly, writing as therapy is used by organisations counselling clients for grief, torture and trauma. But of course, your group may get together for no other reason than your shared passion for writing and your common need for constructive criticism. One such group which used to meet in Canberra has seen three of its members published to high acclaim — Sara Dowse, Margaret Barbalet and Dorothy Johnston.

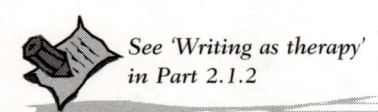

See 'Writing as therapy' in Part 2.1.2

Writing groups can approach the work of their members in different ways. One approach is for some members to be allocated a nominated time at each meeting for a discussion of their work. The size of the group and the length of the meetings will determine whether everyone in the group gets the opportunity to have their work discussed at each meeting. Copies of a selected prose passage or poem can be distributed to every person, who then comments on it during a general discussion. Comments and suggestions could also be written on the copy and handed back to the writer at the end of the discussion. An alternative is for the group to read the entire manuscript of one of its members and to devote one or more sessions to a thorough discussion of it.

Writers showing their work to others may initially feel timid and vulnerable. Considerable rapport needs to be developed among members of writing groups to encourage an atmosphere of mutual trust and respect.

Starting your own writing group

You could start your own writing group, especially if you live in a regional area where there are no writers' centres to assist you (although they can always provide advice by phone, fax, email or letter).

Firstly, find the writers and those interested in writing who are living in your area. Your nucleus could be like-minded writing friends or fellow students from a course who want to continue writing together. Alternatively, contact your local newspaper or radio station to publicise your first meeting or give out a telephone number for people to contact. You can also post notices at your local library, your school, the community centre, supermarket, university, pub, and bookshop and anywhere else where there may be a notice board to advertise your intention. And don't forget that word-of-mouth may take longer but will eventually attract people interested in writing.

You don't need too many people: a group of ten, of whom five or six come regularly, is about the right size. Once you have collected interested people together, discuss the best meeting times for members of the group and where to meet. Some writing groups meet once a week, others once a month, depending on the availability of group members. Check out the venues for a meeting, preferably one where there are desks or tables to sit at, good lighting and comfortable seats.

Many people in your group may be just beginners. It is worthwhile in the first session to set some parameters and to agree that the aim of the group is to help improve one another's writing and that all criticism should be undertaken in this spirit.

As the members of the group get to know one another, it will be possible to branch out and undertake new activities. For example, the group could invite an established writer and experienced tutor to give a workshop on a particular style of writing, such as family history, short stories or articles. Funding may be available from the local council or community centre or from a writers' centre for such a workshop.

After the group has been working together for a while, you might like to hold a public reading of selected works which you have workshopped together. The local library or bookshop is an appropriate place to promote and host the reading. Remember that group members will need practice if they have not read their work in public before.

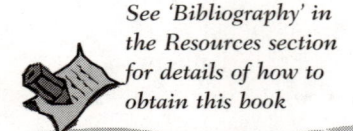

See Part 4.9 'DIY publishing or self-publishing'

At some point the group may consider publishing a book of the work of its members. Discuss what kind of publication it will be — how long, whether it will include both prose and poetry, whether there should be a theme.

See 'Bibliography' in the Resources section for details of how to obtain this book

One useful publication which will help you to set up a writers' group is *Round Table Writing: a Workbook for Writers' Groups, All you need to know to start and run a successful writing group*.

3.6.5 The Regional Writers' Network

Established by enterprising Victorian regional writer Paul Vander Loos, the Regional Writers' Network (RWN) is an email-based information service that allows Australian writers who have email access to interact with other writers across the country. It is of special benefit to regional writers' groups and isolated writers.

Writers on the network can publicise literary events and competitions based in their areas; put out a call for specific information relating to writing pursuits; let others know when they will be visiting their areas so they can set up a welcome and organise billets. If you have a skill to share in some area of writing, you can set up workshops and billets/accommodation in other areas where the network is operating. If you are a professional author/publisher/writer, then writers on the network want to know when you visit their areas. All this can be publicised on the RWN newsgram.

Paul invites writers to contact him at his email address (paulv@wackado.com.au) and tell him what information they want to supply or what request they wish to make. He sends out a newsgram when sufficient new information comes to hand. There is no cost to belong to RWN, and the more who decide to join the better, as there will be more information to share. Paul hopes that more writers Australia-wide will come to know about this service and add their email addresses to the list.

Do not submit documents done on a word processor as an attachment to the email because this requires the recipient to have the same word-processing applications as the sender in order to open it. All information must be forwarded as email text only and kept brief to facilitate an easy transfer to the newsgram, which is compatible with all email programs.

3.6.6 Starting your own reading group

Reading groups are an exciting and informative way of sharing critical opinions on the books that interest you, and this will have the valuable role of helping you to develop your skills as a writer and your analytical skills as a critic.

A reading group can be started in the same way as a writing group, with several individuals who agree to meet regularly in order to discuss a selected reading list.

Rather than choose a number of titles at random, it may be more interesting to select books on the basis of some kind of theme, by date, or by subject matter, in order to give you a point of comparison between the titles. For example, a reading list might consist of a selection of twelve women writers living over the last 300 years, or Shakespeare's comedies, or twentieth-century American poets, or the entire works of a particular writer. Librarians can help you choose authors to include on such a list, or you could obtain a reading list from an English Department of a university, or follow the guides for reading groups such as those put out by some publishers such as Hodder Headline, Vintage, Transworld and Penguin. Whatever you choose, the final list should take into account the interest of the members of the reading group. In Victoria, the College of Adult Education runs a Reading Group scheme which has proven to be very popular. Perhaps there is a similar scheme operating in a college near you?

Once the group has decided on a list of authors, it should come to some agreement about how to conduct the meetings. You may choose to spend just one meeting on a particular book or deal with it in detail over several meetings. A member who has had experience in leading discussions about literature might be called on to kick off the discussions. Someone could be nominated each time to give a short presentation about the life of the author under discussion, and another person could select a particularly fine passage to read aloud to the group.

The most important thing about a reading group is that it allows participants to improve their critical skills by systematically discussing a selected list of published authors. The surroundings should be comfortable and allow each member to clearly hear what others are saying. Discussion will falter in an environment that is cold, unfriendly or noisy.

3.6.7   Courses and workshops

Writing is such a popular form of recreation that there are many courses and workshops available, both for beginners and for those wishing to improve their skills and develop their writing to a high professional standard.

Accredited writing courses are offered through some learning institutions as full-time, part-time or correspondence courses, while non-accredited courses and workshops in poetry, fiction and non-fiction are offered through community colleges, writers' centres and other arts organisations.

If no course or workshop is available near where you live, you may have to consider correspondence courses or even start a group of your own.

There are three levels of writing courses available.

Courses at tertiary institutions

Increasing numbers of tertiary institutions offer writing courses in Australia and New Zealand. These are available at undergraduate, post-graduate, diploma and certificate levels. It is also possible to enrol in some of these courses as a non-degree student, a correspondence student, or at a summer school. Courses cover a wide range of genres, from creative writing (fiction), playwriting, journalism, and children's writing, to multimedia, professional writing, editing and translation.

> 'For me it [the Masters Creative Writing course at the University of Queensland's English Department] was an opportunity to hang around with a bunch of people who were as passionate about writing as I was. I had no contacts in the writing community and here were these people who were very talented writers who could offer me a lot of support and help.'
>
> Mary-Rose MacColl quoted in 'Creative Masters', *Courier-Mail*, 27 April 1996.

Continuing and open education programs

Semester-based courses are offered through continuing and open education programs (connected to universities), community colleges and private colleges. These courses are usually given to enthusiastic amateurs by professional writers well-known in their field. They cover a broad range of subjects and approaches; for instance the 2002 autumn program offered by the University of Sydney's Continuing Education included such courses as 'An introduction to play writing', 'Creative non-fiction writing', 'Writing for children', and 'Screenwriting'.

Some private colleges, such as the Australian College of Journalism, offer accreditation in writing or journalism.

See 'Organisations' in the Resources section

Workshops, seminars and short courses

All writers' centres and some other writing organisations offer short workshops, seminars and courses on different aspects of writing, and these are available to anyone interested in developing their writing skills. The topics covered by such workshops and courses are endlessly variable, from specific genres such as travel writing, scriptwriting, autobiography and poetry, to broad topics such as distinctions between truth and fiction and ways of accessing your imagination. Ask your local writers' centre, community education centre, or college for details of such courses. Check that specific courses meet your requirements, and inquire about tutors and fees before making a decision about which one to enrol in.

Many writers have benefited greatly from attending some kind of creative writing course. Such courses may, if you are a beginner, help you to avoid the most common mistakes of writing in a particular genre, give you useful guidance on structuring your articles or stories, teach you how to approach your family history, or simply encourage and support you in your endeavour. Of course, they also have the advantage of bringing you into contact with others interested in the same field, and out of this you may develop an ongoing writers' group or stay in touch with individuals for mutual assistance in your development as writers.

3.6.8 Mentorships

Mentorships are offered by some writing organisations, such as the Australian Society of Authors and many writers' centres, to give assistance to new writers by matching them with a more experienced writer, who is paid for the mentoring work.

These relationships work in different ways, depending on the needs of the novice writer and the methods of the senior writer. Often, the novice is working on a major work, usually a novel. The senior writer will read a section of the work and discuss it with the novice, commenting on such things as structure, style, consistency and so on, but will not generally copy edit the piece.

Novice writers who have received a mentorship award comment on the close personal relationship they develop with

---

'I see mentoring as helping the writer to find her own voice, by asking the right sort of questions and thereby teasing out intentions, by suggesting certain techniques to help break through the usual stalemates that happen, and affirming rather than criticising . . . this mentorship resulted in a pleasant friendship and has given me faith in my teaching methods . . . mentorship is actually a most ancient tradition — giving time, energy and knowledge to a protégé one has faith in — and has always been one of the best ways of encouraging talent. And I think it is also to do with the mysterious process of creativity — how writers can inspire each other so powerfully once the dynamic is set up.'

Rosie Scott, paper delivered at the 'Getting Published' seminar, NSW Writers' Centre, 18 September 1998.

their mentor, and value the trust that develops between them during the course of the project. All I have spoken to say they have benefited tremendously from the experience and skills of the professional writer and have felt privileged to be selected for the scheme. Mentors have also enjoyed the scheme, which gives them the opportunity to test their teaching and communication skills.

3.7 PERFORMANCE SKILLS

You can share your work with a wider public in various ways. Writing need not be always a solitary enterprise, and for those writers with a dramatic flair, public readings provide an alternative method of reaching your 'readers' via oral presentation.

The revival of interest in the oral traditions of old cultures resulted in the flowering of public readings during the 1990s. Regular performance venues offer writers ample opportunities to test their work in public before publication or, in some cases, before recording.

See also 'Readings' in Part 2.1.3 and Part 2.2.4 'Performance poetry'

Reciting your work before an attentive audience helps you to recognise the weak and strong points in your writing by giving you instant feedback, and as you become more familiar with public presentation you will learn to gauge the subtle reactions of your listeners. You sense when you are holding the audience's attention and when you are losing it, when you are repeating yourself and going on for too long, and when you need to expand and clarify something.

Writers' centres and other writing organisations occasionally offer workshops in public reading and performance skills, and various acting institutes run short courses that provide training in stage presentation. Of course, many writers have recorded their works for broadcast and on audio books and these are obtainable from selected record shops and libraries and on the internet. By listening to writers reading from their own work you can learn by example how to use your voice expressively, how to give the right dramatic pauses in the text, and what tone of voice is best suited to your work. You can practise too by recording your reading on audio or video cassette and playing the recording back to yourself.

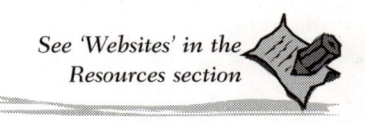

See 'Websites' in the Resources section

Storytelling guilds in Australia and New Zealand also help writers develop the art of storytelling in public. These guilds offer not only tuition in the art of storytelling, but also give accreditation based on numbers of performance hours and assessment by expert judges.

See 'Organisations' in the Resources section for contact details

3.8   TRANSLATION SKILLS

Writers of non-English-speaking background (NESB) or, indeed, English speakers fluent in another language, may find opportunities to use their translation skills in the service of literature. Some Australian publishers are prepared, with or without financial assistance, to publish translations or bilingual editions of literary works, and the establishment of prizes for a literary translation has made it easier for NESB writers to find readers in the general marketplace. A number of Australian magazines (*Ulitarra, Heat*) publish translations (either bilingual or in English only) among their contributions.

In Australia, translation skills can be acquired at various universities and colleges through special training programs, usually conducted by modern languages departments. There are several organisations to assist applicants wishing to develop their translation and interpretation skills and gain formal accreditation.

Writers interested in literary translation should contact the following organisations to find out about professional training and job opportunities, as well as to meet practitioners working in the field.

> 'Translators have the special skill of passing meaning through themselves. They control the turnstiles of our knowledge of other cultures; they are gatekeepers of our cross-cultural awareness. They reveal to the literate illiterate what goes on in the presumptive privacy of another culture, selecting words and whole texts for translation . . . Translation lets outsiders overhear conversations behind the drawn shutters of other societies.'
>
> Alison Broinowski, 'Assisted passages', *The Australian's Review of Books*, June 1998.

3.8.1 Australian Institute of Interpreters and Translators (AUSIT)

Established in 1987, with branches in all states and territories, the Australian Institute of Interpreters and Translators (AUSIT) is the national association of interpreters and translators.

One of AUSIT's aims is to increase awareness of the professional nature of interpreting and translating. It also works to promote members' interests, keeps them informed of new developments in the field, and holds workshops, conferences and seminars for on-going professional development.

AUSIT publishes a journal and a newsletter for its members which cover all the latest issues and news in interpreting and translating. It manages a database, which is marketed Australia-wide, and a website to open up job opportunities for its members.

AUSIT branches welcome inquiries from writers wishing to have their work translated. Alternatively, writers can advertise in the quarterly newsletter.

3.8.2 National Accreditation Authority for Translators and Interpreters (NAATI)

The National Accreditation Authority for Translators and Interpreters (NAATI) is an independent organisation for interpreters and translators which provides accreditation in 47 languages.

NAATI produces various publications, including the newsletter *NAATI News*.

3.8.3 Australian Literary Translators' Association (ALiTrA)

The Australian Literary Translators' Association (ALiTrA) has, since its formation in 1991, promoted literary translation in Australia in order to improve the public profile of this complex art. It acts as a

> 'Translators deploy their ears and eyes in one language and their mouths and pens in another . . . No computer has been taught to replace them, yet their ability is treated as if it were of no more value than a stretched string between two cans.'
>
> Alison Broinowski, 'Assisted passages', *The Australian's Review of Books,* June 1998.

focal point for literary translators, editors, publishers, critics, writers, and others interested in literary translation, as well as promoting the exchange of information and the improvement of work conditions on the job.

ALiTrA's professional database of members allows the organisation to establish contacts between literary professionals and translators, and will help to create more work opportunities for practitioners.

As part of its work ALiTrA publishes *ALiTrA Journal,* a magazine containing short and excerpted translations, articles, information (especially on recent book publications) and advertisements.

3.8.4 Translation grants

> 'Translators can play a key role in enriching our literary canon . . . Both translators and publishers act as gate-keepers . . . who determine which foreign writers and foreign works are presented to Australian audiences and which Australian works are presented abroad.'
>
> Judy Wakabayashi, 'The translator's voice', *Antipodean,* no. 1, October 1997.

The Premier's Translation Prize is offered biennially to an outstanding translator, rather than a particular work of translation, by the New South Wales Ministry for the Arts and the Community Relations Commission for a Multicultural New South Wales in association with International PEN (Sydney Centre). The prize is intended to acknowledge the contribution made to literary culture by Australian translators. It is offered only to translators who translate works into English from other languages. The award is valued at $5000 and the winner also receives a commemorative medallion, sponsored by International PEN (Sydney Centre). To be eligible for nomination, translators should be able to show evidence of a body of literary work that has been published or performed in recent years. This work may include poetry, stage and radio plays, and fiction and non-fiction works of literary merit. The award is not made for the sub-titling of films or television programs.

The Prize is judged by an independent committee appointed by the Premier on the advice of the Ministry for the Arts, the Community Relations Commission for a Multicultural New South Wales and International PEN (Sydney Centre). The committee comprises literary translators, writers, academics and/or critics. The judges give preference to translators who have had a substantial work either published or performed in Australia or overseas in the two years prior to the closing date of the competition. Translators may nominate themselves or be nominated by authors, agents, translation and literary associations, publishers, theatre companies or radio broadcasters, and they must be Australian citizens or hold permanent resident status. For further details contact Program Manager, Literature and History, New South Wales Ministry for the Arts (02) 9228 4745, email ministry@arts.nsw.gov.au.

The Dinny O'Hearn/SBS Prize for Literary Translation of $12 000 was first given in 1992 and has been offered triennially since 1994. The prize, subject to funding, will be next awarded in 2003. It is offered to a translator for a work translated into English, in any category of literature (including theatre, radio script and screen play), which has been published, performed or made available for sale in Australia in the eligible period. Eligible translators must be Australian citizens (residing anywhere in the world) or permanent residents of Australia. Guidelines and nomination forms for the 2003 Award will be available in February 2003. The eligible period for the 2003 award will be 1 May 2000 to 30 April 2003. For further details contact Victorian Premier's Literary Awards Project Officer (03) 8664 7277, email pla@slv.vic.gov.au.

PART FOUR
GETTING PUBLISHED

4.1 RESEARCHING YOUR READERS/AUDIENCE/MARKET

Irrespective of what you have written, you will, if you are interested in sharing your work with others, be trying to find your ideal reader, your most responsive audience, your most appropriate market.

Your readership will, of course, depend on what you have written. You may already have determined your market or readership if, for example, you are writing a newsletter which is aimed at a particular group of people, such as the Society of Editors or the National Trust newsletter.

In other cases your readership may be more elusive. The better you research your market, the more likely you will have success in finding the right outlet for your material. Whether you are writing fiction or non-fiction, ask yourself the following:

- Who am I writing for?
- Where are my readers likely to be found?
- Which outlets, both publications and net addresses, would be suitable for my particular form of writing?
- Do I want to be paid for my writing? If so, what is the best outlet for me? If not, what choices do I have?
- Do I have a good enough publishing résumé to approach a commercial publisher with my work?

Many different kinds of publications accept short items such as articles, essays, interviews, reviews, opinion pieces, short stories and other material for publication; there are specialist companies which help writers with self-publishing ventures; there are publishing companies large and small, multinational and independent, specialist and general, which publish non-fiction and fiction, educational material, children's books, trade publications, self-help books and anything else you can think of.

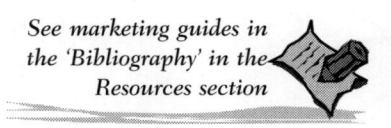

See marketing guides in the 'Bibliography' in the Resources section

Contact your local writers' centre for details of these publications and companies, see 'Organisations' in the Resources section

You can save time, money, effort (and rejection slips!) by sending your work to the magazines or publishers most likely to accept it. Do some market research to determine who these are:

- Browse in newsagents, bookshops and libraries to find out who is publishing work similar to yours and may be interested in it.
- Consult publications such as *The Australian Writer's Marketplace*, *Literary Market Place* and *Writers' and Artists' Yearbook*, available in writers' centres and the reference sections of public and university libraries. These have comprehensive contact lists of agents, and book and magazine publishers throughout the world. For more literary guides, try the *Small Press Guide* and the NSW Writers' Centre's *Journals Directory* for listings of literary publications.

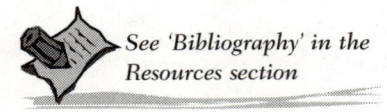

  See 'Bibliography' in the Resources section

- Check out *Books in Print* (US), *Whitakers* (UK) and *Australian Books in Print* (D. W. Thorpe), *New Zealand Books in Print* (D. W. Thorpe), and *Ulrich's Periodicals Guide*.
- Consult the *Australian Book Publishers Association Directory of Members*, which lists the contact details of the major commercial publishers in Australia and the types of work they publish and is usually available at writers' centres and other writing organisations.

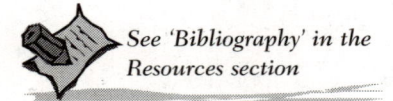

  See 'Bibliography' in the Resources section

4.2 FINDING SUITABLE AVENUES FOR PUBLICATION

If you are just beginning your publishing career, start small with short pieces entered in competitions or submitted to periodicals such as literary journals, commercial publications, local newspapers, specialist magazines, and so on. The point of starting with the publication of shorter pieces is to build up your publishing résumé to establish your credentials as a writer and to show prospective editors or publishers where else your work has appeared. Such a résumé is also vital if you want to apply for a writing grant from government or private bodies and sometimes it is a requirement for a job in journalism. Funding bodies usually require evidence of extensive publication to be submitted with applications.

4.2.1 Periodicals

Choosing the right periodical

Writers' centres, public libraries, university libraries and newsagents hold a huge range of periodicals for you to research. Some large libraries even set aside a special room for the latest issues of journals and magazines.

There are also numerous marketing guides for Australia and New Zealand, as well as for other English-language countries such as the United States, Canada and the United Kingdom, that publish comprehensive listings of literary and academic journals, specialist and general commercial magazines, newspapers, and other outlets for short fiction and non-fiction. Some of these guides list details such as desirable length of contributions, whether unsolicited material is accepted, whether work is paid for in cash or in kind (usually with copies of the publication), and whether you should send illustrative material to accompany your contribution. Two extensive market directories you will find helpful in locating and identifying your market are Rhonda Whitton's *The Australian Writer's Marketplace*, published annually, and the NSW Writers' Centre's *Journals Directory*, with a listing of mostly literary publishing outlets.

See 'Bibliography' in the Resources section for details

Every periodical, whether specialist or general magazine, literary journal or newspaper, has its own distinctive style, tone and readership. The better you know the publication, the more likely you are able to gauge whether a piece you have written is suitable for it. It is a waste of your time and money to send, say, a short article on local history to a publication with a national focus. Nonetheless, if you're prepared to take the risk and send your piece to an unlikely publication, there's always an outside chance that the editor might publish it because it just happens to suit that particular issue.

If you have a particular literary or popular magazine in mind before you write your piece, first read the stories and articles published in it, taking note of their length, style and content, and craft your own material to suit the publication. However, be wary of falling into the trap of producing stories and articles about fashionable themes because you think they have a better chance of

The Writer's Guide

being published. It is the quality of the writing, rather than the subject matter, which is of most importance to discerning editors.

Some writers write their material first and then seek an appropriate outlet for it. This is risky for non-fiction pieces as your work may not fit a magazine's style, word count, subject matter, etc. For short stories or poems, however, the field is much wider. Writer Michael Wilding says of his own experience in writing short stories:

> In terms of the literary market-place, my own practice has always been to write the story first, and then to look for a suitable place for publication afterwards. I have never written fiction with a particular magazine or publisher in mind. I have always believed that writing has its own demands, that the work has to take its own direction and shape and not be deformed by commercial pressures . . . Once you write for the market you have surrendered unconditionally to those pressures ('Writing short stories', address by Michael Wilding to the Society of Women Writers, NSW Writers' Centre, March 1997).

> 'When an issue appears in the newspapers and magazines (e.g. AIDS, child abuse, divided families), we know that we'll get a welter of stories on the subject within three weeks. A story which has been created on the basis of moral outrage remains a diatribe. Leave such instant sociology to the platitudinous slogans of the American evangelists. A good writer may well use any of these themes within a story but the characters remain more important than the Seven Nightly News. A good writer doesn't search out an item and hang a story on it like a cardboard suit.'
>
> Bruce Pascoe, publisher of *Australian Short Stories* (quoted in *600 Markets for Australian Writers*, by Edwina Toohey, Qld, 1996).

Submitting material to periodicals

Most publications have submission guidelines and you should follow these carefully when submitting your work. Handwritten work is definitely *out*. So is work presented scrappily on odd-sized sheets of paper, or with errors in spelling, punctuation and grammar. Submission guidelines are sometimes printed in the publication itself or can be obtained from the editor.

Remember that the deadlines for some of these publications can be months ahead of the actual publication date, so get in early. Contact the editor by phone or letter to ask if he or she would like an article on a particular topic and mention what particular 'angle' you are going to give it. Also send some samples of other articles you have written (see listing in the 'Bibliography' in the Resources section for *Guidelines for Publishing in Periodicals*, a brochure produced by the New Zealand Society of Authors, for useful information).

If you are going to attract the attention of the editor of a periodical, the title of your piece must be interesting. Try to find a catchy title which will stick in the mind of the editor. It could make the difference between your article and another as good being accepted for publication.

The opening sentences of your article must also make compelling reading. Editors have little time to peruse all the material they receive, and they will not waste time reading the rest of a submission if the introduction is poor. Similarly, editors who have specified a word count will discard submissions that are well above or below the word count because they will not fit into the allocated space in the publication.

If you haven't heard from the editor within a week or so of submitting your article, telephone or email to find out whether it has been read and, if so, whether it has been accepted for publication. You should also inquire about the rates at which you will be paid: in 2002 they varied from $100 per 1000 words to $1000 or more for 1000 words depending on the kind of publication, your experience, the quality of the writing, and whether your name is known to the editor. The Media Entertainment and Arts Alliance and the Australian Society of Authors have established fee rates for freelance writers and will be able to provide you with a copy. However, please be warned: many publications take no notice of the recommended rates and will pay as little as possible. It's a buyers' market.

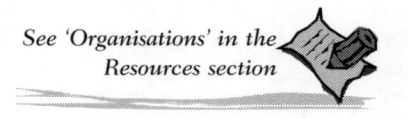

See 'Organisations' in the Resources section

If you are invited to contribute to a particular publication, do so. Only when you are inundated with requests can you afford to be more choosy.

Some magazine or journal editors may like your piece but ask you to lengthen or shorten it or even rewrite it to include new material, or else they may edit it themselves to fit the space or for other considerations. Whether you agree will depend on how committed you are to the form and content of your original piece, how much you want your piece to appear in that particular publication, and how much you are being paid for it, if at all. There is little you can

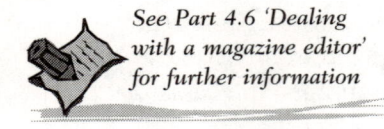

See Part 4.6 'Dealing with a magazine editor' for further information

do about this unless your agreement is to publish it as submitted. If the editor commissions your piece and decides not to publish it, even though it has met all the criteria, you should expect some payment as your 'kill' fee, that is, a fee to be paid if the piece is satisfactory but is not published. The best time to negotiate a kill fee is before you start work, so get an agreement in writing which stipulates the rate of payment, the kill fee and which of your expenses will be covered (if any).

If you have original pictorial material to accompany your article, find out what format the editor would like it in (slides, laser printout, bromides or finished artwork, or some electronic format) and make sure it is of a quality suitable for reproduction. Ensure the match of pictures and captions is clear by submitting a list of captions and marking the pictures or artwork with the number of the caption.

See Part 4.7.10 'Permission fees'

Colour prints are not usually acceptable for publication. If you are submitting pictorial material that is not your own, you must get permission from the copyright holder for its use. You, or the magazine you write for, may have to pay for this. And remember that you should receive extra payment for use of your pictorial material.

4.2.2   Literary competitions

Many small literary competitions held across Australia and New Zealand are, for beginning writers, an excellent way of starting a writing career. These competitions often provide a designated theme for a short story, a poem or an essay, and this will give you the starting point for your subject matter, as well as a word limit and deadline by which you have to complete it. All writers' centres produce publications with details of such competitions, so one of the best ways of finding out about them is to become a member and to receive a regular newsletter.

Although most literary competitions are legitimate, and the organisers are genuinely interested in promoting good writing, it is just as well to check certain details of the competition. Writers can be deceived in the excitement of the moment when told they have won a competition and their work has been selected for publication in a book. One such organisation was investigated by the Department of Consumer Affairs in Queensland because it told all writers who had submitted poems, in what looked like a standard letter, that their work had qualified them as a 'semi-finalist . . . on the basis of your unique talent'. Writers were then invited to purchase the book of winning entries which cost 'only' $70. If you want to avoid this kind of 'vanity' publishing, which preys on unsuspecting writers and robs them of a genuine opportunity to submit their work to a reputable outlet, make sure you check the following details when entering competitions:

- The name of the competition and the address to which entries must be sent. Note that many competitions do not provide phone numbers because they are run by small groups of voluntary staff who do not have the time to answer telephone queries.
- Categories of entries (short story, poetry, essay, etc.).
- Qualifications for entry (e.g. residency of a particular country).
- Length of entry.
- Format of entry (e.g. on A4 paper, single-sided, name or pen-name and address on separate page).
- Amount of fee per entry. Except in major competitions run by a well-known publisher or magazine, when fees could be as much as $25 per entry (in 2002), entry fees will not usually be more than about $5 per entry.
- Maximum number of entries to be submitted.
- Whether the work must be unpublished, or not previously broadcast or performed.
- List of prizes to be awarded in different categories.
- Closing date of competition or last postmark date.
- Names of judges.
- Date of announcement of competition results.
- Whether a stamped self-addressed envelope is required for return of entry.
- Copyright is to remain with the author even if the competition reserves the right to publish the winning entries. The condition of winning a prize in some competitions is that the entry will be published once in a particular publication.

Writers' centres will be able to tell you which competitions are reputable, which not.

4.2.3 Submitting book-length manuscripts

Many writers aspire to seeing their work, whether fiction or nonfiction, published as a book, but there is a lot more to it than just packing off your labour of love to a publisher. The competition is so intense that the more you understand about publishing trends as well as the selection and publishing processes the better your chances.

Large commercial publishers receive hundreds and even thousands of unsolicited manuscripts each year. Some, such as HarperCollins, read only half of them, and of those that are read, only about five end up on the shelves of a bookstore. In 1998, Penguin publisher Julie Gibbs noted that her company received an average of 70 unsolicited manuscripts per week — that is, some 3640 a year — of which only three or four were considered worthy of publication.

For this reason, consider having your work professionally assessed or edited before sending it to a publisher, funding body, or producer. An editor or assessor can critique your work, and suggest improvements where necessary; some even offer to comment on its commercial viability. Some publishers and funding bodies prefer to see manuscripts that have been assessed prior to submission and request that a reader's (sometimes also an agent's) report accompany the manuscript or script.

Publishers are most likely to take on a new writer if the work is written well, if the content is good, and, most importantly, if it is recommended by a literary

> 'We receive every kind of material imaginable — some of it good, some of it so-so and some of it absolute dross. Some people think because they happen to have generated 500 pages of typescript, they've written a novel. Others are sure that the 50 000-word story of their life constitutes a must-read. But, at least, the envelope is opened and each manuscript is given a fair hearing. One would hope that this process will make talent rise to the top.'
>
> Penguin publisher Julie Gibbs quoted in 'Thanks, but no thanks', 'Sunday Life', *Sun-Herald*, 14 March 1998.

See Part 3.5.5 'Manuscript assessment services' and 'Assessment' in the Resources section

See Part 4.8 'The role of agents' and 'Agents' in the Resources section agent or some other respected reader. Approach agents with the same proposal you would send to a publisher and ask them to read and assess it. Some agents charge a reading fee for this service, and not all welcome unsolicited manuscripts. Your local writers' centre can tell you which agents are willing to receive — and read — unsolicited manuscripts.

Commercial publishers (and agents) will be more interested in your manuscript if you have a publishing record, whether in fiction or non-fiction. This is where your publication in periodicals, magazines, newspapers, and so on, becomes a valuable stepping stone to the publication of something more substantial. If you have won prizes or were commended in literary competitions, so much the better. Don't forget to include these on your publishing résumé.

One sure way of getting your novel published is to win a competition for an unpublished novel which guarantees publication of the winning entry. The competition is great, but why not give it a go? Someone's got to win! Lillian Ng is a gynaecologist who submitted her first work of fiction to the inaugural Angus & Robertson Bookworld Prize for Fiction in 1993. She was a runner-up and her manuscript *Silver Sister* was subsequently published. That launched her on her literary career. She has since published her second novel, *Swallowing Clouds*, and is now working on a third.

> 'Don't be discouraged by rejection because there is always a chance. We are publishing a first-time novelist this year, Georgia Blaine. That's the thrill for me — to see something wonderful just bob up out of the mediocrity.'
>
> Penguin publisher Julie Gibbs quoted in 'Thanks, but no thanks', 'Sunday Life', *Sun-Herald*, 14 March 1998.

Finding the right publisher

Before you begin a book-length manuscript, research your market to find out what has already been published in the field. Study publishers' and booksellers' catalogues to see what individual publishers are currently producing. You could also visit a large bookshop and look at the relevant section to make a list of local publishers

See Part 4.1 'Researching your market'

producing work similar to yours, or visit a large library to look at the current listings of Australian or New Zealand books in print.

Directories of Australian and New Zealand publishers will help you find the right publishing company for your particular manuscript. Certain publishers specialise in non-fiction general books, some are exclusively educational publishers, while others concentrate on fiction.

Just because a particular publisher has not published anything like your work in the past does not mean that it never will. For example, even though Penguin Books Australia had not published science fiction for years, writer Paul Collins approached the company with a proposal for a science fiction anthology and was offered a contract for three. Of course, if there is already a recent book published on your topic, you may have to think of a new angle or discard the idea for another.

Most publishers have guidelines for submission of manuscripts which can be obtained by telephoning the editorial section of the company or writing in with a request for a copy. It is important to follow these guidelines: manuscripts which ignore them could be rejected unread.

The best way of keeping in touch with current trends in book publishing is to read the arts and review pages of newspapers and literary magazines. By paying attention to who is publishing what, you will be able to target your manuscript to the most appropriate publisher.

International publishers

It is wisest to begin your search for a publisher within Australia or New Zealand. As a general rule, international publishers are not interested in unknown antipodean writers, and if you have no publishing record or profile, your manuscript has even less chance of being accepted for publication in a market other than your own. Some writers do succeed overseas, but usually only after success in their home country.

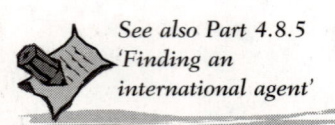

See also Part 4.8.5 'Finding an international agent'

However, rules are there to be broken, and it is just possible that your manuscript may appeal to an international publisher. NSW Writers' Centre member Tim Griggs tried to get his novels published for 30 years and, after failing in his attempts in Australia, returned to his native UK and landed a six-figure deal for his novel *Redemption Blues*.

4.2.4 Internet publishing

Although internet publishing has been regarded with some scepticism by the publishing industry, it is gradually becoming accepted as a legitimate form of publishing and a breeding ground for new talent. For example, in 1998, a novel first published on the web — Patricia Le Roy's *Angels of Russia* — was accepted as one of 125 entries for the Booker Prize. Le Roy published her book with an internet publisher called Online Originals. In Australia, HarperCollins took on a crime novel by Lindy Cameron, called *Golden Relic*, which was first published on the net.

Most mainstream publishers will not take up the net as a form of distribution until they can work out some way of making money from it, but smaller publishers and individuals are increasingly using it to trawl for exciting new writers. Sydney writer Alan Gold intends to use his site to attract literary talent and then forward selections of the submissions to publisher acquaintances. He states with conviction that 'Publishing houses are missing out on a wellspring of serious future talent by turning their backs on the Internet as a breeding ground for future writers' (quoted by Suzy Freeman-Greene in 'Writers put their pens to cyberspace', *The Age*, 17 October 1998).

It has been suggested that internet publishing may spark a renaissance in poetry because it does not incur the high costs of production and distribution of conventional publishing. John Tranter, editor of the literary zine *Jacket*, says: 'The problem for poetry is the cost of distribution for a book with inherently small sales, and the

> 'If claims about netizen politics are true, we can expect that Internet users will not accept the prevailing view that self-published literature is not worth reading. If it is possible for entire novels to be published on the Internet, then netizens will seek them out and read them. If the current problems with copyright and making payments on the Internet are resolved, then authors will no doubt move to exploit this market.'
>
> Glenn Phillips, 'Bad press: political views of self-published literature in contemporary Australia', *Redoubt*, no. 25, 1997, pp. 130–3.

The Writer's Guide

unwillingness of the book stores to stock poetry titles. The Net solves all that. It also has a global reach. You wouldn't want to read a novel on the Net — you'd go blind. But poetry is ideal — most poems are short' (quoted by Suzy Freeman-Greene in 'Writers put their pens to cyberspace', *The Age*, 17 October 1998).

Internet publishing services

Some specialist companies have established services to help writers self-publish and distribute their books on the internet. They perform many of the same tasks as companies which offer to help writers self-publish their books. This form of publishing potentially allows authors to reach a global market.

See 'Websites' in the Resources section for details of several internet publishers

After receiving a copy of your manuscript electronically or on disk, the internet publisher may refer you to, or provide, editing, desktop formatting, graphic design and other services required to make the text suitable for presentation on the net.

Once the text has been prepared, the publisher places the text on a dedicated site on the web. Interested readers may purchase the electronic version of the book on the strength of an opening chapter or blurb on the net and download it onto their system after paying for it. The reader can then peruse the book on-screen or read it in hard copy.

See 'Payment' on opposite page

Such publishers usually charge for production costs plus a commission, the standard being about 10 per cent, a one-off registration fee of about $500 (in 2002), and a fee for hire of annual 'shelf space' on the web bookstore site. They will provide an ISBN (International Standard Book Number) for your 'book', and offer to display it in the virtual bookstore together with your résumé and a synopsis of your work. They will also process orders for the book and pay royalties at regular intervals.

See 'ISBN' in Part 4.9.2

If you are not interested in making money from the sale of your text you may choose to freely present it entirely on the web to anyone who wishes to read it. However, you will still incur costs whether you attach your page to an existing website or develop your own site. In the latter case, you will need to pay a service provider for a web address and will require expertise, your own or someone else's, to design the website.

> *See 'Websites' in the Resources section*

Software

Preparing your text for internet publication requires two stages. Firstly, you will need

> *See Part 2.5 'Internet and multimedia writing' and Part 5.5 'Your own website'*

to desktop-publish the book, that is, present it on the screen in the best possible layout. Secondly, you will need to make sure others, whatever the computer equipment they use, can read your work.

For desktop publishing, you could use one of the popular industry-standard software packages, such as Claris Home Page, Adobe Pagemill or Microsoft Frontpage, which allows you to format a home page with comparatively little expertise. Alternatively, you could create your book as a file in a popular word program such as Microsoft Word, the latest version of which allows you to save a document as 'html' or hypertext mark-up language suitable for placing on a website.

In order for others to read your work exactly as you have formatted it, they will need to have Adobe Acrobat Reader, a common formatting tool, installed on their computer. Most people who surf the web would have such a program.

Although this process may seem complicated to a novice, it is not difficult: with some expert advice or a short course in website production you can design your own website and gain great satisfaction from seeing your work on the screen and available to readers around the world.

Payment

How do you get payment before readers download your book onto their computers for later perusal? You could have your book file on a hidden web page or on a site that is controlled by a password. If you know how to design forms and set up interactive sites to send data back to your host computer, online orders can be sent to you, complete with credit-card details. Payment is by 'E-cash', an encrypted electronic credit-card payment system which is supposed to protect the credit-card holder. Once you receive an order, you give the user the password to download the file or send a disk.

The password needs to be changed often. Many web design companies can create sites like this.

But it is not necessarily so simple. Fair remuneration for work produced on the web is an ongoing problem for writers. Writers presently cannot, with any measure of certainty, protect their work from being reproduced directly from the web. In addition, there are manifest difficulties in collecting royalties for work in multiple platforms and delivery systems. For example, a work could be produced on the web, and transformed from a video game to a website to a feature film, which could in turn be broadcast via cable television, high-definition television, direct satellite systems, digital video disc set-tops, DVD (digital video disc) ROM and others yet to come on the market.

The question of royalties for web products is far from being resolved, and professional writers' organisations in Australia and New Zealand are campaigning vigorously to make sure writers' rights are protected in the current electronic revolution. It might have been comparatively easy for pop musicians to win their case against NAPSTA, but writers face far greater difficulties in protecting both the integrity of their work and their legal right to royalties.

Marketing

Internet publishers will market the book for you if you have decided to use their services. Advertisements on the web can be supported by additional forms of marketing and publicity, such as fliers and other promotional material sent to specialist magazines and publications interested in reporting on net books. The NSW Writers' Centre has entered into an arrangement with distributor John Reed whereby the centre advertises members' books on its website and they are distributed from Reed's warehouse in Sydney.

4.3 THE BUSINESS OF BOOK PUBLISHING

Book publishing is expensive and speculative and entails making calculated decisions about what will sell, what readers will buy, and what the marketplace will absorb. If your goal is to have your work published in book form at any stage, then an understanding of the basic business, the processes involved, and some of the issues facing the publishing industry, will help you in your pursuits.

4.3.1 An overview of the industry

With so many alternatives to occupy leisure time in the early 2000s, the book has suffered from stiff competition. Publishers are taking fewer risks, and are much more selective and disciplined about what they publish. In 1998, Peter Field, then managing director of Penguin Books Australia, said that the business of publishing was like 'going to the casino every day' to emphasise the uncertainties of his profession, although the then executive director of the Australian Publishers Association, Sue Blackwell, believed that the Australian publishing industry was more resilient and stable than its overseas counterparts.

Of the 9755 books published in Australia during 1999–2000, about one-third did not sell. The number of unsold books that booksellers return to publishers (called the rate of returns) has been averaging between 25 per cent and 35 per cent. In the United States it averages 45 per cent. The sheer volume of books offered on the market each year presents difficulties for publishers: limited shelf space in bookshops, competition for reviews and media attention, and rivalry for the attention of readers. Hilary McPhee, former chair of the Australia Council and former publisher of McPhee Gribble, says there are too many books on the market and too many poor-quality books being published. Her sentiments are echoed by others in the business and they are acting on it. Hodder Headline's Australian list has been cut in the last two years from 150 titles to 80 in 2002, while HarperCollins' local titles have been reduced from 270 to 220. Hodder Headline publishing director Lisa Highton identifies a world trend for 'publishing fewer titles but publishing harder'. She says that publishers generally make 80 per cent of their money from 20 per cent of their books.

Some blame has been attributed to the takeover of small publishing companies by multinational conglomerates, which often lack the editorial expertise to select and foster talent or are reluctant to

> 'There is a lot of rubbish published. Hundreds of books come onto the market every month which are crap. The level of mistakes is too high. If 40 per cent of the products manufactured by a company like Nike were dogs, the executives would be slashing their wrists.'
>
> Former General Manager of Dymocks, Tony Aduckiewicz, quoted by Sally Loane, 'Publish and be drowned', *Sydney Morning Herald*, 22 November 1997.

> 'Where once an editor with flair could spot an emerging talent and nurture it through several books which could boast only modest reviews and sales, in the hope that he or she would eventually write the big book that would break through and earn for author and publisher both revenue and reputation, that is now virtually unknown. A book published by all but the smaller, fringe houses must now have a guaranteed readership before the publishing businesses will invest their resources. Fat advances to a few, sure-fire bestselling authors accompanied by massive hype and a big marketing budget are the order of the day. Editing is less important; the key factor is not the quality of the text but the image on the cover; not the prose style but the dress sense and photogenic features of the author.'
>
> Jane Hill, 'Fact or Fiction: The Changing Role of the Book Editor', *Mattoid 51*, 1997.

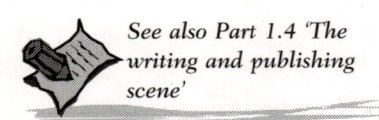

See also Part 1.4 'The writing and publishing scene'

put resources into editorial support. In this climate, writers may be pushed towards publication before they are ready for it, and if their first or second novel bombs, they are likely to be dropped by their publisher.

Nonetheless, small independent publishers such as Brandl and Schlesinger and Duffy and Snellgrove, and some of the new poetry publishers such as Five Islands Press, publish short print-run, specialised books appealing to a niche market. These publishers are much more likely to concentrate on producing quality publications which attract, and retain, loyal readers among the educated class. Because the survival and success of such publishers depends on the quality of their product, they are likely to provide the intensive editorial services that every writer needs before releasing a book on the market, not to mention particular attention to design and illustration.

One such company which provides a large amount of editorial support for its writers is Text Publishing, whose publisher Michael Heyward says: 'Because we are a new company, we do a lot of first books and I love doing first books. We really want to find writers who can grow with us. Their growth will be our growth; they'll make us and we'll make them. I'm into first books.' This may explain the extraordinary success Text has had in its publishing program with such writers as Shane Maloney, Linda Jaivin, Gideon Haigh and Helen Garner, all edited by Michael Heyward himself.

4.3.2 The stages of publication

Publishing is labour intensive, with many people exercising their skills along the way from first draft to finished product. The writer is the starting-point of the whole operation, but before the book comes to the reader's attention there is a bevy of editors, illustrators, designers, production managers, and marketing and salespeople who work on it at different stages of production, distribution and publicity. It will help you in your publishing ventures if you know how a book is published and why publishers make certain decisions.

Author Alan Gold believes that successful publishing relies on four principles: the quality of the writing, the quality of the packaging, the display of the book, and the 'packaging' of the author.

The following section describes the typical stages of production in a commercial publishing operation as distinct from a self-publishing venture initiated by an author.

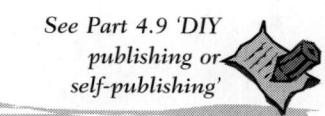

See Part 4.9 'DIY publishing or self-publishing'

Selecting material

A book comes into being either when an author has a bright idea and successfully puts a proposal to the publisher or managing editor of a publishing company, or when a commissioning editor approaches a writer to produce a book to fit certain specifications. If it is a non-fiction work, the editor may suggest material to be included in the book and work with the writer to develop an appropriate contents list of subjects or topics to be covered.

The role of publishers' editors

After deciding to go ahead with the publication of a book, most publishers assign either an in-house or a freelance editor to edit the manuscript. (This is usually a different person from the acquisitions or commissioning editor, who commissions books but does not perform the hands-on role of editing the book, except in small companies such as Text Publishing.) This editor either takes your manuscript and edits it alone or, more rarely, works closely with you on getting it to a publishable standard. Editors either work with a pen on hard copy or take your manuscript on computer disk and edit it on-screen.

Most publishing companies produce style guides that cover

The Writer's Guide

> 'Nowadays editors must be all-rounders, must keep acquiring new publishing skills. And I'm not referring to updating their obvious editorial knowledge but rather a willingness to understand the role of the other publishing departments. Money is expensive, whatever the interest rate, so advances must be judiciously negotiated; contracts must be carefully understood, particularly in these days of ever-expanding technological spin-offs; all subsidiary, book club and overseas rights have to be exploited; budgets and costings must be second nature; schedules understood and kept; balance sheets mustn't blow the mind; authors must be found, bullied, cosseted and loved.'
>
> Richard Smart, 'Changing directions in publishing and the role of the editor', *Blue Pencil*, January/February 1997.

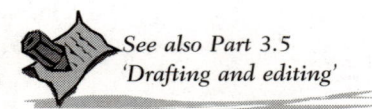

See also Part 3.5 'Drafting and editing'

conventions in spelling, punctuation, typefaces, titles, references, layout, and so on. Such guides assist you to achieve the desired presentation of your manuscript for your particular publisher.

Professional editors are skilled in the various forms of editing that they are required to do for publishers. Fiction and non-fiction editing have different emphases; the former requires a sensitivity to the authors' distinctive styles, for example, their tone, language and rhythm. Non-fiction editing, on the other hand, requires a tight focus on clear and cogent presentation of the subject matter.

The publisher's editor performs the following steps:

- edits the structure of the 'argument' in non-fiction or the storyline in fiction
- confirms that the author has checked the facts
- edits for length and reading level
- edits for consistency and continuity
- copy edits for errors of spelling, grammar and punctuation
- proofreads for literals, or errors which have crept in during the process of rewriting and editing.

Publishers' editors must also be on the look-out for potentially defamatory statements in manuscripts dealing with current affairs, and even in fiction, although the responsibility of anything defamatory appearing in the published work is usually contractually shared between the author and publisher. When a public figure identified himself from Amanda Lohrey's novel *The Reading Room*, the novel was removed from bookshops and pulped. A new version omitting the identifying features of the character was issued, at great cost to the publisher and inconvenience to the author. In a more recent example, publisher Random House was sued by two politicians and their wives after publishing comments by writer Bob Ellis in his Labor Party memoirs *Goodbye Jerusalem*. Ellis, however, was not sued.

Most professional editors are trained to be sympathetic and sensitive to the text and do not make changes unless they believe that they will improve the quality and marketability of the work. Most writers are grateful for the work of editors who, unlike the writer, are able to stand back dispassionately and assess the overall effect of a work. Sometimes an editor skilled in non-fiction will make inappropriate changes (to punctuation, sentence construction, etc.) in fiction. You do not have to accept the changes. Treat them as suggestions and negotiate on those you are unhappy about. If you have serious problems working with your editor, you could, in theory, ask that another be assigned to you. In practice, this would be a most unusual occurrence. Remember that the editor the publisher has assigned to you is probably the one regarded as being most capable of dealing with your particular manuscript.

> See Part 4.7.11 *'Defamation' for further information*

> 'A successful author–editor relationship can be crucial to the success of the book and, like most important human relationships, it must be based on mutual trust. The author trusts the editor to help him or her make the book as good as it can be; the editor trusts the author to discuss directly any problems that arise — that is, not to complain about the editing all over town or to bitch to the publisher behind the editor's back.'
>
> Jacqueline Kent, 'On Editing and Invisible Mending', *Voices*, Summer 1996–97, vol. VI, no. 4.

Design

The design of the book takes place when the manuscript is well-advanced and the content has been finalised. The designer has responsibility for the design of the type (font), for the layout of each page of text, for the cover and preliminary pages (such as title and contents pages), as well as for the presentation of graphics such as photographs, illustrations, charts and diagrams. Authors are usually shown the design for the cover and contents of their book, and asked for comment.

Novelist Amanda Lohrey commented on her own experience with a book cover:

> You can usually veto the cover. You can't veto all of it, but you have an input. If you absolutely hate it, then you have a power of veto. But if you basically like it and want to rearrange the print they may well tell you to get lost . . . The print was too small in my book. I had no power over that. The layout was too cramped, I had no say in that . . . Milan Kundera has a lovely essay in which he says that white space in fiction is as important as the print . . . He writes into his contracts, as he can, that he gets to lay out his work. I wish I had that.' (Interviewed by Amanda Galligan, *Imago*, Summer 1997, vol. 9, no. 3.)

Pre-press

When the manuscript is finalised and the design completed, the manuscript and all illustrative material are converted to page proofs, that is, a version of the final pages as they will appear in the printed book. At this stage, the author and editor check the proofs for final corrections and produce an index before the proofs are sent to the printer. If there are major changes, a second set of proofs will be produced for final checking. Most writers find it difficult to resist the temptation to rewrite just a little bit here and there when the book is at proof stage. To discourage this, most publishers stipulate in their contracts that if you want to make significant changes to page proofs, the costs incurred will be deducted from your royalties.

Production

From the page proofs or from a disk containing the same material, the printer produces plates which are then used on the printing press to print the pages as they will appear in the book. After the pages are printed, they are collated and bound, and the book is then ready for distribution. This technology will inevitably be superseded by electronic production, which sends the page layout of the book directly from the computer to the printer.

Refer to Part 4.9.2 'Parts of a book' for information about standard ways of laying out a book

Marketing, distribution and promotion

Long before the book is printed, the marketing and sales division of the publishing house starts work on publicity by preparing leaflets and fliers and pursuing other forms of promotion. Sales staff are briefed on the book so that they can deliver a 'pitch' on it to booksellers.

Once the book is distributed through a distribution company to its outlets, the publicity department implements the promotional strategy for the book. In the case of high-profile writers, this may include reviews and media interviews with the author, and appearances by the author at literary festivals or special functions such as literary lunches. These occasions, which usually include readings and discussion, provide opportunities for major authors to boost sales of their books by directly interesting the public in their work.

Most writers receive what could be considered routine promotion — the inclusion of the title in the publisher's catalogues and fliers and promotion of the book in media outlets that may review it. The publicity and promotion that your book receives depend on your own profile and the size and resources of the publishing company.

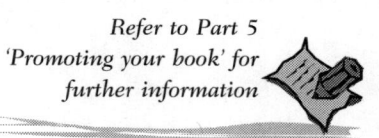

Refer to Part 5 'Promoting your book' for further information

4.4 PRESENTING YOUR WORK

When your manuscript hits the desk of the editor of a magazine or an in-house publishing editor, along with dozens of other submissions, how are you going to make it stand out from the crowd and demand to be read? Editors will reject sloppy submissions, so pay attention to the way you present your manuscript. A good-looking, well-organised manuscript will make a much better impression and give the editor some confidence in your ability as a writer to meet the demands of the professional world of publishing. The following general guidelines apply to both fiction and non-fiction manuscripts, including material for periodicals, with the exception of poetry where layout is highly individual.

4.4.1 Covering letter

The first thing an editor will read is your covering letter, which must be persuasive, polite and professional. It should make a case for the publication of your work: what it is and why it should be published. Above all, keep it brief and to the point — the less extraneous material editors and publishers have to read the better. If you don't have your own letterhead, design one for yourself on your computer so that your letter will look professional.

Find out the name of the most appropriate person in the firm to submit your manuscript to — for example the fiction editor, the non-fiction editor, literature publisher — and address the letter directly to them by name.

The covering letter should be no more than one page long, and should include:

- the title, theme and genre of your submission
- the number of words in the manuscript or article
- your contact details
- some information about yourself, such as your literary credentials
- a brief description of any previously published work
- any other information you think the editor may find interesting and useful
- the reasons why you think your piece is suitable for that particular publication or publisher (for example, if you have written a self-help manuscript on chronic fatigue syndrome and there is no book on the market which covers the topic, explain that such a book is needed and give some details about how many sufferers there are to indicate the potential readership)
- a photo if the publication requires it
- the relevant details if your piece has previously been published or won a competition.

'Shepparton, April 4th, 1897

Dear Sir,

Circumstances compel me to solicit a private reply to two or three words only.

   I have just finished writing a full-sized novel: title, Such is life; scene, Riverina and northern Vic; temper, democratic; bias, offensively Australian.

   Now what publishing firm should I communicate with — Melbourne preferably, but not necessarily? I am absolutely in the dark here and have no other referee. I am Sir,

          Yours very truly,
          JOSEPH FURPHY
          (Tom Collins)'

Mitchell Library, MSS. collection A1964: *On Submitting the manuscript of* Such is life *to J. F. Archibald, editor of the* Bulletin.

> **Sample covering letter for a short work**
>
> Stephanie Kovacs Christina Columbus
> Editor 149 Pacific Drive
> *Travel Australasia* Sunrise Beach
> 23 View Street
> Newmarket
>
> 30 June 1999
>
> Dear Ms Kovacs,
>
> I am offering the first Australasian [or Australian or New Zealand] rights of my short story 'Returning to the New Old World' for your consideration for the 'Tall Tales' section of *Travel Australasia*.
>
> The story is about a contemporary ocean-going sailor who takes the same route as Christopher Columbus did more than 500 years ago, and her adventures along the way.
>
> I have published many travel stories in popular magazines and journals, including *Geographic Australasia, New Zealand Holidays, Asian Destinations,* and in several in-flight airline magazines including *Qantas Travel* and *Continental Traveller* (samples enclosed).
>
> At 1505 words, the story meets your requirements for length.
>
> If you select my story for publication I would like it to be published under my pen-name 'Kris Colombo'.
>
> I look forward to hearing from you.
>
> Yours sincerely,
> Christina Columbus

4.4.2 Title page or cover sheet

The title page (or cover sheet) should contain the following information:

- title of work
- author's name and any pen-name used (centred on page)
- number of words in the article or manuscript

Sample covering letter for a full-length manuscript

Ms Nikki Malone
Publisher
Picador
GPO Box 456
Sydney NSW 2001
30 June 1999

Moira Simpson
3 High Street
Wellington NSW 2464
Phone (02) 9876 5432
Fax (02) 1357 2468
Email moira@ozemail.com.au

Dear Ms Malone,

I am enclosing for your consideration two sample chapters and a synopsis of my historical manuscript titled 'A Devil at My Table'. It is a fictional account of a true story of a convict woman who, despite her origins and many difficulties, established one of the finest restaurants in Sydney in the middle of the last century. Some of her original recipes are included in the text of the novel.

This is my first full-length novel manuscript (total 90 000 words) but I have published many short stories, poems, interviews, articles and reviews and won numerous literary competitions (see attached résumé).

I am forwarding this manuscript to you as I believe it will fit very well into your publishing list which includes not only several volumes of historical fiction but also several very fine cook books.

Please also find enclosed a reader's report from Ms Rosemary Creswick, an agent with the CJC Literary Agency.

I have enclosed a stamped self-addressed envelope for return of my sample chapters.

I look forward to hearing from you.

Yours sincerely,
Moira Simpson

- copyright line, with the symbol © (from your computer or by hand)
- author's name and year the manuscript was completed
- name, address, phone, fax and email numbers (towards the bottom of the page).

> **Sample title page or cover sheet**
>
> 'Returning to the New Old World'
> A short story
> by Kris Colombo (pen-name)
>
> Number of words: 1505
>
> © Christina Columbus 1999
>
> Contact details
> Christina Columbus
> 149 Pacific Drive
> Sunrise Beach
> Phone (01) 9753 2446
> Fax (01) 8697 6453
> Email kris@clear.co.nz

4.4.3 Typing and formatting

Clean copy that is neatly set out is easy to read and gives the impression that you are a competent writer. Submit your manuscript on white A4 paper on one side of the paper only. Good quality photocopies are acceptable, carbon copies are not. Don't forget to keep a copy of the original manuscript.

- Leave generous margins on each page (3–4 cm).
- Indent each paragraph.
- Do not leave extra line spaces between paragraphs.
- Use one and a half or double spacing to allow editors room for comments and to make the manuscript easier to read.
- Leave your text unjustified (ragged right edge) as it is easier to read; the publisher will justify the text after editing.

Some publishers request manuscripts on disk or by electronic transmission, so be prepared to submit your material in the requested format.

If you are sending your piece by email it is better to send it as an attached document in order to retain the formatting, but your recipient will need the correct software to open the document. If you are sending your piece on disk, state whether it is a Mac or IBM compatible disk and which application you used to produce it (for example Microsoft Word, Word Perfect, and which versions).

4.4.4 Binding and pagination

Put loose leaves in a manila folder or wallet-type folder secured with a heavy-duty elastic band, cloth tape or paper clips, rather than staples. In case of separation, all pages (whether paper or electronic) should be numbered and carry a header or footer with the title of the work (or an abbreviation of the title) and the pen-name or last name of the author. For example a story titled 'Returning to the New Old World' by Christina Columbus with the pen-name of Kris Colombo can have a footer 'New Old World/Colombo . . . page 1', usually in smaller type to distinguish it from the text.

Don't send the only copy of your manuscript. Publishers take no responsibility for lost manuscripts.

4.4.5 Synopsis and contents page (for book-length manuscripts)

Your synopsis should be a brief overview of no more than one page outlining the essence of the manuscript without necessarily telling the whole story. Also provide a contents page with chapter headings (not necessary for works of fiction where chapters are not titled). For non-fiction works include sub-headings as well.

4.4.6 Sample chapters and chapter outline (for book-length manuscripts)

Send two or three sample chapters. These should be consecutive so that the publisher can get some idea of the development of the theme; they should demonstrate some of the important elements of your work, such as style, use of language and subject matter. With non-fiction manuscripts, include an outline of one short paragraph per chapter.

4.4.7 Return postage

If you want your manuscript returned, include a stamped, self-addressed envelope (SSAE) with sufficient postage, or an international reply coupon (IRC) available from your post office if you are submitting overseas. If you don't include an SSAE, the manuscript will not be returned, nor will you be told if it has been rejected.

The envelope should be large enough to hold the manuscript flat. Don't bend or fold your manuscript, and make sure it will open easily when being read.

If you do not want your manuscript returned (because the postage costs more than the photocopying of your manuscript), say so, but still enclose an SSAE for a letter to be sent to you.

4.4.8 Records

Keep detailed records of where you have sent your piece, including date, name of publication or publisher, and title of the work. This will help you remember what you have sent and to whom, so you don't submit your work to the same place twice, or fail to send it to a likely outlet.

It is also useful to keep records of who responded to your submission, so that you know where to send the revised version in a couple of years!

4.4.9 Multiple submissions

Authors are usually advised to submit their work to one publication or publisher at a time, but if your goal is to be published, then you could avoid the long wait for a reply by sending your work off to several outlets concurrently. Be sure to inform the others if one accepts. You may even try resubmitting a work if you know there has been a change in editorial personnel. As editors and publishers change, it may well be that a successor in that position will publish your work when a previous incumbent has rejected it. Keep yourself up-to-date with editors' and publishers' names if you intend to do this.

4.5 CHILDREN'S BOOK MARKETS

There are two major fields of children's publishing: trade, or general, publishers and educational publishers.

4.5.1 Trade or general publishers

Trade or general publishers produce books for the general book trade, largely through retail bookshops. These include well-known publishers such as Pearson Australia and Random House.

See 'Children's book publishers' in the Resources section

Trade publishers require the highest-quality writing and illustrating and are very selective in their choice. They are looking for a fresh voice, original subject matter, well-crafted characterisations and plot and, of course, 'child appeal'. 'Recycled' story-lines and derivative plots and narrative styles will always be spotted, so a new children's writer or artist must work hard to avoid clichés.

> 'Children's literature is part of the mainstream of literature. I think the qualities of a good book for adults are the same qualities, exactly, as a good book for children.'
>
> Libby Hathorn quoted in 'Truth and consequence', 'Good Weekend', *Sydney Morning Herald*, 25 July 1998.

As trade publishing is fiercely competitive and the production costs of illustrated books are high, most children's publishers take on very few new titles each year, often preferring to stick with authors whose works have an established readership.

Before sending off your text, check that the publisher does have a children's list: some do not. Check the publication details on imprint pages to confirm where a book was first published. Many children's books are imported, so search for those which were originated locally, then concentrate on finding the publisher whose list seems most appropriate for your work.

Some children's book publishers receive more than 2000 unsolicited manuscripts each year, so don't take it too personally if your manuscript is not accepted.

If you have written text for a picture book, it is not necessary to have it illustrated before submitting it. In fact, unless the illustrations are spectacularly good, it is better to submit the text on its own. If publishers decide to take on your manuscript, they will find the right illustrator for you. Neither is it necessary to send directions for the illustrator unless your concept for the book cannot be understood without explanation.

See Part 4.5.3 'Tips for aspiring illustrators' for further information

If you are one of the rare breed of writer-illustrators and your artwork is of a publishable standard, enclose a sample illustration or two at most. Don't send original artwork through the post as it may be damaged or lost in transit. Black-and-white or colour photocopies will do. If publishers are interested in your artwork, they will ask to see the originals.

Many writers hold the mistaken belief that writing a picture book is easier than writing a book for children in chapters, with no illustrations. There may be fewer words in a picture book, but successful communication of a story in simple, brief text is an art form that requires much skill.

4.5.2 Educational publishers

Educational publishers produce books especially for the school market, both domestic and for export. They must meet the needs of classroom teachers and curriculum content for each state in Australia, so their requirements are specific. Educational publishers usually commission books from a pool of well-known authors with the requisite expertise. Before submitting material or sample artwork to an educational publisher, telephone and ask if they provide copies of guidelines.

Some publishers produce anthologies or books in series, especially reading or history books, and they commission a variety of authors to contribute. If they seek you out, they will give you a strict brief. In

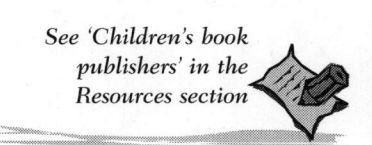

See 'Children's book publishers' in the Resources section

other words, you'll be writing 'to order', for example, a play for teenagers on current social issues.

While the name 'educational publishing' might be deceptive, these publishers are not seeking didactic texts; they always stress that they are after the best writing and illustrating possible.

4.5.3 Tips for aspiring illustrators of children's books

If you are an illustrator, the following advice will help you produce the sort of material required by children's book publishers.

Illustrating children's books, like writing for children, is a highly specialised field. It is essential that new illustrators really want to focus on children's books and are not simply looking for a vehicle for their graphic work. Illustration is not a decorative art but, rather, an interpretive one. The informed illustrator is a voracious reader and is inspired by the written word. If you like drawing or painting but you are not a bibliophile, then reconsider whether you are really a book illustrator at heart.

Study children's books in the same way as any writer must; cultivate a relationship with specialist children's booksellers and librarians, and read widely from their recommendations.

See Part 2.3.3 'Children's book illustration' and 'Websites' in the Resources section for the address

If you want to publicise your work, there is a website dedicated to professional illustrators at Authors and Illustrators. It lists names and contact details, but does not display samples of the work of individual illustrators.

Approaching publishers and editors with illustrative material

Publishers and editors will need to see a folio of your work. They are always looking for new illustrators but are pressed for time, so you may have difficulty making an appointment to show them your originals. Instead, send them a collection of photocopies. Black-and-white will be fine, but include a couple of colour copies or photographs if you can afford to. The publisher or editor can then keep your folio on file for future reference.

Children's book publishers and editors are looking for specific qualities in an illustrator's folio. They want competently drawn images with warmth, vivacity and a life of their own. Make sure to include a lot of figure drawing, especially of children engaged in activity. Static portraits will not interest the children's book editor.

It is a good idea to find a story that you really love (from a previously published book) and to make some sample drawings to go with a couple of paragraphs of the text. This will show publishers or editors what they could expect from you on any particular job.

Illustrators are engaged by publishers and editors, not by writers. If a writer approaches you to illustrate a work, don't go ahead until the writer has contracted the book to a publisher. Wait until the publisher or editor approaches you if you want to be sure to be paid for your work.

Some publishers provide technical guidelines for new artists. However, some are poorly written and are confusing for a novice illustrator. If you are commissioned by a publisher or editor, speak with the art director or designer before you proceed to finished artwork.

Educational publishing is great training for illustrators. Make approaches to educational publishers when you are starting out. They will be your most likely source of work, and you will learn the ropes at the same time. Join the Society of Book Illustrators, the Society of Children's Book Writers and Illustrators, the Illustrators Association of Australia, or the New Zealand Children's Illustrators and Authors, and ask your local writers' centre for advice about which publishers to approach.

See 'Children's book publishers' and 'Organisations' in the Resources section

4.6 DEALING WITH A MAGAZINE EDITOR

Once your contribution has been accepted by a particular publication, ask the editor to provide an agreement in writing on the terms of publication, such as the amount to be paid for the item and when it is going to be published. Too many writers are caught out with nothing but an oral agreement, and they spend frustrating weeks and even months waiting for the appearance of their article or story in a publication, only to be eventually told that it was not suitable, by which time, of course, it may be quite out of date and too late to send it to another publication. Most agreements with periodicals will be for first Australasian rights, meaning a once-only publication in Australia and the other countries of the region. If you want to submit the same work to another publication in Australia or New Zealand, inform the editor of where it was first published. You may be required to alter it substantially.

If the publication wants to use your material in any other way — reproducing it in other editions of the publication, translating it for sale to other publications — your agreement should make it clear whether you or the publishing company holds copyright in your work, exactly how many outlets it will be appearing in, and how much you will be paid for each part or whole reprint.

See Part 4.7.6 'Copyright'

If a dispute with the editor arises, you can contact the Australian Society of Authors or the New Zealand Society of Authors if you are a member and set out in detail on paper the nature of the problem. These two professional associations have a long history of dealing with publishers and may be able to solve your problem.

4.6.1   Reminder letter

If you have not heard from the magazine editor within two weeks of sending your article or short story, write a tactful and courteous letter or email to remind her or him of your manuscript and to ask whether he or she intends to publish it. If you receive no reply to your first reminder letter, forward another with the words 'Second reminder' written at the top. If you receive no reply to this one, try another publication.

Sample reminder letter

Moira Simpson
3 High Street
Wellington NSW 2464
Phone (02) 9876 5432 Fax (02) 1357 2468 Email lisa@ozemail.com.au

Ms Nikki Malone
Editor
Monthly Forum Magazine
GPO Box 456
Sydney NSW 2001
30 June 1999

Dear Ms Malone,

Re: [Title of work]

On (date), I forwarded my short story/article to you and would like to know whether it is suitable for your publication.

If it is not, I would be grateful if you would return it in the SSAE forwarded with it.

Alternatively, please fill in the form below and return with your comments in the enclosed SSAE.

I look forward to hearing from you.

Yours sincerely,
Moira Simpson

Title of work
By Moira Simpson

❏ Your manuscript is unsuitable, please find it enclosed.
❏ We need more time to consider your manuscript.
❏ Your manuscript is suitable and we will forward a letter soon.

4.7 DEALING WITH A BOOK PUBLISHER

Book publishers and editors work in a variety of ways, so to give your work the best possible chance of a reading, call your chosen

> 'I think I was lucky with [my first novel] Blue Kisses. Publishers don't seem to like reading unsolicited manuscripts. Both Penguin and Random House turned it down with only a cursory glance. Random House actually declined it on the grounds that their nonfiction list was full for the next eighteen months! Geoff Walker at Penguin apologised and did read it in the end. Just when I was wondering what to do next Ian Watt at HarperCollins advertised in this newsletter, I sent it in, and he liked it. He was excellent to work with — perceptive, had some useful suggestions. I'm very happy with how the book turned out, and now it's out there for people to enjoy.'
>
> Novelist/filmmaker Keith Hill interviewed in *Write Up*, April 1998.

publishing company before submitting your manuscript to find out exactly what they want from you. Some publishers want to see the whole manuscript, others a synopsis (summary of your story) and several chapters. Sometimes they simply want a proposal letter from you (particularly in the case of non-fiction) to see if they are interested in your idea.

If a publisher accepts your proposal and wants to see the rest of the manuscript, make sure it is in a presentable form, following the points given in Part 4.4 'Presenting your work', and conforms with the guidelines issued by the publishing company itself. Before sending your manuscript off, read it through once again for errors of fact, style, consistency, structural coherence, and so on. Some publishers acknowledge receipt of manuscript, some do not.

It may take some time for the publisher to make a final decision on whether or not to publish your manuscript, and you are entitled to ring up and find out about the progress of the decision. Many publishers are overworked and respond only when asked. Alternatively, you may want to send a reminder letter. Modify the sample given in Part 4.6.1 'Reminder letter' to suit your book-length manuscript. If your book requires a quick decision — for example, if the material is going to be out of date within a year — let the publisher know, and be prepared to take your manuscript to another publisher if the first does not respond within, say, one month.

Sometimes publishers commission individuals to produce a non-fiction book on a particular theme according to guidelines established by the publisher. In this case, your job will be made much easier as it is likely you will be in contact with the publisher or an editor during the course of writing the book.

If a publisher is interested in your book proposal, make sure you sign a contract or agreement before you do any substantial work on the manuscript.

See Part 4.7.1 'Contracts'

4.7.1 Contracts

A contract between an author and a publisher is a legal and binding document about the publishing partnership which sets out the rights and responsibilities of both author and publisher.

Contracts are written by publishers and are lengthy (usually at least six or seven pages), complex, detailed documents. They have been transformed in recent years as electronic communication and information technology have opened up many new publishing media, while marketing of associated products has become part of the publishing business.

First-time writers can be confused by the terms of a contract and may be tempted to accept any kind of contract from a publisher just to see their work in print. This is not prudent, as you may lose rights which later on you wish you had retained. Too many novice writers, swept away by the euphoria of having someone agree to put their opus between covers, sign on the bottom line and unwittingly do themselves out of a fair deal.

> 'Trading in intellectual property has now become a key component in the GATT accords [General Agreement on Trade and Tariffs] and many decades of old practices in publishing, such as market monopolisation by region, have been outlawed. Countries are rewriting their intellectual property laws — copyright, trade marks and design statutes — to conform to this new regime, and these changes do not necessarily take account of the needs of writers. Increasingly writers are obliged to fall back on the only enforceable protection that they have — their contract.'
>
> The Business of Writing: An Annotated Model Standard Contract, New Zealand Society of Authors, 1995.

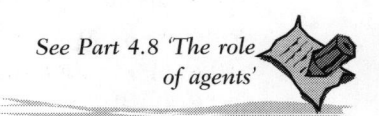

If you are not inclined to read the fine print in long documents, if you have difficulty understanding legal terminology, if you have no desire to negotiate strenuously on your own behalf, or if you are uncertain about your rights, then get advice before you sign anything. There are several ways of obtaining contractual advice:

- Seek the services of a literary agent, who can negotiate with the publisher on your behalf to get you the best possible deal.

See Part 4.8 'The role of agents'

☞ Join a professional writers' organisation, such as the Australian Society of Authors or the New Zealand Society of Authors, to obtain the benefit of their experience in the field. The Australian Society of Authors provides a contract reading service for members at a reasonable charge.

☞ Join the Arts Law Centre of Australia which offers its members free contract advice from experienced lawyers. (There is no equivalent organisation in New Zealand.)

> 'Some people have this romantic notion that reading their contract is beneath them. A lot of Australian authors are quite infantile in that respect — they don't understand the industrial side of publishing.'
>
> Tim Winton, quoted in *Fine Line*, no. 4, Autumn 1998.

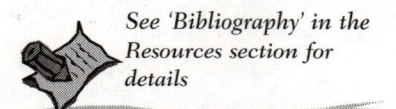

Even if you engage the services of a literary agent, try to familiarise yourself with the terminology and conditions of your contract so that you understand exactly what publishers want you to sign over to them. Both the New Zealand Society of Authors and the Australian Society of Authors have produced publications to help you understand publishing contracts, as well as providing model contracts for writers to use in their negotiations with publishers.

See 'Bibliography' in the Resources section for details

4.7.2   Beware unscrupulous publishers!

The New Zealand Society of Authors was asked to help out in the case of writer Gilian Painter, who was astonished to hear her book being advertised on a local radio station at $20 less than the retail price. Inquiries with the publisher revealed that 1500 copies of her book had been remaindered, that is, sold off at discount rates, probably because the publisher wanted to clear the shelves for new stock. Her contract stipulated that her books could be remaindered only after they had been offered to her at the remaindered price. Painter had lost the opportunity to make at least $10 per book over time on 1500 books (she was a lecturer and could sell them to her students), and the radio station had made a profit of at least $21 000.

She approached the NZSA's legal advice committee, which engaged a solicitor to act on her behalf. The solicitor requested compensation for her loss of opportunity to earn money from the books because her publishing contract had been broken. The chief executive of the publishing company replied with an offer of full royalties on the remaindered books as well as the 236 free books remaining in stock. After this, Painter wrote:

> He gave no apology and in a patronising way wrote he hoped this would 'alleviate my disappointment'. As well as being angry, I was disappointed that a large international publishing company would break any author's publishing contract and that the chief executive did not have the grace to apologise. ('Contract Corner', The New Zealand Author, September 1998.)

4.7.3 Rights

The publishing contract gives the publisher certain rights to publish your work under certain conditions in exchange for a payment. The exact nature of the rights and conditions are spelled out in detail. The list is usually long, including rights to publish and sell the work, translation rights, serialisation rights, film rights and electronic rights.

See Part 4.7.5 'Royalties and advances'

The most important right to retain in a contract is your copyright. If you have written an original manuscript, that manuscript belongs to you by law in both Australia and New Zealand unless you sign it over to someone else. Publishers should not ask you in their contracts to hand over, or assign, copyright.

See Part 4.7.6 for further information about copyright

The following clause appears in many contracts and needs some comment: 'The Proprietor hereby grants to the Publisher for the full legal term of copyright in the work, the sole and exclusive licence to produce, publish, sell and exploit the work in all forms and media and languages across the world.'

Do you realise that publishers who persuade you to license your work 'for the full legal term of copyright in the work' obtain a licence for your lifetime plus 50 years? The Australian Society of Authors recommends you license your work for fifteen years only.

See Part 4.7.7 'Protecting electronic rights'

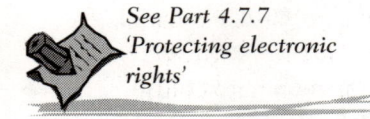

If you agree to license your work 'in all forms and media' you may be signing away very valuable electronic rights in media which have not yet been developed. It is advisable to ask if your publisher has any plans for exploiting electronic rights. If the answer is affirmative, then ask for a separate contract to cover these rights.

You're wrong if you think the English-speaking world is the largest consumer of books. China is a growing market, and even Germany does larger print runs than the United Kingdom. Giving away your rights 'in all languages' may lose you much-needed income. If your publisher has no intention of translating your work into other languages, there is no need to sign this clause.

Some contracts ask for world rights, some ask for world rights just in English, and some for rights in only Australia and New Zealand. Many Australian and New Zealand publishers, including branches of transnationals, in fact publish only in Australia and New Zealand, so there is no need to give them world rights. Inquire whether they are going to negotiate world sales. Ask for a clause in the contract that stipulates that these rights will revert to you after a specified period, say, one year. This will leave you free to exploit rights in other countries with another publisher.

4.7.4 Responsibilities

Remember that your contract is a legally binding document and that under its terms you have certain obligations and responsibilities. These include producing a manuscript to a certain standard and a stipulated length, delivering the final manuscript by the date stated in the contract and, in some contracts, paying certain costs such as permission fees, and editorial and indexing costs. The author must also give a warranty that the work does not infringe the copyright of others or defame anyone.

4.7.5 Royalties and advances

Once your work is published, you are entitled to payment on copies sold. This is called a royalty. The royalty is usually a proportion of the recommended retail price (RRP) or the jacket price. This can vary but is usually set at a minimum of around 10 per cent of RRP, rising to 12 per cent after a certain number of copies. Some crafty publishers offer a percentage of net receipts rather than a percentage of the RRP. The net receipts refer to the amount the publisher gets paid by the bookshops for copies sold. Bookshops usually pay around 60 per cent of the RRP, and so 10 per cent of net receipts will be considerably less than 10 per cent of RRP.

Publishers often, but not always, give the author an advance against royalties in expectation that the book will sell. Some publishers do not offer an advance until a writer asks for it. The amount varies but it is usually about half of what you could expect in royalties on the first print run. An advance is a sign of commitment on the part of the publisher, but it is not usually sufficient to support an author to work on the book full time.

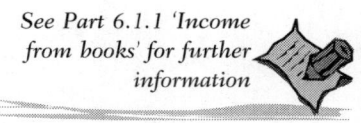

See Part 6.1.1 'Income from books' for further information

4.7.6 Copyright

In both Australia and New Zealand, your work is automatically protected under copyright law from the time it is written down or otherwise recorded in some way. There are no formalities to be completed, such as registration or payment of fees, in order to safeguard your work. Internationally, the Berne Convention for the Protection of Literary and Artistic Works and the Universal Copyright Convention, to which both Australia and New Zealand are signatories, protect your work in those countries that are also signatories. Note that there is no copyright in ideas *per se*. Rather, copyright protects the way ideas are expressed (for example, in writing, on disk, taped, saved as a computer file or filmed).

To give you an example, one writer sent off an idea to a television channel for a five-minute poetry reading before the evening news. Although his particular proposal was not taken up, the channel took up the idea with its own production. This writer has no recourse to compensation under copyright law because, as was mentioned above, there is no copyright in ideas. (There may, however, have been a right to recover damages under the law of confidential information.)

Some writers, especially those writing for the screen, will ask potential producers to sign a confidentiality agreement before reading proposals and treatments in an attempt to protect their work from being used without their permission. Producers take this seriously if they want to protect their reputations. The New Zealand Writers Guild provides a confidentiality agreement for use by members at no cost, while the Australian Writers' Guild offers a script registration service (see below).

While copyright law applies to written works, it is unlikely to provide protection for a book or article title or for a pseudonym. In some cases, you may have some protection against other people using the same or a similar title or name if you register it as a trade mark or business name. In other cases, laws such as the Trade Practices Act may allow you to take action if people use your title or name in a way that might confuse, mislead or deceive the public. Alternatively, in some cases, the law of passing off may help you stop other people passing off their work under your name or title.

Copyright in photographs generally lasts for 50 years.

Copyright rights

Ownership of copyright entitles you to control whether other people do such things as:

- perform the work in public
- reproduce it in some form, such as by printing or photocopying
- 'communicate it' to the public (for example, by using it on TV or radio, or by emailing it or by posting it to a website or intranet)
- translate it into another language, and
- convert it to another form such as a dramatised or a pictorial version.

Your rights as a copyright holder can either be sold outright or you can license your rights by agreement, such as the right to publish a German language version of your work. Ensure that such agreements specify very clearly which rights you are signing over and for what period, as well as any special conditions you wish to attach to the agreement. It is also advisable to ensure that all agreements are in writing and signed by both parties. Breaches of oral agreements are much harder to prove in court. It is usually a good idea to get legal advice before signing any agreement.

Exceptions to copyright ownership

In general, the person who creates copyright material will be the first owner of copyright in that work, but some exceptions apply. These include employees generally (including employees of newspapers and other periodicals) and people creating material under the direction or control of government departments or entities. Both the general rule and the exceptions may be altered by agreement.

Use of copyright material for educational purposes

Copyright material can be used for private study, and may be quoted in reviews or academic or other works, provided the use is 'fair' (these exceptions are generally referred to as 'fair dealing' exceptions).

Libraries and educational institutions are also allowed, under the Act, to make copies of material for the purposes of study. In some cases, fees are collected on the basis of samples of copied material and paid to the Copyright Agency Limited or to Copyright Licensing Ltd in New Zealand for distribution to copyright owners.

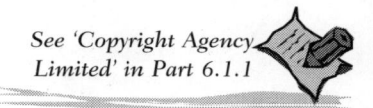

See 'Copyright Agency Limited' in Part 6.1.1

Script registration services

There is no registration of copyright in either Australia or New Zealand. Nonetheless, authors should be aware that the Australian Writers' Guild provides a script registration service for both Australian Writers' Guild and Australian Screen Directors Association members. This service seeks to establish priority of authorship if a copyright infringement dispute should arise. This can be useful in writing for television and film production.

Evidence that you created something

It is very unusual for people to have to prove that they, and not somebody else, created a work protected by copyright. Generally, if somebody else tried to convince a court that he or she had written a work that you created, the court would have to decide who was telling the truth by taking evidence from both sides. Apart from statements about how you came to create the work, your evidence might include your drafts.

When you distribute your material, use the 'copyright notice' to alert others to your ownership and to remind them that it is protected. The notice also provides a contact name if someone wants to use your material. The copyright notice consists of the copyright sign, followed by your name and the year of production or first publication, for example © Irina Dunn 2002. You could put this at the bottom of the first page of your manuscript. (The '©' mark is available on most word processing programs as a 'Symbol' to be inserted in the text wherever you designate.)

Duration of copyright

In both Australia and New Zealand, copyright in a written work lasts from the time the work is created until 50 years after the creator dies. Estates of writers can therefore continue to benefit from royalties payable during the 50-year period after a writer's death. If a work is not published at all until after an author's death, copyright in Australia lasts for 50 years from that first publication. (In New Zealand and the United Kingdom it lasts only for 50 years after the year of death).

Internationally, the length of copyright varies from country to country (for example, in Europe and the United States, copyright generally lasts for 70 years after the creator dies). However, some countries, such as Papua New Guinea, do not have copyright laws at all. International pressure is being placed on these countries to sign, and adhere to, the conventions because of the huge losses resulting from theft of intellectual property when unauthorised copying of original works takes place.

Public domain

Once material has passed out of copyright it goes into what is referred to as the 'public domain' and may be reproduced without the necessity of clearing copyright or paying permission fees. Some websites contain collections of literature that are in the public domain.

Australian Copyright Council

The Australian Copyright Council assists creators with their queries in relation to copyright and produces a range of publications about copyright, including an information sheet and practical guide, both entitled *Writers and Copyright*. The information sheet and details about ordering the practical guide are available on its website at www.copyright.org.au. In a number of cases, the Copyright Council is also able to offer free legal advice for professional creators, arts organisations and members of affiliated organisations on:

Getting Published

- how to identify who owns copyright
- how long copyright lasts
- whether permission is needed and whose permission must be obtained
- whether copyright has been infringed
- what a copyright contract (such as a book publishing contract) means, whether it is acceptable and what changes should be negotiated.

It also periodically runs seminars on copyright issues, including seminars for writers.

4.7.7 Protecting electronic rights

Electronic publishing introduces an entirely new and as yet uncharted field in the world of publishing. The ease with which material can be transmitted, reproduced and modified electronically has caused professional writers' organisations some concern about how to protect the electronic rights of creators when exploitation is not as clear-cut as in book publishing.

It is now becoming the norm in book publishers' contracts to have a clause which grants the publisher world electronic rights (rather than country by country rights). Authors need to be aware that electronic rights may be very valuable and should not be easily surrendered. The Australian Society of Authors has published an informative booklet on the question of electronic rights and contracts called *Electronic/Digital Rights: A Handbook for Authors*.

See 'Bibliography' in the Resources section

The Australian Copyright Council makes the following points in relation to electronic rights.

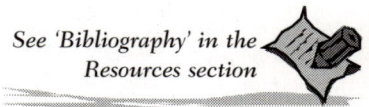

- Ideally, there should be no 'blanket' granting of electronic rights such as in the clause 'The illustrator/author grants the publisher the exclusive right to print, publish, produce or sell the work in any form throughout the world'.
- As in print publishing, authors should only license rights, not assign them. Assigning rights means transferring them to someone else, that is, losing total control over them.

- Authors are advised to negotiate an agreement only when a specific use is proposed. Some publishers ask for rights 'just in case' but do not have the expertise or intention to use them.
- Any rights, including print rights, should have a reversion clause built in such as 'If this right has not been utilised within a period of three years, or royalty level falls below $50 per annum, this right reverts to the author'.

4.7.8 Moral rights

In contrast to copyright, which provides creators of works with an economic return on their work, moral rights are personal creative rights that are not transferred if copyright is transferred, but allow creators, including writers, to promote and protect their reputations by obliging people who use their work to attribute the creator, and to respect the integrity of the work they have produced.

Moral rights in Australia

Under the *Copyright Act* as enacted in 1968, a creator was protected from having another person's name put on their work, and from having an altered work published or sold as an unaltered work. More comprehensive moral rights were introduced in Australia by amendments to the *Copyright Act*, which came into operation in December 2000. As a result of the amendments, in addition to the rights relating to false attribution, creators also have the right:

- to be identified as the creator (the right of attribution); and
- to have the integrity of their work respected (that is, not to have the work subjected to treatment that is prejudicial to the creator's honour or reputation).

Writers are among the types of creators who have moral rights in their work. Screenwriters have moral rights not only in their scripts but in the resulting film (the director and producer of the film will also have moral rights in the film).

Moral rights generally last until copyright expires, but the right of integrity in films lasts only until the creator dies.

Unlike the situation in New Zealand, in Australia a creator does not have to assert his or her moral rights. Rather, like copyright, moral rights under Australian law exist from the time the work is created. Moral rights in a work remain with the creator (or his or her personal legal representative) even if he or she does not own copyright in the work.

There are a number of situations in which people do not have to attribute a work to an author or respect the integrity of works, including when it is 'reasonable' in all the circumstances not to do so. People wanting to use a work in a way that would otherwise infringe a moral right may also get consent from the creator.

Creators whose moral rights have been infringed can take action against the person who has infringed the right—you should only do this, however, once you have legal advice on your position.

For more information, see the Australian Copyright Council's information sheet *Moral Rights* (available for free from its website at www.copyright.org.au) or its detailed practical guide, which is also entitled *Moral Rights*.

Moral rights in New Zealand

Moral rights were introduced into New Zealand's intellectual property laws in the *Copyright Act* of 1994. Under this legislation, an 'author' has the right:

- to be identified as the author of the work;
- not to be identified as the author of the work;
- to object to any modification or derogatory treatment of the work which would be prejudicial to the author's honour or reputation.

These rights are often referred to as:

- the right of attribution;
- the right against false attribution;
- the right to object to derogatory treatment.

The first two rights are generally not available to employees who create a work in the course of their employment. The right to object to derogatory treatment of the work is limited to the term of copyright in the work, and does not cover translations or apply to any work created for the purposes of reporting current events.

In New Zealand a moral right must be asserted in writing for it to be relied on. Although moral rights cannot be assigned they can be waived. A waiver is an agreement not to enforce particular moral rights and may refer to a particular work or to any future works deriving from the original, such as a screenplay made from a novel.

4.7.9 Plagiarism

Plagiarism is the use in print of someone else's words without attribution or acknowledgment. Plagiarism is obvious if the exact sequence of words is reproduced from the original, but is more debatable, and certainly less detectable, if the original wording is paraphrased. Plagiarism is not only embarrassing for an author; it could also be a breach of copyright and cost the plagiarist his or her reputation and any further contracts with publishers.

Certain amounts of other people's text may be used without breaching copyright provisions, although permission may need to be obtained. If you are drawing on someone else's published work, then you must cite the work by indicating the original source and providing full details of authorship, title of the work, publication details, date of publication, and page numbers. Put any quoted passage in quotation marks. Plagiarism annoys, but citation and acknowledged quotations are appreciated. There are various citation indexes for academic work, such as the Social Citation Index and the Scientific Citation Index, and these indicate the number of times a scholarly work is referred to. A high level of citations helps promotion!

> 'How to describe this eerie infringement? It feels as if your brain has been burgled. The pirating from my book includes images, precise phrasings and paraphrasings, the copying of a unique setting for a particular scene, an identical descriptive metaphor, and exact lines of conversation — plus third-person quotations and other examples of a more minor nature. To see this as a coincidence demands a stretch of the imagination that I confess is beyond my capacity, even as a poet.'
>
> American author Robin Morgan on Helen Darville's *The Hand that Signed the Paper*, 'Dear Helen, just give me back my words', *Sydney Morning Herald*, 23 March 1996.

> 'The broad effect of copyright law is that writers can plunder other writers' work as freely as they please (historians and biographers do this all the time) — so long as they rewrite. If they don't rewrite, if they use another's words, they risk breaching copyright. Actually, good literary manners will keep writers out of most trouble with copyright. If they courteously acknowledge their debts to others' work they will probably be okay.'
>
> Ken Methold, *A–Z of Authorship: A Professional Guide*, Australian Society of Authors, Sydney, 1996.

4.7.10 Permission fees

Authors have an obligation under publishing contracts not to breach legal copyright provisions (see above) or to include defamatory material (see Part 4.7.11) and have an ethical obligation to acknowledge material quoted from other sources. If the amount of this material is extensive, then the author will have to seek permission to reproduce it, and this may be costly.

Permission fees are payable to copyright owners whose work, or part of a work, is being reproduced in any form. The fees vary widely depending on where it is being reproduced, how much of a work is being reproduced and whether it is written material, graphics, a sound recording or film.

Some publishing companies allocate specialised staff to determine copyright ownership and pay the appropriate permission fees for material reproduced in any of their publications, but they often ask the author to negotiate these rights on the grounds that authors can negotiate a lower fee. Your responsibility as the author is to provide these staff with full details of the material to be reproduced, including the precise source of the material and contact details of the publisher.

Other publishers' contracts specify that it is the author's responsibility to clear copyright with the owners and to pay permission fees for the reproduction of their work. If, for example, you intend to include substantial quotations from copyright material, or numerous illustrations or graphics (for example, for your book cover), you are required under copyright law to obtain permission for its reproduction in your work and may also be required to pay any fees required by the copyright holders (who may not, by the way, necessarily be the creators of the work). This can be a time-consuming task, and may cost you a considerable amount of money which you are expected to pay or have deducted from your royalties. I did not, however, need permission to use the quote from Ken Methold in the box accompanying the 'Plagiarism' section above as it contains only 70 words and it is, of course, acknowledged. Students researching for their courses are able to quote freely from copyright material provided that their work is not published, while reviewers may quote short extracts for the purposes of a review. If the material is longer than about 250 consecutive words it would be prudent to obtain permission to reproduce it.

If you are unable to locate the copyright owner and wish to reproduce textual material, the convention is to state as much in the acknowledgments section of the publication. Of course, if the source material is in the public domain or out of copyright, there is no need to obtain permission or pay permission fees.

Quotations from poetry and song lyrics can be more difficult. Publishers often severely restrict the number of words quoted from a poem unless a fee is paid. Some song publishers refuse permission for lyrics altogether. English novelist David Lodge wanted to use a Cole Porter line for the title of a novel but the song publisher refused so the book was called *The British Museum is Falling Down* — rather than 'losing its charm', as in the song.

4.7.11 Defamation and obscenity

If you are writing a controversial work, be careful that it does not breach obscenity or defamation laws. If you are not sure whether passages in your book are obscene or defamatory, think whether what you have said may offend the community's 'standards of decency' (and these are debatable) or harm someone's reputation.

In relation to defamation, simply naming someone in your book is not a cause for concern, but if you have been critical it may be worthwhile seeking the opinion and advice of an organisation such as the Arts Law Centre or a specialist lawyer.

A publisher who is concerned that material in your manuscript may be defamatory can get the firm's lawyers to check it. However, most contracts require the author to warrant that the work contains nothing defamatory. The author must also agree to fully indemnify the publisher against any suits, claims or proceedings which may be taken against the publisher if the work is defamatory. Some professional writers' organisations have raised this matter with publishers as they think this is an unfair burden to place on writers.

4.8 THE ROLE OF AGENTS

Often known in the publishing world as 'literary' agents, agents today represent a range of creative artists, including adult and children's fiction authors, scriptwriters, script editors, illustrators, producers, directors, composers, actors, designers, playwrights and journalists.

Some represent a wide field of literary endeavour; others specialise in certain genres, and many do not accept poetry, short stories, romance and science fiction. Most will consider non-fiction, such as autobiography, biography, historical works and cook books, but exclude educational material. However, the exception proves the rule and it is difficult to generalise about an agent's preferences. One Sydney agent deals only in romance and popular fiction and does not accept any unsolicited manuscripts or material in any other genre.

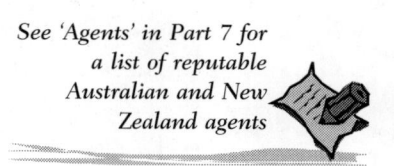

See 'Agents' in Part 7 for a list of reputable Australian and New Zealand agents

4.8.1 What can agents do for you?

If you are an established writer, or a new author with an unsigned contract in your hand, a literary agent can take a lot of the worry out of selling your work by approaching publishers for you and negotiating publishing deals on your behalf. Agents can also provide marketing advice, find new markets for you, and negotiate film, television and multimedia rights, as well as overseas, foreign-language or translation rights.

The specific work of a literary agent is to:

- find suitable publication outlets for your work
- negotiate favourable terms with a publisher and confirm them in a contract
- handle correspondence relating to contractual matters
- negotiate terms for the reproduction of your work in different territories and in different media such as film or television
- manage the receipt of royalties
- generate work opportunities for you.

Be wary of individuals who set themselves up as agents without any track record. They are unlikely to have the contacts in the book trade nor the experience in dealing with manuscripts. Check with your nearest writers' centre for a list of reputable agents.

See 'Agents' in Part 7 of the Resources section for a selection of the better-known agencies

4.8.2 Are agents necessary?

In some countries, such as the United States, you cannot get a foot in the door of a publishing house without an agent. It is different in Australia and New Zealand, where some publishers will at least consider unsolicited manuscripts submitted by a writer. However, because publishers receive so many unsolicited manuscripts, they are increasingly relying on the recommendations of literary agents, so it is almost inevitable that you will have to approach an agent if you wish to publish a book. An agent's recommendation will certainly help your manuscript rise to the top of a publisher's reading pile.

> 'The fiction [for our list] generally does not come from the unsolicited pile because it's not physically possible to read all those manuscripts. It's not through lack of respect for good writing but in terms of work load and staff load, unsolicited manuscripts are looked at only when people have time. Other people's recommendations help me to filter . . .'
>
> Sophie Cunningham, Trade Publisher, Allen & Unwin, in 'Agents, Publishers and Writers', *Write On*, vol. 9, no. 4, May 1998.

If you are an established author you may need a literary agent if you:

- have trouble approaching and negotiating with publishers and would prefer to work through a third party
- believe that you're not receiving as much as you might for your writing
- are finding that administering your writing finances and contracts is a burden
- believe that you have a commercial manuscript but are not able to access the market.

If you disagree with the editor, designer or publisher about anything during the long and complex process of producing your book, it is often better sorted out through an agent so that the relationship between you and the publisher is left in good shape.

Not all published writers use agents. A number of successful authors, such as Bryce Courtenay, negotiate their work themselves, or use solicitors for contracts. If you are accustomed to reading fine print and have well-developed negotiating skills and time to spare, you might consider handling your own contract and all the correspondence which arises from the publication of your work. This will save you the agent's fees and give you total control of the process.

4.8.3 Looking for an agent?

Most agents make their living from established writers with a contract in hand and an established readership and market. They rarely undertake to represent first-time book writers unless they have produced an exceptional manuscript, or are already known to them, or are recommended by someone in the business.

Although agents are reluctant to read unsolicited manuscripts, they are all, nevertheless, always on the look-out for exceptional work of quality. To prevent your manuscript being returned unread, your best approach is to telephone, write or fax first to give them some idea of your proposal before sending anything through the post. Some agents have submission guidelines and business terms which they will send you if you forward a stamped self-addressed envelope.

> 'We take on about five clients a year from people who just submit manuscripts cold to us and we often work a long time with them until we think the work is good enough to be submitted to a publisher.'
>
> Jenny Darling, Australian Literary Management, in 'Agents, Publishers and Writers', *Write On*, vol. 9, no. 4, May 1998.

If an agent agrees to look at your work, send a covering letter (see next page for sample) and include your publishing résumé, a synopsis of the work, and two or three sample chapters, preferably the first three to give some idea of the content and development of your piece. If you have no history of publication either in book form or in periodicals, you are unlikely to be taken on by an agent. A history of successful literary prizes can persuade an agent to look at your manuscript, so start entering the numerous competitions advertised each month in writers' centres' newsletters.

Don't forget to include a sufficiently large stamped self-addressed envelope for the return of your manuscript. If you do not wish your manuscript to be returned to you, say so and send a smaller stamped self-addressed envelope for the agent's letter to you.

A few agents charge a modest fee for reading unsolicited manuscripts to see if they are publishable but will not provide critical comments on the manuscript. Most will let you know of their decision within six to eight weeks.

Sample covering letter to an agent

Moira Simpson
3 High Street
Wellington NSW 2464
Phone (02) 9876 5432 Fax (02) 1357 2468
Email lisa@ozemail.com.au

Ms Cathy Barton
Barton Literary Agency
GPO Box 123
Sydney NSW 2001
30 June 1999

Dear Ms Barton,

    I am enclosing for your consideration three sample chapters and a synopsis of my historical novel titled *A Devil at My Table*. It is a fictional account of a true story of a convict woman who, despite her origins and many difficulties, established one of the finest restaurants in Sydney in the middle of the last century. Some of her original recipes are included in the text of the novel.

    This is my first full-length novel manuscript (total 90 000 words) but I have published many short stories, poems, interviews, articles and reviews and won numerous literary competitions (see attached résumé).

    Please also find enclosed a reader's report from Ms Rosemary Creswick, a well-known fiction writer, academic and book reviewer.

    I have enclosed a stamped self-addressed envelope for return of my sample chapters.

    I look forward to hearing from you.

Yours sincerely,
Moira Simpson

4.8.4 What does an agent charge?

Agents' terms vary, but generally they take a commission (ranging from 10 to 20 per cent) on any money that you earn, whether from a manuscript, a short story, a public speaking engagement, or overseas sales. Some agents also charge a fee for reading your manuscript and for postage and photocopying expenses.

Certain agents ask you to sign an agency agreement outlining the terms and conditions of the arrangement. Others are satisfied with an oral agreement. If you are unsure about anything you are asked to sign in such an agreement, the Australian Society of Authors and the New Zealand Society of Authors can offer advice.

4.8.5 Finding an international agent

Most local agents have contacts or reciprocal arrangements with agents or agencies overseas. An agent who thinks you have a manuscript which is marketable overseas will forward it, together with a letter of recommendation, to their overseas colleague.

If you wish to contact an overseas agent directly, you can find lists in books such as the *Writers' and Artists' Yearbook* or *International Literary Market Place*. Remember, however, that you are unlikely to obtain the services of an overseas agent if you are an unpublished author: it is extremely unusual for an overseas publisher to take on an Australian or New Zealand writer with no profile and no previous publications.

See 'Bibliography' in the Resources section

See 'International Publishers' in Part 4.2.3

4.9 DIY PUBLISHING OR SELF-PUBLISHING

Self-publishing is an option taken by some people who cannot find a commercial publisher to accept their work or who choose to retain control over the production and distribution of their book. Self-publishers pay for that control and its attendant risks by covering all the costs involved in production and distribution of their work. Self-publication is also a practical alternative for writers who want to produce a relatively small number of copies for family and friends or a select group of people.

'Vanity publishing' is a different matter altogether. If a publisher

> 'I self-published Token Koori in 1998. But the financial reward was not the only reason for doing it myself. More importantly I can now hold the work in my hands today and honestly say I love what's in it and the way it looks. I chose what poems stayed and which ones went. I chose the artist and the art work. I chose the colours of the cover . . . and the font. I chose who would speak at my launch at the Sydney Writers' Festival. I choose where it goes. I own all of the work, and feel both proud and empowered to say that.'
>
> Anita Heiss, paper delivered at the NSW Writers' Centre's Spring Writing Festival, 13 September 1998.

> 'Vanity publishers promise the book and the glitter. Self-publishers get a printer to make the book and then make the glitter as best they can.'
>
> Paul Brennan, 'Print Me: when authors self-publish', *Australian Author*, vol. 29, no. 3, Summer 1997.

offers to produce and distribute your book for you but requests that you pay the costs, or a significant proportion of them, it is a case of vanity publishing. With this type of publishing you are paying for the privilege of being published by a commercial publishing house. Put bluntly, you are paying to have someone else put your work between covers.

Self-publication can be profitable, and some writers have had great success. Abraham H. Biderman's autobiography *The World of My Past* was first self-published in a small print run and went on to win the National Book Council Banjo Award for Non-Fiction in 1996. Sandra Cabot's *The Liver Cleansing Diet* is another wildly successful venture which raked in a large profit for the author and was taken up by a commercial publisher, while Karen Halliday's self-published *A Workaway Guide* has sold 24 000 copies to date. Lyn Bloomfield invested six years of her time and more than $300 000 to produce a book of the etchings of artist Norman Lindsay. Less than a month after publication, she had sold nearly half of the 500 deluxe editions at $800 each, and 2000 copies of the standard hardback edition at $190 each.

With more people writing than ever before, and quality self-publishing services available, the old prejudice that a self-published work must be amateur and lacking literary merit is on the wane. The Australia Council has recognised this and as of 2001 extended its grants criteria to include self-published works which meet certain conditions. As commercial publishers reduce their risk-taking by publishing only the most popular writers, writers for niche markets will increasingly turn to the self-publishing alternative.

There are advantages and disadvantages to self-publishing, and you should know about these before you take this step. D.W. Thorpe's booklet *Publish It! A guide for self-publishers* (which is listed in 'Bibliography' in the Resources section) has useful information on 'Producing your book', 'Your rights and responsibilities' and 'Selling your book', among other things.

Obviously the biggest advantage of self-publishing is that you emerge at the end of the process with your own book in hand. It is, however, not easy or cheap. To be successful, you must have a fair knowledge of the publishing scene and be well aware of all the important steps of the self-publishing process.

> 'A rise in the number of quality self-published books will make the current negative view of the work untenable, especially when those books are awarded prizes and signed up by prestigious publishers.'
>
> Glenn Phillips, 'Bad Press: political views of self-published literature in contemporary Australia', *Redoubt*, no. 25, 1997, pp. 130–3.

4.9.1 Editing

It is certainly worthwhile seeking the services of a professional editor before you go to print. A good editor will correct any inconsistencies or continuity problems or other structural flaws in your manuscript, as well as grammatical, spelling and punctuation errors. Money spent on editing your manuscript may well save you considerable embarrassment after the book is published. The Society of Editors (NSW and Vic.) produce registers of editors which list members of the organisation and describe their individual experience, specialities and computer skills, among other things.

> See Part 3.5 'Drafting and editing' and 'The role of publishers' editors' in Part 4.3.2 for further information, as well as 'Bibliography' and 'Assessment' in the Resources section

4.9.2 Parts of a book

A self-published book must include certain pages dictated by convention as well as specific information such as ISBN and Cataloguing-in-Publication data specifically assigned to it. The following sections will lead you through the information you need to include in a self-published work.

Half-title page

This usually contains only the brief title of the book but may sometimes incorporate the blurb from the cover or an author biography. For example, the half-title page of this book carries an author photo and brief biography. This is generally regarded as page 1 of the manuscript although no page numbers appear until the Contents page. Pages appearing before the first chapter are usually called 'preliminary pages' and are either unnumbered or numbered with roman lower-case numerals.

Title page

This page shows the full name of your work, your name, and place of publication. For example:

Sample title page

THE WRITER'S GUIDE

A companion to writing for pleasure or publication

Irina Dunn

ALLEN & UNWIN

Imprint page

This page, also called the reverse title page, is found on the other side of the title page. Imprint pages vary from book to book but usually provide the year of the first edition and any subsequent editions, information about the publisher, including name and address, the copyright symbol '©' with the name of the author alongside, Cataloguing-in-Publication (CiP) information and ISBN number, and the names of the typesetter, designer and printer. The imprint page will also usually contain a paragraph like this: 'All rights reserved. No part of this publication may be reproduced, stored in

See following pages for information about CiP and ISBN

a retrieval system, or transmitted in any form or by any means, electronic, mechanical, photocopying, recording or otherwise, without the prior written permission of the publisher.'

Some authors include a 'moral rights' statement on the imprint page, as follows: 'The author [your name] asserts the moral right to be identified as the author of this work.'

See Part 4.7.8, 'Moral rights'

You could also include on this page some information, such as an address, fax or phone number, or email address for people who would like to obtain another copy of the book. You might also consider giving your 'publishing company' a name that is different from yours as the author. This requires that you register a trade name, which then appears on the imprint page as the publisher.

Look at several books to get an idea of how to lay out the imprint page.

Cataloguing-in-Publication information

Cataloguing-in-Publication, or CiP, provides a catalogue entry for books which is usually printed on the imprint or reverse title page. Although it is not compulsory, it is useful in that it gives advance notice of books to be published and their subject category for those who may be interested, and if the book is published by a small publisher the address of that publisher is included in the CiP listing.

The National Library of Australia provides a free CiP service based on information provided by the publisher to the library's CiP Unit.

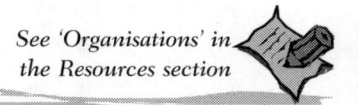

See 'Organisations' in the Resources section

All publishers, including self-publishers, are required to provide the title page, the table of contents, preface and introduction of a book to assist in the accurate compilation of a CiP entry. All information appearing on the title page must be shown on the CiP form. If details change, publishers should inform the CiP Unit. CiP entries are returned to publishers by fax or priority-paid mail where available.

No CiP is required in New Zealand.

ISBN

The International Standard Book Number (ISBN) is a worldwide code which is assigned to an individual book to assist in identifying it when recording or communicating information about it. Although it is not mandatory, it is important to obtain this number for your book because without it you are not eligible to receive Public and Educational Lending Right payments.

See 'Public and Educational Lending Right Schemes' in Part 6.1.1 for information

ISBNs allow individual books to be easily located and identified. The ISBN is incorporated into a book's barcode.

An ISBN should be given to:

- printed books, booklets and pamphlets
- book readings on cassettes and educational videos
- microfiche publications
- Braille publications
- computer software
- multimedia kits containing printed material.

The ISBN must be printed somewhere in the book, either on the imprint page, at the bottom of the title page, on the back cover of the book, or some other prominent location. It must also be printed on the dust jacket if there is one.

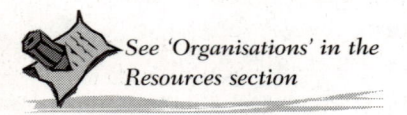

See 'Organisations' in the Resources section

To obtain an ISBN in Australia, contact D. W. Thorpe which will provide an ISBN. If you are a new publisher or self-publisher, you must pay the ISBN Agency a registration fee of $25. All publishers need to be allocated a block before ISBNs can be issued, and there is no expiry date on the numbers. If you are publishing one title, you will need to buy a block of five numbers for $25; if you are publishing 2–3 titles per year you will need to buy a block of 10 numbers, which will cost you $40, and so on.

It is worth mentioning here that many shops will not accept a book without a barcode. An ISBN barcode can be programmed into a shop's computer with the recommended retail price. Barcodes can be obtained from the ISBN Agency.

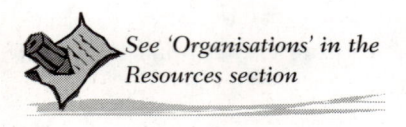

See 'Organisations' in the Resources section

In New Zealand ISBNs are assigned free of charge to books published in New Zealand by the New Zealand Standard Book Numbering Agency, located in the National Library.

See 'Organisations' in the Resources section

If you substantially change the text of your publication in a revised or updated edition, you will need a new ISBN.

ISSN

An International Standard Serial Number is a worldwide identification code assigned to serial publications or periodicals in the same way that ISBNs are assigned to books.

A serial is defined as a publication intended to continue indefinitely, made up of a number of parts linked by the same title, and issued in a sequence. Serial publications include periodicals such as newspapers, newsletters, magazines and annual publications, but may also include other formats such as microfiche, microfilm, CD-ROM and online electronic journals. Multi-volume books and series with a limited number of parts are not considered to be serials, but require an ISBN for each volume as well as an ISBN for the whole set of volumes. Series with ongoing titles are eligible for ISSNs.

A different ISSN is required for:

- each serial title
- each continuing, separately numbered supplement to a serial
- each numbered monograph series
- some serials where the issuing body changes its name
- each format in which a serial is issued (for example, print, CD-ROM).

Publishers and authors must remember to obtain an ISSN before the publication goes to the printer so that it can be included on the front cover or some other prominent part of the publication.

In Australia, information about ISSN and allocation of numbers is provided as a free service by the National Library of Australia. In New Zealand, information about ISSN and allocation of numbers can be obtained from the National Library of New Zealand.

See 'Organisations' in the Resources section

4.9.3 Design and layout

Before you approach a printer, store your manuscript on a computer unless you want to pay for transcribing it from handwritten or typewritten copy. If you are skilled in word processing, you can experiment with type styles and sizes to see what appeals to you, how your work looks on the page, and how many pages it makes.

It is important to determine the size and shape of the page when doing your layout. There are several standard sizes for books, depending on their genre and intended market. Carefully examine the layouts of various books to see what you think works best. Pay attention to the margins on your pages and leave sufficient space around the text. If you are doing a layout on an A4 page for an A5 book (that is, half the size of an A4 page), leave at least 60 mm above and below the text (including page numbers), and 55 mm on either side of the text. The resulting 'text box' will leave enough room for the gutter (or space between the text and the spine), the edges, and top and bottom margins.

Some printers who specialise in helping self-published authors offer additional services that will assist you if you are not skilled in type design and layout. It is practical to take advantage of these services because a skilled designer and desktop publisher can make a book much more readable by making it look attractive.

Alternatively, if you would like outside help with designing your book, check out your local phone book or local newspaper to find contact details for designers and desktop publishers. Discuss with them your own ideas or the sorts of books you like the design of. Don't forget to clearly establish how much the job will cost you and how long it will take.

4.9.4 Costing your book

Before your book is printed, ask yourself how many you think you could sell and at what price. (If you are printing your book to give away, this is not a consideration.) To recoup your expenses, base the unit cost of the book on your total expenses divided by the number of books printed; you can add a mark-up for profit. It is financially safer to print only as many books as you think you will be able to sell: you can always print more if your book takes off.

Another way of working out the appropriate price is, as a general rule of thumb, to charge five or six times the total cost of producing your book. This will help absorb the costs of distributing your books to retail outlets and discounts to bookshops (see Part 4.9.8 'Distribution' for further information on these costs). With a recommended retail price (RRP) set at five or six times the production cost, you should be able to make your money back when you have sold half of the print run.

Remember to set aside some money for designing the cover (about $300 in 2002 for a cover for which you provide the photos). When printing the price on the cover, remember to include 'RRP' after the price because it is illegal to fix the price.

4.9.5   The cover

Despite the adage 'don't judge a book by its cover', most people do to some degree. The front cover should contain the title, subtitle (if there is one) and the author's name. You can include other information, but too much writing on the front cover can be a turn-off. If you wish to use an image on the cover such as a painting or photograph, remember you will need to obtain permission to use someone else's copyrighted work. This may incur a fee.

See Part 4.7.10 'Permission fees'

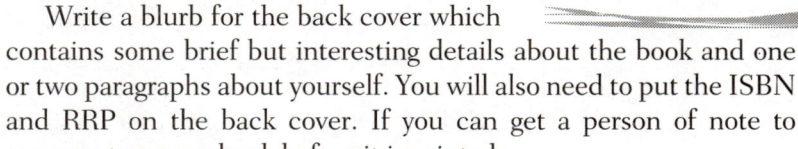

Write a blurb for the back cover which contains some brief but interesting details about the book and one or two paragraphs about yourself. You will also need to put the ISBN and RRP on the back cover. If you can get a person of note to comment on your book before it is printed, you could include a sentence or two from the quote on the back cover, or even on the front cover.

The spine is also important because it is likely to be the only part of your book visible on the bookshelf. It should contain the title, author's name and the publisher's name or logo. It should also be easy to read from a distance.

> 'Paying a publisher to publish for you is vanity publishing, but self-publishing the right number of books makes you a successful small business person.'
>
> Pat Woolley, 'Fast Books' website, 1998.

4.9.6 Printers

Having obtained all this information and performed these steps, you are now ready to approach a printer. With computer disk and printout in hand, phone several printers for information on costs. You will need to tell the printer the format for your book (that is, the size and shape of the printed page and how many pages it makes) and how many copies you want to print. Writers' centres will be able to advise you on selected printing companies with a proven record in helping writers to publish their books.

Some companies that offer special services to self-publishing authors charge a large amount of money to print your book. Although they may offer to distribute your work to various outlets such as bookshops, this may not be your best option as they do not usually have access to mass markets. This type of company is working more along the lines of vanity publishing. Many local printers can offer you exactly the same services at a much cheaper rate, but they will not distribute your work for you.

If you are able to produce camera-ready artwork either in hardcopy or electronically, that is, every page of your book is ready to be printed and requires no further alterations, you will save yourself some money, but you will either have to produce the work yourself on a word-processing or desktop-publishing package or pay someone else to do it for you.

In order to raise some money for the printing of your book you might consider a special pre-publication offer which gives purchasers a discount if they buy the book before it is published. This will help you to gauge interest in the book, as well as raising some cash for its production. This is not a new idea: subscription publishing was routinely done last century by authors publishing their own works.

> 'In the Australian market, an easy way to separate a vanity publisher from one offering the purely commercial service some authors seek, is to look at their prices and the quality of their products. Ask: How good are the books and what is their unit price? Vanity prices are usually inflated. For example, while an A5 page of type can easily be set for $5 (and at times $1 per page from disk), one Australian vanity publisher has charged $50 per page. If in doubt, avoid publishers who are cagey and vague about editing and promotion. Better to ask a printer for real costs.'
>
> Paul Brennan, 'Print Me: when authors self-publish', *Australian Author*, vol. 29, no. 3, Summer 1997.

4.9.7 An unusual twist to self-publishing

With a 30-year career in writing behind him, well-known Australian author Frank Moorhouse came up with a scheme which bypassed a commercial operation to publish his work in an unusual fashion — and to make money from it. After writing his erotic androgynous novel *Sonny*, he decided to offer it by prospectus and release it by advance subscription in a limited edition to subscribers who could afford to pay the price. The prospectus was accompanied by a statement from Moorhouse and a shareholder agreement document.

Five hundred copies of the novel, numbered 1 to 499, were to be offered for sale at $250 each, while another 26 copies were marked A to Z and signed by Moorhouse. Of these, twenty were reserved for investors prepared to pay $1000 per copy to finance the production, their money to be refunded after the project was successfully completed. The remaining copies were reserved by Moorhouse and the five members of the publishing board controlling the venture. All copies were hand-bound in leather and printed on special imported paper to the highest standard.

It seems that this unusual method of selling one's work has paid off for Moorhouse and intrigued the literary critics. Some claim that this form of limited edition publishing is akin to censorship. Surely it is more about creating a demand for your work and providing yourself with an assured income? Moorhouse gets much better returns than if he published through a large commercial publishing house, and his investors eventually get their money back and receive a beautiful copy of the book for lending Moorhouse the money.

4.9.8 Distribution

The biggest problem faced by self-published authors is the distribution of their books, that is, getting books into the bookshops or other outlets where they can be sold. To do this successfully, develop your own unique, creative distribution plan, taking into account all possible readers and outlets for your book.

It is almost impossible to sell your book through ordinary bookshops unless they are prepared to promote self-published books. Bookshops that accept self-published books usually insist on a 'sale or return' arrangement, usually within a specified period, and few will make a firm (non-returnable) purchase. The standard practice is for bookshops to pay you 55–60 per cent of the recommended retail price for each copy sold, that is, they get a 40–45 per cent discount.

Your local bookshop is the one most likely to take your books, especially if you can drum up local publicity. After that it is a time-consuming and painstaking task to go around to as many other bookshops as possible. You may find that your book is rejected by the large shops and chains who try to limit the number of accounts they have and will not deal with small suppliers and self-publishers. A more comprehensive approach would be to engage the services of a distributor.

There are a number of independent distributors, some with national, some with state-based, services, who will distribute books from small presses, independents and self-publishers, although many distributors are not keen on taking a single title from a self-publisher as there is a lot of paperwork for comparatively little return. If you have only one book to sell, your best bet is to find a distributor who specialises in selling a particular genre of writing (such as children's literature, travel, New Age books, or non-fiction) or specialises in a particular type of outlet (such as airport shops, tourist information centres, national park shops). They usually take books on consignment and charge about 60–70 per cent of the recommended retail price (of which bookshops take about 40 per cent).

Distributors pay only for books they sell, and you can expect to receive the money 90 days after the end of the month of sale. About 35–40 per cent of books 'sold' by publishers and distributors to bookshops are returned two or three months later. Consult a copy of *The Directory of NZ Book Publishers and Distributors* or the *Australian Booksellers Association of Members/Book Distributors in Australia,* which contains the contact details of Australian distributors, as well as a list of Australian bookshops belonging to the Australian Booksellers Association.

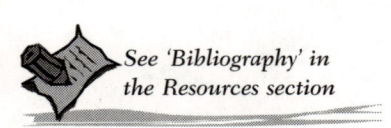

See 'Bibliography' in the Resources section

4.9.9 Legal deposit requirements

All publishers, including self-publishers, are legally required to deposit copies of their books with nominated 'legal deposit' libraries in the country in which they are published.

Australia

Under the Australian *Copyright Act 1968* and various state acts, a copy of any work published in Australia must be deposited with the National Library of Australia and the appropriate state library. In New South Wales, Queensland and South Australia, a copy must also be deposited with more than one specified library.

Legal deposit extends not only to commercial publishers but also to private individuals, clubs, churches, societies and organisations. Legal deposit of the material is the sole responsibility of the publisher or author. It ensures that the works of authors and publishers will survive for the use of future generations. The comprehensive collections of Australian publications formed in this way provide the basis for research into all aspects of Australian life, history, culture, and artistic, commercial, technical and scientific endeavour.

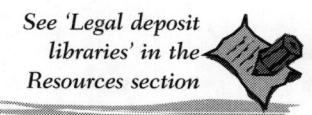

See 'Legal deposit libraries' in the Resources section

New Zealand

Under the legal deposit provisions of New Zealand's *National Library Act 1965* authors and publishers are required to deposit three copies of every work published in New Zealand with the National Library's Legal Deposit Office.

One copy is made available for public use in the library, one is placed in the Parliamentary Library, and the third is permanently preserved in the Alexander Turnbull Library.

See 'Legal deposit libraries' in the Resources section

4.9.10 Publicity and promotion

There is no point in your book sitting on the shelf of a bookshop unless people know it is there for purchase. Make lists of organisations and individuals who may be interested in your work and send them fliers and press releases about it. Include information about the price of the book, where it can be obtained, some interesting details about the author (yourself), and a short punchy synopsis of the subject of the book. You may have to approach media outlets or organisations to offer yourself for interviews or talks and this will have to be handled with delicacy as you don't want to get a reputation for being pushy. Writer Marele Day offers much good advice for writers in her book *The Art of Self-Promotion: Self-Promotion by Writers*.

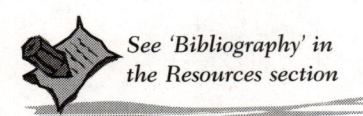

See 'Bibliography' in the Resources section

If you are printing more than about 200 copies of your book, set aside a certain number, say about 10 per cent or twenty copies, as review copies. Be prepared to hand them out liberally: they are your best publicity. It is cheaper to give away copies for review, as samples or as complimentary gifts, than to pay for advertisements. When you give away complimentary copies of your book, include a slip with the name of the author, title of the book, the price, and address, phone, email and fax for readers interested in purchasing your book. Add a line which says, 'Please order this book for your local library and bookshop'. It works!

Two important avenues of publicity are your local newspaper and local bookshops. Approach them with your publicity material. The local paper will probably run a story on the 'local author' while the bookshop may even want you to come in to meet your readers for an advertised booksigning.

See also Part 5 'Promoting your book' for further information on working with a publicist, your own promotion strategy, preparing for interviews, book launches, creating a website and getting reviews

You may need to think of hiring a publicist at a cost of anywhere between $2000 and $5000 (in 2002) and decide whether the income generated by the publicity will cover the costs. To find the right publicist for your book, call your local writers' centre for some contacts, or check out publicists listed in the phone book.

4.10 GETTING YOUR SCRIPT PRODUCED

4.10.1 Film and television

Film and television production is an expensive and competitive enterprise. Most television, film, video and CD-ROM producers require fully professional scripts with a strongly commercial flavour for production and, at the risk of sounding negative, it is a waste of your time and money (and theirs) to forward a script which is poorly developed, badly laid out, and has little regard for commercial potential.

It is virtually impossible to get a feature-length film produced before you have first made a number of shorter films. There are opportunities for makers of short films in the many short film festivals staged around Australia and New Zealand. With a script in hand, a cheap video recorder, and willing participants in your project, you can begin to experiment with the medium in making and submitting entries to these festivals.

See 'Festivals and events' in the Resources section

There are many production companies, government organisations and educational institutions that need writers for educational or promotional films and videos, and these provide the bread and butter for scriptwriters while they wait for the jam of feature production. It is hard to break into the industry and you may have to find a mentor prepared to take you on without pay so that you can get the experience, and the credits, before you apply to write a film of your own.

Like film, television writing is also a highly specialised area that is difficult to break into. Opportunities arise for experienced writers in this medium when the Australian Broadcasting Corporation and TV New Zealand call for project submissions or program ideas. The best way to find out about these is to join one of the specialist organisations which publish newsletters containing such information for their members.

Encore, a directory of film, television and video personnel, contains the names and contact details of Australian screen producers, directors, writers, and editors, among others, and lists their credits. It is an invaluable reference if you wish to contact producers, directors and writers directly.

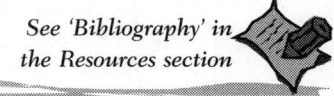

See 'Bibliography' in the Resources section

Professional help

If you believe you have a marketable product, your first stop will be the Australian or New Zealand Writers' Guild to get advice about agents or producers who are looking for fresh new scripts.

Sometimes they advertise in the newsletters of writing organisations, and it is worthwhile checking the back issues to search out these opportunities. In Australia, contact the Australian Film Commission and the NSW Film and Television Office for information about script development grants and other programs for new scriptwriters. In New Zealand contact the NZ Film Commission.

The Australian Writers' Guild offers its members a Script Assessment and Script Clinic. The script assessment service provides a written assessment of the strengths and weaknesses of your work. It is couched in friendly, constructive terms, covering topics ranging from basics such as formatting and presentation to structure, characterisation and marketability. The assessment will be sent to you within six weeks. First and second assessments cost $137.50 each, third and subsequent assessments cost $275 each. The Script Clinic offers a two-hour (but often goes longer) face-to-face assessment of your work, held at a date and time to suit you. It is open to writers in Adelaide, Brisbane, Melbourne, Perth and Sydney. The first and second clinics cost $192.50, third and subsequent clinics cost $385 each. If a quick written assessment is required an additional $55 will be charged, which is passed directly to the assessor.

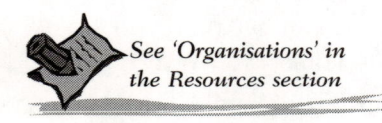

See 'Organisations' in the Resources section

4.10.2 Opportunities for playwrights

There are many theatre groups, including multicultural, experimental, youth, and local amateur groups catering to different audiences such as the elderly, which welcome new scripts and are prepared to try them out in workshops.

See also Part 2.2.2 'Writing for the stage' and Part 6.1.9 'Awards, competitions, residencies and festivals for scriptwriters' and 'Assessment' in the Resources section

Mainstream drama companies sometimes look for new scripts to develop, so contact them individually to find out if they do so and how to submit your work.

In addition, the following organisations may be helpful.

Australian National Playwrights' Centre

The Australian National Playwrights' Centre has a Script Assessment and Dramaturgy Program offering a variety of professional development options for both members and non-members.

Through the script assessment service playwrights receive a written report containing valuable professional comment on their plays. In addition, there are face-to-face sessions in which a dramaturg — a kind of artistic midwife — helps the novice playwright to realise the full potential of the work before it is submitted to a theatre company (or is workshopped or rehearsed) by asking searching questions about structure, dialogue and character, among other things.

See 'Assessment' and 'Organisations' in the Resources section

Through this program the applicant is also considered for the Playwrights' Program and the work may be selected for workshopping at the annual National Playwrights' Conference and this may lead to production with a theatre company. To access the script assessment service, playwrights need to contact the centre and obtain a script entry form.

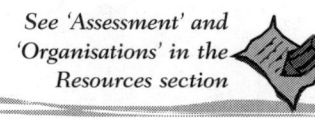

Playworks

Based in Sydney, the Playworks Script Development Program for Australian women playwrights supports experienced, emerging and new writers. All scripts submitted are read by the Director of Script Development, and many are also read by the Artistic Director. All receive a written assessment from a professional practitioner. Scripts may take the form of a playscript or, in the case of a physical work, a video or treatment may be submitted.

Playlab

A Queensland organisation called Playlab Inc. promotes and supports playwriting as an art form by providing resources and professional services to playwrights to facilitate the creation of new work.

Playlab's Script Development Network is a script assessment service offered to theatre and performance writers to provide comprehensive and informed comment on developing texts.

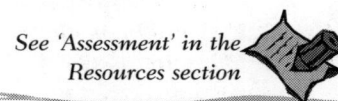

See 'Assessment' in the Resources section

There are three options: the snapshot assessment, which provides a brief overview with recommendations for development (cost in 2002 $70 and $60 for members); a full assessment, which offers an extended analysis, suggestions for improvement and recommendations (cost in 2002 was $110 and $95 for members) and the face-to-face assessment, which is delivered in a meeting with a dramaturg (cost $140). Playlab also assesses musicals (book and score) for the cost of $125. All these prices include GST.

Playlab is also a publisher. Plays must have been professionally produced, or produced in a significant community context. Playlab also publishes other drama-related material. Publication is by submission. Playlab can also assist member playwrights in a range of activities such as contracting, representation, and funding applications.

Playmarket

New Zealand's Playmarket offers a range of script advisory services for New Zealand playwrights. To be eligible for Playmarket assistance you must be a New Zealand citizen or resident.

The usual first step towards a production of your script is through Playmarket's assessment service. Scripts are read by at least two people involved in New Zealand professional theatre. They assess the production potential of scripts written for the stage and provide a written report which identifies the script's strengths, weaknesses and production potential. This usually takes about four weeks.

4.10.3 Radio markets

ABC Radio

In Australia, the Australian Broadcasting Corporation allocates time to the production of drama for radio. In 2002, the ABC broadcast two weekly drama programs, details of which are available in the ABC's magazine *24 Hours*. The programs were: *Airplay* and *Saturday Night Drama*, both on ABC Radio National. *Airplay* is Radio National's showcase for new Australian writing and performance. It presents half-hour audio performance works which experiment with form and explore a wide range of subjects, genres and narrative styles. The ABC encourages writers to submit half-hour scripts that are lively, diverse, and intellectually and emotionally engaging. These may include comedy scripts. *Saturday Night Drama* broadcasts one-hour plays and series from Australian and world writers, and productions by overseas broadcasting organisations including the BBC. The ABC also offers commissions to writers and commissions stage and screenwriters to adapt their work for radio production.

Writers are encouraged to listen to current radio drama to become familiar with the programs before sending scripts. As ABC Radio head Richard Buckham advises: 'The best advice we can give to anyone who wants to write for radio is to *listen* to radio'. Writers interested in sound are also advised to tune in to *The Listening Room* produced by the Acoustic Art Unit and broadcast every Monday night on ABC Classic FM.

Community radio

Radio broadcast opportunities exist for writers of all kinds on Australian community radio.

Community stations are almost as diverse as they are numerous. In 2002 there were over 230 licensed stations in Australia, with more than 80 in New South Wales. Their numbers are still increasing and they vary in size from those with full city-wide coverage to much smaller groups of suburbs or stations covering a regional area. Some city-wide stations favour a particular demographic while typically suburban, rural and regional stations are more general in focus.

Some stations already have writers' programs, but most don't. However, many will be eager to build ongoing partnerships with arts groups and individuals. Few have drama departments as such but are likely to be enthusiastic when approached and some will have already produced plays.

Bigger stations such as 2SER (Sydney) and 2NUR (Newcastle) have a long history of working with writers and recording plays. Other stations such as 2MCE (Bathurst), 2BBB (Bellingen) and many others have broadcast live or recorded original comedy.

New stations are usually full of optimism and keen to hear ideas, so give them a go.

The Writer's Guide

Many, but not all, stations like shorter pieces (serials, micro-dramas, micro-documentaries, short stories and poems) which can be run in the breakfast time-slot as well as during the morning and afternoon shows. Most stations have an arts program but if you want to jump out of the arts radio ghetto think about how to make your work approachable to a general audience at the most popular listening times (6 am–6 pm Monday to Friday).

The Community Radio Satellite (ComRadSat) comprises 150 stations and is increasing in numbers. ComRadSat broadcasts two writers' programs and its administrator is always on the look-out for original drama and comedy. For example, in one year ComRadSat commissioned a Radio Drama Mentorship Scheme funded by the NSW Arts Ministry, recorded and broadcast short plays from the Belvoir Street Theatre and a group of monologues recorded at 2RES and 2SER, and successfully sought Australia Council funding for a radio play from Newcastle. The Community Broadcasting Association of Australia (CBAA) has produced *A Practical Handbook for Arts Participation in Community Radio*, which covers issues such as management, funding, writing, producing and directing radio drama, copyright and public liability.

See 'Bibliography' in the Resources section

See 'Organisations' in the Resources section

If you are having trouble finding a station or want more information on community radio, contact the Community Broadcasting Association of Australia or check out the website at www.cbaa.org.au.

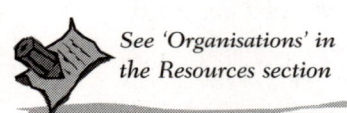

Approaching New Zealand radio producers

Radio New Zealand Drama welcomes unsolicited radio scripts from New Zealand residents or New Zealanders living abroad. Scripts should be up to 55 minutes of radio fiction. Stage scripts with strong radio potential are also considered.

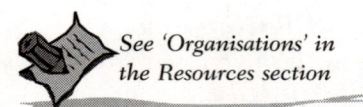

See 'Organisations' in the Resources section

In early 2002, there were two regular programs broadcast each week for drama on National Radio, with a mix of Radio New Zealand productions and overseas productions, as well as other non-drama programs.

Getting Published

Both titled *Playhouse*, one was slotted at 8.06 pm on Wednesday nights, the other on Sunday afternoons at 4.03 pm. Changes in drama programming, and probably an expansion of drama opportunities, are expected to occur in mid–2002.

4.11 SURVIVING REJECTION

Don't expect that your work will be instantly accepted. Acceptance depends on your piece being offered to the right outlet at the right moment: it may simply be that your work does not fit that particular publisher's list or producer's schedule at the time. Many commercially successful writers recall the days when the volume of rejection slips they had received could have wall-papered a room in their house. At this stage, it will take time and determination to find an appropriate outlet for your work.

> 'The important thing is not to despair. When something is returned and rejected, don't waste energy being emotional about it, simply send it off somewhere else. (I wish I could follow my own advice here.) Nothing is gained by having a story sitting around submitted nowhere. Some of my most anthologised stories suffered rejection after rejection before they were first published: but once they finally appeared, they were reprinted and translated again and again.'
>
> Michael Wilding, 'Writing Short Stories', address to the Society of Women Writers at the NSW Writers' Centre, March 1997.

PART FIVE
PROMOTING YOUR BOOK

Promoting Your Book

5.1 WORKING WITH A PUBLICIST

After you've checked the page proofs of your book and returned them to the publisher for production and printing, there is still a fair amount of work ahead of you, but don't be disheartened: the kind of work required of you at this stage can be a lot of fun.

If your publisher is a major commercial outfit, you can except that the publicity department will put some effort into marketing and promoting your work. Several months ahead of publication date, make an appointment with the publisher's publicist in charge of your book to discuss the details of the promotion strategy. This will allow your publicist time to organise a feature article about you as deadlines for some newspapers and magazines are often two or even three months ahead of the publishing schedule. If a current issue in the media relates to the topic of your work, let the publicist know and work out an 'angle' to link your work to that issue. This may present some unexpected publicity avenues for you.

> 'It doesn't seem undue to ask a writer — no matter how high-minded — to figure skate and turn cabaret artist now and again in helping to sell and promote their work. An alternative, I suppose, is to hole up in his high-tech garret and send his manuscript around to his friends or distribute via his web site.'
>
> James Hall, Literary Editor, *The Australian*, 4 March 1998.

You will make the publicist's job much easier if you supply:

- several good quality black and white and colour author photos
- about a page description of yourself
- a list of contacts who may be interested in the book
- a list of your ideas for publicising the book
- publications which might be prepared to print a review of your book
- a list of your book's main features and what you think are its major selling points for the reps who visit the bookstores.

Most commercial publishers will give you a long questionnaire to fill out prior to publication of your book, and you will be asked to provide myriad details about your publishing history, your activities, your professional occupations and personal

See 'Publicity Questionnaire (Allen & Unwin)' in the Resources section

191

> 'I love all the attention. After two years of solitude it makes a really nice change. It's so strange: you spend two years glued to the word processor. But in the end I was doing 12-hour days, six days a week, trying to get this [her first novel The Service of Clouds] delivered in time.'
>
> Delia Falconer quoted by Jane Freeman, *Sydney Morning Herald*, 25 October 1997.

See also Part 4.9.10 'Publicity and promotion' for further information on undertaking your own book promotion

interests — anything that could be used to publicise, market and sell the book. Present material that is interesting, useful for the publicist, and memorable for the media, and try to ensure that your 'pitch' is the same as the sales and publicity personnel.

Media exposure is wonderful for a writer selling a new title, but publicists usually work on wide media coverage only for high-profile authors. If you are a previously unpublished author, then the promotion your book receives may be low-key. You need to be realistic about how much publicity the publisher will provide. Think of how many books the firm publishes and imports each month and how many publicity staff it has. It works out to about five minutes of staff time for each book with some of the large publishers. Despite this, you should always pressure for good marketing strategies.

If you are organising some of your own publicity, consult with your publicist as duplication or crossed-wires with her efforts is a waste of everybody's time. Your publicist will be only too glad that you are taking such an interest in promoting and publishing your book.

5.2 YOUR PERSONAL PROMOTION STRATEGY

If you are published by a small publisher, or are self-published, you will probably have to arrange much of the publicity yourself. In either case, if you take an active role in publicising your book you will have some control over how and where it is promoted.

Draw up a list of ideas of possible outlets for your book. Include all the journals and magazines and other publications that might be interested in publishing articles on you or your work or might ask you to contribute an article about your book. Also make up a list of any professional, community and special-interest organisations that might invite you to speak on the subject of your book before a selected audience. Don't forget that local bookshops where the staff know you may agree to display your book prominently and possibly hold a book signing.

Radio programs are also worth considering, especially those which invite visiting speakers to the studio for an extended interview, but even a five-minute phone interview will stimulate interest in you and your book. Don't forget to leave publicity material with the producer of the program on which you are interviewed.

> 'Being a writer doesn't end when your book hits the shelves. It's your book, your passion, your creation — and you are the best person to tell people about it.'
>
> Jen McVeity, *Fine Line*, no. 4, Autumn 1998.

Handy references for your publicity and promotion work are Margaret Gee's *Australian Media Guide*, and the *Bookman Media Guide*, both of which are updated annually. These guides list all the major media outlets in Australia, including metropolitan newspapers, ethnic press and suburban newspapers, regional and country newspapers, radio, television, newsletters, photoagencies, representatives of overseas media and magazines, together with all personnel and contact details. You may be surprised at the large number of potential publicity outlets for your book in the comprehensive listings supplied in these publications. You will also find Marele Day's *The Art of Self-Promotion: Self-Promotion by Writers* a useful guide for tips on media presentation.

See 'Bibliography' in the Resources section

If you have written a literary work, remember that many of the literary magazines listed in marketing guides are not available in newsagents but can be found in large university or public libraries or at writers' centres. A review in one of these, even if its circulation is tiny, will alert readers to your work, and every bit of publicity counts, including word-of-mouth.

Make your own media contacts by approaching the relevant people and posting or faxing material to them. They will be the editors of the appropriate sections of magazines and newspapers, or the producers of particular radio or television programs. Follow up with a phone-call to find out if they have received the material and whether they are interested in interviewing you or promoting the book or giving you some other publicity.

For your publicity material, which you could attractively package as a press kit, write a few interesting paragraphs of biographical data about yourself and arrange for good black-and-white or colour photographs of yourself to be taken by a competent friend, relative or professional photographer. Remember to clear the copyright so that it can be reproduced without charge. On the back of each print stick a label with your contact details and the name of the photographer and note that it can be reproduced for publicity purposes. If you want it back, put a return address on the sticker and ask for the return of the photo. Sometimes they *are* returned, so make it easier for those who use your picture to do the right thing. Prints can be expensive, so try to keep track of them, perhaps in a notebook where you can record the names of people you have sent them to.

5.3   PREPARING FOR INTERVIEWS

Whether commercially published or self-published, you should be prepared for interviews with newspapers, radio, and possibly television, as well as for face-to-face meetings with professional bodies, schoolchildren, community organisations, and anyone who could have an interest in hearing you speak about or read from your work.

If you are not used to handling interviews by journalists, now is the time to start practising. Use every opportunity to develop your skills for public speaking by accepting every invitation you receive. Make your own arrangements to be interviewed on a local community radio station. Even if no-one seems to be listening, it is still good practice in familiarising yourself with radio studio procedure and becoming less nervous.

The first thing to do is to acquaint yourself with the particular format of the interview — who will be conducting the interview, where and when it will appear or be broadcast, what kind of publication or program it will be (whether specialist or general interest, talk show or review pages of a newspaper), and its likely audience or readership. These considerations will help you to determine the kinds of responses you give, and to make your interview appropriate for the outlet.

Think about the salient selling-point of your work and write a few catchy lines about it for interviews or for your written publicity material or press releases. If your book is likely to be controversial, prepare yourself for challenges from the media by anticipating questions and writing out succinct responses in advance of the interview. You may be asked about other books in your field, so to avoid appearing ignorant read widely in case this occurs. Reread 'Interview techniques' in Part 3.4.1 to check on the types of interview you may be facing and what you can expect from an interviewer.

5.4 YOUR BOOK LAUNCH

Most publishers these days claim they cannot afford to pay for a launch, and there is some doubt whether launches actually help to sell many copies of a book unless you are famous or the book's subject captures media attention.

If you're prepared to pay for your own modest launch (mainly for food and alcohol), I suggest holding it in your local bookshop where guests have the opportunity to buy the book on the spot — and have the privilege of obtaining the author's signature at the same time. So much the better if you can persuade a well-known public figure to launch it as this may attract publicity in the local or even the mainstream media.

In any case, go ahead and organise your own launch party! You've earned it after all that hard work. You can at least enjoy the pleasure of receiving congratulations from your friends, relatives and colleagues who will, of course, all purchase your book, and you can bask in the recognition of having reached the goal of publication.

5.5 YOUR OWN WEBSITE

Whether or not you're a computer whiz, advertising your work on a website could bring additional sales from unexpected quarters, especially if you have more than one title to offer.

You have the choice of attaching publicity about your latest creation to an existing website or, if you're already hooked up to the net, establishing a dedicated site for your work as many authors have done.

You need to think visually when developing your website, rather than in terms of linear print. The site will be overwhelmed if you try to fill it with too many words. Study other websites to see what works best. If you are not an experienced web designer,

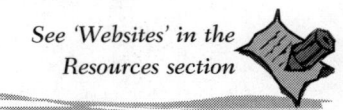

See 'Websites' in the Resources section

you can seek the services of a professional who will create your site and present your material attractively for the virtual visitor. You need to think carefully, however, whether the costs of a professional design company will be covered by subsequent sales of the book. However, it's not all that expensive to establish a simple website if you find a freelance designer or even a student willing to create one for you.

Your site could include a short and interesting paragraph about yourself, your work, your interests, and your skills as well as samples of your work. You could, if you want to get fancy, record yourself reading from your work and accompany your text with colourful graphics. Don't forget to list your contact details: email, street address, phone and fax, and include an order form for those readers who wish to purchase a copy of your book. You may want to insert a counter to show how many people have visited your site, and if you're interested in maintaining contact with your web readers, you could dedicate a part of your site as a chat page. Certainly include a hotlink on your email address for people wishing to contact you.

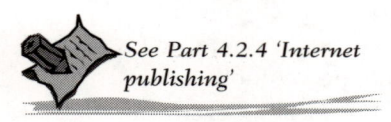

See Part 4.2.4 'Internet publishing'

Some organisations, such as the Australian Society of Authors, offer members their own web page for a small fee with the opportunity to put up a résumé and advertise their work.

5.6 ON GETTING REVIEWS AND BEING REVIEWED

The book review is the culmination of a long process that may have begun years before when you or your publisher first got a bright idea for a book. It is the moment when your book is launched into the world, when it becomes public for the first time, when its merits and faults are debated openly for all to read. This can be a thrilling experience for the author who gets a good review, or it can be horribly disappointing if the book is panned.

Whatever the possible outcome, authors recognise that there are practical reasons for seeking a book review, and that is, you need people to buy and read your book. Unless you have already established who your readers are, and presented them with or sold them

Promoting Your Book

copies of your book, you will have to let people know that your book is available, what it is about, and how to get it. This is the purpose of a book review.

A review of your book does not follow automatically on publication and, given the large numbers of newly published works competing for space on the literary pages of newspapers and periodicals, you can consider yourself lucky if a major paper decides to give your new book some room. If you are extraordinarily lucky, you may also be interviewed in a feature article as the author of an exciting new work.

If your book is non-fiction, you may have more success in getting reviews in special-interest media (such as computer journals or gardening magazines). Reviews in these types of publications are likely to be effective as they appeal to your target audience.

If you are published commercially, the publicist will probably send review copies of your book to the major press and book review magazines. You are entitled to ask which publications have received copies of your book, but you can also do your own research and suggest additional outlets to which the book could be sent. Investigate a large newsagent for the range of magazines on the market, as well as buying one of the marketing guides which list all kinds of publications produced in Australia.

Publishers and writers can never be sure when and, indeed, whether their books will be reviewed. The backlist of reviews is usually lengthy and it may take weeks if not months after publication before a review appears, if it appears at all. This can be a very frustrating time for a writer who, naturally, after all the hard work involved in writing the book, wants it to reach its readers as soon as possible.

> 'You love to play God,
> To toy or to praise,
> To brandish your rod,
> To destroy and to raise,
> But the Lord took the dust
> And made it a man,
> While you earn your crust
> By the opposite plan.'
>
> David Martin, 'To a Critic', in response to a review by A. D. Hope.

> 'I'm not going to win the Booker Prize . . . But I'm disappointed if I am ignored by the critics.'
>
> Jon Cleary interviewed by Tony Stephens, *Sydney Morning Herald*, 15 November 1997.

See 'Bibliography' in the Resources section

See also Part 4.9.10 'Publicity and promotion'

5.6.1 Major review publications

In Australia the major national review publications are *The Weekend Australian's* arts pages, the *Australian Book Review*, and the new magazine *Good Reading*. Capital-city newspapers also carry arts pages, and local press will occasionally publish book reviews or interviews with an author. Numerous literary and academic journals publish reviews, and special interest magazines may wish to review your book for their readers.

Other practical references are *The Australian Writer's Marketplace* and the NSW Writers' Centre's *Journals Directory*. The former lists all the major periodical outlets in Australia, while the latter concentrates on literary journals.

In New Zealand the major review publications are the national quarterly *New Zealand Books*, as well as the papers *The Listener* (weekly), *The Weekend New Zealand Herald*, *The Saturday Dominion*, *The Sunday Star-Times*, *The Evening Post*, *The Press* and the literary journals *Landfall*, *Allsorts*, *Journal of New Zealand Literature*, *Poetry New Zealand*, *Takahe Magazine* and *Sport*.

See 'Magazines' in the Resources section

5.6.2 Reviews of self-published works

If you have self-published your book you will have to work a lot harder at getting a review for it.

Many publications refuse to publish reviews of self-published work unless the author is well-known or the book is unusual. Nonetheless there are other publications, such as specialist journals, which will consider reviewing self-published works if the topic interests their readers, so it may not matter if you cannot get a review in a major newspaper providing that your target market finds out about your book. For example, if you have self-published a self-help book for asthma sufferers, your target market will be readers of newsletters published by asthma societies, popular magazines, especially family and health magazines, and any publication which reviews or at least notes the latest titles in the self-help category.

After making inquiries with the editor of the particular publication, forward a copy of your book with a letter outlining its theme, and request that it be considered for review. Mention any interesting details about its content, why you wrote it, why you self-published it, and where readers can obtain a copy. Some self-published books, such as lawyer Sean Flood's successful *Mabo: a symbol of sharing*, initially achieved a wide reputation by word-of-mouth. It was subsequently reviewed and Flood was appointed to the Native Title Tribunal on the strength of this publication. Once a book has achieved good sales it is likely that it, and subsequent books by the same author, will be treated seriously and reviewed.

Finding a reviewer for a self-published novel is much more difficult than for non-fiction unless one of your readers likes it so much that he or she spontaneously writes a review and sends it off to a periodical which accepts reviews of self-published works. However, many papers will not publish unsolicited reviews. The alternative is to obtain quotes from well-known writers who have read the book and print them on a flier which you can then use to publicise the book among your potential buyers and readers. If they have commented favourably on your manuscript prior to publication, ask them for permission to reproduce their comments in whole or part on the back cover of your book. That way, the book will carry its own reviews wherever it goes!

5.6.3 Is a bad review better than no review?

Is a bad review better than no review? This is hard to answer. Writer Michael Wilding facetiously answered this question by saying that it doesn't matter 'as long they spell my name right!' If ignored by the critics, certain books, such as novels, are unlikely to sell well unless the author has already developed a devoted following clamouring for the next work. If a work of non-fiction has a niche market which doesn't rely on reviews for sales it,

> 'Writers will inevitably wish they had been ignored rather than "clubbed" by the reviewer's ignorance.'
>
> Claire Murdoch, 'One degree of separation', *New Zealand Books*, August 1998.

too, may do well. Some publishers may promote their own titles in paid advertising and this will fetch sales.

Being reviewed well is probably most important for creators of serious literary works, that is, of novels, volumes of poetry, biographies and histories and any book which has some pretensions of style and content. A favourable review of a first novel by an unknown writer can result in a sell-out of the first print run, which in Australia and New Zealand is not likely to exceed 3000.

A bad review may not stop sales of the book if the curiosity of the reading public has been aroused by the review. It may even increase sales. Don Anderson, formerly a regular reviewer for one of the major Australian newspapers, recognised this: 'A review fed on "hatred" or at least respectful demurring is more likely to breed controversy and generate news and possibly even sell books than one deriving from "love" or at least polite admiration.' ('Reviewing Reviewed', *Australian Book Review*, October 1997.)

In some cases reviews may simply be irrelevant to the success of a book. Damning reviews of books by best-selling author Bryce Courtenay have not affected huge sales of his books, which remain popular with his readers despite, or perhaps because of, the bad press. Perhaps his readers do not read reviews.

Regular readers of reviews come to know the particular likes and dislikes of individual reviewers and can read between the lines to find a book they may be interested in reading. In any case, a bad review in one publication may be matched by a good review in another so the overall effect may not be so damaging.

Some literary editors, such as novelist Matt Condon, prefer not to publish bad reviews after having been on the receiving end of them. 'If I don't like a book,' he says, 'I simply won't include it in the pages.' Others are not so gracious. Anna Maria Dell'oso contends that 'what editors of the large dailies prefer is a searing fight, the best copy being a ruthless bastard of a critic ripping into

---

'Therefore, one has to be fairly aware of the cabals and groupings within the writing community in Australia when commissioning reviews. It can frankly be a can of worms. One would hesitate for instance to ask Ken Methold to review any book by Tom Shapcott, and at the risk of being either indiscreet or labelled as a gossip, it is a good idea to keep tabs on the shifting domestic arrangements and emotional entanglements of some writers. All this, of course, has to be done at some remove.'

Former *Sydney Morning Herald* Literary Editor William Fraser, 'Politics of Reviewing', *Australian Author*, Winter 1994, vol. 26, no. 2.

a local artistic tall poppy' ('Confessions of a critic', *Australian Author*, Winter 1994, vol. 26, no. 2).

Few authors, including those who have themselves been critics, have escaped from a bad review at some stage in their career. It goes with the territory. It may be simply bad luck that the reviewer requested to assess a book does not like it, while another might have liked it. Some editors even place books with reviewers who they know will pan a book because that makes good copy. Unfortunately, it's all part of the business of writing, and writers have to take their chances in both the pleasures and pitfalls of the publishing game.

> *'Literary criticism which is fearless, knowledgable, passionate and fair, is a necessity for the vigour of a literary community, and some kind of safeguard that writers' work will be judged on its own merits, however harshly.'*
>
> Debra Adelaide, 'Reviewing the Reviewers', *Australian Author*, Winter 1994, vol. 26, no. 2.

All is not lost if your book is not reviewed, or if it is reviewed badly. According to some booksellers, word-of-mouth can boost sales tremendously and establish a literary reputation as much as any good review can.

PART SIX

WRITING AS A CAREER, OR 'DON'T GIVE UP YOUR DAY JOB'

6.1 SOURCES OF INCOME

6.1.1 Income from books

A study conducted in 1993 found that professional Australian writers earned a median income of $3400 from their writing. In New Zealand, the amount is even smaller. This is not an encouraging figure for those wishing to enter the profession as a full-time career, and suggests that a writer would be unwise to give up regular paid employment if intending to rely on royalties alone for an income.

Most writers must supplement their income from sources other than writing. Few go off to play the stockmarket in the morning, make their millions by lunchtime, and return home for a pleasant afternoon of creative writing in their three-storey waterfront mansion.

More typically, many go through years of comparative poverty if they dedicate most of their time to writing, stitching together a living by giving readings, writing articles, teaching, marking exam papers, editing, translating and interpreting, taxi driving, bar tending, gardening and just about any casual work that gives them the time to write. Writer Peter Robb had lived in poverty for fourteen years and was down to his last $2000 when he won the Victorian Premier's Prize for Non-Fiction in 1997 for his book *Midnight in Sicily*. Many successful writers tell the same story.

Nonetheless, if writers do not live a life of luxury the rewards are to be had elsewhere. Georgia Savage, whose books have been acclaimed internationally, lives in relatively humble circumstances, but she persists with her chosen profession because: 'It gives to me what I ask it to do. I am fulfilling myself. If you can do that you can have a happy life.'

> 'There is deep dissatisfaction among writers over the fact that their incomes have been significantly eroded in recent times. We are also concerned about aspects of publishing, like marketing, the short shelf life of books, the diminution of the vital editing process, electronic publishing.'
>
> Libby Gleeson, Chair of the Australian Society of Authors and children's book author, interviewed by Sally Loane, 'Standing up for our Writes', *Sydney Morning Herald*, 21 March 1998.

> 'In the end, what most Australian writers have to accept is the unalterable fact that they are writing for a base market that is relatively small, i.e. eighteen million people. And although Australians, as you know, buy more books per head of population that any other country, this is not enough to generate an income for their writers.'
>
> Amanda Lohrey interviewed by Amanda Galligan, *Imago*, Summer 1997, vol. 9, no. 3.

Royalties

Royalties are moneys paid to creators of works and are calculated as a percentage of the income received from the sale of the work. Before 1953, British publishers paid Australian writers a 'colonial' royalty of 5 per cent, the equivalent of threepence on a book sold for six shillings. It was Dymphna Cusack who first won a 10 per cent royalty for Australian writers — for her book *Southern Street*.

The standard royalty now paid to Australian authors is 10 per cent of recommended retail price on a hardback or original paperback, or 12 per cent after a certain number of copies have been sold. This figure may be reduced to 7.5 per cent on a paperback reprint.

Your potential income from royalties can theoretically be large, and this is certainly the case for bestsellers such as *The Power of One* (Bryce Courtenay). For the majority of writers, however, the reality is somewhat different. For example, let's say your first novel is being published. The publisher is printing 3000 copies in paperback with a recommended retail price of $16.95. You are receiving a royalty of 10 per cent, that is, $1.70 per copy. Your total possible income from the first print run of your novel is therefore:

$$3000 \times (10\% \text{ of } \$16.95) = \$5100$$

Don't forget that it is likely to take several years for all 3000 copies to be sold, and it is unlikely that your book will be reprinted unless it is a raging success. Publishers generally reckon on selling 50 per cent of the print run in the first year.

See section on 'Advances' on opposite page for information about receiving payment prior to publication

The amount of $5100 does not go a long way when it is spread over the time it takes to write the book as well as the time it takes to sell it.

Authors usually receive a royalty statement from their publisher every six months. The statement shows the performance of a book over the period, including number of copies sold, to whom they were sold (for example, to a book club, export market, remainder sales), the royalty rate, the amount of royalty payable, and the number of copies remaining in stock at the end of the accounting period.

One of the major sources of dissatisfaction with publishers has been that royalty statements are difficult to decipher and contain insufficient information. As a result, the Australian Society of Authors has developed a recommended royalty statement.

Advances

Advances are offered by publishers as a sort of down payment on a manuscript and they are intended to help the author to complete it. They are, literally, an advance against royalties earned. Generally an advance is about half of what the writer can expect to earn in royalties from the first print run. So with your hypothetical first novel you could expect an advance of:

$$50\% \times \$5100 = \$2550$$

Remember that you will not receive a royalty cheque until you have earned back your advance.

Advances are generally paid in stages: when the contract is signed, when the manuscript is delivered and when the book is published. (Don't forget it can take about six months to get the book edited, designed, printed and ready for the bookshops.) Rarely do advances pay for your living expenses during the period of writing.

Some publishers do not offer an advance unless prompted by the author, but well-known writers can command huge advances from publishers on the basis of their past sales. Australian writer Chloe Hooper received about $1 million for her first novel *A Child's Book of True Crime* from an American publisher, far more than she would have received in Australia, where the $600 000 reputed to have been offered by HarperCollins to Peter FitzSimons for his next three biographies is regarded as very generous. Advances represent the publisher's commitment to a book — the higher the advance, the greater the promotion of the book as the publisher strives to earn back the firm's investment. After her first novel manuscript was taken up by the British publishing company Headline, Patricia Shaw was offered £10 000 to produce the second manuscript. 'I nearly fell over,' she said (Review, *Weekend Australian*, 20–21 December 1997). 'That's when I found out about advances.'

Public Lending Right Scheme

Public Lending Right (PLR) is an internationally recognised scheme to compensate eligible creators, editors, illustrators, compilers, translators and publishers of books for income lost from the availability of their books in public libraries. It supports the enrichment of Australian culture by encouraging the growth and development of Australian writing and publishing. If the books weren't in the libraries, the general public might purchase them and therefore the author would get royalties. Payments are not made under this scheme for formats such as audio tapes and other non-book formats of a work.

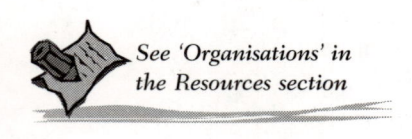

See 'Organisations' in the Resources section

In Australia the scheme is overseen by a Public Lending Right Committee, which includes author, publisher and library appointees, and is administered by the Department of Communications, Information Technology and the Arts. The creators and publishers of books are paid according to the number of copies of their books found by annual sample surveys in public lending libraries.

A creator (including authors, illustrators, editors, compilers and translators) is eligible for PLR if he or she is:

- an Australian citizen (wherever resident) or a permanent resident of Australia
- the sole creator of the book or one of not more than five creators
- eligible to receive royalty payments from the sale of the book.

A publisher is eligible if he or she is:

- a person engaged wholly or substantially in book publishing and the book is published in Australia; or
- a creator or a non-profit organisation which published the book.

Since 1991, publishers have not been able to receive a payment for a book unless the creator received payment for the same book.

Under this scheme, annual payments are made directly to book creators and publishers if there are at least 50 copies of the book estimated to be held in public lending libraries across Australia. Payments are calculated by multiplying the estimated number of copies of each eligible book by the PLR rate of payment (approximately $1.27 in 2000–2001) by the individual's percentage of the PLR entitlement.

In 2000–2001 the average PLR payment to Australian authors was $585. Only ten Australian authors earned more than $20 000 from the scheme, 32 earned between $10 000 and $20 000, 85 earned between $5000 and $10 000, while 7240 earned less than $1000. Nonetheless, considering the statistics for writers' incomes, the amounts earned under this scheme are a significant proportion of many writers' incomes.

Australian creators and publishers can claim PLR by submitting a claim form to the PLR Scheme in the Department of Communications, Information Technology and the Arts before 30 June, the closing date for the annual PLR Program Year. Once a claim for a book has been registered it is not necessary to make further claims for that book unless there are changes to the title or the number or names of the creators, or a new edition is issued.

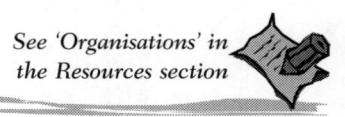

See 'Organisations' in the Resources section

New Zealand Authors' Fund

In New Zealand, the equivalent of PLR is the New Zealand Authors' Fund, established in 1993 to compensate resident New Zealand authors for the loss of royalty income on book sales as a result of their books being in New Zealand libraries. The fund is administered by the New Zealand government arts funding body Creative New Zealand.

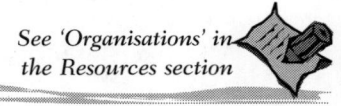

See 'Organisations' in the Resources section

Resident authors are classified as:

- New Zealand citizens who have lived in New Zealand for at least six months prior to registration; or
- authors who are not New Zealand citizens who must be resident in New Zealand for at least two years prior to registration.

Temporary absences of up to three years for a New Zealand citizen, and up to six months for a New Zealand resident, will be permitted without affecting an author's eligibility for the fund. New Zealanders who reside outside New Zealand for longer than the prescribed periods are not eligible. To regain eligibility, authors must be resident for at least 6 months.

A book is eligible for payment if the following requirements are met:

- the author holds copyright and receives royalties from the book
- the author has published the book wholly of his or her own accord (that is, has not paid a third party to publish it) and is eligible to receive income from the sales
- it contains at least 48 pages of prose, or
- it contains 96 pages of illustrations and/or photographs, or
- it contains 24 pages of poetry or drama, or
- it contains 48 pages of combined illustrations and text
- it has been listed in the national bibliographic database of the National Library of New Zealand
- it was published when the author was a New Zealand resident, and
- a minimum of 50 copies are estimated by Creative New Zealand to be held in sampled libraries.

Children's books containing at least 48 pages of prose qualify for full payment, while children's books of at least 24 pages with a combination of both text and illustrations qualify for a payment of 30 per cent.

Books which do not qualify for the scheme include:

- school textbooks
- periodicals, including newspapers
- collections of maps, tables, charts, plans or sheet music
- New Zealand editions of books published overseas
- books written as part of paid employment, under paid contract, or paid for wholly by fee (rather than royalty)
- books by authors who have paid a third party to publish them
- books which have more than three authors.

In 2001 the total allocation for the Fund was NZ$1 000 000, the payout per book was $1.90. The average payment was $739.65. Only 32 New Zealand authors out of 1446 earned more than $5000, most payments were below $1200, and the highest payment was NZ$21 694.38.

First-time applicants must register between January and April of any year and can obtain a registration form from Creative New Zealand. When titles are being registered for the first time, the author must sign the statutory declaration and have it witnessed by a Justice of the Peace, or some other person authorised to take statutory declarations. All new books registered with the fund must have been published before 31 December in the previous year. Applications received after 30 April are not considered for payment at the end of that year.

Authors must re-register each year to continue receiving payments. Re-registration forms, which are sent to authors with the annual payment, need only contain information relating to newly published books as books published in previous years are already registered with the fund.

Educational Lending Right Scheme

The Minister for the Arts and the Centenary of Federation, the Hon. Peter McGauran MP, announced on 20 August 1999 that an Educational Lending Right (ELR) scheme would be introduced by the Federal government. ELR is one element of the four-year $240 million Book Industry Assistance Plan. Funding for ELR commenced in 2000–01 at $8 million, increasing to $11 million in 2003–04.

ELR makes payments to eligible Australian creators and publishers whose books are held in educational lending libraries (that is, school, TAFE and university libraries). It complements the existing PLR, which covers public lending libraries. Australian creators and publishers can claim ELR by submitting a claim form to the ELR Scheme in the Department of Communications, Information Technology and the Arts before 30 June, the closing date for the annual PLR Program Year. Once a claim for a book has been registered it is not necessary to make further claims for that book unless there are changes to the title or the number or names of the creators, or a new edition has been issued.

The first ELR payments were made in June 2001. A total of $7.4 million was paid to 5496 claimants, of which 5314 were creators and 182 were publishers.

No ELR operates in New Zealand.

Copyright Agency Limited

The Copyright Agency Limited (CAL) was set up in 1974 by the Australian Society of Authors and the Australian Book Publishers Association (now the Australian Publishers Association) to represent the copyright interests of authors, publishers and print journalists. CAL administers a number of licence schemes under which users in education, business, government and the general community can copy legally from, and pay for, their copying of writers' copyright material.

CAL surveys a small number of users to identify what and how much they are copying. These users supply records of the copyright material they copy. Writers may be entitled to claim money from CAL if their copyright material appears in records maintained by CAL users.

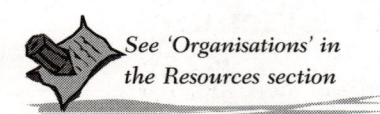

See 'Organisations' in the Resources section

CAL distributes the money it collects to its 'members'. Membership of CAL is free and to be eligible to receive payments you simply need to register with CAL.

Under the terms of reciprocal agreements, CAL also collects payments for Australian copying of the copyright material of authors and publishers from countries such as the United Kingdom, United States and Canada. Some overseas collecting societies likewise collect payment for copying of the copyright materials of Australian authors and publishers. CAL has reciprocal agreements with Canada, Denmark, France, Germany, Iceland, New Zealand, Norway, Republic of Ireland, South Africa, Spain, Switzerland, United Kingdom and the United States.

Copyright Licensing Limited (NZ)

A similar scheme, run by the agency Copyright Licensing Limited (CLL), operates in New Zealand. Established in 1988, CLL is owned by the Book Publishers Association of New Zealand and the New Zealand Society of Authors. It represents the interests of the copyright owners of print-based material, collecting licence fees nationally and internationally for distribution to New Zealand copyright owners.

CLL issues licences to users, largely from the education, government and industry sectors, which are then able to reproduce copyright material within strict guidelines without the need to obtain permission from copyright holders. Annual sampling of selected users establishes the amount of licensing fee to be paid by each user, and copyright owners are paid their share of licensing fees collected.

CLL has reciprocal agreements with Australia, Canada, France, Germany, Greece, Iceland, Norway, Maltese Islands, Ireland, South Africa, Switzerland, United Kingdom and the United States.

Backlists

In the past, recognised authors, particularly novelists, could expect to receive continuing royalties from sales of their books years after first publication as their books were reprinted. The list of an author's books currently in print, but excluding a recently written work still in its first print run, is referred to as a backlist. Having books reprinted and available over a lengthy period (as long as the material doesn't date) is profitable for both the author and the publisher. Writers with a substantial backlist can expect to live off it (that is, the royalties of continually selling books) as they get older, while publishers continue to make money from the sales of their writers' earlier works.

However, not only are the early works of older established writers not being reprinted, but their agents are having difficulty placing their new work with publishers. In this climate older writers claim they are being pushed aside in favour of a younger generation with sex, youth and image to sell in their work. Internationally renowned Australian writer David Malouf is concerned that, in a country where 'virtually all of the classics of Australian literature are out of print', the literary culture will fade and disappear. He wonders if the problem lies with the changing relationship between authors and publishers, who are no longer willing to support their promising writers through several novels until they achieve a significant readership for their works and a healthy level of profit for their publishers.

Publishers claim that their major considerations in relation to backlists are the warehousing costs and accounting procedures whereby warehouse stock is assessed by the tax department as an asset.

See also Part 1.4.2 'The local book market'

> 'If a new book doesn't work within a couple of months of its release, it's pretty much done for unless a prize or a new burst of publicity can get it back on the shelves. In the case of the backlist, the situation is even grimmer. Hardly anyone, it seems, is interested in buying an Australian novel two or more years old; the re-release of a prestigious and important backlist is met with incredulity . . . something has to be done.'
>
> Random House publisher Jane Palfreyman speaking at the 1997 Australian Book Fair.

Another factor influencing backlists in the Australian scene (but not in New Zealand) may be the peculiarity of the 'sale or return' arrangement between booksellers and publishers whereby bookshops can return books that are not sold within the first few weeks. With the huge volume of books being offered to bookshops, managers argue they do not have sufficient space on their shelves to maintain a wide range of titles for longer than several weeks.

Unless there is a healthy interest by the reading public in the backlists of a country's established writers, the works will fall out of print to become rare and treasured collectors' items for those who love books and reading.

An author has a much better chance of retaining a backlist if a work is set as a text for school or university students, or if it is a non-fiction work that does not date, such as cooking and gardening books, or a work that can be easily updated, such as reference material.

Options

Another source of income for writers may come from television, film or theatre producers (or directors or scriptwriters) who wish to adapt your book (fiction or non-fiction) for the screen or stage. They will pay you for the rights to your story for a certain period of time so that they can develop a script to the stage where investment finance can be raised for a full-scale production.

In paying you for an 'option' on your work, the producer has the exclusive rights for the specified option period to adapt your story as specified in an option agreement. This can be any time from six months to several years, and in most cases is renewable. Payment for options varies dramatically (from one dollar to tens of thousands of dollars) depending on how well-known the author is, how well-known the producer is, and how likely it is that the production will come to fruition.

6.1.2 Income from stage productions

Professional companies usually pay playwrights a commissioning fee for a new play being written specifically for that company. This can vary dramatically depending on the size of a company. Amateur companies usually pay a comparatively smaller fee.

In addition to a fee, the playwright receives a royalty on box-office receipts. This is usually about 8 per cent of the net receipts.

6.1.3 Income for screenwriters

The fee paid to a screenwriter for either an original script or an adaptation is usually 2–3 per cent of the total budget. Budgets, of course, can differ widely depending on the genre (documentary, drama), the format (television, film), and the scale of the production (from low to high budget).

Screenwriters also usually get a percentage (up to 3 per cent, depending on the renown of the writer) of what is called the producer's profit. This is a percentage of the profit which is shared with the investors of the film.

6.1.4 Payment to writers for writing-related work

Authors rarely make a living out of royalties and other payments unless they have a remarkably successful writing career and have written sufficient books to collect a living wage from their royalties. Most need to supplement their royalties with other sources of income.

Thus writers usually look to other kinds of writing-related work to boost their income, such as giving readings, lecturing, holding workshops, seminars, tutorials and masterclasses, writing reviews and articles, judging literary competitions, or editing and appraising manuscripts.

Because writers often work alone, and because the field is so competitive, there is room for exploitation by employers or commissioning agents and it is rare for writers to be recompensed adequately for the work they do. While few people would question a dentist's bill or a solicitor's fee, many question the payment of writers at professional rates because they undervalue the work of writers or believe it is an easy matter to write a few thousand words or speak eloquently for 40 minutes. In fact, writers are often expected to do many or all of these things for nothing — out of love for their chosen profession, as a hobby, or perhaps as self-promotion — and many organisations fail to produce a budget to make the payment of writers a bottom-line item as essential as the payment of rent or electricity.

The professional organisations for writers in Australia and New Zealand publish recommended rates and fees for writers performing certain kinds of work. These are guidelines only, but are useful if you are starting out in the profession and would like some idea of what others may be charging. However, the marketplace presents its own conditions and circumstances, and fees vary greatly according to the reputation of individual writers, their experience and publishing record, and their individual bargaining power.

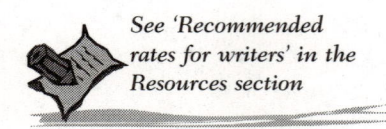

See 'Recommended rates for writers' in the Resources section

6.1.5   Employment opportunities

The employment pages of the newspapers rarely carry job advertisements for writers unless they are for journalists, so writers seeking non-journalistic writing work have to look elsewhere for their job opportunities. Publishing companies such as Reader's Digest and Gregory's employ writers to produce the text for their glossy productions; although they pay their writers well for their efforts, the writers are rarely given attribution for their own work, their names usually appearing in a list of contributors at the beginning of the book.

Writing as a Career

Copywriters are also needed by advertising companies and indeed by any company or organisation with a publicity department. A useful guide for learning the techniques of copywriting is a 200-page manual called *The Copywriter's Companion*, which also contains copywriting exercises that can be returned to the author for assessment.

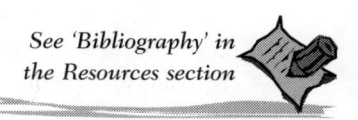

See 'Bibliography' in the Resources section

Apart from literary agents, there are, in Australia, only a few organisations and companies which act as brokers for writers who register with them. The Queensland Writers' Centre has established a program which assists writers to find work with private companies, government organisations and anyone who needs a writer for a particular job. In Sydney, a company called Media Network and Personnel represents newspaper, corporate, features, technical, magazine, broadcast and advertising writers as well as editors, public relations personnel, graphic designers and illustrators and photographers. The company takes a 10 per cent commission (of the first year's salary) from the employer for finding you a job, and 12 per cent of the fee for a casual assignment.

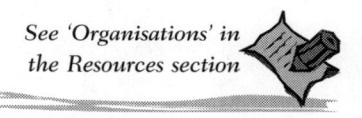

See 'Organisations' in the Resources section

If you are looking for work as a writer, however, you will have to search out your opportunities in company newsletters, by word-of-mouth, by approaching publishers which employ staff or contract writers, by checking the publications of writers' centres, by approaching production companies, and possibly by searching for leads over the internet. Occasionally government departments and agencies advertise for non-fiction writing work in the tenders sections of newspapers, and sometimes corporations advertise for writers to prepare annual reports and perform other types of business writing.

6.1.6 Government literary grants and prizes

Different levels of government in Australia and New Zealand provide assistance to writers through various grant programs. The world of literary grants is highly competitive. Only a small proportion of writers receives any assistance at all, and this is usually sufficient only to help the writer meet basic living costs during the period of the grant. For example, in 2000, the Literature Fund of the Australia Council received 433 applications in the New Work category. Of these, 82 were awarded. Nonetheless, grants not only provide writers with the opportunity to write but also confer status on the recipients, who have usually been competitively selected against dozens of others, and thus draw the attention of potential publishers to their work. Writers who successfully acquit their grants are in turn more likely to receive further grants to assist in their development as writers. Funding bodies generally prefer their support to achieve a tangible outcome such as publication.

If you are applying for a new writer's grant, you have a greater chance of being considered if you have already shown your commitment to writing by developing a substantial publishing record in magazines, journals, newspapers and other periodicals. Applicants with no publishing history are unlikely to be taken seriously by selection panels.

Prospective applicants are advised to read the guidelines of the funding bodies very carefully and ensure they have satisfied all criteria set for the particular grant they are applying for and provided the necessary documentation. A professionally presented grant application will get a much better reception than one prepared sloppily and in haste. Usually funding bodies will not accept late applications under any circumstances, so it is important to be mindful of the closing date and submit your application on time. Don't forget to keep a copy of your application for your own records. If the funding body you are applying to provides for interviews with prospective applicants, take advantage of the opportunity to ask questions and apprise yourself of the requirements of the application and the conditions of the grant.

The Australia Council for the Arts

In Australia, the major source of funding for writers is the Literature Fund of the Australia Council for the Arts, which 'aims to encourage the creation, development, publication, critical appraisal and awareness of high quality contemporary Australian literature'. The Fund provides direct financial support for emerging, developing and established writers under the Australia Council categories of New Work (to support the creation of new work by funding a one-off project), Presentation and Promotion (which funds projects that present, exhibit, publish, distribute and/or promote work), Skills and Arts Development (which provides development opportunities for artists through residencies and mentorships), Key Organisations (for the development of infrastructure such as writers' centres) and Fellowships (a once-only offer to individual artists of funding of $40 000 per year for two years for the production of a creative work). The Australia Council extended its grant program in 2001 to include self-published authors whose works received a review in a major journal or newspaper or had national distribution. Picture book illustrators may apply under any of these programs.

The Council's Partnerships and Initiatives program is not a grant category but 'an invitation to artists, organisations and community members to propose ideas for projects and partnerships that will result in substantial benefits across the artform or to a particular targeted sector'. Check the Australia Council *Support for the Arts Handbook*, which covers all artforms funded.

State Government funding for literature

All the states and territories in Australia have arts ministries or departments which also fund literature by providing grants or fellowships to individual writers, and offering prizes for Fiction, Poetry, History, Non-English-Speaking Background, and Children's Writing. State arts bodies also fund writing organisations, literary events such as festivals and certain publications. Categories vary among states and territories so it is best to contact the relevant body in your state and territory for information.

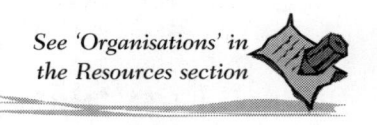

See 'Organisations' in the Resources section

Creative New Zealand

In New Zealand, the major source of funding for writers is Creative New Zealand, the government arts body. Grants are considered for New Zealand writers of fiction, poetry or drama or 'literary' non-fiction such as biography or history. Applicants

'I would be glad to see new prizes and grants. I am quite ready to get on the gravy train. But I will never take off my hat to the driver.'

James K. Baxter, *Landfall*, 14, 1960.

> 'Even when you have a grant, often it isn't enough to survive on so you have to chase other money which slows down the rate at which you work on your fiction, or whatever project it was you got the grant for in the first place. There are times when you feel like a cat endlessly chasing its tail. And the grant is the same for a middle-aged writer trying to support a family as it is for a twenty-year-old with fewer living expenses.'
>
> Amanda Lohrey interviewed by Amanda Galligan, *Imago*, Summer 1997, vol. 9, no. 3.

must have previously published work in magazines and journals, or in book form.

Publishers may apply for subsidies to publish new work by New Zealand authors provided that they have a record in publishing and have proven access to marketing, promotion and distribution networks. Self-publishing is not supported. In particular, grants are offered by the Historical Branch of the Department of Internal Affairs to publishers to assist in the publication of works which make a significant contribution to an understanding of New Zealand's past, but may not be commercially viable. They are assessed by the branch and will provide a proportion (up to 50 per cent) of the production costs.

Like the Australia Council, Creative New Zealand also publishes an annual funding guide booklet.

6.1.7 Other prizes, grants and awards

Australia

There are many non-government literary prizes and awards offered each year at international, national and state level. Some are for unpublished manuscripts while others, such as the English Booker Prize and the Commonwealth Writers' Prize (both for fiction), are awarded to published works. To win, or even be nominated for such prestigious international prizes, is an immediate guarantee of hugely increased sales for the book and lavish publicity for the author.

Writers respond differently when told of their nomination or win. Some react with disbelief, while others acknowledge the random nature of the selection process. 'You're pulling my leg! Bloody hell!' Keri Hulme exclaimed when told she had won the 1985 Booker Prize for *The Bone People*. For many, the dream of at last being recognised is equal to the prospect of filling the coffers with much-needed funds.

In Australia the most prestigious prize, the Miles Franklin Award (2002 prize money $28 000), is offered for a published novel or play 'portraying Australian life in any of its phases'. The award has been dogged by controversy in recent years when Helen Demidenko was awarded the prize for *The Hand that Signed the Paper*, her fictional account of the role of Jewish communists in the Ukrainian famine of the 1930s, and when *Grand Days*, Frank Moorhouse's novel about a young Australian working in Geneva in the early days of the League of Nations, was excluded from consideration.

The winner of the Miles Franklin Award can expect a big hike in sales of the winning book, and possibly even reprints of earlier books. Christopher Koch, who won the award in 1996, commented:

> 'It's just the accident of the coincidence of the taste of the chairman of the judges happening along with the publication of my book. It's a lottery. They [other writers] could win next time. There's no need to get upset about it.'
>
> Expatriate Australian writer Madeleine St John interviewed by Christopher Henning after winning the 1997 Booker Prize for her novel *The Essence of the Thing*, 'The Essence of Being a Writer', 'News Review', *Sydney Morning Herald*, 2 September 1997.

> Quite simply, the biggest impact of my win was the boost in sales. The Franklin, more than any other Australian literary prize, seems to carry some prestige, even abroad. While I've never taken awards as the absolute sign of literary ennobling, the money was like a lottery windfall, and the publicity put a strong focus on the work.

University of Queensland Press publisher Laurie Muller agrees: 'It's a second coming for the winner, which has usually exhausted its promotional impetus from its launch. It gives the book legs.' (Both interviewed by Murray Waldren in 'Great Expectations', *The Australian*, 5 June 1998.)

The major award for an unpublished fiction manuscript is the Vogel Award for writers under 35 years. The Vogel Prize, administered by Allen & Unwin, offered $20 000 in 2001 for an original unpublished manuscript of fiction (or Australian

> 'When a prize is in the offing, you not only allow yourself a few moments of thinking that the world has realised it needs your book. You're also excited because soon your roof won't leak. You'll become the good parent at last. And you won't get sued by the tax department.'
>
> 'Being a loser, as it were', Sue Woolfe writing about her unsuccessful nomination for the 1997 Commonwealth Writers' Prize, 'Writers World', *The Australian's Review of Books*, July 1997.

> 'Because artists are obsessed with money, for good reasons, the awards they want to win are the ones with the biggest payouts, because that's another year's writing.'
>
> Amanda Lohrey interviewed by Amanda Galligan, *Imago*, Summer 1997, vol. 9, no. 3.

history or biography) of at least 30 000 words, with assured publication of the winning manuscript. Publishers are always keen to publish prize winners of major competitions, but may also be interested in publishing a manuscript from the short list, or one that has simply been recommended by a judge of the competition.

The Newcastle Poetry Prize carries one of the largest sums of money for a poetry award. In 2002, the prize offered $10 000 in the Open section. Provided by the City of Newcastle, this annual award was extended in 2001 with the addition of a new media award of $2000 for the best entry or entries using new media.

The David Unaipon Award, administered by the University of Queensland Press, recognises the contribution and talent of Aboriginal and Torres Strait Islander writers in Australia by providing an annual prize of $5000 for any book-length work by an unpublished author.

> 'For an unpublished writer, competitions such as the Vogel award . . . and short story competitions make a big difference. Publishers take notice of them and they are open to everyone. The Vogel judges often say to me, "This person is very talented", even if that particular writer was not shortlisted.'
>
> Sophie Cunningham, Trade Publisher, Allen & Unwin, in 'Agents, Publishers and Writers', *Write On*, vol. 9, no. 4, May 1998.

The Marrwarnging Award is offered annually for published and unpublished Aboriginal and Torres Strait Islander writers of novels, collections of short stories or poems, individual and family oral history collections, histories (including regional histories), biographies and works for children. The author of the winning manuscript wins $5000 and publication by the University of Western Australia Press.

The National Biography Award is awarded biennially for a published work of biography, autobiography, memoirs and similar genres, and in 2002 offered a prize of $12 500.

See Part 6.1.9 for information on prizes and awards for scriptwriters, and Part 3.8.4 'Translation grants'

Prizes are also offered for secondary students, young writers, children's books, short stories, poetry, drama, scriptwriting, science fiction and fantasy writing, mystery novels, women's writing, critical writing, bush verse, legal writing, radio plays, translation, history, journalism, audio books on cassette, best book published in the year, as well as book design and illustration, and there is even an award for an outstanding index.

Funding for screenwriters is provided by such bodies as the Australian Film Commission, NSW Film and Television Office, Film Victoria, Pacific Film and the Television Commission, ScreenWest and the South Australian Film Corporation.

New Zealand

In New Zealand, the major literary prize is offered by the Montana New Zealand Book Award for the categories of fiction, poetry, history, biography, reference and anthology, environment, lifestyle and illustrative. Each category winner (except for fiction) gets a $5000 award and is eligible for the Montana Medal for an outstanding book of non-fiction and a further award of $10 000. In the Fiction category a long list of five titles will be drawn up and from these judges will select a winner who will get the Deutz Medal and a prize of $15 000. Two runners up will be awarded $2500 each.

The Creative New Zealand Writers' Residency in Berlin was set up in 2000 by the Arts Board to provide a residency for a New Zealand writer working in the areas of fiction, poetry, drama, biography or history (of national significance to New Zealand). The residency is open to any established New Zealand writer of New Zealand literature who has been resident in New Zealand for at least three years.

The New Zealand Post Children's Book Awards are given for high quality children's literature, while the *Sunday Star Times* Bruce Mason Playwright's Award is given to a promising playwright at the beginning of his or her career.

The University of Otago offers the one-year Robert Burns Fellowship for New Zealand or resident writers of fiction or non-fiction. Other writers in residence programs of one-year's duration are offered at the University of Canterbury, Victoria University of Wellington, the University of Auckland and the University of Waikato. All of these are partnered by Creative New Zealand, which provides a half contribution to the writers' stipend. A similar partnership exists between Dunedin College of Education and Creative New Zealand to provide a six months' children's writing residency. All residencies are administered by the institutions themselves and subject to different conditions and closing dates, so intending applicants should directly approach each university or college.

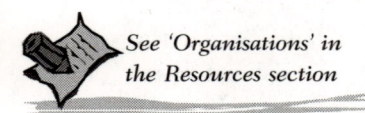

See 'Organisations' in the Resources section

The New Zealand History Research Trust Fund, under the auspices of the Ministry of Culture for Heritage, offers financial support for researching and writing New Zealand history and offers awards in Oral History.

For other awards, check the events, awards, courses section of the NZ Book Council website at www.bookcouncil.org.nz.

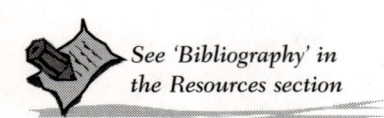

See 'Bibliography' in the Resources section

D. W. Thorpe's *Australian Literary Awards and Fellowships* provides the most comprehensive listing of Australian literary awards, prizes and fellowships. D. W. Thorpe's *New Zealand Books in Print* (published annually) provides a detailed list of New Zealand literary awards.

6.1.8 Residencies

Writers' residencies are offered by several institutions across Australia, including Booranga Writers' Centre at Wagga Wagga and the Varuna Writers' Centre in the Blue Mountains west of Sydney. Writers are provided with food and accommodation, and sometimes a small stipend, for the period of their residency. In exchange they are usually asked to give a reading or workshop, or to be available for other writers to consult, but are free the rest of the time to work on their own projects.

See also Part 6.1.9 'Awards, competitions, residencies and festivals for scriptwriters'

International residencies are offered by the Australia Council at Cambridge University, the Keesing Studio in Paris, the B. R. Whiting Library in Rome, the Tyrone Guthrie Centre in Ireland or at the Yaddo Artists' Colony in Saratoga Springs, New York. Information is available from the Australia Council annual handbook.

Introduced in 1996, the Asialink Literature Residency program provides opportunities for Australian writers to work in the region, to enable long-term involvement with the host country, and to encourage ongoing contacts between Australian and Asian writers. The residencies are four months long with the writer attached to an institution such as a university or literary organisation. A similar residency was jointly launched in late 1998 by the Insearch Language Centre, the University of Technology (Sydney) and the Australia Council for the Arts. This program gives two developing Australian writers the chance to live and write in Asia, with intensive language training and access to the resources of Australia Centres in Thailand and Indonesia.

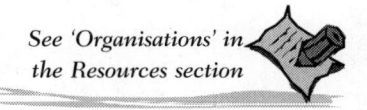

See 'Organisations' in the Resources section

6.1.9 Awards, competitions, residencies and festivals for scriptwriters

There are several competitions for playwriting, including the Awgie Awards which are offered annually by the Australian Writers' Guild for outstanding scripts by Australian film, stage, radio and television writers. The Jill Blewett Playwright's Award is offered as part of the South Australian Festival Awards program, and awards for drama and television scripts are offered under both the Queensland and NSW Premier's Literary Awards programs. The Fellowship of Australian Writers runs a Radio Play Competition and the Adele Shelton Smith Award for Play, Radio or Television Scripts for Young Writers 18–25 years. Published plays may also be considered for *The Age* Book of the Year Awards.

Interplay, the International Festival of Young Playwrights, selects entries received from around Australia to be performed and workshopped during the annual Interplay Festival in Townsville.

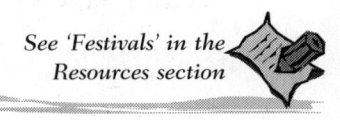

See 'Festivals' in the Resources section

Playwrights have the opportunity of entering the Playbox/ Asialink Annual Asian-Australian Playwriting Competition, a national public competition which aims to encourage playwrights to develop themes from the general area of Asian-Australian involvement. Playwrights may choose their own form and content and either a domestic or foreign setting. The style may be naturalistic or not, and the material may be contemporary, historical or fantastical.

The date for submissions is 31 March every year. First prize is $5000, with an additional $2000 for redrafting if the script is selected for production. A commended script receives $2000. There is also a special prize of $2000 for a playwright of non-English-speaking background resident in Australia.

There are also Asialink residencies in performing arts, and playwrights can apply to either of these programs. The residencies are for four months with funding of $12 000 for travel and living expenses.

In New Zealand, the *Sunday Star Times* Bruce Mason Playwright's Award of $5000 is made to a playwright of promise in recognition of achievement at the beginning of a career.

6.2   TAX DEDUCTIONS AND KEEPING RECORDS

Once you start earning income from writing, you may be entitled to claim tax deductions for your expenses.

In Australia, if your assessable income exceeds your tax deductions, you will be considered a professional by the Australian tax department and will be eligible for tax deductions. If your tax deductions are greater than your assessable income, the tax department may classify you as a hobbyist and refuse to allow your tax deductions. You are entitled to appeal against such a decision.

In New Zealand, as long as you can prove you are a serious writer putting actual effort into publishing with the aim of making a profit, you can claim expenses against any income.

6.2.1   Writers' income

If you are a full-time writer without major sources of income other than writing and related activities, your income is likely to be derived from many areas and you should apply to the Australian Taxation Office for an Australian Business Number (ABN) or to the New Zealand Commissioner of Inland Revenue for a Registration Number, which you should record on every invoice you send out. In Australia, if your writing income is over $50 000 per annum you are also obliged to register for the Goods and Services Tax (GST) and you will then have to both charge your clients 10% for GST and put aside 10% of your receipts for GST payment to the government.

You will also be obliged to submit a Business Activity Statement (BAS) monthly or quarterly, depending on the type of your business activity and the size of your income. Don't make the mistake of spending the GST that you are obliged to remit periodically to the government. If your income is under $50 000 per annum, you are not obliged to register for the GST and, if you don't, you will, unfortunately, have to pay it on goods and services you purchase and you will not be eligible to claim it back.

A writer is obliged under law to declare all income which, for the purposes of taxation, includes:

- salaries, wages and fees for services rendered
- work benefits and allowances
- commissions
- competition prizes related to your occupation or profession
- royalties and advances on royalties
- social security receipts
- interest, dividends and rent received, and
- grants (including government grants).

6.2.2 Writers' expenses

As writers' average annual incomes are not usually large, try to minimise your tax liability by ensuring that you keep accurate records and receipts of your expenditure related to writing and other sources of income if you are not an employee. Your taxable income may be reduced by claiming any expenses incurred in the course of earning that income or in carrying on a business with the aim of profit.

A business diary will help you keep track of income and expenses, business appointments and phone calls and such a record is a legal requirement if you are going to claim deductions for travel expenses for trips of more than five nights away from home.

Record expenses as they occur in your diary, together with details of the method

> 'I've been writing so long that I've forgotten what it is to have a real job with holiday pay on a loading, superannuation and sick leave and my employer paying all the office expenses. My problem is that I love writing so much that I forget to charge for it. But lately I've become tired of having all the fun and none of the profit.'
>
> John Emery, 'The business of writing seminar', *Southern Write*, March 1999.

of payment — cash, cheque, credit card, or direct payment into a bank account — and file your receipts carefully. If the expense is unusual (such as the purchase of a new camera) make a note explaining the need for the equipment, particularly if it relates to a current project. Some expenses, such as telephone bills, may have to be apportioned between private and business use. Large expenses, such as the purchase of a new computer, can be claimed over a period of years as depreciation. For example, if you buy a computer which has a life of five years for $2000, you can claim depreciation of $400 a year for five years. You do not have to keep receipts for small expenses of $10 each to a total of $200 per annum, but they should be recorded in your diary.

You are required to keep your tax records for five years, and they will be essential proof if you are ever audited by the tax department.

Cash payments are not encouraged by the tax department; use cheques and credit cards wherever possible because you will have a record of the transaction. It is a good idea to have a separate credit card for business and professional expenses. Use your business credit card even if the item paid for is only partially used for work. You may consider establishing a separate business bank account to make it easier for yourself and your accountant to calculate your tax deductions at the end of the financial year.

If your business is growing and you find that keeping manual records is too time-consuming, consider purchasing a simple accounting program such as MYOB (Mind Your Own Business) to keep track of your income and expenses. MYOB is suitable for use even by individuals with no accounting experience.

The list of expenses a self-employed writer is allowed to claim usually includes:

- airfares, car hire and accommodation expenses incurred in the course of the work
- bank charges on business accounts
- cinema and theatre admissions (for scriptwriters)
- cleaning costs of your office or studio
- commissions and fees payable to a literary agent
- computers and software programs
- conferences and seminar costs
- courier, postage, photocopying and printing

- depreciation costs on capital equipment such as computers, faxes, answering machines
- donations to listed charities and arts organisations
- electronic diaries
- furniture
- home office expenses such as a proportion of telephone, electricity and gas bills and rates
- insurance premiums for studio or office (usually a proportion of the total home insurance bill if you have an office at home)
- interest payments on, for example, loans for business purposes
- journal and magazine subscriptions if the publications are related to work
- leasing charges for hire of equipment, cars, etc.
- legal, accounting and financial advisory fees
- other travel expenses, such as living away from home expenses related to a writing project if it enhances income
- payments on television and/or video cassette recorder
- photography
- professional library depreciation and purchases
- publicity and promotion expenses
- rent incurred for your office or studio if it is separate from your home
- repairs and maintenance expenses on your equipment
- research fees
- sales tax paid
- stationery
- study expenses related to your profession or occupation
- superannuation payments (if you are self-employed)
- typing costs
- vehicle expenses (subject to log book requirements)
- video cassette hire (usually for scriptwriters).

6.2.3 Averaging income

The Australian government recognises that a writer's income generally is unpredictable and erratic. Consequently you may apply in writing to have your professional earnings averaged over a five-year period. This means that if your income has an unusual increase in any one year, your tax load can be abated by taking an average of your earnings over the previous five-year period. The Australian government will tax either the actual annual net earnings or the five-year average net earnings, whichever is the lesser amount.

New Zealand authors do not have the same concessions from the Department of Inland Revenue.

6.2.4 Seeking help

I suggest that you seek professional accounting assistance as taxation legislation changes frequently and you may disadvantage yourself financially if you are not aware of the constantly varying regulations which apply to your profession. A qualified accountant (a member of the Australian Society of Certified Practising Accountants or the Institute of Chartered Accountants) will be able to help you, and the fee for the service is yet another tax deduction. Both the Australian Taxation Office and the New Zealand Department of Inland Revenue have a telephone advisory service to answer inquiries from the public.

The Australia Council has produced a small booklet called *Arts and Facts: The Arts and Tax*, which answers many questions about artists and tax. The NSW Writers' Centre has a brochure on *Tax and Writers* and the New Zealand Society of Authors has produced a booklet on *Writers and Tax*.

You may not make a great deal of money as a writer, but it is worthwhile protecting what income you do receive by at least understanding some of the principles of taxation, especially how to minimise your tax burden by keeping good records and knowing which concessions are available to you as a professional writer. Try to find an accountant who specialises in clients from the arts sector. Not only will such accountants have the expertise to defend your interests, but they are also likely to be lively conversationalists when you make your annual visit to their office!

POSTSCRIPT

Postscript

Writers write for all kinds of reasons — because they have to write for their job, because they want to report on current affairs, or to tell the story of another person's life, or to create a poem, or to produce an entire fictional work peopled with its own characters living in an imagined world.

If this book has helped you on your journey, given you inspiration or the courage to write, and offered practical advice along the way, I am delighted, because I believe passionately in the pursuit of writing, in the activity of carefully arranging words to create a polished piece of work, whether fiction or non-fiction, that represents as nearly as possible what you want to express, and conveys that with interest and imagination to the reader.

Meanwhile, remember that writing is something you can do all your life with minimal resources, and as it improves with practice, your writing will give you intellectual stimulation, pleasure in refining your work, delight in reading the work of others and, ultimately, the satisfaction of being able to express yourself — your thoughts, ideas, feelings — in a form which can also give pleasure to many others.

May your explorations of the world of writing be pleasurable, productive and rewarding!

> 'Sometimes I have thought that without a good deal of "natural" ability nobody should ever attempt to write. And yet I had myself no such ability and everything over many years had to be learned . . .'
>
> Frank Sargeson, *More Than Enough: A Memoir*, Wellington, 1975, p. 75.

> 'The wonderful thing about writing as a career, or even as a part-time pursuit, is that it does not have a shelf-life or use-by date. So, while sports stars and ballet dancers are hanging up their boots and tutus in their mid-30s, writers can write on.'
>
> Professor Elizabeth Webby, Judge's Report, NSW PAVE 1997 Literary Competition, November 1997.

PART SEVEN
RESOURCES

CONTENTS

Agents	239
Assessment	243
Bibliography	255
Children and youth	271
Children's book publishers	285
Festivals and events	294
Legal deposit libraries	303
Literary websites	307
Search engines	315
Magazines and journals	316
Organisations	331
Poetry publishers	353
Publicity questionnaire (Allen & Unwin)	358
Recommended rates for writers	361

Every effort has been made to check the accuracy of the information in the Resources section at the time of printing. If you know of any alterations or amendments please contact Irina Dunn at the address given on page xv.

AGENTS

The following is a list of reputable Australian and New Zealand literary agents. A list of overseas agents is available from the Australian Society of Authors, PO Box 338, Strawberry Hills NSW 2021, phone (02) 9318 0877, email asa@asauthors.org. Publications such as *Literary Market Place* (R. R. Bowker) and *Writers' and Artists' Yearbook* (A. & C. Black Publishers) list overseas agents and should be available at your local library or writers' centre.

AUSTRALIA

Altair-Australia Literary Agency

Robert Stephenson
PO Box 475
Blackwood SA 5051
Phone: (08) 8278 8994
Fax: (08) 8278 5585
Email: altair-australia@altair-australia.com
Website: www.altair-australia.com/agency

Anthony Williams Management

Anthony Williams, Anthony Blair
PO Box 1379
Darlinghurst NSW 1300
Phone: (02) 9360 3833
Fax: (02) 9360 3189
Email: aawmgt@mte.net.au

Australian Literary Management

Lyn Tranter
2A Booth Street
Balmain NSW 2041
Phone: (02) 9818 8557
Fax: (02) 9818 8569
Email: lyn@austlit.com, alpha@austlit.com
Website: www.almaustlit.com

Barbara Mobbs Literary Agency

Barbara Mobbs
PO Box 126
Edgecliff NSW 2027
Phone: (02) 9363 5323
Fax: (02) 9328 1303

Bryson Agency

Fran Bryson
PO Box 226
Flinders Lane Vic 8009
Phone: (03) 9620 9100
Fax: (03) 9621 2788
Email: agency@bryson.com.au
Website: www.bryson.com.au

Cameron Creswell Agency

Rosemary Creswell, Annette Hughes
Suite 5, Edgecliff Court
2 New McLean Street

The Writer's Guide

Edgecliff NSW 2027
Phone: (02) 9362 0600
Fax: (02) 9363 3317

Christine Nagel Literary Service
Christine Nagel
PO Box 153
Mundaring WA 6073
Phone: (08) 9295 3364
Fax: (08) 9295 0590
Email: nagelhop@bigpond.com
Website: www.nagelliteraryservices.com

Curtis Brown (Australia)
Fiona Inglis, Fran Moore, Tara Wynne, Pippa Masson
PO Box 19
Paddington NSW 2021
Phone: (02) 9361 6161, 9331 5301
Fax: (02) 9360 3935
Email: info@curtisbrown.com.au

Detrusa Promotions Literary Agency
Cleo Pozzo
44 George Street
Fitzroy Vic 3065
Phone/Fax: (03) 9416 1778
Email: detrusaprom@ozemail.com.au

Diversity Management
Bill Tikos
PO Box 1449
Darlinghurst NSW 1300
Phone: (02) 9130 4305
Fax: (02) 9365 1426
Email: bill@diversitym.com.au

Golvan Arts Management
Debbie Golvan
PO Box 766
Kew Vic 3101
Phone: (03) 9853 5341
Fax: (03) 9853 8555
Email: golvan@bigpond.net.au
Website: www.golvanarts.com.au

HLA Management
Hilary Linstead
PO Box 1536
Strawberry Hills NSW 2012
Phone: (02) 9310 4948
Fax: (02) 9310 4113
Email: hla@hlamgt.com.au

June Cann Management
John Cann
PO Box 386
Woollahra NSW 2025
Phone: (02) 9362 4007
Fax: (02) 9327 8553
Email: agency@junecann.com
Website: www.junecann.com

Jenny Darling & Associates
Jenny Darling, Jacinta Di Mase
PO Box 413
Toorak Vic 3142
Phone: (03) 9827 3883
Fax: (03) 9827 1270

Kevin Palmer Management
Kevin Palmer, Jackie Hewitt
258 Bulwara Road
Ultimo NSW 2007
Phone: (02) 9552 1277
Fax: (02) 9660 3121
Email: kevinpalmer@kevinpalmer.com.au

Margaret Connolly & Associates
Margaret Connolly
PO Box 945
Wahroonga NSW 2076

Phone: (02) 9449 6342
Fax: (02) 9449 6352

Margaret Kennedy Agency

Margaret Kennedy
PO Box 1433
Toowong Qld 4066
Phone: (07) 3870 9996
Fax: (07) 3870 5214
Email: mkagency@optushome.com.au

Mary Cunnane Agency

Mary Cunnane
PO Box 781
Terrigal NSW 2260
Phone: (02) 4385 9911
Fax: (02) 4365 1093
Email: mary@cunnaneagency.com

Rick Raftos Management

Rick Raftos, Rachel Skinner, Rhonda Blanch
PO Box 445
Paddington 2021
Phone: (02) 9281 9622
Fax: (02) 9212 7100
Email: raftos@raftos.com.au

RGM Associates

Robin Gardiner, Nelly Flannery
PO Box 128
Surry Hills NSW 2010
Phone: (02) 9281 3911
Fax: (02) 9281 4705
Email: info@rgm.com.au

Sandy Wagner Creative Agents

Sandy Wagner
12/44a Bayswater Road
Kings Cross NSW 2011
Phone: (02) 9356 2213
Fax: (02) 9358 2594

Strictly Literary

John Cokley
PO Box 20
Wellers Hill QLD 4121
Phone: (07) 3848 1141 or 0413 004 138
Fax: (07) 3892 1929
Email: literary@powerup.com.au
Website: www.strictlyliterary.com

NEW ZEALAND

The four literary agencies listed have formed the New Zealand Association of Literary Agents (NZALA) to negotiate more effectively with publishers on behalf of authors. The NZALA expects that the self-regulatory activities of the association will help to assure authors who are unclear about the mutual responsibilities of authors and agents, and has formulated a constitution and a code of behaviour to help clarify ambiguous situations. Michael Gifkins is the spokesman for the association.

Glenys Bean Literary Agency

PO Box 60 509
Titirangi
Auckland
Phone: (09) 812 8486
Fax: (09) 812 8188
Email: g.bean@clear.net.nz

Michael Gifkins & Associates

Michael Gifkins
PO Box 6496
Auckland 1
Phone: (09) 523 5032
Fax: (08) 523 5133
Email: michael.gifkins@xtra.co.nz

Richards Literary Agency

Ray Richards, Nicki Richards Wallace
PO Box 31–240
Milford
Auckland 9
Phone: (09) 479 5681, 410 5681
Fax: (09) 479 5681, 410 6389
Email: rla.richards@clear.net.nz

TFS (Total Fiction Services) Literary Agency

Chris and Barbara Else
PO Box 29–023
Wellington
Phone/Fax: (04) 479 6746
Email: tfs@elseware.co.nz
Website: www.elseware.co.nz

ASSESSMENT

This section contains listings of manuscript assessment services for writers of fiction and non-fiction, and script development and assessment services for playwrights and screenwriters.

AUSTRALIA

Manuscript assessment services

A Decent Proposal
Rhonda Whitton
PO Box 6067
Highton Vic 3216
Phone/Fax: (03) 5241 3971
Email: AustralianWriter@ozemail.com.au
Give your book proposal the best possible chance of impressing a publisher by having it professionally appraised prior to submission. Email or send a stamped self-addressed envelope (large) for guidelines before submitting work.

Affordable Assessments
Sally Odgers
PO Box 90
Devonport Tas 7310
Phone: (03) 6426 1168
Fax: (03) 6426 2276
Email: sodgers@tassie.net.au
Website: www.sallyodgers.com/mentor/htm
Experienced manuscript assessor, specialising in children's books.

AKKA Literary Services
Bernt Vesterberg
5 Wanora Road
Fernvale Qld 4306
Phone/Fax: (07) 5426 6312
Offers support, suggestions and advice on manuscripts (including picture material) for children and young teenagers.

Allison Rushby
Phone: 0409 787 429
Email: allison@bigpond.net.au
Website: www.allisonrushby.com
Manuscript appraisal and editing services for fiction and non-fiction (no poetry). Specialises in assessing and/or editing the outline and first three chapters (or 50 pages) of work in readiness to present to a publisher or agent.

Article Appraisal Service
Rhonda Whitton
PO Box 6067Highton Vic 3216
Phone/Fax: (03) 5241 3971
Email: AustralianWriter@ozemail.com.au
Appraisal of feature and travel articles by an experienced freelance writer and teacher of freelance journalism and

The Writer's Guide

writing. Email or send a stamped self-addressed envelope (large) for guidelines before submitting work.

Between Us
Meredith Whitford
165 Belair Road
Torrens Park SA 5062
Phone: (08) 8274 1531
Fax: (08) 8357 2110
Email: between@bigpond.com
Website: www.users.bigpond.com/between
Handles short stories and book-length works. Specialises in non-fiction and the popular genres of fiction, but no poetry. Provides editing and a complete critique, plus a report which can be submitted to publishers and agents if the work is of sufficient quality. Further details available on the website.

Book Doctor
Margaret Johnson
7 The Vale
Willeton WA 6155
Phone: (08) 9457 4056
Fax: (08) 9259 6520
Email: ask@bookdoctor.com.au
Website: www.bookdoctor.com.au
Assesses, edits and agents works by writers and offers writing instruction.

Christine Nagel Literary Services
Christine Nagel
PO Box 153
Mundaring WA 6073
Phone: (08) 9295 3364
Fax: (08) 9295 0590
Email: nagelhop@bigpond.com
Website: www.users.bigpond.com/nagelliteraryagency/
Provides selected editing and a fully detailed written critique. All work assessed except poetry, technical and children's. Will assess sample or short works up to 7 500 words, or full manuscripts. Also offers literary agency services, but assessment does not imply the agency will represent the author.

Creative Crop
Laurel Cohn
7 Moffatts Road
Billinudgel NSW 2483
Phone/Fax: (02) 6680 3411
Email: laurelcohn@dingoblue.net.au
Assessment, editing, proofreading, manuscript development and desktop publishing services. Provides a written report with detailed feedback and careful evaluation to fiction and non-fiction writers about their work, and an opinion as to publishing potential.

Danielle Ellis
1/10 Peter Street
South Golden Beach NSW 2483
Phone: (02) 6680 3073
Fiction editor and assessor. Short stories, novels, plays. In-text and creative editing, with special attention to structure, which is the backbone of any work of fiction. Assessment rates reasonable.

Detrusa Promotions Manuscript Assessment Service
Cleo Pozzo
44 George Street
Fitzroy Vic 3065
Phone/Fax: (03) 9416 1778
Fax: (03) 9416 1778
Full editing and assessment of manuscripts-in-progress and completed work. All genres accepted. Further information available on request.

Driftwood Manuscripts
Kirsty Brooks
PO Box 6600
Halifax St, Adelaide SA 5000

Assessment

Phone: (08) 8339 1147
Fax: (08) 8211 6838
Email: driftw@ozemail.com.au
Website: www.adelaide.net.au/~driftw/index2.html
Manuscript assessment and editing in all genres for authors and publishers. Provides authors with 10–20 pages of constructive comment on strengths and weaknesses of their work. Exceptional work will receive a separate review for publishers. Further details available on the website.

edit or die

Sarah Endacott
PO Box 1621
South Preston Vic 3072
Phone: (03) 9471 9270
Fax: (03) 9471 9169 (phone first)
Email: kendacot@vicnet.net.au
Website: home.vicnet.net.au/~kendacot/
Offers a full range of editing and writing services for corporate, non-profit and government organisations, and a manuscript development service and assessments for writers and artists. Specialties include fantasy and science fiction, women's knowledge, children's books, genre novels, poetry and short fiction. Further details available on the website.

Enisa Hasic

5/47–53 Hobart Place
Illawong NSW 2234
Phone/Fax: (02) 9541 4491
Email: enisa_h@yahoo.com
Assesses mainly romantic fiction of all lengths and sub-genres. Looks at all aspects of the writing (viewpoint, characterisation, plotting, emotional tension, narrative, dialogue, pacing, conflict, setting, 'show and tell', grammar, punctuation, manuscript presentation, writing style). Provides a personal and prompt constructive critique with advice and suggestions for improvements, if required, with complete confidentiality.

EveryWrite

Carolyne Bruyn
PO Box 21
St Peters NSW 2044
Phone: (02) 9550 5892
Fax: Please ring first
Email: cbruyn@ihug.com.au
Website: www.everywrite.com.au
Manuscript appraisal and editing service. Most genres accepted. Particular interest in history, poetry and children's writing. New and developing writers welcome. Friendly, supportive service from concept to finished manuscript. Reasonable hourly rate and will quote.

FAW Manuscript Assessment Service

Alan Russell
Fellowship of Australian Writers
PO Box 488
Rozelle NSW 2039
Phone/Fax: (02) 9810 1307
Email: faw1@bigpond.com
Website: www.ozemail.com.au/~faw/
Offers critical readings with general criticism and editing. Assesses articles, short stories, poetry and novels.

Grant Caldwell

189 Edward Street
Brunswick Vic 3056
Phone: (03) 9387 7251
Fax: (03) 9344 8462 (during tertiary semesters)
Email: grantcaldwell01@yahoo.com
Assesses novels, stories, poetry and autobiography.

Holly Smith Manuscript Appraisal Service

Holly Smith
6 Park Avenue
Avalon Beach NSW 2107
Phone/Fax: (02) 9918 2265
Manuscript appraisal and editing service. All genres for adults and children including stories, articles, textbooks and other non-fiction, TV and radio scripts, stage plays, resumés, reports and reviews.

Interactive Publications

Dr David Reiter
Treetop Studio
9 Kuhler Court
Carindale Qld 4152
Phone: (07) 3395 0269
Fax: (07) 3324 9319
Email: info@interpr.com.au
Website: www.interpr.com.au
Authors can submit a full manuscript or synopsis and sample for assessment. If publishable, the assessor will prepare a letter of recommendation to an agent or publisher. Alternatively, the assessor will propose how the author can improve the work's publishability. Further details available on the website.

Jim Stephenson

Flat 6, 12 Ronald Avenue
Harbord NSW 2096
Phone/Fax: (02) 9939 6916
Manuscript assessment and development, sub-editing, copy editing and proofreading. Assesses any type of material. Experienced in general books, academic, reference, novels, magazines, and newspapers.

Kerry Davies Publishing Services

Kerry Davies
9 Hubert Street
Leichhardt NSW 2040
Phone/Fax: (02) 9568 6887
Email: k.davies@bigpond.com
Manuscript assessment and development of biography, textbooks, general non-fiction, reference books and fiction.

Learning Wheel

Viki Wright
PO Box 215
Lawson NSW 2783
Phone: (02) 4759 2922
Fax: (02) 4759 2482
Email: learning@pnc.com.au
All types of assessment, excluding technical, business and science writing, and most theses.

Life Stories Manuscript Development Service

Patti Miller
PO Box 4
Hazelbrook NSW 2779
Phone/Fax: (02) 4758 8058
Email: lifestories@hotmail.com
Website: www.lifestories.cjb.net
Manuscript development and general editing, specialising in autobiography and autobiographical fiction and general fiction. Provides a full written report offering assessment and advice on style and structure.

Liz Goodman

26a Sunnyridge Place
Bayview NSW 2104
Phone: (02) 9979 6905
Fax: (02) 9979 6452
Email: fullmeasure@bigpond.com
Editing, proofreading, and indexing. General non-fiction, secondary and tertiary textbooks, manuals. Subject specialities: gardening, cookery, Southeast Asia, technology, engineering and the environment.

Assessment

Lynk Manuscript Assessment Service

Liat Kirby
PO Box 174
Brunswick Vic 3056
Phone: (03) 9381 0302
Fax: (03) 9381 0305
Email: lynkmas@eisa.net.au
Formerly the National Book Council Manuscript Assessment Service. Provides constructive critical comments as a careful evaluation of the work and an idea of publishable standard. Assesses fiction (all genres), non-fiction (all kinds), poetry, playscripts and filmscripts, children's fiction and children's illustrated books. Uses well-established authors and editors throughout Australia as assessors.

Manuscript Appraisal Agency

Brian Cook
PO Box 577
Terrigal NSW 2260
Phone: (02) 4384 4466
Fax: (02) 4384 4600
Email: manu@netspace.net.au
Commercial evaluation and advice on how to get manuscripts to a standard acceptable to literary agents and publishers. All types of manuscripts appraised except for scientific and technical, academic, religious and poetry. Manuscripts thought to be commercially viable may be presented to a publisher through an associated literary agent.

Manuscript Assessment Service

Di Bates
20 Kulgoa Road
Woonona NSW 2517
Email: dibates@bigpond.com
Website: www.users.bigpond.com/billcondon/di.html
Assesses children's and young adult fiction and non-fiction only. Offers comments, copy-editing and advice. Di Bates is the author of over 70 fiction and non-fiction books for children and young adults.

Market Media

Diane Beer
12 Sandford Street
Kensington Gardens SA 5068
Phone: (08) 8332 6085
Email: dyoz@ozemail.com.au
Manuscripts edited, critiqued or polished for publication. Marketing direction, information, career planning and publicist services for writers. Quotes given before work is started. Manuscript appraisals cost between $80–$200. Reports written for agents and publishers.

Michael Giffin

PO Box 167
Paddington NSW 2021
Phone: (02) 9360 9985
Fax: (02) 9331 4653
Email: michaelg@matra.com.au
Manuscript assessment, development, copy editing and proofing for fiction authors and academic writers by a published author of literary criticism.

Nimrod Literary Consultancy

Norman Talbot
PO Box 170
New Lambton NSW 2305
Phone: (02) 4957 5562
Fax: (02) 4950 9658
Email: nimrod@hunterlink.com.au
Advises writers on manuscripts at every stage of development. Specialises in poetry, short fiction and the novel (in particular fantasy, science fiction and young adult fiction), biography and autobiography, literary criticism and

The Writer's Guide

scholarly research papers in various areas of the humanities.

Non-Fiction Manuscript Development Service

Rhonda Whitton
PO Box 6067
Highton Vic 3216
Phone/Fax: (03) 5241 3971
Email: AustralianWriter@ozemail.com.au
Manuscript development service for non-fiction works which provides constructive advice about content, writing style, grammar, word usage and market potential. Email or send a stamped self-addressed envelope (large) before submitting work.

NT Writers' Centre Manuscript Appraisal Service

GPO Box 2255
Darwin NT 0800
Phone: (08) 8941 2651
Fax: (08) 8941 2115
Email: ntwriter@octa4.net.au
Website: www.ntwriters.com.au
Assesses poetry, prose and children's fiction.

Professional Editing Services

Bill Phippard, Susan Rintoul
PO Box 234
Henley Beach SA 5022
Phone: (08) 8235 1535
Fax: (08) 8235 9144
Email: seaview@seaviewpress.com.au
Website: www.seaviewpress.com.au
Clients include Federal, State and local government departments, large and small businesses, publishers and individuals. Send one A4 page for a sample edit. Assessors will then provide you with a quote to edit the complete manuscript. Further details available on the website.

Proof

Belinda Castles
PO Box 16
Brooklyn NSW 2083
Mobile: 0403 166 398
Email: belinda@belindacastles.com
Website: www.belindacastles.com
Assessment and editorial agency with knowledge of fiction and non-fiction markets.

Queensland Writers' Centre Manuscript Appraisal Service

Level 2, 109 Edward Street
Brisbane Qld 4000
Phone: (07) 3839 1243
Fax: (07) 3839 1245
Email: qldwriters@qwc.asn.au
Website: www.qwc.asn.au
Assessment service and editorial consultancy service for members.

Richard Butler Script Consultancy

Richard Butler
PO Box 1401
East Camberwell Vic 3126
Phone: (03) 9830 0011
Fax: (03) 9852 0603
Email: richardbutler@bigpond.com
Provides intensive care for manuscripts rejected by publishers, advice on choosing a publisher and assessments of any written material other than poetry.

Rosanne Dingli Manuscript Assessment Service

Rosanne Dingli
17 Summerhayes Drive

248

Assessment

Karrinyup WA 6017
Phone: (08) 9246 7631
Fax: (08) 9246 7632
Email: rdingli@space.net.au
Website: www.rosannedingli.tripod.com
Assesses completed manuscripts (over 40 000 words) of fiction and non-fiction. Does not assess children's, political or polemical, conspiracy theory, religious, science fiction, horror, poetry or scientific, academic and technical works. Professional and highly experienced editor, and author of three published works of fiction, a writers' handbook and a collection of poetry.

Sid Harta Publishers Manuscript Appraisal Service

Kerry Collison
PO Box 1102
Hartwell Vic 3214
Phone: (03) 9560 9920
Fax: (03) 9560 9921
Email: author@sidharta.com.au
Websites: www.sidharta.com.au, www.publishers-guidelines.com, www.temple-house.com
Offers a full manuscript evaluation service for fiction, including short stories, and all other genres except poetry.

Society of Editors (NSW)

PO Box 254
Broadway NSW 2007
Phone: (02) 9294 4999
Fax: (02) 9913 7799
Email: socednsw@bigpond.com
Website: www.users.bigpond.com/socednsw
Produces an editorial services directory, which lists editors and manuscript assessors, their specialties, experience and qualifications. Available free on the society's website, or as a print edition from the Society of Editors or from the NSW Writers' Centre.

South Australian Writers' Centre Assessment Service

PO Box 43
Rundle Mall
Adelaide SA 5000
Phone: (08) 8223 7662
Fax: (08) 8232 3994
Email: sawriters@sawriters.on.net
Website: www.sawriters.on.net
Assesses any type of writing. Service for members only.

Sonnet Editorial

Loretta Barnard
44 Neptune Road
Newport Beach NSW 2106
Phone: (02) 9997 6463 or 0410 608 956
Fax: (02) 9979 7636
Offers manuscript assessment, project management, copy editing, proofreading, permissions and copyright clearance. Assesses technical and business, arts and humanities, secondary and tertiary texts, and popular/mass market non-fiction.

Strictly Literary

John Cokley
PO Box 20
Wellers Hill Qld 4121
Phone: (07) 3848 1141 or 0413 004 138
Fax: (07) 3892 1929
Email: literary@powerup.com.au
Website: www.strictlyliterary.com
Assesses all kinds of manuscripts, and offers internet publishing. Send a one-page synopsis, one-page profile and return postage for free comments, or send best two to four chapters, full profile, full synopsis and return postage for complete written appraisal.

Suzanne Hemming Editorial Services

Suzanne Hemming
PO Box 1244

Kensington Vic 3031
Phone: (03) 9372 2828
Mobile: 0402 647 257
Email: hemmings@bigpond.com
Editorial service for both published and unpublished writers. Specialising in romance writing.

Tasmanian Writers' Centre Manuscript Assessment Service

77 Salamanca Place
Hobart Tas 7000
Phone/Fax: (03) 6224 0029
Email: ed_taswriters@trump.net.au
Website: www.fearless.net.au/taswrites
Assesses up to 5000 words or 20 pages.

Victorian Writers' Centre Assessment Service

Meat Market Arts House
42 Courtney Street
North Melbourne Vic 3051
Phone: (03) 9326 4619
Fax: (03) 9326 4974
Email: info@writers-centre.org
Website: www.writers-centre.org
Professional assessment by established writers and editors.

Wannabee Publishing

Jean Briggs
PO Box 21
California Gully Vic 3556
Phone/Fax: (03) 5446 2189
Email: publish@wannabee.com.au
Website: www. wannabee.com.au
Services include assessments of short stories and poetry, editing, proofreading and manuscript development (biographies and novels). Does not assess religious work.

Witch Words

Adrianne Fitzpatrick
PO Box 908
Mt Gravatt Qld 4122
Phone: (07) 3219 2699
Email: info@witchwords.com.au
Website: www.witchwords.com.au
Professional manuscript appraisal, proofreading and editing for short stories and novels, including children's. Specialises in speculative fiction and children's literature (fiction and non-fiction).

Working Title

Helen Armstrong
47 Eric Street
Bundeena NSW 2230
Phone: (02) 9527 1525
Mobile: 0408 209 609
Email: jarmstro@mail.usyd.edu.au
Provides a comprehensive range of services for writers including manuscript appraisal, editing, desktop publishing/layout and computer advisory services, all at highly competitive rates. The writer is supported at every stage of the creative process, including getting a computer package personalised to specific needs and budget. We even make house calls!

WriteSpot Publishers International

The Submissions Editor
PO Box 221
The Gap Qld 4061
Phone: (07) 3300 1948
Email: frontdesk@writersspot.com
Website: www.writersspot.com
Publishers of all fiction genres: crime, thriller, romance, horror, fantasy, etc. Will also consider selected non-fiction. Services include written assessments of all submissions presented for possible publishing. Accepts both novel length and

short story submissions, no poetry at this stage. Reasonable rates. Will assist with self-publishing projects on request. Editing and typesetting services available.

Writing Matters

Pearlie McNeill
PO Box 539
Thirroul NSW 2525
Phone/Fax: (02) 4285 5373 or
0407 064 312
Email: bookworm@wollongong.apana.org.au
A confidential manuscript evaluation service, flexible enough to adapt to individual requirements. Pearlie McNeill is an award-winning author who has been teaching creative writing courses in England and Australia for the past eighteen years.

Script development and assessment services

Australian National Playwrights' Centre Script Assessment and Dramaturgy

PO Box 1566
Rozelle NSW 2039
Phone: (02) 9555 9377
Fax: (02) 9555 9370
Email: info@anpc.org.au
Website: www.anpc.org.au
Available to members and non-members. To access the script assessment service, playwrights need to contact the Centre and obtain a Script Entry Form. There are programs available for new and experienced playwrights.

Australian Writers' Guild Assessment Service

8/50 Reservoir Street
Surry Hills NSW 2010

Phone: (02) 9281 1554
Fax: (02) 9281 4321
Email: admin@awg.com.au
Website: www.awg.com.au
Subsidised assessment service for members only by writers with significant credits to their name.

Embryo Films

PO Box 68
St Pauls NSW 2031
Phone: (02) 9399 6951
Email: workshop@embryo-films.com
Website: www.embryo-films.com

Melbourne Writers' Theatre

PO Box 1049
Carlton Vic 3053
Phone: (03) 9347 2562
Provides script assessment for its members.

National Institute of Dramatic Arts Playwrights' Studio

215 Anzac Parade
Kensington NSW 2052
Phone: (02) 9697 7600
Fax: (02) 9662 7415
Email: nida@unsw.edu.au
Website: www.nida.unsw.edu.au
Workshop for a small group of dedicated and enthusiastic people who wish to write professionally for the theatre. The Studio aims to provide an introduction to the techniques of writing for the theatre.

Playlab's Script Development Network

PO Box 878
Fortitude Valley Qld 4006
Phone: (07) 3852 1400
Fax: (07) 3852 1405

The Writer's Guide

Email: cluster@thehub.com.au
Script assessment service offered to theatre and performance writers to provide comprehensive and informed feedback on developing texts.

Playworks Dramaturgy Program

PO Box A2216
Sydney South NSW 1235
Phone: (02) 9264 8414
Fax: (02) 9264 8449
Email: playwks@ozemail.com.au
Website: www.ozemail.com.au/~playwks
Offers a national script development and dramaturgy service for women playwrights.

Queensland Theatre Company Writing Program

PO Box 310
South Brisbane Qld 4101
Phone: (07) 3840 7000
Fax: (07) 3840 7040
Email: udauth@qldtheatreco.com.au
Website: www.qldtheatreco.com.au
Contact: Ursula Dauth
The company assesses unsolicited manuscripts from playwrights who satisfy the criteria. These are assessed internally, with a view to deciding whether the QTC can program or help develop those of sufficient merit.

NEW ZEALAND

The following assessment services are all members of the New Zealand Association of Manuscript Assessors (NZAMA). The contact for the Association is TFS Assessment Service (see details below).

Anna Rogers

18 Bletsoe Avenue
Christchurch 2
Phone/Fax: (03) 337 3044
Email: a.rogers@clear.net.nz
Specialises in assessing adult fiction (particularly) and non-fiction. Does not deal with poetry or children's material. Anna Rogers has 23 years' experience as a book editor and has written four non-fiction titles.

Editline

Lesley Marshall
PO Box 68
Maungatapere
Phone: (09) 434 6814
Email: editline@xtra.co.nz
Lesley Marshall has been a freelance editor for over 20 years, and will work on any kind of fiction or nonfiction except poetry. References are available, and quotes on request.

Jane Parkin Editorial and Assessment Services

48 Nevay Road
Seatoun
Wellington
Phone/Fax: (04) 388 4535
Email: janep@paradise.net.nz
Offers a range of editorial services, specialising in fiction editing and manuscript development. Jane Parkin is a founding member of the NZAMA and has a long association with the NZ book publishing industry. Inquiries welcome. No unsolicited material, please.

Pen and Ink Services

Loren Teague
18a Taupata Street
Stoke
Nelson
Phone/Fax: (03) 547 5369
Email: pen-ink@netaccess.co.nz
Website: users.netaccess.co.nz/lorenteague/writer.htm

Specialises in manuscript assessment of fiction: romance, crime, fantasy, historical, thriller, young adult and other genres. Publishing advice, including e-publishing. Guidance offered to new and established writers. Editing, freelance writing, synopses and book reviews.

Marigold Enterprises

Barbara Murison
PO Box 22–180
Khandallah
Wellington
Phone/Fax: (04) 479 5538
Email: barbaram@clear.net.nz
Specialises in stories and novels for children and teenagers. Does not assess poetry, although picture books in rhyme are welcome. Flyer available.

Norman Bilbrough Manuscript Assessments

191 Wilton Road
Wilton
Wellington
Phone: (04) 475 8151
Email: norman.b@paradise.net.nz
Offers a detailed objective report on your writing project, noting strengths and weaknesses and commenting on characterisation, style, dialogue and validity of story line. Gives suggestions on reworking your manuscript towards a publishable form.

Scope Manuscript Services

Maria Jungowska
PO Box 109
Whangamata
Email: m.j.scope@xtra.co.nz

Scope offers to help new writers increase their chances of publication. Manuscripts can be assessed, as well as edited and prepared for submission to publishers, by an editor of many years' experience with major publishing houses. Scope also undertakes book projects, providing editorial and camera-ready production services.

TFS Assessment Service

PO Box 29–023 Ngaio
Wellington NZ
Phone/Fax: (04) 479 6746
Email: tfs@elseware.co.nz
Website: www.elseware.co.nz
TFS has helped new and established writers improve their work. Writers receive an objective report with constructive comment relating directly to the text. Over 97% of clients say they would use our service again and recommend it to others. For more details, check the website or send a stamped self-addressed envelope for a brochure.

Write Right

Graeme Lay
50 Lake Road
Takapuna
Auckland
Email: graemelay@xtra.co.nz

Write Right

Stephen Stratford
PO Box 56–112
Dominion Road
Auckland
Email: stephen.stratford@xtra.co.nz

Script development and assessment services

Playmarket Script Advisory Service

PO Box 9767
Te Aro
Wellington
Phone: (04) 382 8462
Fax: (04) 382 8461
Email: info@playmarket.org.nz
Website: www.playmarket.org.nz

Playmarket provides a range of script advisory and script development services for New Zealand playwrights, including readings, workshops and paid script assessments. Scripts submitted for assessment are read by an assessor who is involved in New Zealand professional theatre. A written report provides an assessment of the script's strengths, weaknesses and production potential. For an additional fee playwrights can also obtain a script consultation with the assessor.

BIBLIOGRAPHY

This list includes references mentioned in the text as well as other references. Many of these references can be found in writers' centre libraries. Where an organisation is listed as the publisher of a particular work, the contact details are supplied in the 'Organisations' list in the Resources section.

GENERAL PUBLICATIONS ON WRITING

Amis, Kingsley. *The King's English: A Guide to Modern Usage*, HarperCollins, 1997.

Aronson, Linda. *Writing With Imagination: A Practical Guide*, Macmillan Education Australia, Melbourne, 2000.

Beazley, Malcolm, and Marr, Grahame. *The Writer's Handbook: Words, Grammar, Usage, Style, Purpose*, Phoenix Education, Melbourne, 1994.

Cutts, Martin. *The Plain English Guide: How to Write Clearly and Communicate Better*, Oxford University Press, New York, 1995.

Delton, Judy. *Twenty-Nine Most Common Writing Mistakes and How to Avoid Them*, Writer's Digest, Cincinnati, Ohio, 1991.

Dillard, Annie. *The Writing Life*, HarperPerennial, New York, 1989.

Dumbrell, Laurel. *You Can Write—Here's Proof. Laurel Dumbrell in Conversation With Twenty Writers*, Talver Pty Limited, Parramatta, 1997.

Dupré, Lyn. *Bugs in Writing: A Guide to Debugging Your Prose*, Addison Wesley, Reading, Massachusetts, 1995.

Eagleson, Rob. *Writing in Plain English*, Australian Government Publishing Service, Canberra, 1997.

Fowler, H. R., and Aaron, J. E. *The Little, Brown Handbook*, HarperCollins College Publishers, New York, 1995.

Fox, Mem, and Wilkinson, Lyn. *English Essentials: That Wouldn't-Be-Without-It Guide to Writing Well*, Macmillan Education, Melbourne, 1993.

Goldberg, Natalie. *Writing Down the Bones*, Shambhala, Boston, 1986.

——*Wild Mind: Living the Writer's Life*, Bantam Books, New York, 1990.

Grenville, Kate. *Writing From Start to Finish: A Six Step Guide*, Allen & Unwin, Sydney, 2001.

Hughes, Barrie (ed.). *The Penguin Working Words: An Australian Guide to Modern English Usage*, Penguin Books, Ringwood, Vic., 1993.

Ivers, Michael. *The Random House Guide to Good Writing*, Random House, New York, 1991.

James, Neil (ed.). *Writers on Writing*, Halstead Press, 1999.

King, Stephen. *On Writing: A Memoir of the Craft*, Hodder & Stoughton, 2000.

Kinross-Smith, Graeme. *Writer: A Working*

Guide for New Writers, Oxford University Press, Melbourne, 1992.
Lane, Barry. *Writing As a Road to Self-Discovery,* Writer's Digest, Cincinnati, Ohio, 1992.
Lindsay, Hilarie. *Learn to Write,* Ansay, Sydney, 1992.
Lodge, David. *Practice of Writing,* Secker & Warberg, London, 1997.
Marsden, John. *Everything I Know About Writing,* Pan Macmillan Australia, Sydney, 1998.
Neale, Robert. *Writers on Writing: An Anthology,* Oxford University Press, Auckland, 1992.
Parv, Valerie. *The Idea Factory: A Guide to More Creative Thinking and Writing,* Allen & Unwin, Sydney, 1995.
Petelin, Roslyn, and Durham, Marsha. *The Professional Writing Guide: Writing Well and Knowing Why,* Longman Professional, Melbourne, 1992.
Provost, Gary. *100 Ways to Improve Your Writing,* Mentor, New York, 1985.
Renton, N. E. *Good Writing Guide,* The Business Library, Melbourne, 1994.
Roberts, James, Mitchell, Barry and Zubrinich, Roger (eds). *Writers on Writing,* Penguin Books, Melbourne, 2002.
St George, Frank, and St George, Andrew. *Clear English: How to Improve Your Style,* Bloomsbury, London, 1996.
Walsh, Barbara. *Communicating in Writing,* Australian Government Publishing Service, Canberra, 1989.
Whitebeach, Terry. *Handbook for Central Australian Indigenous Writers,* Northern Territory Writers' Centre, 1998.
Whitton, Rhonda, and Hollingworth, Sheila. *A Decent Proposal,* Common Ground Publishing, Melbourne, 2001.
Wood, Monica. *Description,* Writer's Digest, Cincinnati, Ohio, 1995.
Zinsser, William. *On Writing Well: The Classic Guide to Writing Non-Fiction,* 6th edn, HarperPerennial, New York, 1998.

ADAPTIONS

McFarlane, Brian. *Novel to Film: An Introduction to the Theory of Adaption,* Oxford University Press, Oxford, 1997.

ANTHOLOGY

ASA Prose and Poetry Anthology Policy, Australian Society of Authors, Sydney, 1998.

ARTICLES

Owen, Jane Duncan. *Writing and Selling Articles: Australian/NZ Guide,* Hale & Iremonger, Sydney, 1997.

AUTOBIOGRAPHY

Miller, Patti. *Writing Your Life: A Journey of Discovery,* Allen & Unwin, Sydney, 2001.
Moon, Ken. *Write Your Life: A Guide to Autobiography,* Wrightbooks, North Brighton, Melbourne, 1994.
Smith, Nancy. *Writing Your Life Story: A Step-By-Step Guide to Writing Your Autobiography,* Piatkus, London, 1993.

BIOGRAPHY

Brooks, Barbara. 'Writing Biography', *Australian Author,* vol. 27, no. 3, Spring 1995.
Brooks, Barbara, with Clark, Judith. *Eleanor Dark: A Writer's Life,* Macmillan, Sydney, 1998.
Heilbrun, Carolyn. *Writing a Woman's Life,* Women's Press, London, 1989.
Homberger, Eric (ed.). *The Troubled Face of Biography,* Macmillan, Basingstoke, 1998.
Huggins, Jackie, with Huggins, Rita. *Auntie Rita,* Aboriginal Studies Press, Canberra, 1994 (essays on biography).

Marr, David. *Patrick White: A Life*, Vintage, Sydney, 1992.
Modjeska, Drusilla. *Poppy*, Picador, Sydney, 1996.
Rowley, Hazel. *Christina Stead*, Heinemann, Melbourne, 1993.
Sykes, Roberta. *Snake Cradle*, Allen & Unwin, Sydney, 1997.
—— *Snake Dancing*, Allen & Unwin, Sydney, 1998.
—— *Snake Circle*, Allen & Unwin, Sydney, 2000.

BOOK LAUNCHES

Rintoul, Susan, and Phippard, Bill. *Book Launching for Authors: Making the Most of Your Sales*, Seaview Press, Adelaide, 2001.

BROADCASTING

A Practical Handbook for Arts Participation in Community Radio, Community Broadcasting Association of Australia, Sydney, 1998.
Broadcasting Arts, Community Broadcasting Association of Australia, Sydney, 1998.

CHILDREN'S BOOKS AND MAGAZINES

Amoss, B., and Suben, E. *Writing and Illustrating Children's Books for Publication*, Writer's Digest, Cincinnati, Ohio, 1995.
Bates, Dianne. *The New Writer's Survival Guide*, Penguin Books, Ringwood, Vic., 1989.
Children's Book Publishers (Trade/General), NSW Writers' Centre, Sydney, 2000 (brochure).
Clarke, Margaret. *Writing for Children*, A. & C. Black, London, 1997.
Dunkle, Margaret (ed.). *The Storymakers*, vol. 1 & 2, Oxford University Press, Oxford, 1989 (a bibliography).
Educational Publishers, NSW Writers' Centre, Sydney, 2000 (brochure).
Edwards, Hazel, and Alexander, Goldie. *The Business of Writing For Young People*, Hale & Iremonger, Sydney, 1998.
Fisher, Margery. *Matters of Fact: Non-fiction for Children*, Brockhampton, Chicago, 1972.
Gleeson, Libby. *Writing Hannah: On Writing for Children*, Hale & Iremonger, Sydney, 1999.
Lees, Stella, and Macintyre, Pam (eds). *The Oxford Companion to Australian Children's Literature*, Oxford University Press, London, 1993.
Matthews, Stephen. *The Eye of the Soul: 17 writers on writing for children and young adults*, Magpies, Queensland, 1998.
McVitty, Walter. *Authors and Illustrators of Australian Children's Books: A Bibliography*, Hodder & Stoughton, Sydney, 1989.
Morris, Jill. *Writing for the Children's Book Market*, Australian Society of Authors, Sydney, 1998.
Nilsson, Eleanor. *Writing for Children*, Penguin Books, Ringwood, Vic., 1992.
Odgers, Sally Farrell. *Storytrack: Writing for Children*, Kangaroo Press, Sydney, 1989.
Wagner, Jenny. *On Writing Books for Children*, Allen & Unwin, Sydney, 1992.
Who's Who of Australian Children's Writers, D. W. Thorpe in association with the National Centre for Australian Studies, Melbourne, 1996.
Writing and Illustrating Children's Books, NSW Writers' Centre, Sydney, 2000 (brochure).
Writing and Illustrating for Children: New Zealand Publishers' Requirements and Addresses, 1997, 9th edn, Canterbury Public Library, Christchurch, 1998.

COMEDY

Helitzer, Mel. *Comedy Writing Secrets*, Writer's Digest, London, 1992.
Wolfe, Ronald. *Writing Comedy: A Guide to Scriptwriting*, Robert Hale, London, 1996.

COMMUNITY WRITING

Clarke, Sherryl. *In Others' Words: Writing in a Community Context*, Blackwood Street Neighbourhood House, Melbourne, 1994.

COMPETITION GUIDELINES

Guidelines for Literary Competitions, New Zealand Society of Authors, Auckland, 1997.

CONTRACTS

Arts Law Centre of Australia: Options and Purchase Agreement, Arts Law Centre of Australia, Sydney, 1998 (sample agreement between author and producer for use in low budget and film and video production).
ASA Minimum Approved Contract, Australian Society of Authors, Sydney, 1996.
ASA Upfront Contract, Australian Society of Authors, Sydney, 1996.
Australian Book Contracts, Keesing Press, Sydney, 2001.
Methold, Ken. *Commissioned Works and Contracts*, Australian Society of Authors, Sydney, 1995.
New Zealand Society of Authors. *The Business of Writing: An Annotated Model Standard Contract*, New Zealand Society of Authors, Auckland, 1995.

Society of Book Illustrators. *Illustrator's Contract*, Australian Society of Authors, Sydney, 1998.

COPYWRITING

Burton, Ron. *Copywriter's Companion*, Ron Burton, 35 Folkstone Avenue, Albany Creek, Qld, phone (07) 3264 4647, fax (07) 3264 8010.

CRIME

Bintliff, Russell. *Police Procedural: A Writer's Guide to the Police and How They Work*, Writer's Digest, Cincinnati, Ohio, 1993.
Blythe, H., Sweet, C., and Landret, J. *Private Eyes: A Writer's Guide to Private Investigators*, Writer's Digest, London, 1993.
Day, Marele. *How to Write Crime*, Allen & Unwin, Sydney, 1996.
Grant-Adamson, Lesley. *Writing Crime and Suspense Fiction and Getting Published*, Hodder & Stoughton, London, 1996.
Knight, Stephen. *Continent of Mystery: A Thematic History of Australian Crime Fiction*, Melbourne University Press, Melbourne, 1997.
Mactire, Sean. *Malicious Intent*, Writer's Digest, Cincinnati, Ohio, 1995.
Newton, Michael. *Armed and Dangerous: A Writer's Guide to Weapons*, Writer's Digest, Cincinnati, Ohio, 1990.
Page, David W. *Body Trauma: A Writer's Guide to Wounds and Injuries*, Writer's Digest, Cincinnati, Ohio, 1996.
Raco Chase, Elaine, and Wingate, Anne. *Amateur Detectives: A Writer's Guide to How Private Citizens Solve Criminal Cases*, Writer's Digest, Cincinnati, Ohio, 1996.
Roth, Martin. *The Writer's Complete Crime Reference Book*, Writer's Digest, Cincinnati, Ohio, 1993.

Stevens, Serita Deborah. *Deadly Doses: A Writer's Guide to Poisons,* Writer's Digest, Cincinnati, Ohio, 1990.
Wilson, Keith D. *Cause of Death: A Writer's Guide to Death, Murder and Forensic Medicine,* Writer's Digest, Cincinnati, Ohio, 1992.
Wingate, Anne. *Scene of the Crime: A Writer's Guide to Crime Scene Investigation,* Writer's Digest, Cambridge, Massachusetts, 1992.

DIALOGUE

Turco, Lewis. *Dialogue,* Writer's Digest, Cincinnati, Ohio, 1989.

DICTIONARIES AND THESAURUSES

Australian Concise Oxford Dictionary, 3rd edn, Oxford University Press, Melbourne, 1997.
Basset, J. (ed.). *The Concise Oxford Dictionary of Australian History,* Oxford University Press, Melbourne, 1986.
Bryson, W. *The Penguin Dictionary of Troublesome Words,* Penguin Books, Ringwood, Vic., 1987.
Concise Oxford Dictionary, 7th edn, Oxford University Press, Oxford, 1982.
Deverson, Tony (ed.). *New Zealand Pocket Oxford Dictionary,* 2nd edn, Oxford University Press, New Zealand, 1997.
Ehrlich, E. (ed.). *Le Mot Juste: The Penguin Dictionary of Foreign Terms and Phrases,* Viking, London, 1988.
Macquarie Dictionary, 3rd edn, Macquarie Library, Macquarie University, Australia, 1997.
Macquarie Thesaurus, Macquarie Library, Macquarie University, Australia, 1986.
Murray-Smith, Stephen (ed.). *The Dictionary of Australian Quotations,* Heinemann, Melbourne, 1984.
Orsman, H. W. (ed.). *Dictionary of New Zealand English: New Zealand Words and their Origins,* Oxford University Press, New Zealand, 1997.
Orsman, Harry, and Moore, Jan (eds). *Heinemann Dictionary of New Zealand Quotations,* Heinemann, Auckland, 1988.
Oxford Dictionary for Scientific Writers and Editors, Clarendon Press, Oxford, 1991.
Oxford Dictionary of New Zealand English, Oxford University Press, New Zealand, 1997.
Penguin Macquarie Dictionary of People and Places, Penguin Books in association with Hamish Hamilton, Ringwood, Vic., 1987.
Purchase, S. (ed.). *Australian Writers' Dictionary,* Oxford University Press, Melbourne, 1997.
Roget's Thesaurus of English Words and Phrases, Longman, London, 1982.
Shorter English Dictionary on Historical Principles, 2 vols, Oxford University Press, Oxford, 1973.
Wilkes, G. A. *A Dictionary of Australian Colloquialisms,* Oxford University Press, Melbourne, 1996.

EDITING

Butcher, J. *Copy-editing: The Cambridge Handbook for Editors, Authors and Publishers,* 3rd edn, Cambridge University Press, Cambridge, 1992.
Kaplan, Bruce. *Editing Made Easy,* Bruce Kaplan, Melbourne, 1999.
Council of Biology Editors. *Scientific Style and Format: The CBE Manual for Authors, Editors and Publishers,* Cambridge, 1994.
Editing, NSW Writers' Centre, Sydney, 2000 (brochure).
Flann, Elizabeth, and Hill, Beryl. *The Australian Editing Handbook,* Australian Government Publishing Service, Canberra, 1994.
Getting Help With Your Manuscript: Editing, Assessing and Using an Agent,

New Zealand Society of Authors, Auckland, 1998 (brochure).
Mandell, J. *Book Editors Talk to Writers,* John Wiley & Sons, New York, 1995.
Plotnik, Arthur. *The Elements of Editing: A Modern Guide for Editors and Journalists,* Collier Books, New York, 1984.
Ross-Larson, Bruce. *Edit Yourself: A Manual for Everyone Who Works With Words,* W. W. Norton & Company, New York, 1996.
Sharpe, L. T., and Gunther, S. *Editing Fact and Fiction,* Cambridge University Press, Cambridge, 1994.

EDITORS

Editorial Services Directory, Society of Editors (NSW), Sydney, 2001.
Freelance Register, Society of Editors (Vic.), Melbourne, 1999.

EDUCATION

Spender, Dale, *Writing for the Educational Market,* Australian Society of Authors, Sydney, 1998.

ELECTRONIC RIGHTS

Spender, Lynne. *Electronic/Digital Rights: A Handbook for Authors,* Australian Society of Authors, Sydney, 1997.

EROTIC FICTION

Francis, Louise. *Writing Erotica for Women,* Oracle Press, Montville, Queensland, 1998.
Parker, Derek. *Writing Erotic Fiction,* A. & C. Black, London, 1995.

ESSAY

Craven, Peter (ed.). *Best Australian Essays 2001,* Black Ink, Melbourne, 2001.
Fraser, Morag (ed.). *Seams of Light: Best Antipodean Essays,* Allen & Unwin, Sydney, 1998.
Salusinszky, Imre (ed.). *The Oxford Book of Australian Essays,* Oxford University Press, Melbourne, 1997.

FAMILY HISTORY

Edwards, Hazel. *Writing a 'Non-Boring' Family History,* Hale & Iremonger, Sydney, 1997.
Kyle, Noeline, and King, Ron. *The Family History Writing Book,* Allen & Unwin, Sydney, 1993.
Miller, Patti. *Writing Your Life,* Allen & Unwin, Sydney, 2001.
Price, Bob. *Book of Family Memories: How to Preserve Your Living History,* Australian Consolidated Press, Melbourne, 1987.
Reakes, Janet. *How to Trace Your English Ancestors for Australians and New Zealanders: Including Wales,* Hale & Iremonger, Sydney, 1987.
——*How to Trace Your Family Tree (And Not Get Stuck on a Branch),* Hale & Iremonger, Sydney, 1992.
——*How to Trace Your Missing Ancestors Whether Living, Dead, or Adopted,* Hale & Iremonger, Sydney, 1992.
——*How to Trace Your Scottish Ancestors: An A–Z Approach,* Hale & Iremonger, Sydney, 1988.
——*How to Write the Family Story,* Hale & Iremonger, Sydney, 1993.

FEATURES

Blundell, William E. *The Art and Craft of Feature Writing,* Plume/Penguin Books, New York, 1988.

FICTION

Bacia, Jennifer. *Creating Popular Fiction: How to Write Novels That Sell*, Allen & Unwin, Sydney, 1994.
——*Chapter One: Everything You Want to Know About Starting Your Novel*, Allen & Unwin, Sydney, 1998.
Bird, Carmel. *Dear Writer: The Classic Guide to Fiction Writing*, Vintage, Sydney, 1996.
——*Not Now Jack—I'm Writing a Novel*, Picador, Sydney, 1994.
Boylan, Clare. *The Agony and the Ego: The Art and Strategy of Fiction Writing Explored*, Penguin Books, Ringwood, Vic., 1993.
Card, Orson Scott. *Characters & Viewpoint*, Writer's Digest, Cincinnati, Ohio, 1988.
Disher, Garry. *Writing Fiction: An Introduction to the Craft*, Allen & Unwin, Sydney, 2001.
Frank, T., and Wall, D. *Finding Your Writer's Voice: A Guide to Creative Fiction*, St Martins, New York, 1994.
Grenville, Kate. *The Writing Book: A Workbook for Fiction Writers*, Allen & Unwin, Sydney, 1998.
——*Writing from Start to Finish: A Workbook for Fiction Writers*, Allen & Unwin, Sydney, 2002.
Grenville, Kate, and Woolfe, Sue. *Making Stories: How Ten Australian Novels Were Written*, Allen & Unwin, Sydney, 2001.
Lodge, David. *Art of Fiction*, Penguin Books, New York, 1992.
Martin, Rhona. *Writing Historical Fiction*, A. & C. Black, London, 1995.
McRobbie, David. *Gumshoe: Creative Writing Through Mystery Stories*, Longman, Melbourne, 1989.
McRobbie, David, and Vanzet, Gaston. *What Next?: Creative Writing Through Adventure Stories*, Longman, Melbourne, 1991.
Moon, Ken, and Moon, Elaine. *Writing Quality Fiction: A Guide*, Wrightbooks, Elsternwick, Victoria, 1996.
Ray, Robert J., and Remick, Jack. *The Weekend Novelist*, Dell Books, New York, 1994.
Smith, Nancy. *Fiction Writers' Handbook*, Piatkus, London, 1991.
Swain, Dwight V. *Creating Characters*, Writer's Bookcase, Cincinnati, Ohio, 1994.
Tobias, Ronald B. *20 Master Plots (And How to Build Them)*, Writer's Digest, Cincinnati, Ohio, 1993.
Turcotte, Gerry. *Writers in Action: The Writer's Choice Evenings*, Currency Press, Sydney, 1990.
Walker, Brenda (ed.) *The Writer's Reader*, Halstead Press, NSW, 2002.
Zuckerman, Albert. *Writing the Blockbuster Novel*, Little, Brown & Co., London, 1994.

FOOD

Laurence, Janet. *Craft of Food and Cookery Writing*, Allison & Busby, London, 1994.

FREELANCE WRITING

Moore, Chris. *Freelance Writing*, Robert Hale, London, 1996.

GRAMMAR, PUNCTUATION AND SPELLING

Bernard, J. R. *A Short Guide to Traditional Grammar*, Sydney University Press, Sydney, 1986.
Bolitho, Robert, and Lutton, Russell. *Collins Guide to Australian Usage and Punctuation*, Collins Dove, Melbourne, 1993.
The Cambridge Grammar of the English

Language, Cambridge University Press, Cambridge, 2002.
Carey, G. V. *Mind the Stop: A Brief Guide to Punctuation*, Penguin, Harmondsworth, 1986.
Collins Gem Dictionary of Spelling and Word Division, Collins, London, 1968.
Dykes, Barbara. *Grammar Made Easy*, Hale & Iremonger, Sydney, 1992.
Dykes, Barbara, and Thomas, Constance. *Spelling Made Easy*, Hale & Iremonger, Sydney, 1989.
Garner, M. *Grammar: Warts and All*, 2nd rev. edn, River Seine Press, Melbourne, 1989.
Stern, Dr George. *Choosing Your Mark: A Guide to Good Expression and Punctuation*, Australian Government Publishing Service, Canberra, 1995.
—— *Using Grammar in Your Prose*, Australian Government Publishing Service, Canberra, 1997.

HANDBOOKS FOR WRITERS

Beaton, Hilary (ed). *Word for Word*, Queensland Writers' Centre, Brisbane, 2000.
Britton, Anne-Maree (ed.). *Writers' Services Directory*, ACT Writers' Centre, Canberra, 2001.
Community Broadcasting Association of Australia, *A Practical Handbook for Arts Participation in Community Radio* (1998), available from the CBAA at the price of $15 including postage. Send cheque to CBAA, PO Box 564, Alexandria, NSW 1435 and mark for the attention of the Program Services Manager.
Handbook for South Australian Writers, South Australian Writers' Centre, Adelaide, 2001.
Methold, Ken. *A–Z of Authorship*, Keesing Press, Sydney, 1992.
Parsons, J. *NZ Writers' Handbook*, David Bateman, Auckland, 1998.

Playwrights' Handbook, Australian Writers' Guild, Sydney, www.awgcom.au (free for members).
Victorian Writers' Centre. *Directory of Writers' Services*, Melbourne, 2002.
Whitebeach, Terry Anne. *A Handbook for Central Australian Indigenous Writers*, NT Writers' Centre Inc., Darwin, 1998.

INDEXING

Mulvany, Nancy. *Indexing Books*, University of Chicago Press, Chicago, 1994.
Wellisch, Hans. *Indexing from A to Z*, H W Wilson, New York, 1996.

INDIGENOUS WRITING

Mudrooroo. *The Indigenous Literature of Australia*, Hyland House, Melbourne, 1997.

INTERNATIONAL

Herman, Jeff. *Writer's Guide to Book Editors, Publishers and Literary Agents 1998–1999*, Prima Rocklin, California, 1997.

INTERNET

Crawford, Kathryn, and Ziebell, M. *The Beginner's Guide to the Net*, Allen & Unwin, Sydney, 1997.
Spender, Dale. *Nattering on the Net: Women, Power and Cyberspace*, Spinifex, Melbourne, 1995.
The Friendly Grrrls Guide to Getting on the Net, Geekgirl, Sydney, 1996.

JOURNALISM

Edgar, Patricia. *The News in Focus: The Journalism of Exception*, Macmillan, Melbourne, 1980.

Gill, E. M. *Writing for a Living: Practical Beginnings for Journalist and Author*, Pearson, New York, 1992.

Pearson, Mark, and Johnston, Jane. *Breaking into Journalism: Your Guide to a Career in Journalism in Australia and New Zealand*, Allen & Unwin, Sydney, 1998.

White, Sally A. *Reporting in Australia*, Macmillan Education, Melbourne, 1996.

LETTERS

Wood, John. *How to Write Attention-Grabbing Query and Cover Letters*, Writer's Digest, Cincinnati, Ohio, 1996.

LITERARY AGENTS

Literary Agents, NSW Writers' Centre, Sydney, 2000 (brochure).

Literary Agents List, Australian Society of Authors, Sydney, 1998.

LITERARY AWARDS AND GRANTS

Australian Literary Awards and Fellowships, 10th edn, D. W. Thorpe, Melbourne, 2002.

Summers, Julie (ed.). *The Australian Grants Register*, 2nd edn, Australian Scholarly Publishing, Melbourne, 2002.

MANUSCRIPT ASSESSMENT

Manuscript Assessment Services, NSW Writers' Centre, Sydney, 2001 (brochure).

MARKETING GUIDES

Cohn, Laurel (ed.). *NSW Writers' Centre Journals Directory*, 4th edn, NSW Writers' Centre, Sydney, 2001 (containing 200 publishing outlets).

Holm, Kirsten. *Writer's Market 1998*, Writer's Digest, Cincinnati, Ohio, 1997.

Literary Market Place: The Directory of the American Book Publishing Industry, R. R. Bowker, New Providence, New Jersey, 1997.

MacDonald, Eris. *Australian Competitions and Markets for Young Writers of Poetry and Short Fiction*, Eris MacDonald, Midland, WA, 2002.

MacDonald, Eris. *Australian Poetry Markets and Competitions: A Guide to Publications and Events for Poets*, Eris MacDonald, Midland, WA, 2002.

MacDonald, Eris. *Australian Short Fiction Competitions*, Eris MacDonald, Midland, WA, 2002.

MacDonald, Eris. *Australian Short Fiction Markets: A Marketing Guide for Writers of Short Stories*, Eris MacDonald, Midland, WA, 2002.

Walton, Ian (ed.). *Small Press Guide: A Detailed Guide to Poetry and Small Press Magazines*, Writers' Bookshop, London, 1997.

Whitten, Rhonda. *Australian Writer's Marketplace 2002*, Bookman, Melbourne, 2001, published annually.

Writers' and Artists' Yearbook, A. & C. Black, London, 2002, published annually.

MARKETING, PROMOTION AND PUBLICITY

Bromby, Robin. *Writing for Profit in Australia*, Simon & Schuster, Sydney, 1992.

Budrys, Algis. *Writing to the Point: A Complete Guide to Selling Fiction*, Unifont, Evanston, 1994.

Collins, Paul. *Selling Your Fiction and Poetry Made Easy*, TAFE Publications, Melbourne, 1997.

Day, Marele. *The Art of Self-Promotion: Successful Promotion by Writers,* Allen & Unwin, Sydney, 1993.
Ditrich, Julie. *Promoting Your Book,* Australian Society of Authors, Sydney, 1998.
Kaplan, Cyndi. *Publish for Profit: How to Write, Market & Promote Your Own Book,* Cyndi Kaplan Communications, Sydney, 1997.
Kremer, J. *1001 Ways to Market Your Books,* Open Horizons, Iowa, 1997.
Methold, Ken. *Writing as a Business,* ABC Books, Sydney, 2002.
Oberlin, L. H. *Writing for Money,* Writer's Digest, Cincinnati, Ohio, 1995.
Palmer, Robert. *1000 Markets for Freelance Writers,* Piatkus, London, 1993.
Schwarz, Samantha. *Australian Guide to Getting Published,* Hale & Iremonger, Sydney, 1995.
—— *Getting Published: The Aotearoa New Zealand Guide,* Lincoln University Press and Daphne Brassell Associates, Canterbury, 1997.
Steps towards Getting Published, 3rd edn, Australian Society of Authors, Sydney, 1997.

MEDIA GUIDES

Bookman Media Guide 2000, Bookman Directories, Melbourne, 1999.
Margaret Gee's Australian Media Guide, Information Australia, 45 Flinders Lane, Melbourne, Vic. 3000 (comprehensive media guide to all sectors of the Australian media).

MEMOIRS

Ellis, Bob. *Goodbye Jerusalem,* Vintage, Random House, Sydney, 1997.
Malouf, David. *12 Edmonstone Street,* Penguin Books, Ringwood, Vic., 1986.

MULTICULTURAL WRITERS

Caro, Marisa. *Directory of Multicultural Writing Groups,* NSW Writers' Centre, Sydney, 1999.
Cano, Marisa. *Across Words: A Guide for Facilitators of Creative Writing Workshops for NESB groups,* Liverpool Migrant Resource Centre, 2001.
Gunew, Sheila, Houbein, Lolo, Karakostas-Seda, Alexandra, and Mahyuddin, Jan. *A Bibliography of Australian Multicultural Writers,* Deakin University Press, Victoria, 1992.

MULTIMEDIA WRITING

Aston, R., and Schwarz, J. (eds). *Multimedia: Gateway to the Next Millennium,* AP Professional, Boston, 1994.
Averill, M., and Heidtman, D. *Multimedia Contracts Handbook: An Industry Guide,* Prospect Publishing, Sydney, 1996.
Bonime, Andrew, and Pohlmann, Ken C. *Writing for the New Media: The Essential Guide to Writing for Interactive Media, CD-ROMS, and the Web,* John Wiley and Sons, New York, 1998.
Cawkell, A. *The Multimedia Handbook,* Routledge, London, 1996.
Cotton, B., and Oliver, R. *The Cyberspace Lexicon: An Illustrated Dictionary of Terms from Multimedia to Virtual Reality,* Phaidon, London, 1994.
Feldman, Tony. *An Introduction to Digital Media,* Routledge, London, 1996.
Goldberg, R. *Multimedia Producer's Bible,* IDG Books Worldwide, Indianapolis, 1996.

NEWSPAPERS

O'Connor, Terry. *Hold the Front Page,* Queensland Newspapers, Brisbane, 1993.

PAYMENT

Guidelines for Paying Writers for Writing-Related Work, New Zealand Society of Authors, Auckland, 1998.

PLAYWRITING

Carroll, Dennis. *Australian Contemporary Drama*, Currency Press, Sydney, 1995.
Playwrighting, NSW Writers' Centre, Sydney, 2000 (brochure).
Playwrights' Handbook, Australian Writers' Guild, Sydney, 1998.

POETRY

2000 Australian Poetry Catalogue, Poets Union, 2000.
Bugeja, Michael J. *Art and Craft of Poetry*, Writer's Digest, Cincinnati, Ohio, 1994.
Chisholm, Alison. *Craft of Writing Poetry*, Allison & Busby, London, 1992.
——*Practical Poetry Course*, Allison & Busby, London, 1997.
Drury, John. *The Poetry Dictionary*, Writer's Digest, Cincinnati, Ohio, 1995.
Poetry Book Club of Australia, PO Box U34, Wollongong University, Wollongong, NSW 2500 (quarterly newsletter).
Poetry Publishers, NSW Writers' Centre, Sydney, 2000 (brochure).
Purcell, Brian. *Writing for the Poetry Market*, Australian Society of Authors, Sydney, 1998.
Sweeney, Matthew, and Williams, John. *Writing Poetry and Getting Published*, Hodder & Stoughton, London, 1997.
Tunica, Mandy. *For the Love of Poetry*, PETA, Sydney, 1995.
Walker, Brenda (ed.). *The Writer's Reader*, Halstead Press, NSW, 2002.

PUBLIC LENDING RIGHT

Outline of Public Lending Right: Information Paper Prepared to Assist Individuals and Organisations Making Submissions to an Evaluation of the PLR Scheme, Department of Communications and the Arts, Canberra, 1997.

PUBLISHING AND PUBLISHERS

Aprhys, Alison. *Careers in Publishing and Bookselling*, Hale & Iremonger, Sydney, 1997.
Australian Publishers Association Directory of Members, Australian Publishers Association, Sydney, 2001 (published annually).
Cultural Trends in Australia No. 5: Australian Book Publishers, 1995–96, Department of Communications and the Arts, Canberra, 1997.
Derricourt, Robin. *Ideas into Books: A Guide to Scholarly and Non-fiction Publishing*, Penguin Books, Ringwood, Vic., 1996.
Directory of NZ Book Publishers and Distributors, Book Publishers Association of New Zealand, Auckland, 1998.
Introduction to Book Publishing, Australian Publishers Association, Sydney, 1996.
Jefferis, Barbara. *The Good, the Bad and the Greedy: How Australian Publishers Are Rated by Their Authors*, Australian Society of Authors, Sydney, 1989.
Preparing for Publication, NSW Writers' Centre, Sydney, 2000 (brochure).
WiP Directory of Education and Training for the Publishing Industry, Women in Publishing, Sydney, 1997.

RADIO

Horstmann, Rosemary. *Writing for Radio,* A. & C. Black, London, 1997.
Jolley, Elizabeth. *Off the Air,* Penguin Books, Ringwood, Vic., 1995.
Richards, Keith. *Writing Radio Drama,* Currency Press, Sydney, 1991.
Williams, Christopher. *Notes for Radio Dramatists,* ABC Audio Arts, Sydney, 1995.

RATES FOR WRITERS

ASA Rates for Writers and Illustrators, Australian Society of Authors, Sydney, 1998.

REFERENCE WORKS

Abrams, M. H. *A Glossary of Literary Terms,* 7th edn., Harcourt Brace College Publishers, Fort Worth, Texas, 1999.
Australian Books in Print, D. W. Thorpe, Melbourne (published annually).
Australian Booksellers Association of Members/Book Distributors in Australia, Australian Booksellers Association, Melbourne, (published annually).
Book Distributors in Australia, Australian Booksellers Association, Melbourne, 1996.
Burchfield, R. W. (ed.), and Fowler, H. W. *Fowler's Modern English Usage,* Oxford University Press, Oxford, 1995.
Duwell, Martin, Ehrhardt, Marianne, and Hetherington, Carol (eds). *The ALS Guide to Australian Writers: A Bibliography,* 2nd edn, University of Queensland Press, St Lucia, 1997.
Gowers, Sir Ernest. *The Complete Plain Words,* Penguin Books, London, 1987 (1948).
Hart's Rules for Compositors and Readers at the University Press, Oxford, 39th rev. edn, Oxford University Press, Oxford, 1983.

Hudson, Nicholas. *Modern Australian Usage,* rev. edn, Oxford University Press, Melbourne, 1997.
Looking Good: Desktop Publishing, Australian Government Publishing Service, Canberra, 1990.
Macquarie Aboriginal Words, Macquarie Library, Macquarie University, Australia, 1994.
Miller, C., and Swift, K. *The Handbook of Non-Sexist Writing for Writers, Editors and Speakers,* 2nd edn, Harper & Row, New York, 1988.
Murray-Smith, Stephen. *Right Words: A Guide to English Usage in Australia,* 2nd edn, Penguin Books, Ringwood, Vic., 1990.
New Zealand Books in Print, D. W. Thorpe, Melbourne (published annually).
Partridge, E. *Usage and Abusage: A Guide to Good English,* Penguin Books, Harmondsworth, 1985.
Penguin Working Words: An Australian Guide to Modern English Usage, Penguin Books, Ringwood, Vic., 1993.
Peters, Pam. *Cambridge Australian English Style Guide,* Cambridge University Press, Cambridge, 1995.
Pierce, Peter (ed.). *The Oxford Guide to Australian Literature,* Oxford University Press, Melbourne, 1993.
Purchase, S. (ed.). *The Australian Writers' and Editors' Guide,* Oxford University Press, Melbourne, 1991.
Strunk, W. Jr, and White, E. B. *The Elements of Style,* 3rd edn, Macmillan, New York, 1979.
Sturm, Terry (ed.). *Oxford History of New Zealand Literature in English,* Oxford University Press, Auckland, 1998.
Style Manual for Authors, Editors and Printers, 6th edn, John Wiley & Sons Australia, 2002.
Who's Who of Australian Writers, D. W. Thorpe in association with the National Centre for Australian Studies, Melbourne, 1995.

Write Edit Print: Style Manual for Aotearoa New Zealand, Lincoln University Press and Australian Government Publishing Service Press, Canterbury, 1997.

REPORT WRITING

Oliver, Paul. *Writing Essays and Reports,* Hodder & Stoughton, London, 1996.

Stern, George. *Spot On! Correspondence and Report Writing with Guidelines on Plain English,* Australian Government Publishing Service, Canberra, 1996.

REVIEWS

Baldock, Carole. *Writing Reviews,* How-To Books, Plymouth, 1997.

ROMANCE

Falk, K. *How to Write Romance and Get it Published,* Penguin Books, Ringwood, Vic., 1987.

Jacobs, Sherry Anne. *An Introduction to Romance Writing,* TAFE Publications, Perth, 1995.

McRobbie, David. *Head Over Heels: Creative Writing Through Romantic Fiction,* Longman, Melbourne, 1990.

Parv, Valerie. *The Art of Romance Writing,* Allen & Unwin, Sydney, 1993.

ROYALTIES

ASA Recommended Form of Royalty Statement, Australian Society of Authors, Sydney, 1998.

SCIENCE FICTION, FANTASY AND HORROR

See 'Organisations' for Chimaera Publications, a company that specialises in science fiction titles.

Borcherding, David H. (ed.). *Science Fiction and Fantasy Writer's Sourcebook,* 2nd edn, Writer's Digest, Cincinnati, Ohio, 1996.

Bova, Ben. *The Craft of Writing Science Fiction That Sells,* 1st edn, Writer's Digest, Cincinnati, Ohio, 1994.

Card, Orson Scott. *How to Write Science Fiction and Fantasy,* Writer's Digest, Cincinnati, Ohio, 1990.

Dozois, Gardner (ed.). *Writing Science Fiction and Fantasy,* St Martin's Press, New York, 1993.

Jakubowski, Maxim. *The Profession of Science Fiction: SF Writers on Their Craft and Ideas,* St Martin's Press, New York, 1992.

Kenworthy, Christopher. *Writing Science Fiction, Fantasy and Horror: How to Create Successful Work for Publication,* How-To Books, Oxford, 1997.

LeFanu, Sarah. *Writing Fantasy Fiction,* A. & C. Black, Cambridge, 1996.

Ochoa, George. *The Writer's Guide to Creating a Science Fiction Universe,* Writer's Digest Books, Cincinnati, Ohio, 1993.

McRobbie, David. *What if?: Creative Writing Through Science Fiction Stories and Ideas,* Longman Cheshire, Melbourne, 1989 (for secondary students).

Scott, Melissa. *Conceiving the Heavens: Creating the Science Fiction Novel,* Heinemann, Portsmouth, 1991.

Shaw, Bob. *How to Write Science Fiction,* Allison & Busby, London, 1993.

Strahan, Jonathan, and Bryne, Jeremy. *The Year's Best Australian Science Fiction and Fantasy,* HarperCollins Voyager, Sydney, 1997.

Williamson, J. N. *How to Write Tales of Horror, Fantasy and Science Fiction,* Writer's Digest, Cincinnati, Ohio, 1991.

SCREENWRITING

Aronson, Linda. *Scriptwriting Updated: New and Conventional Ways of Writing for the Screen,* Allen & Unwin, Sydney, 2000.

Aronson, Linda. *Television Writing: The Ground Rules of Series, Serials and Sitcom,* Allen & Unwin, Sydney, 2000.

Brady, Ben. *Principles of Adaptation for Film and Television,* University of Texas Press, Austin, Texas, 1994.

Cram, Alan. *How to Write and Sell TV Scripts in Australia and New Zealand,* William Heinemann, Melbourne, 1985.

Dancyger, Ken, and Rush, Jeff. *Alternative Scriptwriting: Writing Beyond the Rules,* Focal Press, Boston, Massachusetts, 1995.

Drouyn, Coral. *Big Screen, Small Screen: A Practical Guide to Writing for Film and TV in Australia,* Allen & Unwin, Sydney, 1994.

Encore, Reed Publishing, Sydney (a directory of personnel working in film and television, their contacts and credits, published annually).

Field, Syd. *Screenplay,* Dell, New York, 1982.

——*The Screenwriters' Workbook,* Dell, New York, 1988.

——*Selling the Screenplay,* Dell, New York, 1989.

——*Four Screenplays: Studies in the American Screenplay,* Dell, New York, 1994.

——*The Screenwriter's Problem Solver,* Dell, New York, 1998.

Froug, William. *Screenwriting Tricks of the Trade,* Silman James, Los Angeles, 1993.

——*Zen and the Art of Screenwriting,* Silman James, Los Angeles, 1997.

Frensham, Raymond G. *Screenwriting,* Hodder Headline, London, 1996.

Goldman, William. *Adventures in the Screen Trade,* Penguin, Ringwood, Vic., 1989.

——*William Goldman: Four Screenplays,* Applause Books, New York, 1996.

——*William Goldman: Five Screenplays,* Applause Books, New York, 1998.

——*Adventures in the Screen Trade,* Warner Books, Hollywood, 1998.

Haddrick, Greg. *Top Shelf 1: Reading and Writing the Best in Australian TV Drama,* Currency Press and the Australian Film, Television and Radio School, 2001.

——*Top Shelf 2: Five Outstanding Television Screenplays,* Currency Press and the Australian Film, Television and Radio Schooll, 2001.

Hauge, Michael. *Writing Screenplays that Sell,* HarperPerennial, New York, 1991.

Hunter, Lew. *Screenwriting 434,* Berkeley Books, New York, 1993.

King, Vicki. *How to Write a Movie in 21 Days,* HarperPerennial, New York, 1987.

Lucey, Paul. *Story Sense: Writing Story and Script for Feature Films and TV,* McGraw Hill, 1996.

Mamet, David. *A Whore's Profession,* Faber & Faber, London, 1995.

Seger, Linda. *Creating Unforgettable Characters,* Henry Holt, New York, 1990.

——*The Art of Adaptation: Fact and Fiction into Film,* Henry Holt, New York, 1991.

——*Making a Good Script Great: A Guide for Writing and Rewriting,* Samuel French, Los Angeles, 1994.

Screenwriting, NSW Writers' Centre, Sydney, 2000 (brochure).

Stuart, Linda. *Getting Your Script Through the Hollywood Maze: An Insider's Guide,* Acrobat, San Francisco, 1992.

Trottier, David. *The Screenwriter's Bible,* Silman James, Los Angeles, 1996.

Vogler, Christopher. *The Writer's Journey: Mythic Structure for Storytellers and Screenwriters,* Michael Wiese Productions, Studio City, California, 1998.

Vorhaus, John. *The Comic Toolbox,* Samuel French, Los Angeles, 1994.

SCRIPTWRITING

Straczynski, Michael. *Complete Book of Scriptwriting*, Writer's Digest, Cincinnati, Ohio, 1996.

SELF-PUBLISHING

Clark, Sherryl. *Successful Self-Publishing*, Hale & Iremonger, Sydney, 1997.
Methold, Ken. *Self-Publishing*, Australian Society of Authors, Sydney, 1995.
Mitchell, Euan. *Self-Publishing Made Simple*, Hardie Grant Books, Melbourne, 2000.
Poynter, Dan. *Self-Publishing Manual*, 9th edn, Parapublishing, Santa Barbara, 1996.
Publish It! A Guide for Self-publishers, D. W. Thorpe, Melbourne, 1998.
Self-publishing, NSW Writers' Centre, Sydney, 2000 (brochure).

SEX

Benedict, Elizabeth. *Joy of Writing Sex*, Writer's Digest, Cincinnati, Ohio, 1996.
Francis, Louisa. *Writing Erotica for Women*, The Oracle Press, Montville, Qld, 1998.

SHORT STORY

Baker, Donna. *How to Write Stories for Magazines*, Allison & Busby, London, 1995.
Lindsay, Hilarie. *The Short Story*, Ansay, Sydney, 1979.
Sheriff, John. *Practical Short Story Writing*, Robert Hale, London, 1995.

SLANG

Blackman, John, and Fyfe, Andrew. *The Best of Aussie Slang: Great Australian Slang and Phrases Explained in Basic English*, Sun Australia, Melbourne, 1995.
Johansen, Lenie Midge. *The Penguin Book of Australian Slang: A Dinkum Guide to Oz English*, Penguin Books, Ringwood, Vic., 1996.
Lambert, James (ed.). *Macquarie Book of Slang: Australian Slang in the 90s*, Macquarie Library, London, 1996.

SPORTS

Kervin, Alison. *Sports Writing*, A. & C. Black, London, 1997.

STORYTELLING

McKay, Helen, and Dudley, Berice. *About Storytelling: A Practical Guide*, Hale & Iremonger, Sydney, 1996.
Sawyer, Ruth. *The Way of the Storyteller*, Bodley Head, London, 1942.

TAX

Tax and Writers, NSW Writers' Centre, Sydney, 2000 (brochure).
Writers and Tax, New Zealand Society of Authors, Auckland, 1998 (brochure).

TEENAGE MARKET

de Gale, Ann. *Writing for the Teenage Market*, A. & C. Black, London, 1993.

TRAVEL WRITING

Peat O'Neil, L. *Travel Writing: A Guide to Research, Writing and Selling*, Writer's Digest, Cincinnati, Ohio, 1996.

WOMEN'S WRITING

Adelaide, Debra. *Bibliography of Australian Women's Literature, 1795–1990*, D. W. Thorpe, Melbourne, Vic., 1991.

Ferres, Kay. *The Time to Write: Australian Women Writers, 1890–1930*, Penguin Books, Ringwood, Vic., 1993.
McNeill, Pearlie. *Because You Want to Write: A Workbook for Women*, Allen & Unwin, Sydney, 1992.

WRITING COURSES

Writing Courses (Non-Degree Courses: Community and Private Colleges, Continuing and Open Education), NSW Writers' Centre, Sydney, 2000 (brochure)
Writing Courses (Degree Courses at Tertiary Institutions in NSW), NSW Writers' Centre, Sydney, 2000 (brochure).

WRITING GROUPS

Heffernan, Erin, Barnes, Frances, and Rundle, Sharon. *Round Table Writing: A Workbook for Writers' Groups*, Watagan Press, Laguna, 1998.

YOUNG WRITERS

Edwards, Hazel, and Alexander, Goldie. *The Business of Writing for Young People*, Hale & Iremonger, Sydney, 1998.
Henderson, Kathy. *Market Guide for Young Writers: Where and How to Sell What You Write*, Writer's Digest Books, Cincinnati, Ohio, 1993.
Opportunities for Young Writers, NSW Writers' Centre, Sydney, 2000 (brochure).
Young Writers Showcase 2001, Board of Studies, NSW, 2001.

CHILDREN AND YOUTH

AUSTRALIA

The following list contains information about magazines and journals (including online journals) specifically for and/or by young people, as well as some for writers and librarians interested in reviews of books for children and youth. Many other publications accept submissions by young people and details of these are available in the NSW Writers' Centre *Journals Directory* (4th edition), which provides comprehensive information about journals, magazines and newspapers accepting fiction and poetry submissions from Australian writers. The directory is available from the NSW Writers' Centre (see 'Organisations').

Publications

All Write!

PO Box 349
Penneshaw SA 5222
Phone/Fax: (08) 8553 7453
Email: allwrite@kin.net.au
Contact: Editor
Aims to provide young writers with an outlet for creative expression, competitions for monetary prizes and some insight into the writing industry through helpful articles on writing and interviews with authors.

Blast Off, Countdown, Orbit, Touchdown

School Magazines (NSW)
Department of Education and Training
PO Box 1928
Macquarie Centre NSW 2113
Phone: (02) 9889 0044
Fax: (02) 9889 0040
Email: schmag@geko.net.au
Website: www.geko.net.au/~schmag
Contact: Editor
Four magazines aimed at various primary school reading levels. Accepts short stories, plays and articles. Contributor guidelines are available on the website or send a stamped, self-addressed envelope. Subscription forms available from the editorial address.

Bookbeat

Children's Book Council
PO Box 765
Rozelle NSW 2039
Phone: (02) 9818 3858
Fax: (02) 9810 0737
Email: nsw@cbc.org.au
Website: www.cbc.org.au
A junior newsletter published by the Children's Book Council for young writers and readers. Primary school age children can submit poetry, book reviews and short pieces.

Comet, Explore, Challenge, Pursuit

Pearson Education Australia
PO Box 1024
South Melbourne VIC 3205
Phone: (03) 9697 0666
Fax: (03) 9699 2041
Email: magazines@pearsoned.com.au
Website: www.longman.com.au/magazines
Contact: Editors
Comet (5–7 years), *Explore* (8–10 years), *Challenge* (11–14 years), *Pursuit* (12–15 years). Fiction, non-fiction, letters, jokes, drawings. Check website for latest guidelines. Also offers Young Aussie Writers' Awards (YAWA) for 5–15 years. Poetry, prose, non-fiction.

dB Young Writers' Page

PO Box 43
Rundle Mall SA 5000
Phone: (08) 8223 7662
Fax: (08) 8232 3994
Email: sawriters@sawriters.on.net
Website: www.sawriters.on.net
Contact: dB Young Writers' Committee
Produced by the SA Writers' Centre, the dB Young Writers' page is published monthly in *dB Magazine*, a free broadsheet aimed at young people. Contributions of poetry, short stories, anecdotes, graphics, cartoons and reviews invited from SA writers aged 25 and under. Send a stamped self-addressed envelope and covering letter with submissions. Payment: poetry to 15 lines $20; poetry over 15 lines $30; prose 10¢ per word up to 1000 words, $30 min.; graphics and cartoons $30 per item. Applicants need to be SA residents.

Dolly

GPO Box 5201
Sydney 1028
Phone: (02) 9282 8437
Fax: (02) 9267 4911
Email: dolly@acp.com.au
Website: ninemsn.com.au/dolly
Contact: Features Editor
A youth magazine dealing with female lifestyle and entertainment issues, for girls 12–19 years. Accepts articles, interviews, poetry and submissions for the 'Short Pieces' page. Guidelines available. Rarely uses freelancers. No payment for 'Short Pieces' page.

Global Wave

Website: www.cs.bilkent.edu.tr/~david/derya/gw
Contact: Editor
An online magazine published by the Young Writers' Club. Produced entirely by children, featuring children's work. Most authors are 7–15 years old. Contributors must be members of the Young Writers' Club. See website for details. Send articles with the online submission form. Prefer non-fiction items about topics of interest to readers around the globe with images and links.

HighFive News

PO Box 367
Wynnum Qld 4178
Phone: (07) 3396 1522
Fax: (07) 3393 5848
Email: raymason@gil.com.au
Contact: Editor
A general children's newspaper, sold through newsagents and tuck shops. Accepts submissions for articles and reviews to 600 words, preferably with pictures. Payment by negotiation with the editor, plus one copy of the publication.

Inscape

PO Box 3058
Auburn Vic 3123

Phone/Fax: (03) 9819 2651
Email: jwinn@ozemail.com.au
Contact: Editor
A national Year 11 and 12 school students' annual literary magazine. Submissions should cover contemporary issues and themes and may be written in experimental or traditional forms. Annual awards for outstanding submissions. Send a stamped self-addressed envelope for contributor guidelines and details of theme and categories.

Jetsetter

PO Box 132
Hampton Vic 3188
Phone/Fax: (03) 9598 2191
Email: margjsmag@bigpond.com.au
Contact: Editor
A bi-monthly magazine for 6–16 year olds. Verse, short stories, personal anecdotes, interviews, sport, music, recipes, drawings, competitions, hobbies, activities for children.

K Zone Magazine

35–51 Mitchell Street
McMahons Point NSW 2060
Phone: (02) 9464 3120
Fax: (02) 9464 3203
Email: k-zone@pacpubs.com.au
Website: www.kzone.com.au
Contact: Editor
A magazine for children 6–13. Covers music, television, videos, books, fads, entertainment, new products, comics, puzzles, exclusive features, interactive competitions, sport, cooking, craft and more. Interested in hearing from experienced children's writers who can produce material appropriate to the readership. Read the publication before sending work. Accepts articles, interviews, fiction, puzzles, graphics. Most material written in-house but looking for fiction, mainly from September to November.

Send full submission in hard copy or include stamped self-addressed envelope.

Katharsis

Email: Webmaster@Katharsis.org
Website: www.katharsis.org
Contact: Webmaster
An online ezine for young writers. Includes fiction, poetry, forums, articles, exercises and a book club.

Lowdown

11 Jeffcott Street
North Adelaide SA 5006
Phone: (08) 8267 5111
Fax: (08) 8239 0689
Email: lowdown@carclew.org.au
Website: www.carclew.on.net
Contact: Editor
A youth performing arts magazine. Contact editor before submitting articles or reviews on youth arts, political issues affecting the youth arts industry and profiles on young artists. Mainly commissions experienced writers but also endeavours to attract new writers, in particular young people just starting their writing careers.

Magpies Magazine

PO Box 98
Grange Qld 4051
Phone: (07) 3356 4503
Fax: (07) 3356 4649
Email: james@magpies.net.au
Website: www.magpies.net.au
Contact: Editor
A magazine about books for children. Accepts author and illustrator profiles, reviews, articles and thematic bibliographies. Submission information on the website. Payment by negotiation. Includes a New Zealand Supplement.

Midlink Magazine

SAS Campus Drive
Cary NC USA 27513
Email: midlink@sas.com
Website: longwood.cs.ucf.edu:80/~MidLink
Contact: Instructional Technologist
An online magazine by students, for students 8–18 years. Highlights exemplary work from the most creative classrooms around the globe. Detailed guidelines on the website.

One Talk

PO Box 576
Palm Beach Qld 4221
Phone: (07) 5598 4603
Fax: (07) 5598 4605
Email: onetalk@ppau.com.au
Website: www.ppau.com.au
Contact: Editor
A magazine that attempts to bridge cultures through art and literature. Published by the Pacific Cultural Heritage Society. Contributions of writing from 10–18 year olds. Ideal story length to 850 words, other items to 500 words. Contributions must be accompanied by student and school details.

Viewpoint: On Books for Young Adults

Box 4286
University of Melbourne
Parkville Vic 3052
Phone: (03) 9344 8617
Fax: (03) 9344 0025
Email: viewpoint@edfac.unimelb.edu.au
Website: www.edfac.unimelb.edu.au/LLAE/viewpoint/
Contact: Editor
Contains reviews and articles about young adult fiction, authors and readers. Interested in young adult fiction, poetry and non-fiction. Accepts articles, interviews and reviews from 600 to 2000 words. Contributor guidelines available. Include a stamped, self-addressed envelope.

Voiceworks

Express Media
1st Floor 156 George Street
Fitzroy Vic 3065
Phone: (03) 9416 3305
Fax: (03) 9419 3365
Email: editor@expressmedia.org.au
Website: www.expressmedia.org.au
Contact: Editor
A magazine featuring work entirely written, illustrated and designed by young people. Contributors must be under 25 years of age. Accepts features, fiction, poetry, interviews and opinions up to 2000 words, and illustrations, comics and photographs. Each issue has a separate theme. Call for details and deadlines before submitting work. Guidelines available on the website.

Youth writing awards and competitions

The listing below includes annual competitions either specifically for young writers, or with sections for school-aged writers. In addition to these competitions, there are many more that do not specify an age group. Young writers are not excluded although they would be competing against adult writers in 'open' categories. Writers' centres' newsletters and magazines list up-coming competitions.

ABC Central West Banjo Paterson Children's Writing Awards

ABC Central West
PO Box 863
Orange NSW 2800
Phone: (02) 6393 2511
Fax: (02) 6393 2599
Email: orange.regional@abc.net.au
Website: www.abc.net.au/centralwest

Children and Youth

Competition for children 16 years and under. Send a stamped self-addressed envelope for entry forms and conditions.

Clarissa Stein Multicultural Poetry Prize

Contact: Coordinator
Papyrus Publishing
C/- PO Scarsdale Vic 3351
Phone: (03) 5342 2394
Fax: (03) 5342 2423
Email: editor@papyrus.com.au
Website: www.papyrus.com.au
Section for Open Poetry Youth (14 –17 years). Send a stamped self-addressed envelope for entry forms. Entries close July.

Dorothea Mackellar Poetry Awards

Contact: Executive Officer
PO Box 113
Gunnedah NSW 2380
Phone: (02) 6740 2233
Fax: (02) 6740 2237
Email: dorothea@northnet.com.au
Website: www.dorothea.com.au
A competition with an annual topic. Categories are: final certificate year, secondary, primary, and special awards. State/Territory winners receive a prize as well as national winners. Entry forms from February/March from above address. Entries close June.

Eastern Regional Libraries Story Writing Competition

Contact: Youth Services
511 Burwood Highway
Wantirna South Vic 3152
Phone: (03) 9298 8444
Fax: (03) 9298 8424
Email: jill@eastern.erl.vic.gov.au
Website: www.erl.vic.gov.au
Short story writing competition (to 3000 words). Sections include teenage (13–18 years) and junior (9–12 years). Send a stamped self-addressed envelope for entry form. Entries close September.

EJ Brady Short Story Competition

Contact: Competition Co-ordinator
PO Box 201
Mallacoota Vic 3892
Phone: (03) 5158 0890
Fax: (03) 5158 0985
Email: info@mallacootafestival.org
Website: www.mallacootafestival.org
Short stories to 3000 words. No set theme. Youth categories (under 18 years). Send a stamped self-addressed envelope for entry form. Entries close March.

Fellowship of Australian Writers (Vic) Awards

Contact: National Literary Awards Co-ordinator
Fellowship of Australian Writers (Vic)
PO Box 3036
Ripponlea Vic 3183
Phone/Fax: (03) 9528 7088
Website: www.writers.asn.au
Send a stamped self-addressed envelope for entry forms and guidelines after August, or download from the website. All the following competitions close end of October:
FAW Alan Marshall Short Story Award. For 10–14 year olds. No word limit.
FAW CJ Dennis Poetry Award. For 10–14 year olds.
FAW Colin Thiele Poetry Award. For 15–20 year olds.
FAW John Morrison Short Story Award. For 15–20 year olds. No word limit.
FAW Mavis Thorpe Clark Creative Writing Award. Open to secondary school students. All kinds of writing eligible. Work must be original and written in the year of entry. Part 1: for individuals—at least 10 pieces of work required. Part 2:

for a group of students attending the same secondary school—15 to 20 pieces required.
FAW Adele Shelton Smith Award/Di Cranston Award. Awards for a stage play, radio or television script for 18–25 year olds.

FAW (NSW) Hilarie Lindsay Young Writers Award

Contact: Development Officer
Fellowship of Australian Writers (NSW)
PO Box 488
Rozelle NSW 2039
Phone: (02) 9810 1307
Fax: (02) 9810 1307
Email: faw@ozemail.com.au
Website: www.writers.asn.au
A short story competition in four sections: year 4 and under, years 5 and 6, years 7–9 and years 10–12. Send a stamped self-addressed envelope for entry forms, or download from the website. Entries close September.

Greater Dandenong National Writing Awards

Contact: Competition Co-ordinator
City of Greater Dandenong
PO Box 200
Springvale Vic 3171
Phone: (03) 9239 5141
Fax: (03) 9239 5196
Email: cultural.development@cgd.vic.gov.au
Website: www.greaterdandenong.com
Categories include Young Writers Awards: Junior (8–13 years), stories to 500 words, and Youth (14–18 years), stories to 1000 words. Poetry Award youth section: Under 18 years, poems to 36 lines, open theme. For competition guidelines, email, phone or visit the website. Send a stamped self-addressed envelope for entry form. Entries close mid year.

Grenfell Henry Lawson Festival of Arts Awards

Contact: Secretary, Grenfell Henry Lawson Festival
PO Box 77
Grenfell NSW 2810
Phone: (02) 6343 1284
Email: knappdm@tpg.com.au
Two sections: verse and short story, all on an Australian subject. Category for verse by author under 18 years and short story by author under 18 years. Send a stamped self-addressed envelope for entry forms. Entries close March.

Henry Kendall Poetry Award

Contact: Central Coast Poets
PO Box 276
Gosford 2250
Phone: (02) 4362 1662
Email: hawthorn@turboweb.net.au
Open theme, maximum 32 lines. All styles of poetry accepted. Sections include for 13–18 year olds and for 12 year olds and under. Competition followed by an anthology. Send a stamped self-addressed envelope for entry forms. Biennial competition, held in even years.

Henry Lawson Literary Awards

Contact: Secretary
Henry Lawson Society of NSW
PO Box 235
Gulgong NSW 2852
Phone: (02) 6374 2049
Email: brown235@hn.ozemail.com.au
Categories include the Noeline Gaudry Memorial Student Performance Poetry Award, and the Henry Lawson Student Literary Awards for poetry (years 3–6) and short story (years 7–10). Send a stamped self-addressed envelope for entry forms

Children and Youth

and guidelines. Entries close April, announced June.

Laura Literary Awards

Contact: Co-ordinator
PO Box 18
Laura SA 5480
Phone: (08) 8662 2340
Competition held as part of the Laura Folk Fair. The Flinders News Prose Awards (for short story): open section to 1500 words; young adult section (13–18 years) to 1000 words; junior section (to 12 years) to 500 words. CJ Dennis Poetry Award: young adult (13–18 years) and junior section (to 12 years), both up to 60 lines. Entries close mid-February. Send a stamped self-addressed envelope for entry form.

Margaret Connah Bequest Young Adult Poetry Competition

36 Foxglove Street
Mt Gravatt East Qld 4122
Website: www.writers.asn.au
Open to entrants 16–25. Poetry to 60 lines. Forms available on the website. Entries close September.

Maxwell Lakeman & Kerry Wright Poetry Competition

Contact: Competition Organiser
North Shore FAW
PO Box 716
Turramurra NSW 2074
Phone: (02) 9940 3773
Competition in two sections: over 18 and under 10 years. Send a stamped self-addressed envelope for competition guidelines. Entries close September.

Mentor Writing Competition

Children's Book Council (NSW)
Mentor Program
PO Box 765
Rozelle NSW 2039
Phone: (02) 9818 3858
Fax: (02) 9810 1307
Email: nsw@cbc.org.au
Website: www.cbc.org.au
An annual competition for school students and adults in NSW who have not been published professionally. Subject: any text material written for children of any age (no illustrations). Prizes include cash, the opportunity to work with a published author on the text, and evaluation of the work by a professional editor. Send a stamped self-addressed envelope for entry forms. Entries close end of May.

Nescafe Big Break

Phone: 1800 630 630
Email: theManager@nescafe.com.au
Website: www.nescafe.com.au
Grant program for ages 16–24. This is not an achievement award and there are no categories. Can apply for anything from wanting to start a business to writing a film. Any form of writing considered. In 2001, eight awards of $20 000 and ten awards of $2000. Entries accepted from individuals or groups. Phone for guidelines. Entry forms available after March. Entries close end of August.

Nestle Write Around Australia

Contact: Co-ordinator
Community Programs
State Library of NSW
Macquarie Street
Sydney NSW 2000
Phone: (02) 9273 1610
Fax: (02) 9273 1248

Email: vnoake@slnsw.gov.au
Website: www.writearound.com.au
A national writing competition for senior primary school students. 500-word story on any topic. Finalists invited to an extended workshop with a published author. Prizes include certificates, Nestle products, books and computers. Winning stories, writing tips, author information and entry forms on the website. Entry forms also available from public libraries and school from March. Entries close May.

Queensland Theatre Company Young Playwrights' Awards

PO Box 310
South Brisbane Qld 4101
Phone: (07) 3840 7000
Fax: (07) 3840 7040
Email: JCharlton@qldtheatreco.com.au
Website: www.qldtheatreco.com.au
Contact: Jodie Charlton
Annual awards for under 25s in four different age categories. Held as a platform for youth to speak out and be heard. Winners receive cash prizes, books, memberships and professional development of their script. The winning plays are presented as part of the Brisbane Writers Festival. Open to Queensland residents only. Free writing workshops are held in Brisbane for students and teachers. Online dramaturgy is available for regional Queenslanders. Further details on the website.

Somerset National Novella Writing Competition

Contact: Bambi Price
Somerset College
Somerset Drive
Mudgeeraba Qld 4213
Phone: (07) 5530 3777
Fax: (07) 5525 2676
Email: bprice@somerset.qld.edu.au
Website: www.somerset.qld.edu.au
Open to all current secondary school students attending school in Australia aged under 19 years. Send a stamped self-addressed envelope for competition guidelines and entry form. Novellas should be 10 000 to 20 000 words. State finalists are flown to Somerset College for the Somerset Celebration of Literature where the national winner is announced. (See Workshops, Festivals and Events section.)

Sydney Morning Herald Young Writer of the Year Award

Contact: Fairfax Education
Fairfax Publications
GPO Box 506
Sydney NSW 2001
Phone: (02) 9282 1946
Fax: (02) 9282 3703
Email: amann@mail.fairfax.com.au
A competition for senior secondary students in NSW and the ACT. Original short story (700–1000 words) written in the year of the competition. Open theme. Entries open April and close June. Winners announced August.

Sydney Theatre Company Young Playwrights Award

Contact: Manager—Education
PO Box 777
Millers Point NSW 2000
Phone: (02) 9250 1700
Fax: (02) 9251 3687
Email: education@sydneytheatre.com.au
Website: www.sydneytheatre.com.au
For NSW and ACT secondary school students, 19 years of age or under. One winner from Year 7–10 and one from Year 11 and above. Cash prize plus a two-day workshop of script with a staged reading at the Wharf Theatre. Merit awards also

presented in each category at judges' discretion. Entries close July/August.

TalentEd 'Interview with a Scientist' Competition

Contact: Stan Bailey
School of Education
University of New England
Armidale NSW 2351
Phone: (02) 6773 3832
Fax: (02) 6773 5078
Email: sbailey@metz.une.edu.au
Website: scs.une.edu.au/TalentEd/
500–3000 words based on a report of an interview with a scientist. Junior, intermediate and senior awards. Entries close September.

Western Union Young Writing Competition

7 Muirhead Crescent
Werribee Vic 3030
Phone: (03) 9741 3577
Email: margaret_c@optusnet.com
An annual competition with three age groups in both poetry and stories: 10 and under, 11–14 years and 15–18 years. Imagination Creation Trophy awarded to the best class entry from a primary school (stories or poems). Wyndham Books Award for a secondary school-age student's folio of writing. Send a stamped self-addressed envelope for entry form. Winning and selected short-listed entries published. Entries close towards the end of the year.

Wimmera Short Story Competition

Mibus Centre, Wimmera Regional Library
28 McLachland Street
Horsham Vic 3400
Phone: (03) 5382 1777
Fax: (03) 5382 0727
Email: library@wrlc.org.au
Website: www.wrlc.org.au
Sections include teenage (13–18 years) to 3000 words and junior (8–12 years) to 1000 words. Open section to 5000 words. Send a stamped self-addressed envelope for entry form. Entries close May (subject to change).

Woorilla Magazine Annual Poetry Competition

Woorilla Magazine
255 Macclesfield Road
Avonsleigh Vic 3782
Phone: (03) 5968 4291
Fax: (03) 5968 4152
Email: woorilla@nex.net.au
Includes junior section (to 18 years). Poems to 50 lines, reflecting the Dandenongs. Must be original, unpublished and not have won a prize. Send entry with contact details on a cover sheet and a stamped self-addressed envelope. Entries close September.

World Peace Bell Association Poetry Competition

Australian Chapter of The World Peace Bell Association
12 Kendall Street
Cowra NSW 2794
Phone: (02) 6342 2975
Fax: (02) 6341 1217
Sponsored by Rural Press through *The Cowra Guardian*. Sections include: Primary school student (to 10 lines) and secondary school student (to 20 lines). Local section for primary and secondary students. Winning poems read at World Peace Day Ceremony in Cowra in September. Send a stamped self-addressed envelope for entry form. Entries close August.

The Writer's Guide

Young Aussie Writers' Awards

Pearson Education Australia
PO Box 1024
South Melbourne VIC 3205
Phone: (03) 9697 0666
Fax: (03) 9699 2041
Email: magazines@pearsoned.com.au
Website: www.longman.com.au/magazines
Open nationwide to 5–14 year olds. Winners publicised in Victorian school magazines. Submit stories, articles, plays, poems, reports, comics, cartoons and song lyrics. Entry forms available in *Comet*, *Explore* and *Challenge* magazines or on the website. Entries close 30 June.

Festivals, workshops and organisations for young writers

Australian National Playwrights Centre National Young Playwrights Weekend

PO Box 1566
Rozelle NSW 2039
Phone: (02) 9555 9377
Fax: (02) 9555 9370
Email: info@anpc.org.au
Website: www.anpc.org.au
Runs weekend workshops for people aged 25 years and under. Held in nine capital cities every two years.

Australian Theatre for Young People

The Wharf Pier
4/5 Hickson Road
Walsh Bay NSW 2000
Phone: (02) 9251 3900
Fax: (02) 9251 3909
Email: atyp@atyp.com.au
Website: www.atyp.com.au
Conducts workshops for young people to 25 years in drama/acting, playwrighting, directing, design and lighting. Scholarships available.

Books North—the North Qld Children's Literature Festival

CBC North Qld
C/- Young People's Librarian
Aitkenvale Library
PO Box 132
Aitkenvale Qld 4810
Phone: (07) 4727 8314
Fax: (07) 4727 8936
Email: mrh@townsville.qld.gov.au
Held bi-annually in the Townsville region, in odd-numbered years.

Carclew Youth Arts Centre

11 Jeffcott Street
North Adelaide SA 5006
Phone: (08) 8267 5111
Fax: (08) 8239 0689
Email: carclew@carclew.org.au
Website: www.carclew.on.net
Projects feature courses, training, exhibitions and performances in the arts, including literature.

Children's Book Week

C/- Children's Book Council of Australia (WA)
PO Box 473
West Perth WA 6872
Email: wa@cbc.org.au
Website: www.cbc.org.au

Geelong Children's Book Festival

C/- Children's Book Council (Geelong Branch)
265 Curlewis Road RSD

Children and Youth

Drysdale Vic 3222
Phone: (03) 5250 3194
Fax: (03) 5221 8270
Email: janeparsons@bigpond.com
Website: www.bigpond.com/bookfestival/
Held annually during Book Week in August.

International Board on Books for Young People (Australia)

Unit 1, 85 Yarranabbe Road
Darling Point NSW 2027
Phone: (02) 9363 5075
Email: enanoelibby@hotmail.com

Interplay—International Festival of Young Playwrights

PO Box 2021
Townsville Qld 4810
Phone: (07) 4781 5454, 4781 4993
Fax: (07) 4781 5454
Email: interplay@jcu.edu.au
Website: www.jcu.edu.au/school/comvat/interplay/html
International biennial festival for playwrights aged 18–25. Delegates work with Australian and overseas theatre, film and television professionals. July/August. Brochures and application forms available from the Interplay office or the website.

National Young Writers Festival

Phone: (02) 4927 1475
Fax: (02) 4927 0470
Email: national@youngwritersfestival.org
Website: www.octapod.org.au/nywf/
Part of the 'This is not art' Festival, which attracts over 3000 media makers, writers and creators. Held over five days. Includes discussion panels, workshops, performances and launches.

NSW Association of Gifted and Talented Children

Hilltop Public School
Hilltop Road
Merrylands NSW 2160
Phone: (02) 9633 5399
Fax: (02) 9633 5799
Email: office@nswagtc.org.au
Website: www.nswagtc.org.au
Runs seminars and workshops for gifted children, some of which may include writing activities.

Queensland Theatre Company

Contact: Jodie Charlton
PO Box 310
South Brisbane Qld 4101
Phone: (07) 3840 7000
Fax: (07) 3840 7040
Email: JCharlton@qldtheatreco.com.au
Website: www.qldtheatreco.com.au
Free writing workshops are held in Brisbane for students and teachers. Online dramaturgy is available for regional Queenslanders. Further details on the website.

Shopfront Theatre

88 Carlton Parade
Carlton NSW 2218
Phone: (02) 9588 3948
Fax: (02) 9588 6545
Email: sfront@matra.com.au
Contact: General Manager
Offers support for playwrights aged 8–25 years with workshopping of scripts, and provides newsletters throughout the year.

Somerset College Celebration of Literature

Somerset College
Somerset Drive

Mudgeeraba Qld 4213
Phone: (07) 5530 3777
Fax: (07) 5525 2676
Email: bprice@somerset.qld.edu.au
Website: somerset.qld.edu.au
Contact: Bambi Price
A five-day writers' festival held in March each year. Caters for all ages, from beginner readers to older readers and includes writers from all genres. Activities include meet the author, panel discussions and debates, storytelling, workshops and readings. Winner of the Somerset National Novella Competition announced at the Literary Dinner (see Competitions section).

Voices on the Coast, Youth Literature Festival

C/- Immanuel Lutheran College
Wises Road
Maroochydore Qld 4558
Phone: (07) 5477 3444
Email: voices@immanuel.qld.edu.au
Website: www.immanuel.qld.edu.au/voices/
For south-east Queensland students. Allows students access to authors, poets and performers from all over Australia. Workshops, book talks, storytelling, poetry and drama. Held annually at the University of the Sunshine Coast each autumn/early winter.

NEW ZEALAND

Publications, journals and radio programs

Around the Bookshops

Marigold Enterprises
Box 22 180
Khandallah
Wellington
Phone/Fax: (04) 479 5538
Email: barbaram@clear.net.nz
Aimed primarily at school librarians. Titles selected on the basis of being 'current, appropriate and available'. Short, critical annotations. Themes and year levels indicated for all titles. General information, news, events, authors, awards etc.

Magpies Magazine (New Zealand)

Jabberwocky Children's Bookshop
202 Dominion Road
Mt Eden
Auckland
Phone: (09) 630 6827
Fax: (09) 630 6809
Email: kidsbooks@jabberwocky.co.nz
Website: www.magpies.net.au
Contact: Editor
A magazine about books for children. Eight-page New Zealand supplement in the Australian edition of the magazine. Accepts author and illustrator profiles, reviews, articles and thematic bibliographies. Submission information on the website. Payment by negotiation.

New Zealand Children's Books in Print

PO Box 56–278
Auckland
Phone/Fax: (09) 620 5459
Email: nzcbip@allsorts.co.na
A fully annotated listing of children's and educational books published in New Zealand. Updated annually, the catalogue is an invaluable resource for teachers and librarians maintaining collections of New Zealand children's literature and seeking locally produced teaching resources. Includes comprehensive listings of Maori and Pacific Island publications for children.

Radio New Zealand Storytime

Producer/Presenter
Radio New Zealand

Children and Youth

PO Box 123
Wellington
Email: plangbein@radionz.co.nz
Radio New Zealand runs a New Zealand children's story on Storytime each weeknight at 6.45 pm with an omnibus edition on Sunday mornings between 6–7. Storytime accepts original imaginative stories by New Zealand authors of 4–10 minutes' duration. They should be typed and double spaced. Previously published work accepted (include details of where and when published).

Reading Forum

C/- Joan Gibbons
Education Library
University of Waikato
Private Bag 3105
Hamilton
New Zealand
Phone: (07) 838 4500 ext 7829
Fax: (07) 838 4515
Email: joang@waikato.ac.nz
The official newsletter of the New Zealand Reading Association.

School Journal

Learning Media
PO Box 3293
Wellington 6001
Phone: (04) 472 5522
Fax: (04) 472 6444
Email: info@learningmedia.co.nz
Website: www.learningmedia.co.nz
Published regularly at four different reading levels. Features New Zealand fiction, non-fiction, poetry and drama for children.

Talespinner

C/- Christchurch College of Education
PO Box 31–065
Christchurch
Phone: (03) 343 7746
Fax: (03) 343 7731
Email: doreen.darnell@cce.ac.nz
A 60-page journal of research in children's literature, including general articles and resources for teachers, librarians, parents and anyone with an interest in children and their books. Published twice yearly.

Too Good to Miss

PO Box 22 180
Khandallah
Wellington
Ph/Fax: 04 479 5538
Email: barbaram@clear.net.nz
Published annually in May. Covers the best of children's literature in a particular genre each year (e.g. 2001 New Zealand Children's Books, 2002 Stories to Read Aloud).

Well Read

PO Box 56 278
Auckland
Phone/Fax: (09) 620 5459
Email: wellread@allsorts.co.nz
A bi-monthly journal of reviews of children's books, fiction, non-fiction and poetry, news of books and writers, notice of up-coming visits by overseas children's authors, illustrators and publishers.

Festivals and events

New Zealand Post Children's Book Festival

Booksellers New Zealand
PO Box 11–377
Wellington
Phone: (04) 472 8678
Fax: (04) 472 8628
Email: heathergatley@booksellers.co.nz
Website: www.booksellers.co.nz
Aims to reinforce the importance of reading for children, illustrating the range

and quality of children's books and focusing on New Zealand's cultural identity through literature. Two weeks in April every year. Incorporates *New Zealand Post* Children's Book Awards.

Storylines Festival of New Zealand Children's Writers and Illustrators

PO Box 28–665
Remuera
Auckland
Phone: (09) 522 6822, 0274 599 980
Fax: (09) 522 6825
Email: robin.h@xtra.co.nz
Website: www.clfnz.org.nz/storylines/events/storylines_festival
Aims to celebrate and promote New Zealand children's writers, illustrators and storytellers. Established by the Children's Literature Foundation of New Zealand. Held annually in June.

CHILDREN'S BOOK PUBLISHERS

AUSTRALIA

ABC Books

GPO Box 9994
Sydney NSW 2001
Phone: (02) 9950 3964
Fax: (02) 9950 3888
Email: abcbooks@your.abc.net.au
Website: shop.abc.net.au
Publishes children's fiction and non-fiction books and tapes related to ABC programs, as well as a separate trade list of high quality children's fiction and non-fiction unconnected to ABC programs. Manuscripts should be clearly typed with double spacing. Send a copy of your work with a stamped self-addressed envelope. Evaluation: 6 weeks.

AIATSIS—Aboriginal Studies Press

Archives and Production
GPO Box 533
Canberra ACT 2601
Phone: (02) 6246 1184
Fax: (02) 6249 7310
Email: dfh@aiatsis.gov.au
Website: www.aiatsis.gov.au
Publishes all books relating to Aboriginal and Torres Strait Islander studies, including academic, literature, biographical and children's stories, music, videos and CD-ROMs. Send only complete manuscripts in hard copy and disk format with illustrations. Evaluation: up to 4 months.

Allen & Unwin

East Melbourne Vic 3002
Phone: (03) 9665 5000
Fax: (03) 9665 5050
Email: info@allenandunwin.com.au
Website: www.allenandunwin.com.au
Specialises in children's books. Publishes illustrated picture books, junior novels and young adult novels. Occasionally publishes non-fiction. Unsolicited manuscripts considered for junior fiction (minimum 10 000 words) and young adult fiction only. No unsolicited picture book texts. Send a stamped self-addressed envelope with the full submission for fiction work or proposal and detailed chapter outline for non-fiction. Evaluation: 3–4 months.

Benchmark Publications Management

PO Box 71
Montrose Vic 3765
Phone: (03) 9761 8133
Fax: (03) 9761 8144
Email: benchm@smart.net.au
Specialises in children's picture books, natural history and history. Unsolicited manuscripts considered. Phone first to

285

discuss proposal. Also produces the publishing list for University of Western Australia.

Era Publications

220 Grange Road
Flinders Park SA 5025
Phone: (08) 8352 4122
Fax: (08) 8234 0023
Email: editor@erapublications.com.au
Website: www.erapublications.com.au
Publishes children's picture books, children's novels up to 2000 words, and Big Books of fiction and non-fiction. Most books published are commissioned. First submission should be by emailed synopsis only. Materials should be submitted only following a response to an email synopsis. Mostly seeking manuscripts to fit 'Magic Bean K–2' and 'Junior Novel' lists. Future communication via website. Manuscripts (on disk) should be accompanied by a stamped self-addressed envelope with return postage. No additional material is required. Evaluation: 4–8 weeks.

The Five Mile Press

22 Summit Road
Noble Park Vic 3174
Phone: (03) 9790 5000
Fax: (03) 9790 6888
Email: maggie@fivemile.com.au
Specialises in adult non-fiction and children's picture books (no children's novels). Accepts unsolicited manuscripts. Guidelines available. Send proposal, sample chapters and resumé. Enclose a stamped self-addressed envelope for return of work. Evaluation: up to 10 weeks.

Fremantle Arts Centre Press

PO Box 158
North Fremantle WA 6159
Phone: (08) 9430 6331
Fax: (08) 9430 5242
Email: facp@iinet.net.au
Website: www.facp.iinet.net.au
Publishes Western Australian writers and artists, and non-fiction works with a strong WA focus. Children's picture books and young adult fiction published under the Sandcastle Books imprint. Accepts unsolicited manuscripts. Guidelines available from the publisher or on the website. Evaluation: up to 3 months.

Golden Press (see HarperCollins)

Greater Glider Productions

Book Farm
330 Reesville Road
Maleny Qld 4552
Phone: (07) 5494 3000
Fax: (07) 5494 3284
Email: jillmorris@greaterglider.com
Website: www.greaterglider.com
Publishes children's books and multimedia. Send one-page letter outlining the project and a stamped self-addressed envelope for response. Only high-quality, well-considered and fully developed projects. Evaluation: up to 2 months, depending on potential.

Halstead Press

19a Boundary Street
Rushcutters Bay NSW 2011
Phone: (02) 9360 7866
Fax: (02) 9332 4663
Email: halsteadpress@bigpond.net.au
Phone to discuss relevance of manuscripts. Mostly interested in literary fiction for 8–12-year-olds, but will consider other works. Evaluation: 1–3 months.

Children's Book Publishers

HarperCollins Publishers (Australia)

PO Box 321
Pymble NSW 2073
Phone: (02) 9952 5000
Fax: (02) 9952 5444
Email: luciecrowhurst@harpercollins.com.au
Website: www.harpercollins.com.au
Publishes children's books for ages 7–8 and upwards. All submissions via agent or recommended by a published author, or with a report from an assessment body or workshop/course coordinator. Do not send unsolicited manuscripts. Submit typed synopsis with intended age level, author details, sample chapter and chapter storylines for longer novels. Under the Golden Press imprint, HarperCollins publishes licensed character books, activity books, story books, sight'n'sound books and book'n'tape product for juveniles. All work is commissioned. Send outlines only. Do not send unsolicited manuscripts. Evaluation: 3 months minimum.

Hodder Headline Australia

Level 22, 201 Kent Street
Sydney NSW 2000
Phone: (02) 8248 0800
Fax: (02) 8248 0810
Email: auspub@hha.com.au
Website: www.hha.com.au
Only considers work sent through an agent or that which is commissioned. Publishes fiction, children's to 15 years and non-fiction. Do not send unsolicited manuscripts.

Hyland House Publishing

PO Box 122
Flemington Vic 3031
Phone/Fax: (03) 9376 4461
Email: hyland3@netspace.net.au
Specialises in young adult fiction, and adult non-fiction. Contact the publisher before submitting manuscript proposals. Must include a stamped self-addressed envelope with proposal. Evaluation: 3–6 months.

IAD Press/Jukurrpa Books

PO Box 2531
Alice Springs NT 0871
Phone: (08) 8951 1334
Fax: (08) 8952 2527
Email: publisheriad@ozemail.com.au
IAD Press is the publishing arm of the Aboriginal-controlled Institute for Aboriginal Development. Art, fiction and children's books by Aboriginal authors (or collaborative projects) published under the Jukurrpa imprint. Guidelines available. Send proposal and sample chapters. Evaluation: 6 weeks.

irrePRESSible Press

4 Sunnybar Parade
Queanbeyan NSW 2620
Phone: 02 6299 6875
Email: cambrus@goldweb.com.au
Website: www.irrepressible.com.au
Phone first to discuss proposal. Writers may contribute to production costs.

Koala Books

PO Box 626
Mascot NSW 2020
Phone: (02) 9667 2997
Fax: (02) 9667 2881
Email: admin@koalabooks.com.au
Website: www.koalabooks.com.au
Publishes children's fiction and non-fiction, picture books and bridging books. Specialises in high-quality books for under–10s. Unsolicited typed manuscripts accepted with a stamped self-addressed envelope, but prefers manuscripts via an agent. New writers should have their manuscripts professionally appraised. Do not send email submissions. Illustrators should send portfolio. Evaluation: 3 months.

Little Hare Books

4/21 Mary Street
Surry Hills NSW 2010
Phone: (02) 9280 2220
Fax: (02) 9280 2223
An independent children's publishing house specialising in early childhood, picture books and literary fiction. Manuscripts should be typed and double spaced. Please enclose a stamped self-addressed envelope. Evaluation: 6 weeks.

Lothian Books

Level 5, 132–136 Albert Road
South Melbourne Vic 3205
Phone: (03) 9694 4900
Fax: (03) 9645 0705
Email: books@lothian.com.au
Website: www.lothian.com.au
Publishes juvenile books. Children's picture book format is 32 pages. Enclose sufficient postage for the manuscript to be returned certified mail. No multiple submissions. Evaluation: about 6–8 weeks.

Macmillan Education Australia

Locked Bag 1
Prahran Vic 3181
Phone: (03) 9825 1000
Fax: (03) 9825 1010
Email: mea@macmillan.com.au
Website: www.macmillan.com.au
Macmillan Education Australia (Primary Division) publishes core subject texts, blackline masters, teacher resource books, science, maths and SOSE programs, library and reference books, and some reading programs for all primary school levels.

Magabala Books

PO Box 668
Broome WA 6729
Phone: (08) 9192 1991
Fax: (08) 9193 5254
Email: info@magabala.com.au
Website: www.magabala.com.au
Publishes children's books written by Aboriginals and Torres Strait Islanders. Prefers a query letter first with an outline, brief biographical information, samples and breakdown of material available, if any, including artwork and photos. Do not send full manuscript. Evaluation: 3 months.

Mimosa Publications

8 Yarra Street
Hawthorn Vic 3122
Phone: (03) 9819 0511
Fax: (03) 9819 0524
Email: info@mimosapub.com.au
Specialises in fiction and non-fiction for primary school children. All publications sold to international markets. Send proposal, sample chapters or the full manuscript. Evaluation: 2 weeks.

Murdoch Books

GPO Box 1203
Sydney NSW 1045
Phone: (02) 8220 2365
Fax: (02) 8220 2558
Publishes Cocky's Circle Children's Series: 24-page children's picture paperbacks for years 1–6. Contact for guidelines before submitting work. Evaluation: 1–3 months.

Nightingale Press

PO Box 547
Warners Bay NSW 2282
Phone: (02) 4954 3688
Fax: (02) 4954 3699
Email: pauln@nightingale-press.com.au
Website: www.nightingale-press.com.au
Publishes educational texts in key learning areas of school curriculum. Present manuscript as book as it is to be seen as a finished product. Material must be activity-type books that relate to the school curriculum. Evaluation: 6–8 weeks.

Children's Book Publishers

Omnibus Books (Imprint of Scholastic)

52 Fullarton Road
Norwood SA 5067
Phone: (08) 8363 2333
Fax: (08) 8363 1420
Email: omnibus@scholastic.com.au
Website: www.scholastic.com.au
Publishes fiction and non-fiction in the children's and adolescent book categories. Send outline and sample chapters. Guidelines available. Evaluation: 6–8 weeks.

Pan Macmillan Australia

Level 18, St Martins Tower
31 Market Street
Sydney NSW 2000
Phone: (02) 9285 9100
Fax: (02) 9285 9190
Email: pansyd@panmacmillan.com.au
Website: www.macmillan.com.au
Publishes children's fiction and non-fiction, but not picture books. Obtain submission guidelines for further information. All primary submissions handled by the New Zealand office. Send proposal and sample chapters with a stamped self-addressed envelope to Private Bag 102970, North Shore Mail Centre 1333, 6 Ride Way, Albany, Auckland, phone (64) 9 415 6670 and fax (64) 9 414 2368.

Penguin Books Australia

250 Camberwell Road
Camberwell Vic 3124
Phone: (03) 9811 2400
Fax: (03) 9811 2620
Website: www.penguin.com.au
Obtain a copy of guidelines from the website or from the publisher before sending any work. Unsolicited manuscripts considered, but prefers manuscripts via an agent. Submit proposal, resumé and a stamped self-addressed envelope. Do not email or fax proposals. Specifically looking for fiction and non-fiction for 8–12-year-olds. Evaluation: 3 months.

Random House

1st Floor, 20 Alfred Street
Milsons Point NSW 2061
Phone: (02) 9954 9966
Fax: (02) 9955 3226
Email: random@randomhouse.com.au
Website: www.randomhouse.com.au
Specialises in children's illustrated books and general fiction and non-fiction. Only considers manuscripts submitted through an agent. Do not send unsolicited manuscripts.

Roland Harvey Books

Level 1, 1 Bleakhouse Lane
Albert Park Vic 3206
Phone: (03) 9699 4440
Fax: (03) 9696 5570
Specialises in children's picture books and fiction and non-fiction up to age 12. Unsolicited manuscripts considered. Multiple submissions accepted. Send proposal, sample chapters or full manuscript, author's resumé and a stamped self-addressed envelope. Evaluation: 8–12 weeks.

Scholastic Australia

PO Box 579
Lindfield NSW 2070
Phone: (02) 9413 8341
Fax: (02) 9416 9877
Website: www.scholastic.com.au
Specialises in children's fiction and non-fiction picture books. Unsolicited manuscripts considered. Guidelines available. Evaluation: 6 weeks.

Simon & Schuster Australia

PO Box 507
East Roseville NSW 2169

Phone: (02) 9417 3255
Fax: (02) 9417 4292
Publishes popular non-fiction trade books, and children's books under the imprint Kangaroo Press. Send a written submission to the publisher. Evaluation: 2 months.

University of Queensland Press

PO Box 6042
St Lucia Qld 4067
Phone: (07) 3365 7244
Fax: (07) 3365 1988
Website: www.uqp.uq.edu.au
Publishes children's books from picture books to works for 17-year-olds. Phone first to discuss proposal. Do not send proposals by fax or email. Evaluation: 1–3 months.

University of Western Australia Press

University of Western Australia
Cnr Mounts Bay Rd & Crawley Ave
Nedlands WA 6009
Phone: (08) 9380 3670
Fax: (08) 9380 1027
Email: uwap@cyllene.uwa.edu.au
Website: www.uwapress.uwa.edu.au
Publishes children's books under the imprint Cygnet Books. Contact first for submission requirements. Guidelines available on the website. Send typed hard copy of manuscript for assessment with resumé and a stamped self-addressed envelope. Evaluation: 2–3 months.

Working Title Press

33 Balham Avenue
Kingswood SA 5062
Phone: (08) 8271 6665
Fax: (08) 8271 0885
Email: workingt@esc.net.au
Accepts unsolicited picture book manuscripts. Evaluation: 6 weeks.

NEW ZEALAND

Breaksea Productions

12 York Place
Titirangi
Auckland 7
Phone/Fax: (09) 817 9399
Email: kate@breaksea.co.nz
Website: www.breaksea.co.nz

Bush Press Communications Ltd

PO Box 33–029
Takapuna
Auckland 1309
Phone/Fax: (09) 486 2667
Email: bush.press@clear.net.nz
New Zealand non-fiction, specialising in natural and historical heritage. Publishes 4–5 new titles a year. Query with outline, sample chapters only and a stamped self-addressed envelope.

Cape Catley

PO Box 32–622
Devonport
Auckland
Phone/Fax: (09) 445 9668
Email: cape.catley@xtra.co.nz
Website: www.capecatleybooks.co.nz

Greensmith Books

PO Box 60–506
Titirangi
Auckland 1007
Phone/Fax: (09) 817 7807
Specialises in children's fiction.

HarperCollins Publishers NZ

PO Box 1
Auckland 1

Phone: (09) 443 9400
Fax: (09) 443 9403
Website: www.harpercollins.co.nz
Publishes children's fiction, also under Golden Press imprint.

Huia Publishers

PO Box 17–335
Karori
Wellington
Phone: (04) 473 9262
Fax: (04) 473 9265
Email: huiapubs@huia.co.nz
Website: www.huia.co.nz
Publishes books in Maori or English with a strong Maori focus. Prefers Maori author or illustrator or both. Also publishes Maori-language learning resources as well as readers, science and technology kits, language videos and CDs/tapes. Prefers phone call first but accepts manuscripts in as near a final form as possible with self-addressed return package. Illustrations not accepted. Evaluation: 1 month.

Junior Educational Publications

5 Regents Park Drive
Styx
Christchurch
Phone: (03) 352 8280
Fax: (03) 354 3330
Email: galfam@xtra.co.nz
Specialises in children's picture books.

Kotuku Publishing Ltd

PO Box 22–011
Khandallah
Wellington
Phone: (04) 479 3264
Fax: (04) 479 8226
Website: www.kotuku-books.co.nz

Learning Media: Te Pou Taki Korero

PO Box 3293
Wellington 6001
Phone: (04) 472 5522
Fax: (04) 472 6444
Email: info@learningmedia.co.nz
Website: www.learningmedia.co.nz
Produces well-researched publications, picture packs, audiocassettes and videocassettes to support the New Zealand curriculum.

Longacre Press

PO Box 5340
Dunedin
Phone: (03) 477 2911
Fax: (03) 477 7222
Email: longacre.press@clear.net.nz
Publishes young adult fiction and selected non-fiction.

Mallinson Rendel Publishers

PO Box 9409
Wellington 1
Phone: (04) 802 5012
Fax: (04) 802 5013
Email: publisher@mallinsonredel.co.nz
Publishes for children of all ages. Interested in receiving manuscripts for consideration. Manuscript to be typed, double spaced and single sided, accompanied by a stamped self-addressed envelope. Evaluation: up to 6 weeks.

Nelson Price Milburn

PO Box 38–945
Wellington Mail Centre
Wellington
Phone: (04) 568 7179
Email: npm@xtra.co.nz
Educational and children's books.

Nets NZ

15 Tumanaka Place
Henderson Heights
Auckland 8
Phone: (09) 838 8356
Fax: (09) 838 8093
Specialises in children's stories with parent information.

New House Publishers

PO Box 33-376
Takapuna
Auckland
Phone: (09) 410 6517
Fax: (09) 410 6329
Email: service@newhouse.co.nz
Website: www.newhouse.co.nz
Publishes teenage fiction specifically for high schools. Manuscripts must be appropriate for use as school readers.

Pearson Education NZ

Private Bag 102-908
North Shore Mail Centre
Auckland 10
Phone: (09) 444 4968
Fax: (09) 444 4957
Email: feedback@pearsoned.co.nz
Website: www.pearsoned.co.nz
Publishes educational materials for primary and secondary markets.

Penguin Books

Private Bag 102-902
North Shore Mail Centre
Auckland
Phone: (09) 415 4700
Fax: (09) 415 4701
Website: www.penguin.co.nz
Publishes a select list from picture books to junior and senior fiction. Send in material as typescript. Prefers synopsis not full manuscript. Evaluation: 2 months.

Random House

Private Bag 102-950
North Shore Mail Centre
Auckland 10
Phone: (09) 444 7197
Fax: (09) 444 7524
Email: admin@randomhouse.co.nz
Website: www.randomhouse.co.nz
Publishes limited number of children's titles, particularly in the area of natural history. Send proposal and sample material. Evaluation: 2 months.

Scholastic New Zealand Ltd

Private Bag 94-407
Greenmount
Auckland
Phone: (09) 274 8112
Fax: (09) 274 8114
Email: cdale@scholastic.co.nz
Publishes fiction and non-fiction picture books and novels suitable up to teenage, as well as some teacher and classroom resources.

Shortland Publications Ltd

Private Bag 11-904
Ellerslie
Auckland
Phone: (09) 526 6200
Tollfree: 0800 100 246
Fax: (09) 526 4499
Email: sales@shortland.co.nz
A major publisher of primary educational materials with a large range of titles, series and materials for schools and some retail outlets. Mainly publishes for international primary reading market. Advice to prospective authors is to familiarise themselves with Shortland product. Authors' guidelines can be obtained from the above address.

Stonepress

Postal Centre
Norsewood
Phone: (06) 374 1874
Fax: (06) 374 8686
Email: stonem@xtra.co.nz

Stoneprint Press

Private Bag 55–037
Castle Hill Village
Christchurch 8020
Phone: (03) 318 7377
Fax: (03) 318 7311
Email: info@stoneprint.co.nz
Website: www.stoneprint.co.nz
Publishes children's picture books.

Waiatarua Publishing

PO Box 65–252
Mairangi Bay
North Shore City
Phone: (09) 419 4268
Fax: (09) 419 0641
Specialising in children's books by New Zealand authors.

Wendy Pye Ltd

Private Bag 17–905
Greenlane
Auckland 1130
Phone: (09) 525 3575
       (09) 525 4205
Email: info@sunshine.co.nz
Website: www.sunshine.co.nz/sunkids.html
Publishes reading material that focuses primarily on the first three years in school. International publishing program includes books, CD-ROMs, Internet material.
Present manuscript as finished.
Evaluation: 3–4 weeks.

FESTIVALS AND EVENTS

AUSTRALIA

Adelaide Writers' Week

PO Box 8116
Station Arcade
Adelaide SA 5000
Phone: (08) 8216 4444
Fax: (08) 8216 4455
Email: afa@adelaidefestival.net.au
Website: www.adelaidefestival.org.au
Held in conjunction with the Adelaide Festival of Arts, includes author readings and panel discussions by Australian and international authors. Held in the first week of March, biennially.

Association for the Study of Australian Literature (ASAL)

Department of Humanities and Social Sciences
Faculty of Arts
University of Southern Queensland
Toowoomba Qld 4350
Phone: (07) 4631 2628
Email: leec@usq.edu.au
Website: idun.itsc.adfa.edu.au/asal/
An annual conference that features papers on any aspect relating to Australian literature. Open to academics, writers, publishers and the public.

Australian Book Fair

Expertise Events
PO Box 295
Brookvale 2100
Phone: (02) 9939 4445
Fax: (02) 9939 4229
Website: www.expertiseevents.com
Organised by the Australian Publishers Association, the Fair aims to promote books in Australia and overseas. Held annually in June, in Sydney.

Australian Literacy Educators' Association

PO Box 3203
Norwood SA 5067
Phone: (08) 8332 2845
Fax: (08) 8333 0394
Email: alea@netspace.net.au
Website: www.alea.edu.au
Conference with a focus on education and literacy. Includes author readings, illustrator appearances, presentations, plenary and theme sessions. Held in a different state each year.

Australian Publishers' Bookshow

NSW Writers' Centre
PO Box 1056
Rozelle NSW 2039
Phone: (02) 9555 9757

Fax: (02) 9818 1327
Email: nswwc@ozemail.com.au
Website: nswwriterscentre.org.au
The Australian Publishers' Bookshow features independent Australian publishers and individual self-publishers who are available in a marquee to meet prospective authors and to sell their books. Held in late October in conjunction with the Carnivale Literary Festival (see below) in the heritage grounds of the NSW Writers' Centre in Callan Park, Rozelle. Phone or email for complimentary magazine.

Autumn Writing Festival

NSW Writers' Centre
PO Box 1056
Rozelle NSW 2039
Phone: (02) 9555 9757
Fax: (02) 9818 1327
Email: nswwc@ozemail.com.au
Website: nswwriterscentre.org.au
A lively and interesting weekend writers' festival of readings, panel sessions, book launches and talks by Australian and international writers held annually in early March in the heritage grounds of the NSW Writers' Centre in Callan Park, Rozelle. Also features the Poetry Sprint, a performance poetry competition held each year to find the best performance poet in Sydney. Phone or email for complimentary magazine.

Boroondara Writers Festival

C/- Boroondara City Council
Private Bag 1
Camberwell Vic 3124
Phone: (03) 9278 4773
Fax: (03) 9278 4611
Email: litfest@boroondara.vic.gov.au
Website: www.boroondara.vic.gov.au
Contact: Literary Program Coordinator
Annual literary program consisting of regular readings, writer-in-residence placements and a festival. The festival has components for children, adults and youth, held from May to July each year.

Brisbane Writers' Festival

PO Box 3567
South Brisbane Qld 4101
Phone: (07) 3255 0254
Fax: (07) 3255 0362
Email: writers@qpac.com.au
Website: www.brisbanewritersfestival.com
A celebration of Australian writers and their craft. An annual event held over four days in October as part of the Brisbane Festival.

Byron Bay Writers' Festival

Northern Rivers Writers' Centre
PO Box 1846
Byron Bay NSW 2481
Phone: (02) 6685 5115
Fax: (02) 6685 5166
Email: nrwc@nrg.com.au
Website: www.nrwc.com.au
Aims to present some of Australia's finest writers in a program designed to amuse, challenge and stimulate. Organised by the Northern Rivers Writers' Centre and held annually over three days in winter.

Carnivale Literary Festival

NSW Writers' Centre
PO Box 1056
Rozelle NSW 2039
Phone: (02) 9555 9757
Fax: (02) 9818 1327
Email: nswwc@ozemail.com.au
Website: nswwriterscentre.org.au
A lively and interesting weekend festival of readings, panel sessions, book launches and talks by multicultural Australian and international writers held annually in late October in the heritage grounds of the NSW Writers' Centre in Callan Park,

The Writer's Guide

Rozelle. Held in conjunction with the Australian Publishers' Bookshow (see above). Also features the Poetry Sprint, a performance poetry competition held each year to find the best performance poet in Sydney. Phone or email for complimentary magazine.

Dendy Awards for Australian Short Films

PO Box 950
Glebe NSW 2037
Phone: (02) 9660 3844
Fax: (02) 9692 8793
Email: jneighbour@sydneyfilmfestival.org
Website: www.sydneyfilmfestival.org
For fiction, documentary and other category shorts under 60 minutes made on film and video.

Down South Writers' Festival

PO Box 251
Busselton WA 6280
Phone/Fax: (08) 9752 2991
Three-day youth program and weekend adult program featuring around twenty authors from all over Australia. Workshops, panels, readings and school visits. Held biennially in May.

FEAST

Adelaide Lesbian & Gay Cultural Festival
PO Box 8183
Station Arcade
Adelaide SA 5000
Phone: (08) 8231 2155
Fax: (08) 8231 8793
Email: feast@feast.org.au
Website: www.feast.org.au

Flickerfest International Short Film Festival

PO Box 7416
Bondi Beach NSW 2026
Phone: (02) 9365 6877
Fax: (02) 9365 6899
Email: flickerfest@bigpond.com
Website: www.flickerfest.bigpond.com
Festival of the best international and Australian short films (drama or documentary) 30 minutes or less in 16mm, 35mm and video.

Mardi Gras Film Festival

Queer Screen Limited
PO Box 1081
Darlinghurst NSW 2010
Phone: (02) 9332 4938
Fax: (02) 9331 2988
Email: info@queerscreen/com.au
Website: www.queerscreen.com.au
Queer Screen runs My Queer Career competition for Australian and New Zealand shorts as part of the festival.

Melbourne Fringe

146V Queens Parade
North Fitzroy Vic 3068
Phone: (03) 9481 5111
Fax: (03) 9481 5211
Email: info@melbournefringe.org.au
Website: www.melbournefringe.org.au
Short Stuff film and video festival, open access event screening Australian and international shorts.

Melbourne Queer Film and Video Festival

6 Claremont Street
South Yarra Vic 3141
Phone: (03) 9827 2022
Fax: (03) 9827 1622
Email: info@melbournequeerfilm.com.au
Website: www.@melbournequeerfilm.com.au

Best Australian Film award and Audience Choice award.

Melbourne Writers' Festival

Arts House
117 Sturt Street
Southbank Vic 3006
Phone: (03) 9645 9244
Fax: (03) 9645 9344
Email: info@mwf.com.au
Website: www.mwf.com.au
Seeks to showcase the art and talent of the writer and enhance the pleasure of the reader. Held every spring.

Mildura Wentworth Arts Festival

PO Box 1982
Mildura Vic 3500
Phone: (03) 5023 1930
Fax: (03) 5023 1990
Email: mwaf@bigpond.com
Website: www.mwaf.org.au
Annual festival with literary program in the winter months.

Montsalvat National Poetry Festival

7 Hillcrest Avenue
Eltham Vic 3095
Phone: (03) 9439 7712
Fax: (03) 9431 0290
Email: montsalvat@montsalvat.com.au
Website: www.montsalvat.com.au
A meeting of poets and poetry lovers held every summer.

National Playwrights' Conference

Australian National Playwrights' Centre
PO Box 1566
Rozelle NSW 2039
Phone: (02) 9555 9377
Fax: (02) 9555 9370
Email: info@anpc.org.au
Website: www.anpc.org.au
Workshops and new Australian plays, organised by the Australian National Playwrights' Centre and held annually in April.

National Student Film and Video Festival

PO Box 500
University Union
University of Sydney NSW 2006
Phone: (02) 9563 6159
Fax: (02) 9563 6109
Email: filmfest@usu.usyd.edu.au
Website: www.yap.coom.au/filmfest
Open to students of any discipline who are members of their student union. Winning works tour campuses.

Next Wave Festival

31 Victoria Street
Melbourne Vic 3000
Phone: (03) 9662 1099
Fax: (03) 9662 4922
Email: nextwave@nextwave.org.au
Website: www. nextwave.org.au
Dedicated to supporting young artists and creating dynamic opportunities for young people to experience the arts. Held biennially every even-numbered year.

Over the Fence Comedy Film Festival

Film and Television Institute WA
PO Box 579
Fremantle WA 6959
Phone: (08) 9335 1055
Fax: (08) 9335 1283
Website: www.iinet.net.au/~mindcam/otf

Perth Writers' Festival

C/- Perth International Arts Festival
UWA Festival Centre
University of WA 6907
Phone: (08) 9380 2000
Fax: (08) 9380 8555
Email: festival@perthfestival.com.au
Website: www.perthfestival.com.au
Part of the Festival of Perth, in conjunction with Curtin University. Readings, panel sessions and workshops by Australian and international writers, held biennially in March.

Queensland New Filmmakers Awards

Brisbane International Film Festival
GPO Box 909
Albert Street Post Office
Brisbane Qld 4001
Phone: (07) 3224 4114
Fax: (07) 3224 6717
Email: pftc@pftc.com.au
Website: www.pftc.com.au

Somerset College Celebration of Literature

Somerset College
Somerset Drive
Mudgeeraba Qld 4213
Phone: (07) 5530 3777/7762
Fax: (07) 5525 2676
Email: bprice@somerset.qld.edu.au
Website: somerset.qld.edu.au
Visiting writers, lectures, readings, informal talks. Held annually over five days in March. Three days aimed at primary and secondary school students and two days (weekend) catering for all ages.

Subverse: Queensland Poetry Festival

Fringe Arts Collective Inc
PO Box 5787
West End Qld 4101
Phone: (07) 3891 5118
Fax: (07) 3391 0447
Email: subverse@powerup.com.au
Website: www.fringearts.asn.au
Annual literary event for poets and poetry in Queensland held in October. Features Queensland, interstate and international guest poets.

Sydney Gay and Lesbian Mardi Gras, Literary Events

PO Box 557
Newtown NSW 2042
Phone: (02) 9557 4332
Fax: (02) 9516 4446
Email: reception@mardigras.com.au
Website: www.mardigras.com.au
A series of readings, talks and other events that accompany the Sydney Gay and Lesbian Mardi Gras, held in February every year. Program details on the website.

Sydney Writers' Festival

PO Box 841
Broadway NSW 2007
Phone: (02) 9566 4108
Fax: (02) 9566 4809
Email: swf@zip.com.au
Website: www.swf.org.au
International authors, and local and interstate visitors present author profiles, readings, discussion sessions, workshops, tours and children's activities. Held annually over five days in May/June.

Tasmanian Poetry Festival

PO Box 345
Launceston Tas 7250
Phone: 0416 031 892
Email: sdavis@peoplesource.com.au
Website: www.tassie.net.au/Poetry/
Aims to provide performance venues for poets and allow Launceston people to hear

readings from Australian and international poets. Held annually in October.

Tasmanian Writers' Festival

Tasmanian Writers' Centre
77 Salamanca Place
Hobart Tas 7000
Phone/Fax: (03) 6224 0029
Email: ed_taswriters@trump.net.au
Website: www.fearless.net.au/taswriters/
Features writers from Australia and overseas participating in a program of events, readings and panel discussions. Held annually in March/April.

The Shootout

PO Box 892
Newcastle NSW 2300
Phone: (02) 4962 1855
Fax: (02) 4961 2294
Mobile: 0408 430 275
Email: teresa@theshootout.com.au
Website: www.theshootout.ciom.au
A film-making event in which film crews have to complete a short film within 24 hours.

Tropfest Pty Ltd

Suite 24, 2A Bayswater Road
Kings Cross NSW 2011
Phone: (02) 9368 0434
Fax: (02) 9356 4531
Email: mail@tropfest.com.au
Website: www.tropfest.com.au
Competitive festival for short films less than seven minutes.

WA Lesbian and Gay Film Festival

44 Ethelyn Street
Hilton WA 6163
Phone: (08) 9331 2986
Fax: (08) 9331 2471

Email: fanny@cleo.murdoch.edu.au
Website: www.gfd.net.au
Open to queer filmmakers across Australia. Old and new work accepted.

Waltzing Matilda Bush Poetry Championship

Waltzing Matilda Centre
PO Box 44
Winton Qld 4735
Phone: (07) 4657 1466
Fax: (07) 4657 1886
Email: matilda@thehub.com.au
Bush poets from around the world recite Paterson and their own verse. Section for children.

Warburton Film Festival

Federation of Victoria Film Societies
17 Bruce Street
Mitchan Vic 3132
Email: ian.davidson@netlink.com.au
Non-competitive festival of Australian and international feature films and shorts.

Western Australian Screen Awards

92 Adelaide Street
Fremantle WA 6160
Phone: (08) 9335 1055
Fax: (08) 9335 1283
Email: fti@fti.asn.au
Website: www.imago.com.au/fti
Annual competition and showcase for emerging and independent filmmakers.

White Gloves National Film Festival

PO Box 1218
St Kilda Vic 3182
Phone: (03) 9534 8678
Fax: (03) 9537 1276
Email: wgmotionpicturesinc@operamail.com

Website: www.musicpost.com
International event for amateur and professional filmmakers.

Word Festival Canberra

Gorman House Arts Centre
Ainslie Avenue
Braddon ACT 2612
Phone/Fax: (02) 6249 7068
Email: wordfest@cyberone.com.au
Website: www.lib.adfa.edu.au/wordfest
Organises various literary events including a literary festival, book launches, Writers at Tilleys and other readings.

Word of Mouth Writers' Festival

WA State Literature Centre
PO Box 891
Fremantle WA 6160
Phone: (08) 9432 9559
Fax: (08) 9430 6613
Email: slo@fremantle.wa.gov.au
Website: www.writerswritingwa.org
A one- or two-day event held annually in November with a focus on local writers. Interstate writers and occasionally international writers also involved. Panels, readings and workshops.

NEW ZEALAND

Auckland Writers and Readers Festival

The Old Sitting Room
1B Ponsonby Rd
Newton
Auckland
Phone: (09) 376 8074
Fax: (09) 376 8073
Email: aucklandwriters@xtra.co.nz
Biennial event held in May in odd-numbered years, alternates with the *New Zealand Post* Writers and Readers Week in Wellington. Aims to provide unprecedented access to local and international authors, academics and intellectual debate.

Books and Beyond: The Christchurch Book Festival

PO Box 845
Christchurch
Phone: (03) 377 2365
Email: festpro@clear.net.nz
An annual writers' and readers' festival held around the Queen's Birthday weekend in early June. Events are designed for every sector of the community, from kids to grandparents.

Christchurch Arts Festival

PO Box 705
Christchurch
Phone: (03) 365 2223
Fax: (03) 365 5569
Email: admin@chchartsfestival.org.nz
Website: www.artsfestival.co.nz
Biennial Arts Festival held July/August in odd-numbered years. Includes a Readers' and Writers' Season.

Glistening Waters Festival of Storytelling

PO Box 444
Masterton
Phone: (06) 377 1200
Email: tui@wise.net.nz
Website: wairarapa.co.nz/storytellers/
A festival of workshops, classes and activities for anyone interested in the art of storytelling. Showcases and sessions for those who just wish to listen to stories told by world class storytellers from many countries. Held biennially over three days on Labour Weekend in late October in even-numbered years.

Festivals and Events

Going West Literary Festival

C/- Waitakere City Council
Private Bag 93109
Waitakere City
Phone: (09) 836 8000 ext. 8780
Fax: (09) 836 8087
Email: barbara.cade@waitakere.govt.nz, naomi.mccleary@waitakere.govt.nz
Annual two-day festival of writers, performers and critics held in September each year. Profiles new writers of substance and the great writers of New Zealand. Includes a second-hand and rare book fair and fringe theatre.

Montana Poetry Day

Booksellers New Zealand
PO Box 11–377
Wellington
Phone: (04) 472 8678
Fax: (04) 472 8628
Website: www.booksellers.co.nz/poetry
Coordinated by Booksellers New Zealand. Aims to broaden and strengthen the appeal of poetry. Held annually.

New Zealand Post Writers' and Readers' Week

PO Box 10–113
Wellington
Phone: (04) 473 0149
Fax: (04) 471 1164
Email: nzfestival@festival.co.nz
Website: www.nzfestival.telecom.co.nz
Aims to present the very best New Zealand artists and performers alongside the very best the world has to offer. Part of the biennial New Zealand International Festival of the Arts held in Wellington for a week in February/March.

Taranaki Arts Festival

PO Box 4251
New Plymouth
Phone: (06) 759 8412
Fax: (06) 759 8458
Email: taranakifest@xtra.co.nz, roger.king@xtra.co.nz
Website: www.taranakifest.org.nz
Held biennially in odd-numbered years in February/March. Events include music, theatre, dance, the visual arts and a range of literary events.

Tauranga Arts Festival

PO Box 13011
Tauranga
Phone: (07) 577 6862
Fax: (07) 577 6864
Email: taurangafest@xtra.co.nz, roger.king@xtra.co.nz
Website: www.taurangafestival.co.nz
Held biennially in odd numbered years in October/November. Events include music, theatre, dance, the visual arts and a range of literary events.

Women's Book Weekend

Women's Bookshop
105 Ponsonby Road
Auckland
Phone: (09) 376 4365
Fax: (09) 376 4399
Email: books@womensbookshop.co.nz
Website: www.womensbookshop.co.nz
Features all New Zealand women writers with new books published that year. Held in October, alternate years to the Listener Festival.

World Book Day Aotearoa

Booksellers New Zealand
PO Box 11–377
Wellington
Phone: (04) 472 8678

The Writer's Guide

Fax: (04) 472 8628
Website: www.booksellers.co.nz/
bookday1.htm

Created, funded and administered by
Booksellers New Zealand.

LEGAL DEPOSIT LIBRARIES

Under the Australian *Copyright Act 1968* and various state acts, a copy of any work published in Australia must be deposited with the National Library of Australia and the appropriate State library. In New South Wales, Queensland and South Australia, a copy must also be deposited with more than one specified library.

NATIONAL

National Library of Australia
Legal Deposit Unit
Canberra ACT 2600
Phone: (02) 6262 1312
Fax: (02) 6273 4322
Email: legaldep@nla.gov.au
Website: www.nla.gov.au/1/services/ldeposit.html

NEW SOUTH WALES

Legal deposit is required under the New South Wales *Copyright Act 1879–1952*, sections 5–7. The act requires that a copy of every book first published in New South Wales be lodged within two months of publication. 'Book' is defined in the act as any book, newspaper, pamphlet, leaflet, music, map, chart or plan separately published and bound, sewed or stitched together.

State Library of New South Wales
Legal Deposit Librarian
Collection Development
Macquarie Street
Sydney NSW 2000
Phone: (02) 9273 1489
Fax: (02) 9273 1246
Email: library@slnsw.gov.au
Website: www.slnsw.gov.au

NSW Parliamentary Library
Parliament House
Macquarie Street
Sydney NSW 2000
Phone: (02) 9230 2384
Fax: (02) 9230 2640
Email: elaine.sinclair@parliament.nsw.gov.au

University of Sydney Library
Legal Deposit Officer
University of Sydney NSW 2006
Phone: (02) 9351 7268
Fax: (02) 9351 7305
Email: legaldeposit@library.usyd.edu.au
Website: www.library.usyd.edu.au

NORTHERN TERRITORY

Legal deposit legislation is under consideration and it will require the deposit with the Northern Territory Library of one copy of any book, pamphlet, newspaper, periodical, sheet music, map, plan, chart, printed sheet, film, videocassette, audiocassette and audio-disk published in the Northern Territory.

Northern Australia Collection
Legal Deposit Librarian
Northern Territory Library
GPO Box 42
Darwin NT 0801
Phone: (08) 8999 7364/7177
Fax: (08) 8999 6927
Email: larraine.shepherd@nt.gov.au
Website: www.ntlib.nt.gov.au

QUEENSLAND

Legal deposit is required under the Queensland *Libraries and Archives Act 1988*, Part VI. The act requires that material published in Queensland be deposited within one month of publication with the State Librarian and the Librarian of the Parliamentary Library.

Material is defined as every part or division of a book, periodical, piece of sheet music, map or chart as well as non-print material (audiotape, film, video-recording, disk, microfilm or microfiche). Material is considered to have been published if reproductions of the material or edition have been supplied (whether by sale or otherwise) to the general public.

State Library of Queensland
Library Deposits (Queensland)
PO Box 3488
South Brisbane Qld 4101
Phone: (07) 3840 7893
Fax: (07) 3846 2421
Email: jol@slq.qld.gov.au
Website: www.slq.qld.gov.au

Parliamentary Library
Parliamentary Librarian
Parliament House
George & Alice Streets

Brisbane Qld 4001
Phone: (07) 3406 7199
Fax: (07) 3210 0172
Email: library.inquiries@parliament.qld.gov.au
Website: www.parliament.qld.gov.au/parlib

SOUTH AUSTRALIA

Legal deposit is required under the South Australian *Libraries Act 1982*, section 35, and the *Libraries Act Amendment Act 1989*. The acts require that material published in South Australia be deposited within one month after publication. Material includes books, or a part or division of a book, newspapers, magazines, journals or pamphlets, maps, plans, charts or tables, printed music, records, cassettes, films, videos or audiotapes, disks or other items made available to the public, designed to store and facilitate the reproduction of visual images, sound or information.

All items received by the State Library of South Australia under legal deposit are listed in Mortlock miscellany, acquisitions received by the Mortlock Library of South Australia.

State Library of South Australia
Legal Deposit Unit
GPO Box 419
Adelaide SA 5001
Phone: (08) 8207 7338
Fax: (08) 8207 7287
Email: gilbert.mark@slsa.sa.gov.au
Website: www.slsa.sa.gov.au

Parliamentary Library
GPO Box 572
Adelaide SA 5001
Phone: (08) 8237 9300
Fax: (08) 8212 1797
Email: kathy.sherriff@parliament.sa.gov.au

Legal Deposit Libraries

TASMANIA

Legal deposit is required under the Tasmanian *Libraries Act 1984*, section 22. The act requires that a book published in Tasmania be deposited within one month of publication. 'Book' means any book, periodical, newspaper, printed matter, map, plan, music, manuscript, picture, print, motion picture, sound recording, photographic negative or print, microphotography, videorecording and any other matter or thing whereby words, sounds or images are recorded or reproduced.

State Library of Tasmania
Legal Deposit Unit
91 Murray Street
Hobart Tas 7000
Phone: (03) 6233 7502
Fax: (03) 6233 7506
Email: helen.jones@education.tas.gov.au
Website: www.statelibrary.tas.gov.au

VICTORIA

Legal deposit is required under the Victorian *Libraries Act 1988*, section 49. The act requires the deposit within two months of every new publication published in Victoria. Publication includes every book, periodical, newspaper, musical score, map, chart, plan, picture, photograph, print and any other printed matter, any microfiche or microfilm, and a range of other types of publication.

State Library of Victoria
Legal Deposit Unit
328 Swanston Street
Melbourne Vic 3000
Phone: (03) 8664 7000
Fax: (03) 9663 1480
Email: lcolquho@slv.vic.gov.au
Website: www.statelibrary.vic.gov.au

WESTERN AUSTRALIA

Until 1994, legal deposit was required in Western Australia under the *Copyright Act 1895*, sections 4, 7–9. The act required that a book published in Western Australia be deposited within two months of publication. A 'book' means and includes every volume, part or division of a volume, newspaper, pamphlet, sheet of letterpress, sheet music, map, chart or plan, separately published.

This act was repealed in 1994. Until new legislation is introduced and proclaimed, the Library Board of Western Australia hopes that publishers will abide by the spirit of legal deposit. Deposit material is housed in the J. S. Battye Library of Western Australian History.

Library Board of Western Australia
Acquisitions
Alexander Library Building
Perth Cultural Centre
Perth WA 6000
Phone: (08) 9427 3111
Fax: (08) 9427 3276
Email: info@mail.liswa.wa.gov.au
Website: www.liswa.wa.gov.au

NEW ZEALAND

Legal Deposit is required under the *National Library Act 1965*, section 30A, amended 1994. The act requires publishers to deposit up to three copies of all publications with the National Library of New Zealand's Legal Deposit Office for inclusion in the New Zealand National Bibliography and Subscriber Services. Publications include books and booklets, brochures, pamphlets, leaflets, conference papers, directories, guidebooks, discussion documents, magazines, journals, microfiche, newsletters, maps, newspapers, reports, sheet music and a range of other printed documents.

The Writer's Guide

National Library of New Zealand
Legal Deposit Office
PO Box 12–340
Wellington
Phone: (04) 474 3104

Fax: (04) 474 3161
Email: legal.deposit@natlib.govt.nz
Website: www.natlib.gov.nz/en/services/publishers/legal/index.html

LITERARY WEBSITES

The sites listed here represent a range of literary output from writing courses to online bookshops, dictionaries and thesauruses, to search engines that will help you navigate your way around the web, to numerous poetry sites, as well as academic and general arts sites. The sites listed below were active at the time of writing, but be aware that many fall into oblivion either because it becomes too expensive to run them or the editors do not have time to maintain them.

ABORIGINAL SITE

Info Koori
www.slnsw.gov.au/koori
Index to Australian indigenous information.

AUSTRALIAN ARTS SITES (GENERAL)

Arts Info:
www.artsinfo.net.au
General arts information site

Australia's Cultural Network
www.acn.net.au
Gateway site to hundreds of online Australian cultural organisations. Includes an events calendar, internet development guides and online collaborative projects.

Community Cultural Development Training Directory
www.createaust.com.au
Provides a comprehensive listing of accredited and non-accredited training and training resources available throughout Australia.

dLux media arts
www.dLux.org.au
Arts site.

RealTime
www.realtimearts.net
Australian bi-monthly arts online.

Signal
arts.abc.net.au/signal/
This collaboration between the Australia Council and ABC Online, includes a searchable listing of arts events taking place around Australia and links to online resources for artists and arts organisations.

State of the Arts
www.stateart.com.au
Magazine guide to visual and performing arts in Australia and New Zealand.

AUSTRALIAN STUDIES

Australian Studies Network
austudies.org
Links to Australian studies associations and programs around the world.

AUTHOR SITES

Hundreds of individual authors have their own websites. These can be found through a search engine (see the list of search engines later in this section). Listed below are gateways that provide links to authors. Refer also to some of the general writing resource sites as these often have links to authors.

Authors and illustrators
www.dymocks.com.au/asp/links.asp
Links to home pages of authors and illustrators.

Awards
www.asauthors.org/award
The Australian Writers' And Readers' Database set up by the Australian Society of Authors to promote Australian writers around the world.

Biography
www.biography.com
Biographies of 25 000 personalities (American site).

Internet Book Information Centre
www.internetbookinfo.com

BOOKSHOPS

Abebooks
www.abebooks.com
US-based network of independent booksellers specialising in rare, second-hand and out-of-print books.

Alibris
www.alibris.com
Rare book search.

Amazon.com
www.amazon.com

Australian Online Bookshop
www.bookworm.com.au
General bookshop with special interest sections on Australian books, computing books, science fiction and fantasy.

Barnes and Noble
www.barnesandnoble.com
Online American bookshop.

Dymocks Bookshop
www.dymocks.com.au

Gleebooks
www.gleebooks.com.au
Bookshop in Sydney.

Internet Bookshop
www.bookshop.co.uk
Europe's largest online bookstore.

Writer's Bookcase
www.writersbookcase.com
Specialises in books for writers and editors.

CHILDREN AND YOUNG WRITERS

A Plus Research and Writing for High School and College Students
www.ipl.org/teen/aplus/
Detailed step-by-step writing and research tips on writing essays and research papers.

Aaron Shepard's Young Author Page
www.aaronshep.com/youngauthor/index.html
Articles and links, tips and tricks for young authors.

Creative Writing for Teens
kidswriting.miningco.com
Lists and links to writing tips, publishing resources, forums, articles and author sites.

Katharsis
www.katharsis.org
'The place for young writers to gather on the Web'. Short stories, poetry, sagas, forums, articles, exercises.

Web Topics—Writing
www.dimensional.com/~janf/wtwriting.html
Links to a variety of resources and fun sites for young writers.

Young Writers' Clubhouse
www.realkids.com/club.shtml
How to get started, FAQs, chat, contests, critique group and more for young writers.

Literary Websites

Young Authors Workshop
www.planet.eon.net/~bplaroch/index.html
Children in grades 4–7 are taken through the writing process step by step, from how to find ideas for stories to finding online markets for those stories.

Young Girl Writers
home.talkcity.com/WooHooWay/scanner_death/index.html
Writing and reading activities for girls, including a bulletin board, interviews with authors, book excerpts, newsletters, and more.

The Young Writers Club
www.cs.bilkent.edu.tr/~david/derya/ywc.html
This site contains Global Wave, an online magazine (see entry under Ezines), poems, stories, activities, film reviews, chat page, tips and resources.

COMPETITIONS

Literature Awards
www.literature-awards.com
A-Z of international book awards.

US Awards
www.kimn.net/contests
US awards.

COPYRIGHT

Australian Copyright Council
www.copyright.org.au

The Copyright Website
www.benedict.com
Copyright law and the internet from San Francisco lawyer Bernard Maloney.

World Intellectual Property Organisation
www.wipo.org
Information about intellectual property, including copyright issues, and the system of international treaties designed to protect intellectual property around the world.

DICTIONARIES AND THESAURUSES

Australian Dictionary
www.australia-online.com/dictionaussie.html

Larry's Aussie Slang and Phrase Dictionary
members.tripod.com/~thisthat/slang.html

Macquarie Dictionary
www.dict.mq.edu.au

Oxford English Dictionary
www.oed.com/

Thesaurus
www.thesaurus.com

Thesauruses and Quotations
www.refdesk.com/factquot.html
Roget's thesaurus and links to various quotation sites and other thesauruses.

Webopaedia
www.pcwebopedia.com/
Online computer dictionary for Internet terms and technical support.

Webster Dictionary and Thesaurus
www.m-w.com/dictionary

World Wide Words
www.quinion.com/words
Michael Quinion's language page devoted to the English language, its history, quirks, curiosities and evolution.

EDITING

Editorial Freelancers Association (US)
www.the-efa.org/
A range of information and resources for editors and freelancers.

Council of Australian Societies of Editors
www.editorscanberra.org/case.htm

ENCYCLOPAEDIAS

Encyclopaedia Britannica Online
www.eb.com

Encyclopedia Mythica
www.pantheon.org
An encyclopedia on mythology, folklore and legend.

Macquarie Encyclopaedia
www.dict.mq.edu.au
Australian online encyclopaedia.

FOLKLORE AND MYTHOLOGY

Folklore and Mythology Archives
www.humnet.ucla.edu/humnet/folklore/archives/

GENEALOGY

Family History, NSW State Library
www.slnsw.gov.au/links/

GRAMMAR

HyperGrammar
www.uottawa.ca/academic/arts/writcent/hypergrammar

Online English Grammar
www.edunet.com/english/grammar/index.html

ILLUSTRATORS

Illustrators' Australia
www.netspace.net.au/~soniak/

Society of Children's Book Writers and Illustrators
www.scbwi.org
Based in the US, with a branch in Australia.

LIBRARIES

Australian Libraries Gateway
www.nla.gov.au/libraries

British Library
www.bl.uk

Canterbury Public Library, New Zealand
library.christchurch.org.nz

Internet Public Library
ipl.sils.umich.edu

Library of Congress US
www.loc.gov

National Library of Australia
www.nla.gov.au

New York Public Library
www.nypl.org

State Library of New South Wales
www.slnsw.gov.au

UK Public Libraries on the Web
dspace.dial.pipex.com/town/square/ac940/weblibs.html

US National Library of Poetry
www.kiosk.net/poetry/

WWW Virtual Library
www.vlib.org

MARKETPLACES

The following sites aim to bring writers and publishers together. Authors usually pay a fee for their work to appear on the site.

eLitt
www.eLitt.com.au

Writerfind (NZ)
www.writerfind.com

Writers Display
www.writersdisplay.com

Literary Websites

ONLINE BOOKS

Bartleby.com
www.bartleby.com/
Online references, verse, fiction and non-fiction.

SE Books
www.ebooks3.com
Classic and modern titles.

OnLine Book Page
digital.library.upenn.edu/books
Index of books available online, including a list of banned books.

Project Gutenberg
www.gutenberg.net
A site that provides more than 5000 classic texts that are in the public domain.

Project Gutenberg (Australia)
www.gutenberg.net.au
A site that provides classic Australian texts in the public domain.

POETRY

Electronic Poetry Centre (State University of New York)
epc.buffalo.edu

Ida's Poetics
www.idaspoetics.com.au
Reviews, poetry, links, sales of books and journals.

Internet Poetry Archive
metalab.unc.edu/ipa/index.html

Kukai Report
cc.matsuyama-u.ac.jp/~shiki/kukai.html
Bi-weekly update of the haikus posted to the site from around the world.

Poetry Australia Foundation
paf.scriptmania.com

Poetry Daily
www.poems.com
Anthology of contemporary poetry.

The Poetry Kit
www.poetrykit.org
Online poetry resources.

Poetry Society of America
www.poetrysociety.org
Details about membership, awards, resources and the journal *Crossroads*.

W3PX
www.w3px.com
Poetry exchange.

Web Poetry Corner
www.dreamagic.com/poetry/
Features 1850 poets from over 50 countries.

PUBLISHERS

Hundreds of individual publishing companies have their own websites. These can be found through a search engine (see list of search engines later in this section). Listed below are gateways that provide links to publishers. Refer also to some of the general writing resource sites, as these often have links to publishers.

Australian Publishers Association
www.publishers.asn.au/

Publishers' Catalogues Home Pages
www.lights.com/publisher/
Links to publishers all over the world.

PUBLISHING ONLINE

bob-e-books
www.bob-e-books.com

Interactive Publications
www.interpr.com.au
Publishing assessment and editing services.

Jacobyte Books
www.jacobytebooks.com

Spinifex Press
www.spinifexpress.com.au

QUOTATIONS

The Quotations Page
www.starlingtech.com/quotes/

REVIEW SITES

Book Browser
www.bookbrowser.com
Guide for avid readers—fiction reading lists, reviews, forthcoming titles, author information.

New York Review of Books
www.nybooks.com/nyrev/index.html

SCIENCE FICTION AND FANTASY (SPECULATIVE FICTION)

Fantasy and Science Fiction Links
www.ozemail.com.au/~pjcsjc/fantasy.htm

Science Fiction
www.scifi.com
Information about sci-fi programs (TV, film and online), the magazine *Science Fiction Weekly* and chat rooms.

Science Fiction and Fantasy Search Engine
www.computercrowsnest.com/
Links to magazines, publishers, discussion groups, comics, conferences, film and TV.

Science Fiction and Fantasy Writers Association of America (SFWA)
www.sfwa.org

Science Fiction in Australia
home.vicnet.net.au/~sfoz/

SpecFicWorld.com
www.geocities.com/Area51/Shire/1524/index.html
Resource guide for science fiction, fantasy and horror writers.

Speculations
www.speculations.com
Market listings, news and articles on the craft of speculative fiction.

Ultimate Science Fiction Web Guide
www.magicdragon.com/UltimateSF/
Links to web science fiction resources.

Voyager—Science Fiction and Fantasy Books
www.fireandwater/genres/sf.asp
News on science fiction books and authors published by HarperCollins.

SCREENWRITERS AND PLAYWRIGHTS

Filmnet
filmnet.org.au
Free daily film and TV industry news.

The Playwriting Seminars
www.vcu.edu/artweb/playwriting/
A professional manual (230-page site) of the playwright's craft, with an excursion into film. Quotes from 400 playwrights, screenwriters and others in the business.

Screen Network Australia
www.sna.net.au
Gateway site to Australian film and television industries.

Screenwriters Online
www.screenwriter.com
Masterclasses, screen plays, script analysis, news.

TV Writer
www.tvwriter.com
Dedicated exclusively to TV writing. Includes a TV University with online TV writers' workshops and professional critiques.

Urban Cinefile
www.urbancinefile.com.au
Australian online journal about the film industry.

Literary Websites

SHAKESPEARE

Internet Shakespeare Editions
web.uvic.ca/shakespeare

Shakespeare: Complete Works
tech-two.mit.edu/Shakespeare/
The complete works of Shakespeare.

SONGWRITING

Writing Songs
www.writingsongs.com
Features advice, resources, classified ads and links.

STYLE MANUALS

Acronyms and abbreviations
www.ucc.ie/info/net/acronyms/acro.html

Bartleby.com
bartleby.com/
Online references include Fowler's *The King's English* and Strunk and White's *The Elements of Style*.

Word Processing Style Guide
ourworld.compuserve.com/homepages/timg/

WOMEN WRITERS

A Celebration of Women Writers
digital.library.upenn.edu/women/

WRITING AND ILLUSTRATING BOOKS FOR CHILDREN AND YOUNG ADULTS

Children's and Adolescent Literature Resources
www.indiana.edu/~eric_rec/comatt/childlit.html

Children's Literature Web Guide
www.ucalgary.ca/~dkbrown/index.html
Internet resources related to books for children and young adults.

Children's Writing Resource Centre
www.write4kids.com

Fairrosa Cyber Library of Children's Literature
www.dalton.org/libraries/fairrosa
Support room, articles, tips, interviews, links.

The Institute of Children's Literature, for Writers
www.institutechildrenslit.com/
General information site and courses.

Society of Children's Book Writers and Illustrators
www.scbi.org
Based in the US and has a branch in Australia.

WRITING GROUPS

Rural Women Writers Network
www.ozemail.com.au/~rwwn

WRITING RESOURCES (GENERAL)

Australian Journals Online
www.nla.gov.au/oz/ausejour.html

Australian Literary Gateway
www.austlit.edu.au
Information on Australian authors and Australian literature. Access by subscription.

Bonfire
www.homeusers.prestel.co.uk/jordanhill/focus.htm
Resources for writers of poetry and prose.

Bookwire
www.bookwire.com
Online information source for book industry.

313

The Writer's Guide

Communication Game
communicationgame.com
A site that allows writers to establish their own page and display their work gratis.

Dooyoo
www.dooyoo.co.uk
A site for offering opinions and ranking products and services.

Editforce
www.editforce.com.au
Writers submit ideas for articles and if they are accepted author receives payment if article is sold.

English Literature on the Web
www.lang.nagoya-u.ac.jp/~matsuoka/
A gateway site to English literature sites including British authors, E-text archives, Medieval (and Anglo-Saxon), 17th century (and Renaissance), 18th century (and Restoration), 19th century (Romantics and Victorian) and 20th century.

For Writers
www.forwriters.com
References, site lists, markets, conferences, agents, awards, writing groups, etc.

Geocities
www.geocities.com
A site that invites writers to establish their own presence by submitting their work gratis.

MoleSearch
www.molesearch.com
A search engine dedicated to aspects of publishing, including resources, publishers, manufacturing and publicity.

New Zealand Writers' Website
www.nzwriters.co.nz
Writing competitions, book reviews, noticeboard, chat room and monthly e-zine with up-to-date news of writing and publishing in New Zealand and overseas.

OzAuthors
www.ozauthors.com.au
Resources for readers, those working in education and writers.

OzLit: Australian literary resources on the internet
home.vicnet.net.au/~ozlit
Includes a magazine, Book of the Month, e-texts and links to similar writing.

rememory.com
www.rememory.com
A membership-based site that includes competitions, message board and author profiles.

Society for the History of Authorship, Reading and Publishing
www.sharpweb.org

Soul Food Café
www.dailywriting.net
Cyber writing café.

trAce: Online Writing Community
Website: trace.ntu.ac.uk/
News, resources, forums, workshops, projects.

Writelinks
www.writelinks.com
Writers' resources including critique groups and chatlines.

Writers Display
www.writersdisplay.com
A website dedicated to bringing writers and publishers together.

Writers Weekly
www.writersweekly.com
A site for those writing for websites or publications.

Writers Write
www.writerswrite.com
A compendium of writing resources.

Writing-World
www.tipsforwriters.com
Articles, links, fantasy and science fiction resources, contests, critique groups, books, electronic publishing, freelancing column.

Writers.com
www.writers.com
Offers online writing classes in all genres, writers groups, newsletter, information about competitions and an online bookstore.

Writers.net
www.writers.net
Internet resources for writers, editors, publishers and agents. Includes directories of agents, editors and publishers, discussions, writing assignments and a bookstore.

Writer's Block
www.writersblock.ca
Canadian e-zine for the writing trade.

Writing Corner
www.writingcorner.com
Resources, articles, chat room and online magazine for newly published and unpublished writers.

SEARCH ENGINES

AUSTRALIA AND NEW ZEALAND

AltaVistaAustralia
www.altavista.com.au

Anzwers
www.anzwers.com.au
Australia and New Zealand.

Looksmart Australia
www.looksmart.com.au

Yahoo! Australia and New Zealand
www.yahoo.com.au

OTHER

AltaVista
altavista.com

Ask Jeeves
www.askjeeves.com

Excite
www.excite.com

Google
www.google.com

Hotbot
www.hotbot.com

Infoseek
www.infoseek.com

Looksmart
www.looksmart.com

Lycos
www.lycos.com

Metafind
www.metafind.com

Webcrawler
www.webcrawler.com

Yahoo!
www.yahoo.com

MAGAZINES AND JOURNALS

Literary magazines are often run by only one or two people from their dining-room table and, as a result of insufficient finances, many go out of print after several issues. Every effort has been made to check that the following titles are still being published. Many magazines do not provide a telephone number and are tardy in responding to letters. Check with your local writers' centre to see which magazines are current, and subscribe to your favourite magazines to help them stay afloat.

AUSTRALIA

ACT Write
Gorman House Arts Centre
Ainslie Avenue
Braddon ACT 2612
Phone/Fax: (02) 6262 9191
Email: director@actwriters.org.au
Website: www.actwriters.org.au
Newsletter of the ACT Writers' Centre.

Adelaide Review
PO Box 2294
Kent Town SA 5071
Phone: (08) 8362 7699
Fax: (08) 8362 7878
Email: adelrev@camtech.net.au
Publishes poems, fiction, reviews and discussion of heritage and architecture, visual arts, music and theatre, food and wine.

Altair
PO Box 475
Blackwood SA 5051
Phone: (08) 8278 8995, 0409 838 100
Fax: (08) 8278 5585
Email: altair@senet.com.au
Website: www.altair-australia.com
Quarterly magazine of science fiction writing.

Ambitious Friends
Liverpool Migrant Resource Centre
PO Box 435
Liverpool NSW 2170
Phone: (02) 9601 3788
Fax: (02) 9601 1398
Email: editor@af.asn.au
Website: www.af.asn.au
Multicultural magazine for women.

Antipodean: The Australian Translation Journal
C/- AUSIT
PO Box 185
Sydney South NSW 1235
Phone: (02) 9626 7046
Fax: (02) 9626 7046
Email: national@ausit.org
Website: www.ausit.org
Journal of the Australian Institute of Interpreters and Translators.

Magazines and Journals

Antithesis
Department of English and Cultural Studies
University of Melbourne
Parkville Vic 3052
Phone: (03) 8344 5280
Email: antithesis@english.unimelb.edu.au
Postgraduate journal.

Aurealis
Chimaera Publications
PO Box 2164
Mount Waverley Vic 3149
Phone: (03) 9534 1569
Fax: (03) 9534 1569
Email: straz@fhills.hotkey.net.au
Australian fantasy and science fiction.

AUSIT National Newsletter
43 Newborough Street
Scarborough WA 6019
Phone: (08) 9245 1474
Fax: (08) 9245 1430
Email: wa@ausit.org
Website: www.ausit.org
Newsletter of the Australian Institute of Interpreters and Translators.

Australasian Drama Studies
School of English, Media Studies and Art History
University of Queensland
St Lucia Qld 4072
Phone: (07) 3365 2501
Fax: (07) 3365 2799
Email: v.kelly@mailbox.uq.oz.au,
r.fotheringham@mailbox.uq.oz.au
Website: www.uq.edu.au/drama/adsj/journal_frame.htm
Academic journal on aspects of drama.

Australian Author
PO Box 1566
Strawberry Hills NSW 2012
Phone: (02) 9318 0877
Fax: (02) 9318 0530
Email: asa@asauthors.org
Website: www.asauthors.org
Quarterly journal of the Australian Society of Authors.

Australian Book Review
PO Box 2320
Richmond South Vic 3121
Phone: (03) 9429 6700
Fax: (03) 9429 2288
Email: abr@vicnet.net.au
Website: www.vicnet.net.au/~abr/
Reviews and articles on matters of interest to professional writers.

Australian Bookseller and Publisher
18 Salmon Street
Port Melbourne Vic 3207
Phone: (03) 9245 7370
Fax: (03) 9245 7395
Email: bookseller.publisher@thorpe.com.au
Website: www.thorpe.com.au
Magazine of the Australian publishing industry.

Australian Haiku Anthology
Email: haikuoz@yahoo.com
Website: users.mullum.com.au/jbird/haiku.html
Online production of the Australian Haiku Society.

Australian Humanities Review
Email: AHR@latrobe.edu.au
Website: www.lib.latrobe.edu.au/AHR
An interdisciplinary peer-reviewed electronic journal.

Australian Literary Studies
PO Box 6042
Brisbane Qld 4072
Phone: (07) 3365 2452
Fax: (07) 3365 1988
Email: rosichay@uqp.uq.edu.au
Website: www.uq.edu.au/~enldale
Critical, biographical and historical material on Australian literature.

The Writer's Guide

Australian Multicultural Book Review
Papyrus Publishing
C/- PO Scarsdale Vic 3351
Phone: (03) 5342 2394
Fax: (03) 5342 2423
Email: editor@papyrus.com.au
Website: www.papyrus.com.au
A journal devoted to the work of multicultural writers.

Australian Poets' and Writers' Reflections
1a Coomber Street
Bundaberg Qld 4670
Phone: (07) 4154 1663
A publication that gives writers a chance to reflect on their work.

Banksnotes
Chanceart Publications
PO Box 252
Padstow NSW 2211
Phone: (02) 9773 7347
A small literary magazine of fiction, poetry and non-fiction.

Bardfly Magazine
PO Box 301
Enmore NSW 2042
Phone: (02) 9558 4350
Email: bardflys@hotmail.com
Website: go.to/bardfly
Performance poetry magazine.

Blast
PO Box 3514
Manuka ACT 2603
Phone: (02) 6239 4727
Fax: (02) 6073 5081
Email: b.tully@nla.gov.au
A Canberra cultural and literary journal with a political edge.

Blue Dog
PO Box 434
Wollongong University NSW 2500
Phone: (02) 4221 3867
Email: kpretty@uow.edu.au
Journal devoted to the best in Australian poetry.

broad seat
PO Box 2211
Mail Delivery Centre
Bendigo Vic 3554
Poetry magazine.

Centoria
PO Box 2211
Mail Delivery Centre
Bendigo Vic 3554
Poetry magazine.

Central West Writers' Centre Newsletter
PO Box E156
Orange NSW 2800
Phone: (02) 6393 8125
Fax: (02) 6393 8100
Email: writing@netwit.net.au
Website: www.netwit.net.au/~writing
Newsletter of the Central West Writers' Centre.

Colloquy
PO Box 11A
Monash University Vic 3800
Phone: (03) 9905 9009
Email: colloquy@arts.monash.edu.au
Website: www.arts.monash.edu.au/others/colloquy
A web journal of academic work by postgraduates in Literary and Cultural Studies.

Coppertales
Humanities, Faculty of Arts
University of Southern Queensland
Toowoomba Qld 4350
Phone: (07) 4631 1045
Fax: (07) 4631 1063
Email: leec@usq.edu.au

Magazines and Journals

Website: www.usq.edu.au/users/leec/copper.htm
Annual journal of rural arts.

Cordite Poetry Review
PO Box 14022
Melbourne City MC Vic 8000
Email: cordite@optusnet.com.au
Website: cordite.org.au
Online poetry and poetics review.

Crime Factory
C/- Preston Lower Post Office
3 Gilbert Road
Preston Vic 3072
Phone: (03) 9443 7943
Fax: (03) 9443 7943
Email: editor@crimefactory.net
Website: www.crimefactory.net
Crime fiction magazine.

Divan
C/- Professional Writing and Editing
Vocational Access and Education
Box Hill Institute
PO Bag 2014
Box Hill Vic 3128
Phone: (03) 9286 9222
Email: e.livings@bhtafe.edu.au
Website: www.bhtafe.edu.au/Divan/
Online poetry e-zine.

dot.lit
Creative Writing
Creative Industries Faculty
Queensland University of Technology
GPO Box 2434
Brisbane Qld 4001
Phone: (07) 3864 1005
Fax: (07) 3864 1810
Email: dotlit@qut.edu.au
Website: www.dotlit.qut.edu.au/
Online journal of creative writing produced through the Queensland University of Technology.

Eidolon
Eidolon Publications
PO Box 225
North Perth WA 6906
Email: eidolon@eidolon.net
Website: eidolon.net
Journal of Australian science fiction and fantasy.

EMPOWA
PO Box 16
Scarborough WA 6922
Phone: (08) 9254 3587
Fax: (08) 9336 2540
Email: kapetas@gunada.curtin.edu.au
Website: www.aceonline.com.au/~db/
Published by Emerging Poets WA.

engagé
PO Box 4389
University of Melbourne
Parkville Vic 3010
Email: jimaubrey@hotmail.com
Primary focus on writing of political or issue-oriented nature.

Famous Reporter
Walleah Press
PO Box 368
North Hobart Tas 7002
Email: ahugo@tassie.net.au
Website: www.tassie.net.au/~ahugo/fr/
Famous Reporter is a biannual Australian literary journal featuring poetry, prose, haiku, essays, reviews, interviews and news.

Five Bells
PO Box 91
Balmain NSW 2041
Phone: (02) 9818 5366
Email: poetinc@ozemail.com.au
Website: www.ozemail.com.au/~poetinc
Magazine of the Poets Union.

four W
Charles Sturt University

319

The Writer's Guide

Wagga Wagga NSW 2678
Phone: (02) 6933 2688
Fax: (02) 6933 2107
Email: booranga@csu.edu.au
Website: www.csu.edu.au/faculty/arts/
humss/booranga/index.html
Annual anthology from Booranga Writers' Centre.

FreeXpresSion
PO Box 4
West Hoxton NSW 2171
Phone: (02) 9607 5559
Fax: (02) 9607 6612
Email: frexprsn@bigpond.com.au
A journal devoted to original writing, with hints and tips for writers.

Gangway
PO Box 522
Strawberry Hills NSW 2012
Phone: (02) 9280 2120
Fax: (02) 9280 2130
Email: gangway@gangan.com
Website: www.gangway.net
Contemporary literature from Australia and Austria (bilingual: English and German).

Going Down Swinging
PO Box 24
Clifton Hill Vic 3068
Email: gds@vicnet.net.au
The best in new Australian writing for the page, stage and stereo.

Good Reading Magazine
GPO Box 3835
Sydney NSW 2001
Phone: (02) 9810 2477
Fax: (02) 9810 2488
Email: editor@goodreading
magazine.com.au
Website: www.goodreading
magagzine.com.au
Monthly magazine featuring author profiles, book extracts, reviews and news.

GrinSpin
Phone: 0408 246 245
Website: www.grinspin.com
Australian online magazine with humour as its driving force.

Heat
PO Box 752
Artarmon NSW 1570
Phone/Fax: (02) 9419 7934
Email: heat@newcastle.edu.au
Website: www.mypostbox.com/heat
A literary journal featuring Australian writers alongside overseas writers.

Hecate
Department of English
University of Queensland
PO Box 99
St Lucia Qld 4072
Phone: (07) 3365 3146
Fax: (07) 3365 2779
Email: c.ferrier@mailbox.uq.edu.au
Website: www.english.uq.edu.au/awsr/main.html
International, interdisciplinary journal of women's liberation.

Hecate's Australian Women's Book Review
Department of English
University of Queensland
PO Box 99
St Lucia Qld 4072
Phone: (07) 3365 3146
Fax: (07) 3365 2779
Email: c.ferrier@mailbox.uq.edu.au
Website: www.english.uq.edu.au/awsr/main.html
Internet publication. Reviews by women of new publications by women.

Heist
PO Box 2
Newcastle University Union
Callaghan NSW 2308
Phone: 0419 316 625

Magazines and Journals

Email: heist@mockfrog.com
Website: www.mockfrog.com
Short fiction in the style of the 1950s and 1960s.

Hunter Writer
PO Box 71
Hamilton NSW 2292
Phone: (02) 4940 0003
Fax: (02) 4962 3959
Email: puzzleprod@bigpond.com
Website: www.mockfrog.com/hwc
Hunter Writers' Centre newsletter.

Ideation
Griffith University School of Arts
PMB 50
GCMC Qld 9726
Email: ideation_hq@hotmail.com
Publication producing new promotional tactics for emerging artists.

Idiom 23
Faculty of Arts
Central Queensland University
Rockhampton Mail Centre Qld 4702
Phone: (07) 4930 9511
Fax: (07) 4930 9501
Email: l.huf@cqu.edu.au
Named for the Tropic of Capricorn, *Idiom 23* seeks creative writing from as varied backgrounds as possible and endeavours to reflect fictional representations of marginalised or non-privileged positions and values. *Idiom 23*'s Bauhinia Annual Literary Awards welcome entries from Australia and overseas.

Island Magazine
PO Box 210
Sandy Bay Tas 7005
Phone: (03) 6220 2325
Fax: (03) 6220 7631
Email: island@tassie.net.au
Website: www.tased.edu.au/tasonline/island/island.html
A general literary journal of fiction, poetry, articles and reviews.

Jacket Magazine
C/- Australian Literary Management
2A Booth Street
Balmain NSW 2041
Phone: (02) 9818 8557
Fax: (02) 9818 8569
Email: jtranter@jacket.zip.com.au
Website: www.jacket.zip.com.au/
Online quarterly review of new writing.

JAS Review of Books
Australian Studies, Division of Humanities
Curtin University of Technology
GPO Box U 1987
Perth WA 6845
Phone: (08) 9266 4788
Fax: (08) 9266 4787
Email: ffion@iinet.net.au
Website: www.api-network.com/jasreview/
Journal produced by the Australian Studies Centre in association with the Australian Public Intellectual Network.

Journal of Australian Studies
Australian Studies, Division of Humanities
Curtin University of Technology
GPO Box U 1987
Perth WA 6845
Phone: (08) 9266 4788
Fax: (08) 9266 4787
Email: s.dudley@curtin.edu.au
Website: www.api-network.com
International quarterly published by UQP in partnership with Curtain University as part of the Australian Public Intellectual Network.

Joussour Poetry Magazine
PO Box 211
Hazelbrook NSW 2779
Phone: (02) 4758 9965
English and Arabic editions.

The Writer's Guide

Kalimat
PO Box 242
Cherrybrook NSW 2126
Phone: (02) 9484 3648
Fax: (02) 9484 3648
Email: raghid@ozemail.com.au
Australian–Arabic quarterly.

LiNQ
School of Humanities
James Cook University
Townsville Qld 4811
Phone: (07) 4781 4451
Fax: (07) 4781 5655
Email: jcu.linq@jcu.edu.au
LiNQ is a bi-annual journal with a strong and established reputation as a forum for the publication of poetry, fiction, critical essays and book reviews authored by both new and renowned writers.

Literature and Aesthetics
School of English A20
University of Sydney NSW 2006
Phone: (02) 9351 2374
Fax: (02) 9351 2434
Email: william.christie@english.su.edu.au
Journal of the Sydney Society of Literature and Aesthetics.

Mattoid
School of Literary and Communications Studies
Deakin University
Geelong Vic 3217
Phone: (03) 5227 1100
Fax: (03) 5227 2018
Email: bje@deakin.edu.au
A refereed journal of literary and cultural studies that publishes essays, fiction, poetry, reviews and graphics.

Meanjin
University of Melbourne
Parkville Vic 3052
Phone: (03) 9344 6950
Fax: (03) 9347 2550
Email: meanjin@unimelb.edu.au
Website: www.meanjin.unimelb.edu.au
Australia's oldest literary periodical. The editor reads all submissions sent in hard copy and returns them with comment when a stamped self-addressed envelope is supplied. Three issues per year with a central theme, but accepts poetry and fiction unrelated to the theme.

Metaphysical Review (The)
59 Keele Street
Collingwood Vic 3066
Phone: (03) 9419 4797
Fax: (03) 9419 4797
Email: gandc@mira.net
A magazine of reviews and articles about the popular arts (genre literatures, film), general literature and music, and 'personal journalism'. Its letter column is a major feature. Despite its title, the magazine rarely discusses metaphysics.

Micropress Oz
12 Elgata Street
Petrie Qld 4502
Email: gloriabe@powerup.com.au
Exclusively poetry magazine willing to publish poems that have appeared elsewhere.

Muse
B-Block, Gorman House
Ainslie Avenue
Braddon ACT 2612
Phone: (02) 6247 6298
Fax: (02) 6247 7739
Email: muse@interact.net.au
Website: www.muse-arts.com.au
Multi-arts magazine focusing on the arts in the ACT and region.

Navigations
Blue Crow Press
35 Learoyd Street
Mount Lawley WA 6056
Phone: (08) 9272 1192

Magazines and Journals

Fax: (08) 9272 1192
Poetry broadsheet from Western Australia.

New England Review
PO Box U241
University of New England
Armidale NSW 2351
Phone: (02) 6772 2036
Email: jvicars@optusnet.com.au
Broadsheet of poetry, fiction and reviews.

New England Writers' Centre Newsletter
PO Box 1219
Armidale NSW 2350
Phone/Fax: (02) 6772 7210
Fax: (02) 6772 7210
Email: newc@northnet.com.au
Website: www.northnet.com.au/~newc
Newsletter of the New England Writers' Centre.

New Writer
KT Publishing
PO Box 584
Caboolture Qld 4510
Email: admin@kt-p.net
Website: www.kt-p.net
The online magazine for new writers.

Newswrite
PO Box 1056
Rozelle NSW 2039
Phone: (02) 9555 9757
Fax: (02) 9818 1327
Email: nswwc@ozemail.com.au
Website: www.nswwriterscentre.org.au
NSW Writers' Centre monthly magazine.

Orb: Speculative Fiction
PO Box 1621
South Preston Vic 3072
Phone: (03) 9471 9270
Email: kendacot@vicnet.net.au
Website: home.vicnet.net.au/~kendacot/Orb
A speculative fiction magazine.

Overland
PO Box 14146
Melbourne City Mail Centre
Melbourne Vic 8001
Phone: (03) 9688 4163
Fax: (03) 9688 4883
Email: overland@vu.edu.au
Website: www.vulgar.com.au
Contemporary literature, comment and ideas from a broad left standpoint.

Overland Express
9 David Street
Footscray Vic 3011
Email: overland@vu.edu.au
Website: www.overlandexpress.org
An online journal of Australian writing.

Papers: Explorations Into Children's Literature
School of Literature & Communication Studies
Deakin University
221 Burwood Highway
Burwood Vic 3125
Phone: (03) 9244 6487
Fax: (03) 9244 6755
Email: clarex@deakin.edu.au
Scholarly journal on children's literature.

papertiger
PO Box 5532
West End Qld 4101
Phone: (07) 3846 0976
Email: papertiger@rescueteam.com
Australia's first CD-ROM journal of poetry.

Pendulum Magazine
Chisholm Institute
Berwick Campus
71 Clyde Road
Berwick Vic 3806
Phone: (03) 9212 4603
Fax: (03) 9212 4999
Email: enquiries@chisholm.vic.edu.au
Website: www.chisholm.vic.edu.au

The Writer's Guide

Produced by students and staff of the Diploma of Art (Professional Writing) at Chisholm Institute.

PixelPapers
6 Cross Street
Swanbourne WA 6010
Phone: (08) 9384 1971
Fax: (08) 9384 1971
Email: pixpress@iinet.net.au
Website: www.iinet.net.au/~pixpress
PixelPapers publishes and re-publishes on the net poems, shorts, first chapters, reviews, news and views for no charge and no payment.

Poetrix
PO Box 532
Altona North Vic 3025
Phone/Fax: (03) 9314 1082
Bi-annual magazine of women's poetry.

Poets' Narrator
1a Coomber Street
Bundaberg Qld 4670
Phone: (07) 4154 1663
Published by the Bundaberg Poets Society.

QWC Newsletter
Level 2, 109 Edward Street
Brisbane Qld 4000
Phone: (07) 3839 1243
Phone: (07) 3839 1245
Email: qldwriters@peg.apc.org
Website: www.qwc.asn.au
Newsletter of the Queensland Writers' Centre.

Readers' World
PO Box 301
Joondalup WA 6919
Phone: (08) 9300 8247
Fax: (08) 9300 8247
Email: admin@readersworld.com.au
Website: www.readersworld.com.au
Each issue contains a single essay of at least 20 000 words as well as correspondence relating to the previous essay.

Reading Time
PO Box 62
Ashmont NSW 2650
Phone/Fax: (02) 6925 4907
Email: jacohen@ozemail.com.au
Non-profit educational journal from the Children's Book Council.

Red Lamp
5 Kahana Court
Mountain Creek Qld 4557
Email: evans_baj@hotmail.com
Website: www.geocities.com/red_lamp
A printed/online journal of realist, socialist and humanitarian poetry.

Redoubt
C/- University of Canberra
PO Box 1
Belconnen ACT 2616
Phone: (02) 6201 2945
Fax: (02) 6201 5300
Email: redoubt@comserver.canberra.edu.au

Science Fiction: A Review of Speculative Literature
Department of English
University of Western Australia
Crawley WA 6009
Phone: (08) 9380 2280
Fax: (08) 9380 1030
Email: vikin@cyllene.uwa.edu.au
A journal exploring the latest in science fiction and fantasy writing.

SF Commentary
59 Keele Street
Collingwood Vic 3066
Phone: (03) 9419 4797
Fax: (03) 94194797
Email: gandc@mira.net
A magazine of reviews and critical articles

Magazines and Journals

about science fiction and fantasy literature first published 1969. It has been nominated three times for the Hugo Award (World SF Award), and has won several Ditmar Awards (Australian SF Award).

Shortz
38 Warringah Grove
Petrie Qld 4502
Phone: (07) 3285 2887
Fax: (07) 3285 8011
Email: pauliner@powerup.com.au
Short story magazine.

SideWaLk
PO Box 58
Endfield Plaza SA 5085
Email: sidewalkpoe@hotmail.com
Poetry magazine.

South Coast Writers' Centre News Sheet
PO Box 32
Wollongong East NSW 2520
Phone/Fax: (02) 4228 0151
Email: scwc@1earth.net
Website: www.1earth.net/~scwc
Newsletter of the South Coast Writers' Centre.

Southerly
School of English A20
University of Sydney NSW 2006
Phone: (02) 9351 2569
Fax: (02) 9351 2434
Email: david.brooks@english.usyd.edu.au
Website: www.arts.usyd.edu.au/arts/departs/english/southerly
Literary magazine of poetry, short stories, articles, reviews and essays.

Southern Write
PO Box 43
Rundle Mall
Adelaide SA 5000
Phone: (08) 8223 7662

Fax: (08) 8232 3994
Email: sawriters@sawriters.on.net
Website: www.sawriters.on.net
Newsletter of the South Australian Writers' Centre.

Southern Review
Faculty of Art, Design and Communication
RMIT University
GPO Box 2476V
Melbourne Vic 3001
Phone: (03) 9925 9549
Fax: (03) 9639 1685
Email: southern.review@rmit.edu.au
Interdisciplinary journal focusing on the connections between communication and politics, cultural technologies, their histories, producers and audiences, policies and texts.

Steam Engine Time
59 Keele Street
Collingwood Vic 3066
Phone: (03) 9419 4797
Fax: (03) 9419 4797
Email: gandc@mira.net
Publishes long reviews and major articles about science fiction and fantasy literature.

Studio
727 Peel Street
Albury NSW 2640
Phone/Fax: (02) 6021 1135
Email: pgrover@bigpond.com
A journal of writing by Christians.

Stylus Poetry Journal
GPO Box 1931
Brisbane Qld 4000
Mobile: 0415 421 868
Email: editor@styluspoetryjournal.com
Website: www.styluspoetryjournal.com
A bi-monthly e-zine which publishes contemporary poetry and haiku and its related forms.

Swag of Yarns
PO Box 235
Albert Park Vic 3206
Phone: (03) 9690 0894
Fax:(03) 9690 0894
Email: bunyip@netspace.net.au
Website: www.netspace.net.au/~bunyip/
Australia's national storytelling magazine.

Swyntax
PO Box 218
Hawthorn Vic 3122
Phone: (03) 9214 8941
Email: opavlinov@swin.edu.au
Website: www.swin.edu.au/swyntax

Tamba
230 Old Dookie Road
Shepparton Vic 3630
Phone: (03) 5821 6663
Magazine of the Goulburn Valley Writers' Group.

Tasmanian Writers' Centre Newsletter
77 Salamanca Place
Hobart Tas 7004
Phone/Fax: (03) 6224 0029
Email: ed_taswriters@trump.net.au
Website: www.fearless.net.au/taswriters

TEXT
School of Arts, Gold Coast Campus
Griffith University Qld 9726
Phone: (03) 9244 3956
Email: text@mailbox.gu.edu.au
Website: www.gu.edu.au/school/art/text/
Australian Association of Writing Programs e-journal.

Tirra Lirra
Phoebe Publishing
PO Box 305
Mount Evelyn Vic 3796
Phone: (03) 9736 1377
Email: phoebus@netlink.com.au
Website: www.netlink.com.au/~phoebus

Tirra Lirra is an independent, well-produced, literary magazine.

Unsweetened
Publications Coordinator
UNSW Union
PO Box 173
Kingsford NSW
Phone: (02) 9931 3153
Fax: (02) 9662 6340
Email: unsweetened@unsw.edu.au
An annual journal by students of the University of New South Wales.

Varuna Writers' Centre Newsletter
141 Cascade Street
Katoomba NSW 2780
Phone: (02) 4782 5674
Fax: (02) 4782 6220
Email: varuna@varuna.com.au
Website: www.varuna.com.au

Verandah
C/- Arts Faculty
Deakin University
221 Burwood Highway
Burwood Vic 3125
Phone: (03) 9251 7134
Email: verandah@deakin.edu.au
Published and edited by students of Deakin University's Professional Writing and Editing course.

Vernacular
PO Box 598
Torrensville Plaza SA 5031
Phone: (08) 8431 3352, 8443 8675
Email: vernacularlit@hotmail.com
Website: www.vernacular.com.au
Adelaide-based streetwise literary compilation committed to brave new writing.

ViewPoint: On Books for Young Adults
PO Box 4286
University of Melbourne Vic 3052

Magazines and Journals

Phone: (03) 9344 8617
Fax: (03) 9344 0025
Email: viewpoint@edfac.unimelb.edu.au
Website: www.edfac.unimelb.edu.au/LLAE/viewpoint/
Contains reviews and articles about young adult fiction, authors and readers.

WA State Literature Centre Newsletter
Fremantle Arts Centre
PO Box 891
Fremantle WA 6160
Phone: (08) 9432 9559
Fax: (08) 9430 6613
Email: slo@fremantle.wa.gov.au
Website: www.writerswritingwa.org

Wagga Wagga Writers Writers Newsletter
Charles Sturt University
PO Box 588
Wagga Wagga NSW 2678
Phone: (02) 6933 2688
Fax: (02) 6933 2792
Email: booranga@csu.edu.au
Website: www.csu.edu.au/faculty/arts/humss/booranga/index.html
Newsletter of Booranga Writers' Centre.

Wagtail
Picaro Press
PO Box 853
Warners Bay NSW 2282
Phone: 0438 659 868
Email: jandr@hunterlink.net.au
Poetry magazine.

Weekly Book Newsletter
18 Salmon Street
Port Melbourne Vic 3207
Phone: (03) 9245 7370
Fax: (03) 9245 7395
Email: blue.newsletter@thorpe.com.au
Website: www.thorpe.com.au
Weekly newsletter aimed at the publishing industry.

Westerly
Department of English
University of Western Australia
Nedlands WA 6907
Phone: (08) 9380 2101
Fax: (08) 9380 1030
Email: westerly@cyllene.uwa.edu.au
Website: www.arts.uwa.edu.au/westerly
Publishes lively fiction and poetry as well as intelligent articles. Aims to generate interest in the literature and culture of Australia and its neighbouring regions.

Western Word
PO Box 312
Cottesloe WA 6011
Phone: (08) 9384 4771
Fax: (08) 9384 4854
Email: fawwa@iinet.net.au
Website: www.iinet.net.au/fawwa/
Official magazine of the Fellowship of Australian Writers WA.

Winedark Sea
PO Box 367
Southgate
Sylvania NSW 2224
Email: editors@winedark.com
Website: www.winedark.com/index.html
A journal of the surreal, the fantastic and the magically real.

Woorilla
Woorilla Farm
255 Macclesfield Road
Avonsleigh Vic 3782
Phone: (03) 5968 4291
Fax: (03) 5968 4152
Email: woorilla@nex.net.au
Woorilla is an irregular literary magazine accepting well-written but accessible articles on current sociological/political issues, poetry, short fiction and black/white graphics. Occasional publications of established and emerging writers are also produced.

The Writer's Guide

Write On
Meat Market Arts House
42 Courtney Street
North Melbourne Vic 3051
Phone: (03) 9326 4619
Fax: (03) 9326 4974
Email: info@writers-centre.org
Website: www.writers-centre.org
Newsletter of the Victorian Writers' Centre.

Write Stuff (The)
PO Box 1846
Byron Bay NSW 2481
Phone: (02) 6685 5115
Fax: (02) 6685 5166
Email: nrwc@nrg.com.au
Website: www.nrg.com.au/nrwc/
Newsletter of the Northern Rivers Writers' Centre.

Write Turn
GPO Box 2255
Darwin NT 800
Phone: (08) 8941 2651
Fax: (08) 8941 2115
Email: ntwriter@octa4.net.au
Website: www.ntwriters.com.au
Newsletter of the NT Writers' Centre Inc.

Writer Writer
8/50 Reservoir Street
Surry Hills NSW 2010
Phone: (02) 9281 1554
Fax: (02) 9281 4321
Email: admin@awg.com.au
Website: www.awg.com.au
Newsletter of the Australian Writers' Guild.

Writers Voice
PO Box 488
Rozelle NSW 2039
Phone/Fax: (02) 9810 1307
Email: faw1@bigpond.com
Website: www.ozemail.com.au/~faw
Bulletin of the Fellowship of Australian Writers NSW.

Writer's Friend
PO Box 7054
Eaton WA 6232
Phone: (08) 9724 1460
Email: penann@iinet.net.au
Website: www.skybusiness.com/writers
Publishes subscribers' poems, stories and articles.

Writing for Success
PO Box A47
Shellharbour NSW 2529
Phone: (02) 4297 6114
Fax: (02) 4297 0819
Email: editor@writing4success.com
Website: www.writing4success.com
Bi-monthly magazine that provides inspiration and industry information for writers in all genres: tips on technique; interviews with editors and agents; articles and columns about e-publishing, screenwriting, running a writing business, marketing your work and how other authors achieve success.

Yuanxiang (Otherland)
PO Box 200
Kingsbury Vic 3083
Phone/Fax: (03) 9467 8169
Email: youyang@bigpond.net.au
Chinese language literary bi-annual.

NEW ZEALAND LITERARY MAGAZINES

Evasion
PO Box 1663
Shortland Street
Auckland
Phone: (09) 630 5895
Email: evasion@lost.co.nz
Website: www.evasion.co.nz

Magazines and Journals

Fresh
6 Smith Crescent
Onehunga
Auckland 1006
Email: kevin.mcivor@xtra.co.nz
kmc39@hotmail.com
Poetry magazine.

JAAM
26 Grant Road
Thorndon
Wellington
Website: headworx.eyesis.co.nz
National literary journal run by an independent publishing collective.

Kite
English Department
University of Otago
Dunedin
Phone: (03) 479 1100
Email: heather.murray@stonebow.otago.ac.nz
Produced by the Association of New Zealand Literature.

Landfall
University of Otago Press
PO Box 56
Dunedin
Phone: (03) 479 8807
Fax: (03) 479 8385
Email: landfall@otago.ac.nz
In May and November publishes the best new art and quality writing (articles, essays, fiction, reviews, photographs and poetry) by New Zealand and international artists and writers.

New Zealand Books
Level 5, Old Wool House
139–141 Featherton Street
Wellington
Phone: (04) 499 1569
Fax: (04) 499 1424
Email: nzbooks@bookcouncil.org.nz
Website: www.bookcouncil.org.nz
A review of new books published in New Zealand.

New Zealand Books in Print
PO Box 34–198
Birkenhead
Auckland
Phone: (09) 480 9562
Fax   (09) 480 9584
Email: nzbip@ix.net.nz
Website: www.thorpe.com.au
A comprehensive review of New Zealand books.

Southern Ocean Review
PO Box 2143
Dunedin
Email: treeves@es.co.nz
Website: www.book.co.nz
Online and print literary and arts magazine.

Sport
PO Box 11–806
Wellington
Phone: (04) 463 6526
Fax: (04) 463 6581
Email: fergus.barrowman@vuw.ac.nz
New Zealand new writing.

Takahe
Takahe Collective Trust
PO Box 13 335
Christchurch
Promotes the work of emerging New Zealand authors, artists and editors.

Turbine
International Institute of Modern Letters
Victoria University of Wellington
PO Box 600
Wellington
Email: turbine@vuw.ac.nz
Website: www.vuw.ac.nz/turbine
Online literary journal.

The Writer's Guide

Valley Micropress
PO Box 48 002
Silverstream
Upper Hutt
Poetry magazine.

Write Now
76 Saxby Road
Deanwell
Hamilton
Magazine of short fiction and rhyming poetry.

ORGANISATIONS

The organisations listed below were correct at the time of writing, but if you find that they are no longer in existence or have changed address, please let us know. Tollfree numbers can usually only be used in the state in which the organisation is based. TTY phone numbers (available for some government organisations) cater for those who are deaf.

WRITERS' CENTRES

ACT Writers' Centre

Gorman House Arts Centre
Ainslie Avenue
Braddon ACT 2612
Phone/Fax: (02) 6262 9191
Email: director@actwriters.org.au
Website: www.actwriters.org.au

Booranga Writers' Centre

Locked Bag 588
Wagga Wagga NSW 2678
Phone: (02) 6933 2688
Fax: (02) 6933 2688
Email: booranga@csu.edu.au
Website: www.csu.edu.au/faculty/arts/humss/booranga/index.html

Broken Hill Writers' Centre

Broken Hill City Library
Blende Street
Broken Hill NSW 2880
Phone: (08) 8088 3317
Fax: (08) 8087 8055
Email: bhcl@ruralnet.net.au

Central West Writers' Centre

PO Box E156
Orange NSW 2800
Phone: (02) 6393 8125
Fax: (02) 6393 8100
Email: writing@netwit.net.au
Website: www.netwit.net.au/~writing

Hunter Writers' Centre

PO Box 71
Hamilton NSW 2303
Phone: (02) 4940 0003
Fax: (02) 4962 3959
Email: puzzleprod@bigpond.com
Website: www.mockfrog.com/hwc

New England Writers' Centre

PO Box 1219
Armidale NSW 2350
Phone/Fax: (02) 6772 7210
Email: newc@northnet.com.au
Website: www.northnet.com.au/~newc

NSW Writers' Centre

PO Box 1056
Rozelle NSW 2039
Phone: (02) 9555 9757
Fax: (02) 9818 1327
Email: nswwc@ozemail.com.au
Website: www.nswwriterscentre.org.au

Northern Rivers Writers' Centre

PO Box 1846
Byron Bay NSW 2481
Phone: (02) 6685 5115
Fax: (02) 6685 5166
Email: nrwc@nrg.com.au
Website: www.nrwc.com.au

NT Writers' Centre

GPO Box 2255
Darwin NT 0801
Phone: (08) 8941 2651
Fax: (08) 8941 2115
Email: ntwriter@octa4.net.au
Website: www.ntwriters.com.au

Queensland Writers' Centre

Level 2, 109 Edward Street
Brisbane Qld 4000
Phone: (07) 3839 1243
Fax: (07) 3839 1245
Email: qldwriters@qwc.asn.au
Website: www.qwc.asn.au

SA Writers' Centre

PO Box 43
Rundle Mall
Adelaide SA 5000
Phone: (08) 8223 7662
Fax: (08) 8232 3994
Email: sawriters@sawriters.on.net
Website: www.sawriters.on.net

South Coast Writers' Centre

PO Box 32
Wollongong East NSW 2520
Phone/Fax: (02) 4228 0151
Email: scwc@1earth.net
Website: www.1earth.net/~scwc

Tasmanian Writers' Centre

77 Salamanca Place
Hobart Tas 7000
Phone/Fax: (03) 6224 0029
Email: director@tasmanianwriters.org
Website: www.tasmanianwriters.org

Varuna Writers' Centre

141 Cascade Street
Katoomba NSW 2780
Phone: (02) 4782 5674
Fax: (02) 4782 6220
Email: varuna@varuna.com.au
Website: www.varuna.com.au

Victorian Writers' Centre

Meat Market Arts House
42 Courtney Street
North Melbourne Vic 3051
Phone: (03) 9326 4619
Fax: (03) 9326 4974
Email: info@writers-centre.org
Website: www.writers-centre.org

WA State Literature Centre

Fremantle Arts Centre
PO Box 891
Fremantle WA 6160
Phone: (08) 9432 9559
Fax: (08) 9430 6613
Email: slo@fremantle.wa.gov.au
Website: www.writerswritingwa.org

AUSTRALIAN ARTS BODIES

Federal

Aboriginal and Torres Strait Islander Unit of Arts

PO Box 5300
Cairns Mail Centre Qld 4870
Phone: (07) 4048 1411
Fax: (07) 4048 1410
Email: CairnsAQ@arts.qld.gov.au
Website: www.arts.qld.gov.au

Australia Council for the Arts

PO Box 788
Strawberry Hills NSW 2012
Phone: (02) 9215 9000
Tollfree: 1800 226 912
Fax: (02) 9215 9161
Email: info@ozco.gov.au
Website: www.ozco.gov.au

Department of Communications, Information Technology and the Arts

PO Box 2154
Canberra ACT 2601
Phone: (02) 6271 1000
Artsinfo: 1800 241 247
Fax: (02) 6271 1901
Email: dcit.mail@dcita.gov.au
Website: www.dcita.gov.au

State

Arts ACT

GPO Box 158
Canberra ACT 2601
Phone: (02) 6207 2384
Fax: (02) 6207 2386
Email: Caroline.Fulton@act.gov.au
Website: www.arts.act.gov.au

Arts Queensland

PO Box 1436
Brisbane Qld 4001
Phone: (07) 3224 4896
Tollfree: 1800 175 531
Fax: (07) 3224 4077
Email: info@arts.qld.gov.au
Website: www.arts.qld.gov.au

Arts South Australia

GPO Box 2308
Adelaide SA 5001
Phone: (08) 8463 5444
Fax: (08) 8463 5420
Website: www.arts.sa.gov.au

Arts Tasmania

GPO Box 646
Hobart 7001
Phone: (03) 6233 7308
Tollfree: 1800 247 308
Fax: (03) 6223 8424
Email: arts.tasmania@arts.tas.gov.au
Website: www.arts.tas.gov.au

Arts Victoria

Private Bag No. 1
South Melbourne Vic 3205
Phone: (03) 9954 5000
Tollfree: 1800 134 894
TTY: (03) 9682 4864
Fax: (03) 9686 6186
Email: artsvic@dpc.vic.gov.au
Website: www.arts.vic.gov.au

Arts WA

PO Box 8349
Perth Business Centre WA 6849
Phone: (08) 9224 7310
Tollfree: 1800 199 090
Fax: (08) 9224 7311
Email: info@artswa.mca.wa.gov.au
Website: imago.com.au/artswa

The Writer's Guide

NSW Ministry for the Arts

PO Box A226
Sydney South NSW 1235
Phone: (02) 9228 5533
Tollfree: 1800 358 594
TTY: (02) 9228 4869
Fax: (02) 9228 4722
Email: ministry@arts.nsw.gov.au
Website: www.arts.nsw.gov.au

Arts NT (Darwin)

GPO Box 1774
Darwin NT 0801
Phone: (08) 8924 4400
Tollfree: 1800 678 237
Fax: (08) 8924 4409
Email: arts.office@nt.gov.au
Website: www.nt.gov.au/dam

Arts NT (Alice Springs)

PO Box 3521
Alice Springs NT 0871
Fax: (08) 8951 1161
Phone: (08) 8951 1190, 8951 1145

NEW ZEALAND ARTS BODY

Creative New Zealand (Arts Council of New Zealand Toi Aotearoa)

PO Box 3806
Wellington
Phone: (04) 473 0880
Fax: (04) 471 2865
Email: rosemaryw@creativenz.govt.nz
Website: www.creativenz.govt.nz

AUSTRALIAN ORGANISATIONS

ABC Radio Drama

Editorial Co-ordinator
GPO Box 9994
Sydney NSW 2001
Phone: (02) 9333 1335
Fax: (02) 9333 1306
Email: buckham.richard@abc.net.au
Website: www.abc.net.au/rn

Academy of Photogenic Arts International Film School

63 Dickson Avenue
Artarmon NSW 2064
Phone: (02) 9439 9636
Email: carole@apa.edu.au
Website: www.apa.edu.au

Accessible Arts

Pier 4, The Wharf
Hickson Road
Walsh Bay NSW 2000
Phone: (02) 9251 6499
Fax: (02) 9251 6422
Email: aarts@ozemail.com.au
Website: www.central.com.au/aarts/
Organisation for artists with disabilities.

APM Training Institute

Level 1, 33 Chandos Street
St Leonards NSW 2065
Phone: (02) 9436 0155
Fax: (02) 9906 2625
Email: enquiries@apmtraining.com.au
Website: www.apmtraining.com.au
Provides training in marketing and public relations.

Arts Law Centre

The Gunnery
43–51 Cowper Wharf Road

Organisations

Woolloomooloo NSW 2011
Phone: (02) 9356 2566
Tollfree: 1800 221 457
Fax: (02) 9358 6475
Email: info@artslaw.com.au
Website: www.artslaw.com.au

ArtsLink

C/- Performance Media
1st Floor, 382 Pacific Highway
Crows Nest NSW 2065
Phone: (02) 9966 9577
Fax: (02) 9966 8719
Email: media@bigpond.net.au
Website: www.performancemedia.org.au

Asialink

Level 4 Sidney Myer Asia Centre
University of Melbourne Vic 3010
Phone: (03) 8344 4800
Fax: (03) 9347 1768
Email: a.carroll@asialink.unimelb.edu.au
Website: www.asialink.unimelb.edu.au

Association of Australian Writing Programs

C/- Steve Evans
Department of English
Flinders University
GPO Box 2100
Adelaide SA 5001
Email: steve.evans@flinders.edu.au
Website: www.gu.edu.au/school/art/text/

Association of Writers at Work Inc.

PO Box 3329, Village Fair
Toowoomba Qld 4350
Phone: (07) 4633 4903

Australian Booksellers' Association

(with branches in other states)
Suite 65, 3rd Floor
255 Drummond Street
Carlton Vic 3053
Phone: (03) 9349 5766
Fax: (03) 9349 5799
Email: mail@aba.org.au
Website: www.aba.org.au

Australian Bush Poets Association Inc.

PO Box 16
Canowindra NSW 2804
Phone: (02) 6344 1477
Fax: (02) 6344 1962
Email: bushpoet@bushpoetry.com.au
Website: www.bushpoetry.com.au

Australian Centre for Independent Journalism

PO Box 123
Broadway NSW 2007
Phone: (02) 9514 2488
Fax: (02) 9281 2976
Email: acij@uts.edu.au
Website: www.acij.uts.edu.au

Australian Chapter of Romance Writers of America

Warnambool Business Centre
Raglan Parade
Warnambool Vic 3280
Phone: (03) 5560 5054
Fax: (03) 5560 5166
Email: wordcraft@ozzienet.net

Australian College of Journalism

PO Box 1151
Bondi Junction NSW 1355
Phone: (02) 9389 6499 or 1300 309 225
Fax: (02) 9389 4277
Email: principal@acj.edu.au
Website: www.acj.edu.au

335

Australian Copyright Council

PO Box 1986
Strawberry Hills 2012
Phone: (02) 9318 1788
Fax: (02) 9698 3536
Email: info@copyright.org.au
Website: www.copyright.org.au

Australian Film Commission (AFC)

GPO Box 3984
Sydney NSW 2001
Phone: (02) 9321 6444
Tollfree: 1800 226 615
Fax: (02) 9357 3737
Email: info@afc.gov.au
Website: www.afc.gov.au

AFC Victoria Office

PO Box 404
South Melbourne Vic 3205
Phone: (03) 8646 4300
Tollfree: 1800 338 430
Fax: (03) 9696 1476
Email: infomelb@afc.gov.au
Website: www.afc.gov.au

AFC Queensland Office

PO Box 94, Albert Street
Brisbane 4002
Phone: (07) 3224 4114
Fax: (07) 3224 6717
Email: ojohnston@pftc.com.au
Website: www.afc.gov.au

Australian Film Institute

Level 1, 49 Eastern Road
South Melbourne Vic 3205
Phone: (03) 9696 1844
Fax: (03) 9696 7972
Email: info@afi.org.au
Website: www.afi.org.au

Australian Film, Television and Radio School (AFTRS)

National HQ/NSW
PO Box 126
North Ryde NSW 1670
Phone: 1300 13 14 61 or (02) 9805 6611
Fax: (02) 9887 1030
Email: info_nsw@aftrs.edu.au
Website: www.aftrs.edu.au

AFTRS Victoria

PO Box 1008
South Melbourne Vic 3205
Phone: (03) 9690 7111
Fax: (03) 9690 1283
Email: info_vic@aftrs.edu.au
Website: www.aftrs.edu.au

AFTRS Queensland

PO Box 1480
Fortitude Valley Qld 4006
Phone: (07) 3257 7646
Fax: (07) 3257 7641
Email: info_qld@aftrs.edu.au
Website: www.aftrs.edu.au

AFTRS South Australia

SAFC Studios
3 Butler Drive
Hendon SA 5014
Phone: (08) 8244 0357
Fax: (08) 8244 5608
Email: info_sa@aftrs.edu.au
Website: www.aftrs.edu.au

AFTRS Tasmania

5 Trumpeter Street
Battery Point Tas 7004
Phone: (03) 6223 8703
Fax: (03) 6224 6143
Email: info_tas@aftrs.edu.au
Website: www.aftrs.edu.au

AFTRS Western Australia

Film & Television Institute of WA
92 Adelaide Street
Fremantle WA 6160
Phone: (08) 9335 1055
Fax: (08) 9335 1283
Email: info_wa@aftrs.edu.au
Website: www.aftrs.edu.au

Australian Institute of Interpreters and Translators (AUSIT) National Office & NSW Branch

PO Box A202
Sydney South NSW 1235
Phone/Fax: (02) 9626 7046
Email: nsw@ausit.org
Website: www.ausit.org

AUSIT ACT Branch

GPO Box 1732
Canberra City ACT 2601
Phone: (02) 6281 5527
Fax: (02) 6281 5549
Email: act@ausit.org
Website: www.ausit.org

AUSIT Qld Branch

PO Box 10427
Adelaide Street Post Office
Brisbane Qld 4000
Phone: 0407 127 713
Email: qld@ausit.org
Website: www.ausit.org

AUSIT SA and NT Branch

PO Box 6182
Halifax Street
Adelaide SA 5000
Phone/Fax: (08) 8297 0491
Email: sant@ausit.org
Website: www.ausit.org

AUSIT Vic and Tas Branch

PO Box 1070
Blackburn North Vic 3130
Phone: (03) 9877 4369
Fax: (03) 9893 4686
Email: victas@ausit.org
Website: www.ausit.org

AUSIT WA Branch

43 Newborough Street
Scarborough WA 6019
Phone: (08) 9245 1474
Fax: (08) 9245 1430
Email: wa@ausit.org
Website: www.ausit.org

Australian Interactive Multimedia Industry Association (AIMIA)

Level 6, 9–31 Pitt Street
Sydney NSW 2000
Phone: (02) 9252 4938
Fax: (02) 9252 4914
Email: aimia@aimia.com.au
Website: www.aimia.com.au

Australian Literary Translators' Association (ALiTrA)

Melbourne
Judith Rodriguez
Phone: (03) 9244.6760
Email: rodju@deakin.edu.au
Sydney
Barbara McGilvray
Phone: (02) 9953 6845
Email: bmcg@frc.usyd.edu.au

Australian National Playwrights' Centre (ANPC)

PO Box 1566
Rozelle NSW 2039
Phone: (02) 9555 9377
Fax: (02) 9555 9370

Email: info@anpc.org.au
Website: www.anpc.org.au

Australasian Performing Right Association (APRA)

Head Office (NSW)
Locked Bag 3665
St Leonards NSW 2065
Phone: (02) 9935 7900
Fax: (02) 9935 7999
Email: apra@apra.com.au
Website: www.apra.com.au

APRA NT

Membership inquiries to SA office
Licensing inquiries to Qld office

APRA Qld Office

PO Box 21
Spring Hill Qld 4001
Phone: (07) 3257 1007
Fax: (07) 3257 1113
Email: qld@apra.com.au
Website: www.apra.com.au

APRA SA Office

Suite 54, 55 Melbourne Street
North Adelaide SA 5006
Phone: (08) 8239 2222
Fax: (08) 8239 0744
Email: sa@apra.com.au
Website: www.apra.com.au

APRA Vic Office

3 and 5 Sanders Place
Richmond Vic 3121
Phone: (03) 9426 5200
Fax: (03) 9426 5211
Email: victas@apra.com.au
Website: www.apra.com.au

APRA WA Office

177A York Street
Subiaco WA 6008
Phone: (08) 9382 8299
Fax: (08) 9382 8224
Email: wa@apra.com.au
Website: www.apra.com.au

Australian Publishers Association

Suite 60, 89 Jones Street
Ultimo NSW 2007
Phone: (02) 9281 9788
Fax: (02) 9281 1073
Email: apa@publishers.asn.au
Website: www.publishers.asn.au

Australian Science Communicators

PO Box 5009
Nowra DC NSW 2541
Phone: (02) 4422 2205
Fax: (02) 4422 3878
Email: office@asc.asn.au
Website: www.asap.unimelb.edu.au/asc

Australian Script Centre

77 Salamanca Place
Hobart Tas 7004
Phone/Fax: (03) 6223 4675
Email: info@ozscript.org
Website: www.ozscript.org

Australian Society for Technical Communicators (ASTC)

NSW Branch
PO Box R 812
Royal Exchange NSW 1225
Phone: (02) 8250 7056
Fax: (02) 9252 0441
Email: info@astcnsw.org.au
Website: www.astcnsw.org.au

ASTC Vic Branch

PO Box 932
Bayswater Vic 3153
Email: president@astcvic.org.au
Website: www.astcvic.org.au

Australian Society of Authors (ASA)

PO Box 1566
Strawberry Hills NSW 2012
Phone: (02) 9318 0877
Fax: (02) 9318 0530
Email: asa@asauthors.org
Website: www.asauthors.org
Organisation for professional and other writers.

Australian Society of Indexers (AusSI)

PO Box R598
Royal Exchange NSW 2001
Phone: 0500 525 005
Fax: (02) 9358 5593
Email: secretary@aussi.org
Website: www.aussi.org

AusSI NSW Branch

PO Box R598
Royal Exchange NSW 2001
Phone: 0500 525 005
Fax: (02) 9358 5593
Email: nswbranch@aussi.org
Website: www.aussi.org

AusSI ACT Branch

GPO Box 2069
Canberra ACT 2601
Phone: (02) 6286 3259
Fax: (02) 6286 6570
Email: actbranch@aussi.org
Website: www.aussi.org

AusSI Vic Branch

PO Box 1251
Melbourne Vic
Phone/Fax: (03) 9528 2539
Email: vicbranch@aussi.org
Website: www.aussi.org

Australian Society of Speculative Fiction Writers

Email: sfoz@sf.org.au

Australian Storytelling Guild

QVB Post Office
Sydney 1230
Phone/Fax: (02) 9882 8880
Email: dap@mail.hwy.com.au
Website: www.home.aone.net.au/stories/index.html

Australian Writers' Guild (AWG)

Organisation for professional performance writers.

AWG Head Office (NSW)

8/50 Reservoir Street
Surry Hills NSW 2010
Phone: (02) 9281 1554
Fax: (02) 9281 4321
Email: admin@awg.com.au
Website: www.awg.com.au

AWG Qld Office

QPIX
33A Logan Road
Woolloongabba Qld 4102
Phone/Fax: (07) 3391 2809
Email: awgqld@powerup.com.au

AWG SA Office

PO Box 43
Rundle Mall SA 5000
Phone: (08) 8232 6852
Email: sa@awg.com.au

AWG Vic Office

Metropolitan Meat Market
42 Courtney Street
North Melbourne Vic 3031
Phone: (03) 9328 5671
Fax: (03) 9328 5670
Email: awgvic@ozemail.com.au

AWG WA Office

PO Box 492
Leederville WA 6007
Phone: (08) 9201 1172
Fax: (08) 9201 1173
Email: wa@awg.com.au

Barkly Regional Community Arts Officer

PO Box 259
Tennant Creek NT 0861
Phone: (08) 8962 1380
Email: barklyarts@bigpond.com

Brown's Mart Community Arts

GPO Box 2429
Darwin NT 0801
Phone: (08) 8981 5522
Fax: (08) 8941 3222
Email: brownsmart@octa4.net.au
Website: www.brownsmart.com

Canberra Centre for Writing

University of Canberra ACT 2601
Phone: (02) 6201 2321
Fax: (02) 6201 5300
Email: jlw@comedu.canberra.edu.au

Centre for Science Communication

Mary Mulcahy
University of Technology, Sydney
PO Box 123
Broadway NSW 2007
Phone: (02) 9514 2249
Fax: (02) 9514 2260
Email: mary.mulcahy@uts.edu.au

Children's Book Council of Australia (CBCA)

Head Office
PO Box 470
Mount Lawley WA 6929
Phone: (08) 9371 5018
Website: www.cbc.org.au

CBCA ACT Branch

PO Box 48
Hughes ACT 2605
Email: act@cbc.org.au
Website: www.cbc.org.au

CBCA NSW

PO Box 765
Rozelle NSW 2039
Phone/Fax: (02) 9810 0737
Website: www.cbc.org.au

CBCA NT Branch

PO Box 40119
Casuarina NT 0811
Phone: (08) 8927 1636
Fax: (08) 8928 0971
Email: cooperjudith@bigpond.com
Website: www.cbc.org.au/nt

CBCA Qld Branch

PO Box 828
Spring Hill Qld 4004
Phone/Fax: (07) 3217 5155
Email: cbcqld@gil.com.au
Website: www.cbc.org/qld/

CBCA SA Branch

PO Box 2392
Adelaide SA 5001
Phone/Fax: (08) 8332 7025
Email: sa@cbc.org.au
Website: www.cbc.org.au

CBCA Tas Branch

PO Box 113
Moonah Tas 7009
Email: tas@cbc.org.au
Website: www.cbc.org.au

CBCA Vic Branch

PO Box 275
Carlton South Vic 3053
Phone/Fax: (03) 9349 3111
Email: vic@cbc.org.au
Website: www.cbc.org.au

CBCA WA

PO Box 473
West Perth WA 6872
Email: wa@cbc.org.au
Website: www.cbc.org.au

Chimaera Publications

PO Box 2164
Mt Waverley Vic 3149
Phone: (03) 9534 1569
Fax: (03) 9534 1530
Email: straz@fhills.hotkey.net.au

Community Broadcasting Association of Australia

PO Box 564
Alexandria NSW 1435
Phone: (02) 9310 2999
Fax: (02) 9319 4545
Email: office@cbaa.org.au
Website: www.cbaa.org.au

Copyright Agency Limited (CAL)

Level 19, 157 Liverpool Street
Sydney NSW 2000
Phone: (02) 9394 7600
Fax: (02) 9394 7601
Email: info@copyright.com.au
Website: www.copyright.com.au

Council of Australian Societies of Editors

Website: www.editorscanberra.org/case.htm
See also Society of Editors

Crime Writers' Association of Australia

C/- Preston Lower Post Office
3 Gilbert Road
Preston Vic 3072
Email: nedkellynews@yahoo.com.au
Website: members.optusnet.com.au/~honey

Embryo Films

PO Box 68
St Pauls NSW 2031
Phone: (02) 9399 6951
Email: workshop@embryo-films.com
Website: www.embryo-films.com

Fellowship of Australian Writers (FAW) ACT Branch

GPO Box 728
Canberra ACT 2601

FAW NSW Branch

PO Box 488
Rozelle NSW 2039
Phone/Fax: (02) 9810 1307
Email: faw1@bigpond.com
Website: www.ozemail.com.au/~faw

FAW NT Branch

PO Box 37512
Winnellie NT 0820

FAW Qld Branch

PO Box 6338
Upper Mt Gravatt Qld 4122

FAW SA Branch

53 Ozone Street
Victor Harbour SA 5311

FAW Tas South Branch

C/- PO
Margate Tas 7045
Website: www.tased.edu.au/tasonline/fawtas

FAW Tas Nth Branch

8 Olive Street
Burnie Tas 7320

FAW Vic Branch

PO Box 3036
Ripponlea Vic 3183
Phone/Fax: (03) 9528 7088
Email: lori_faw@hotmail.com
Website: www.writers.asn.au

FAW WA Branch

Tom Collins House Writers' Centre
Allen Park, 88 Wood Street
Swanbourne WA 6010
Phone: (08) 9384 4771
Fax: (08) 9343 0072
Email: fawwa@iinet.net.au
Website: members.iinet.net.au/~fawwa

Film Victoria

GPO Box 4361
Melbourne Vic 3001
Phone: (03) 9651 0600
Fax: (03) 9651 0606
Website: www.film.vic.gov.au

Illustrators Australia

PO Box 1174
St Kilda South Vic 3182
Phone: (03) 5956 9587
Fax: (03) 5956 9591
Email: info@webfolio.com.au
Website: www.webfolio.com.au

Insearch Ltd

PO Box K1206
Haymarket NSW 1240
Phone: (02) 9281 4544
Fax: (02) 9281 4675
Email: courses@insearch.edu.au
Website: www.insearch.edu.au

International Board on Books for Young People (Australia)

Unit 1, 85 Yarranabbe Road
Darling Point NSW 2027
Phone: (02) 9363 5075
Email: enanoelibby@hotmail.com

ISBN Agency

Locked Bag 20
Port Melbourne Vic 3207
Phone: (03) 9245 7385
Fax: (03) 9245 7393
Email: isbn@thorpe.com.au
Website: www.thorpe.com.au

Katharine Susannah Prichard Writers' Centre

Old York Road
Greenmount WA 6056
Phone: (08) 9294 1872
Fax: (08) 9294 1372
Website: kspf.iinet.net.au

Macleay College

PO Box 433
Paddington NSW 2021
Phone: (02) 9360 2033
Fax: (02) 9331 7368
Email: enquire@macleay.edu.au
Website: www.macleay.edu.au
Training college for editing, advertising, marketing and public relations.

Media, Entertainment and Arts Alliance

PO Box 723
Strawberry Hills NSW 2012
Phone: (02) 9333 0999
Fax: (02) 9333 0933
Email: federal@alliance.org.au
Website: www.alliance.org.au

Media Network & Personnel

Suite 10, 450 Elizabeth Street
Surry Hills NSW 2010
Phone: (02) 8399 3196
Fax: (02) 8399 3240
Email: greg@ano.com.au
Website: www.mnp.com.au

Media Resource Centre

13 Morphett Street
Adelaide SA 5000
Phone: (08) 8410 0979
Fax: (08) 8410 1787
Email: info@mrc.org.au
Website: www.mrc.org.au

Melbourne Poets Union Inc

PO Box 266
Flinders Lane Vic 8009
Phone: (03) 9386 6259

Melbourne Writers' Theatre

PO Box 1049
Carlton Vic 3053
Phone: (03) 9347 2562

Metro Screen

PO Box 299
Paddington NSW 2021
Phone: (02) 9361 5318
Fax: (02) 9361 5320
Email: metro@metroscreen.com.au
Website: www.metroscreen.com.au

National Accreditation Authority for Translators and Interpreters (NAATI) ACT

PO Box 40
Hawker ACT 2614
Phone: (02) 6255 1888
Fax: (02) 6255 1889
Email: info@naati.com.au
Website: www.naati.com.au

NAATI NSW

PO Box A161
Sydney South NSW 1235
Phone: (02) 9267 1357
Fax: (02) 9267 4720
Email: info@naati.com.au
Website: www.naati.com.au

NAATI NT

PO Box 418
Darwin NT 0801
Phone: (08) 8941 3405
Email: info@naati.com.au
Website: www.naati.com.au

NAATI Qld

PO Box 8179
Woolloongabba Qld 4102

Phone: (07) 3393 1358
Fax: (07) 3393 0745
Email: info@naati.com.au
Website: www.naati.com.au

NAATI SA

PO Box 18
Rundle Mall SA 5000
Phone: (08) 8410 5233
Fax: (08) 8410 5235
Email: info@naati.com.au
Website: www.naati.com.au

NAATI Tas

Room 2, Level 1
McDougall Building
Ellerslie Road Battery Point
Hobart Tas 7004
Phone: (03) 6223 6534
Fax: (03) 6224 4914
Email: info@naati.com.au
Website: www.naati.com.au

NAATI Vic

Suite 14, Level 1
Lonsdale Court
600 Lonsdale Street
Melbourne Vic 3000
Phone: (03) 9642 3301
Fax: (03) 9642 3303
Email: info@naati.com.au
Website: www.naati.com.au

NAATI WA

PO Box 75
West Perth WA 6872
Phone: (08) 9322 7874
Fax: (08) 9322 7878
Email: info@naati.com.au
Website: www.naati.com.au

National Institute of Dramatic Art

215 Anzac Parade
Kensington NSW 2052
Phone: (02) 9697 7600
Fax: (02) 9662 7415
Email: nida@unsw.edu.au
Website: www.nida.unsw.edu.au

National Library of Australia

Canberra ACT 2699

Cataloguing-in-Publication Unit
Phone: (02) 6262 1458
Fax: (02) 6273 4492
Email: cip@nla.gov.au
Website: www.nla.gov.au/services/CIP.html

ISSN Agency
Phone: (02) 6262 1213
Fax: (02) 6273 4492
Email: issn@nla.gov.au
Website: www.nla.gov.au/services/ISSN.html

Legal Deposit
Phone: (02) 6262 1312
Fax: (02) 6273 4492
Email: legaldep@nla.gov.au
Website: www.nla.gov.au/1/services/ldeposit.html

NSW Film and Television Office

GPO Box 1744
Sydney NSW 2043
Phone: (02) 9264 6400
Fax: (02) 9264 4388
Email: fto@fto.nsw.gov.au
Website: www.fto.nsw.gov.au

NT Remote Writers' Group

C/0 NT Writers' Centre
GPO Box 2255
Darwin NT 0801

Phone: (08) 8941 2651
Fax: (08) 8941 2115
Email: ntwriter@octa4.net.au

NRS Training School

11 Lawrie Place
Macquarie ACT 2614
Phone: (02) 6251 6189
Fax: (02) 9251 6240
Email: training.school@nrs.group.com.au
Website: www.nrsgroup.com.au
Training school for media production and communication.

OWNWrite (Writers' Group of Older Women's Network)

35/139 Gold Creek Road
Brookfield Qld 4069
Phone: (07) 3374 0075 or (07) 3848 5552

Pacific Film and Television Commission

PO Box 94
Albert Street, Brisbane Qld 4002
Phone: (07) 3224 4114
Fax: (07) 3224 6717
Email: pftc@pftc.com.au
Website: www.pftc.com.au

Partners in Crime

7 Unwin Street
Bexley NSW 2207
Phone/Fax: (02) 9502 2168
Email: beveges@bigpond.com
Website: www.geocities.com/Athens/styx7255

PEN ACT

Canberra Pen Centre
PO Box 261
Dickson ACT 2601
Phone: (02) 6247 5028
Email: dorothy@dynamite.com.au
Website: plateaupress.com.au/pen

PEN NSW & National Inquiries

Sydney PEN Centre
PO Box 1384
Rozelle NSW 2039
Phone: (02) 9555 9931
Fax: (02) 9555 9927
Website: plateaupress.com.au/pen

PEN Qld, NT

PEN Australia North
PO Box 328
Annerley Qld 4103
Phone: (07) 3359 8647
Email: owlink@telstra.easymail.com.au
Website: plateaupress.com.au/pen

PEN Vic, SA, Tas

Melbourne PEN Centre
PO Box 2273
Caulfield Junction Vic 3161
Phone: (03) 9509 7257
Email: buckrich@netspace.net.au
Website: plateaupress.com.au/pen

PEN WA

Perth PEN Centre
PO Box 1131
Subiaco WA 6008
Phone: (08) 9225 6715
Email: bjosephi@cowan.edu.au
Website: plateaupress.com.au/pen

Playbox Theatre Centre

113 Sturt Street
Southbank Vic 3006
Phone: (03) 9685 5154
Fax: (03) 9685 5112
Email: admin@playbox.com.au
Website: www.playbox.com.au

Playlab Inc.

PO Box 878
Fortitude Valley Qld 4006

Phone: (07) 3852 1400
Fax: (07) 3852 1405
Email: cluster@thehub.com.au

Playworks

PO Box A2216
Sydney South NSW 1235
Phone: (02) 9264 8414
Fax: (02) 9264 8449
Email: playwks@ozemail.com.au
Website: www.ozemail.com.au/~playwks

Poets Union

PO Box 91
Balmain NSW 2041
Phone: (02) 9818 5366
Email: poetinc@ozemail.com.au
Website: www.ozemail.com.au/~poetinc

Prolific Productions

PO Box 2145
Rose Bay North NSW 2030
Phone: (02) 9357 3804
Fax: (02) 9357 3699
Email: prolific@dingoblue.net.au
Website: www.prolificproductions.com.au

Public and Educational Lending Right Schemes

Department of Communication,
Information Technology and the Arts
GPO Box 3241
Canberra ACT 2601
Phone: (02) 6271 1650
Tollfree: 1800 672 842
Fax: (02) 6271 1651
Email: plr.mail@dcita.gov.au
Website: www.dcita.gov.au/plr.html

Qld Multicultural Writers' and Arts Friendship Society

17 Lavinia Street
Sunnybank Qld 4109
Phone: (07) 3345 5108

Queensland Theatre Company

PO Box 310
South Brisbane Qld 4101
Phone: (07) 3840 7000
Fax: (07) 3840 7040
Email: udauth@qldtheatreco.com.au
Website: www.qldtheatreco.com.au

Romance Writers of Australia

PO Box 1236
Neutral Bay NSW 2089
Phone/Fax: (02) 9260 6160
Email: rwasut@powerup.com.au
Website: homepage.powerup.com.au/~rwaust

Screen Production Academy

Briad House, Suite 3A
491–493 Elizabeth Street
Surry Hills NSW 2010
Phone: (02) 9318 2727
Fax: (02) 9310 1475

ScreenWest (Western Australia Film and Television Office)

PO Box 8349
Perth Business Centre WA 6849
Phone: (08) 9224 7340
Fax: (08) 9224 7341
Email: info@screenwest.mca.wa.gov.au
Website: www.screenwest.wa.gov.au

Sisters in Crime

GPO Box 5319 BB
Melbourne Vic 3001
Email: sincoz@hotmail.com
Website: home.vicnet.net.au/~sincoz

Organisations

Society of Book Illustrators

C/- Australian Society of Authors
PO Box 1566
Strawberry Hills NSW 2012
Phone: (02) 9318 0877
Fax: (02) 9318 0530
Email: asa@asauthors.org
Website: www.asauthors.org

Society of Business Communicators

PO Box 8
Paddington Qld 4064
Phone: (07) 3369 2323
Fax: (07) 3369 0883
Email: admin@sbcq.com.au
Website: www.sbcq.com.au

Society of Children's Book Writers and Illustrators (SCBWI)

PO Box 194
Sandringham Vic 3191
Phone: (03) 9598 4232
Fax: (03) 9521 8439
Email: jmcveity@bigpond.net.au
Website: www.scbwi.org

SCBWI NSW

Penny Azar
Phone: (02) 9880 2558
Email: pennylou@ihug.com.au

SCBWI Qld

Cheryl McMaster
Phone: (07) 5590 4961
Email: bungalova@bigpond.com

SCBWI WA

Frané Lessac
Phone: (08) 9430 5479
Email: artbeat@ozemail.com.au

Society of Editors ACT

PO Box 3222
Manuka ACT 2603
Phone: (02) 6282 1993
Fax: (02) 6282 1081
Email: ann.parkinson@atrax.net.au
Website: www.editorscanberra.org

Society of Editors NSW

PO Box 254
Broadway NSW 2007
Phone: (02) 9294 4999
Fax: (02) 9913 7799
Email: socednsw@bigpond.com
Website: www.users.bigpond.com/socednsw

Society of Editors NT

Phone: (08) 8941 2651
Email: editors_nt@yahoo.comlau

Society of Editors Qld

PO Box 1524
Toowong Qld 4066
Phone/Fax: (07) 3369 8681
Email: socedsq@yahoo.com
Website: www.editorsqld.com

Society of Editors SA

PO Box 2328
Kent Town SA 5071
Phone: (08) 8411 6375
Fax: (08) 8232 3994
Email: info@editors-sa.org.au
Website: www.editors-sa.org.au

Society of Editors Tas

PO Box 32
Sandy Bay Tas 7005
Phone: (03) 6225 1941
Email: info@tas-editors.org.au
Website: www.tas-editors.org.au

Society of Editors Vic

PO Box 176
Carlton South Vic 3053
Phone: (03) 9513 6608
Email: camphar@netspace.net.au
Website: www.socedvic.org

Society of Editors WA

PO Box 299
Subiaco WA 6904
Phone: (08) 9383 4782
Email: bdurston@cygnus.uwa.edu.au
Website: editorswa.iinet.net.au

Society of Women Writers (SWW)

GPO Box 1388
Sydney NSW 2001
Phone: (02) 9798 4525
Email: lesleywalter@hotmail.com
Website: www.womenwritersnsw.org

SWW Qld

10 Walsh Street
Newport Quays
Scarborough Qld 4020
Phone: (07) 3203 6667
Email: peban@powerup.com.au

SWW Tas

Email: swwt@tasmail.com
Website: www.tased.edu.au/tasonline/sww

SWW Vic

GPO Box 121A
Melbourne Vic 3001
Phone: (03) 9772 2389
Email: swwvic@vicnet.net.au
Website: www.vicnet.net.au/~swwvic/

SWW WA

PO Box 434
Northbridge WA 6865
Phone: (08) 9361 5895

South Australian Film Corporation

3 Butler Drive
Hendon Common SA 5014
Phone: (08) 8348 9300
Fax: (08) 8347 0385
Email: safilm@safilm.com.au
Website: www.safilm.com.au

Stott's Correspondence College

456 High Street
Prahran Vic 3181
Phone: (03) 9522 0100 or 1300 786 887
Fax: (03) 9522 0111
Email: info@stottsonline.com
Website: www.stottsonline.com

University of Queensland Press

PO Box 6042
St Lucia Qld 4067
Phone: (07) 3365 2127
Fax: (07) 3365 7579
Email: editor@uqp.uq.edu.au
Website: www.uqp.uq.edu.au

University of Technology, Sydney

PO Box 123
Broadway NSW 2007
Phone: (02) 9514 2000
Fax: (02) 9514 1200
Email: info.office@uts.edu.au
Website: www.uts.edu.au

Victorian Federation of Community Writing Groups

RMB 1503 Tulley Road
Lima East Vic 3673
Phone/ Fax:(03) 5768 2405
Email: magwag@cnl.com.au
Website: www.writingismagic.org.au

Vision Science Fiction, Fantasy and Horror Group

5 Lavarak Road
Bray Park Qld 4500
Phone: (07) 3205 6964
Email: scott_robinson@mac.com
Website: welcome.to/vision-writers

Voiceworks Express Media

156 George Street
Fitzroy Vic 3065
Phone: (03) 9416 3305
Fax: (03) 9419 3365
Email: voiceworks@expressmedia.org.au
Website: www.expressmedia.org.au

Women in Film and Television (WIFT)

PO Box 522
Paddington NSW 2021
Phone: (02) 9332 2408
Fax: (02) 9380 4311
Email: info@wift.org
Website: www.wift.org

Women in Publishing (WiP)

PO Box 8190, Angelo Street
South Perth WA 6151
Phone/Fax: (08) 9474 2893
Email: redrobins@bigpond.com.au
Website: www.wipwa.com

Writer's Bookcase

Reply Paid 162
Kippax ACT 2615
Phone/Fax: (02) 6259 2835
Email: keithbin@ozemail.com.au
Website: www.writersbookcase.com
A wide range of Australian and international books for writers and editors. Visit the website for a catalogue.

Writers' Cottage

1 Kelly Street
Battery Point Tas 7004
Correspondence to:
Salamanca Arts Centre
77 Salamanca Place
Hobart Tas 7008
Phone: (03) 6234 8414
Fax: (03) 6224 0245
Email: sacinc@salarts.org.au
Website: www.salarts.org.au

Youngstreet Poets

111 Parkes Road
Collaroy Plateau NSW 2097
Phone: (02) 9971 6206

NEW ZEALAND ORGANISATIONS

Association of New Zealand Literature

English Department
University of Otago
PO Box 56
Dunedin
Phone: (03) 479 8336
Fax: (03) 479 8558
Email: lawrence.jones@stonebow.otago.ac.nz

Australasian Performing Right Association (APRA)

92 Parnell Road
Auckland
Phone: (09) 379 0638
Fax: (09) 379 3205
Email: nz@apra.com.au
Website: www.apra.com.au

Book Publishers' Association of New Zealand Inc. (BPANZ)

PO Box 36–477
Northcote
Auckland 1309
Phone: (09) 480 2711
Fax: (09) 480 1130
Email: bpanz@copyright.co.nz
Website: www.bpanz.org.nz

Booksellers New Zealand

PO Box 11–377
Wellington
Phone: (04) 472 8678
Fax: (04) 472 8628
Email: membership@booksellers.co.nz
Website: www.booksellers.co.nz

Christchurch City Libraries

PO Box 1466
Christchurch
Phone: (03) 379 6914
Fax: (03) 365 1751
Email: library@ccc.govt.nz
Website: library.christchurch.org.nz

Children's Literature Foundation of New Zealand

PO Box 96 094
Balmoral
Auckland 1030
Phone/Fax: (09) 627 9137
Email: childlit@internet.co.nz
Website: www.clfnz.org.nz
There are also several branches throughout New Zealand.

Copyright Licensing Limited

PO Box 36477
Northcote Auckland 1309
Phone: (09) 480 2711
Fax: (09) 480 1130
Email: cll@copyright.co.nz
Website: www.copyright.co.nz

Library and Information Association of New Zealand Aotearoa (LIANZA)

PO Box 12 212
Wellington
Phone: (04) 473 5834
Fax: (04) 499 1480
Email: office@lianza.org.nz
Website: www.lianza.org.nz

National Library of New Zealand

PO Box 1467
Wellington
Phone: (04) 474 3000
Fax: (04) 474 3035
Email: information@natlib.govt.nz
Website: www.natlib.govt.nz

National Library Society

PO Box 12 514
Wellington
Phone: (04) 476 6674

New Zealand Authors' Fund

Grants Process Administrator
Creative New Zealand
PO Box 3806
Wellington
Phone: (04) 498 0735
Fax: (04) 471 2865
Email: bronwynp@creativenz.govt.nz
Website: www.creativenz.govt.nz

New Zealand Book Council

5th Floor, Old Wool House
139–141 Featherston Street

Wellington
Phone: (04) 499 1569
Fax: (04) 499 1424
Email: admin@bookcouncil.org.nz
Website: www.bookcouncil.org.nz

New Zealand Children's Book Foundation

PO Box 96-094
Balmoral Auckland
Phone/Fax: (09) 620 8440
Email: allsorts@iprolink.co.nz
Website: www.nzbooks.com/nzbooks/static/nzcbf.asp

New Zealand Children's Illustrators and Authors

1 Torless Terrace
Thorndon Wellington

New Zealand Copyright Council

PO Box 5028
Wellington
Phone: (04) 384 3523
Fax: (04) 471 0765
Email: ksheat@copyright.co.nz
Website: www.copyright.org.nz

New Zealand Film Commission

PO Box 11 546
Wellington
Phone: (04) 382 7680
Fax: (04) 384 9719
Email: info@nzfilm.co.nz
Website: www.nzfilm.co.nz

New Zealand Guild of Storytellers

C/- Wakapuaka
RD 1
Nelson

Phone/Fax: (03) 545 1646
Email: info@storytelling.org.nz
Website: www.storytelling.org.nz

New Zealand History Research Trust Fund

History Group
Ministry for Culture and Heritage
PO Box 5364
Wellington
Phone/Fax: (04) 496 6334
Email: bronwyn.dalley@mch.govt.nz

New Zealand ISSN Centre

Phone: (04) 474 3090
Fax: (04) 474 3161
Email: issn@natlib.govt.nz
Website: www.natlib.govt.nz/en/services/publishers/isbn.html

New Zealand Poetry Society

PO Box 5283
Wellington
Website: communities.msn.com/NewZealandPoetrySociety

New Zealand Reading Association

Auckland College of Education
Private Bag 92–601
Symonds Street
Auckland
Phone: (09) 623 8899 ext. 8445
Fax: (09) 623 8898
Email: l.limbrick@ace.ac.nz

New Zealand Society of Authors (PEN NZ Inc.)

PO Box 67-013
Mt Eden
Auckland 3
Phone/Fax: (09) 630 8077
Email: nzsa@clear.net.nz
Website: www.arachna.co.nz/nzsa

New Zealand Standard Book Numbering Agency

Phone: (04) 474 3000 ext. 8653
Fax: (04) 474 3161
Email: isbn@natlib.govt.nz
Website: www.natlib.govt.nz/en/services/publishers/isbn.html

New Zealand Writers' Guild

PO Box 47 886
Ponsonby Auckland
Phone: (09) 360 1408
Fax: (09) 360 1409
Email: info@nzwritersguild.org.nz
Website: www.nzwritersguild.org.nz

Playmarket

PO Box 9767
Te Aro
Wellington
Phone: (04) 382 8462
Fax: (04) 382 8461
Email: info@playmarket.org.nz
Website: www.playmarket.org.nz

Playwrights Association of NZ (PANZ)

C/- Post Shop Counter
Wainuiomata
Email: john_dunmore@hotmail.com
Website: homepages.ihug.co.nz/~comberc/panzindex.htm

Professional Historians' Association of New Zealand/Aotearoa (PHANZA)

PO Box 1904
Thorndon
Wellington
Phone: (04) 496 6334
Email: bronwyn.dalley@mch.govt.nz
Website: www.nzhistory.net.nz/PHANZA

Radio New Zealand

PO Box 123
Wellington 6001
Phone: (04) 474 1999
Fax: (04) 474 1459
Email: jdryden@radionz.co.nz
Website: www.radionz.co.nz
For information about drama programs phone (04) 474 1776.

Waikato Children's Literature Association

PO Box 1329
Hamilton
Phone: (07) 856 2737 (home),
       (07) 839 1258 (work)
Fax: (07) 839 1259
Email: paulclark@xtra.co.nz

Wellington Children's Book Association

PO Box 1242
Wellington
Phone: (04) 972 6202
Email: marmac@paradise.net.nz

POETRY PUBLISHERS

The following list of poetry publishers is provided here because of the difficulties poets have in locating publishers who are interested in producing books of poetry.

AUSTRALIAN

Produced by the Sydney-based Poets Union, *The 2000 Australian Poetry Catalogue* is a useful resource for poets and poetry readers. It is available from the NSW Writers' Centre, PO Box 1056, Rozelle NSW 2039, phone (02) 9555 9757, email nswwc@ozemail.com.au.

AIATSIS—Aboriginal Studies Press

GPO Box 553
Canberra ACT 2600
Phone: (02) 6246 1111
Fax: (02) 6249 7310
Email: dfh@clc.aiatsis.gov.au
Website: www.aiatsis.gov.au
Details and ms cover sheet available on website. Unsolicited mss considered.

Arwenbooks

21 Loftus Street
East Geelong Vic
Email: doug@gspp.com.au
Website: www.gspp.com.au

Unsolicited mss considered, and guidelines available on the website.

Black Pepper Press

403 St Georges Road
North Fitzroy Vic 3068
Phone: (03) 9489 1716
Fax: (03) 9489 5318
Specialises in literary fiction and poetry.

Brandl & Schlesinger

PO Box 276
Rose Bay NSW 2029
Phone: (02) 9388 1106
Fax: (02) 9388 1032
Email: books@brandl.com.au
Website: www.brandl.com.au
Specialises in literary fiction and non-fiction, biography, social history, poetry and translations.

Cactus Publishing

PO Box 6266
East Perth WA 6892
Phone: 0419 925 833
Fax: (08) 9277 9518
Email: katrinav@iexpress.net.au
Specialises in poetry. Only considers manuscripts submitted through an agent.

353

Catchfire Press

PO Box 2101
Dangar NSW 2309
Phone: (02) 4926 4029
Fax: (02) 4950 9658
Email: catchfire@idl.com.au
Website: cust.idl.com.au/catchfire
A non-profit, community organisation set up to serve Hunter Region writers.

CopyRight Publishing

GPO Box 2927
Brisbane Qld 4001
Phone: (07) 3229 6366
Fax: (07) 3229 8782
Email: mcrobert@bit.net.au
Website: www.copyright.net.au
Writers may be required to contribute to production costs.

Deadpan Press

Locked Bag 18, STE 205
Newtown NSW 2042
Phone: (02) 9518 3781
Fax: (02) 9518 3781
Email: eroica@bigpond.com
Accepts poetry to 50 pages.

Duffy and Snellgrove

PO Box 177
Potts Point NSW 1335
Phone: (02) 9386 0280
Fax: (02) 9386 1530
Email: info@duffyandsnellgrove.com.au
Website: www.duffyandsnellgrove.com.au

Five Islands Press

PO Box U34
Wollongong University NSW 2500
Phone: (02) 4271 5292
Fax: (02) 4272 7392
Email: kpretty@uow.edu.au
Website: www.5islands.1earth.net

Send stamped self-addressed envelope for information on publishing program and guidelines.

Fremantle Arts Centre Press

PO Box 158
North Fremantle WA 6159
Phone: (08) 9430 6331
Fax: (08) 9430 5242
Email: facp@iinet.net.au
Website: www.facp.iinet.net.au
Publishes writers and artists who live in WA or are of WA origin.

Gangan Publishing

Senior Editor
PO Box 522
Strawberry Hills NSW 2012
Phone: (02) 9319 2443
Fax: (02) 9319 2445
Email: gerald@gangan.com
Website: www.gangan.com
Specialises in contemporary Austrian and Australian literature published in the German language.

Ginninderra Press

PO Box 53
Charnwood ACT 2615
Phone: (02) 6258 9060
Fax: (02) 6258 9069
Email: smgp@cyberone.com.au
Website: www.ginninderrapress.com.au
Publishes poetry under the Indigo imprint.

Hyland House Publishing

PO Box 122
Flemington Vic 3031
Phone: (03) 9376 4461
Fax: (03) 9376 4461
Email: hyland3@netspace.net.au

Poetry Publishers

IAD Press/Jukurrpa Books

PO Box 2531
Alice Springs NT 0871
Phone: (08) 8951 1409
Fax: (08) 8952 2527
Email: publisheriad@ozemail.com.au
Unsolicited manuscripts from Aboriginal authors or on topics relating to Central Australian Aboriginal languages and cultures.

Interactive Press

Treetop Studio
9 Kuhler Court
Carindale Qld 4152
Phone: (07) 3395 0269
Fax: (07) 3324 9319
Email: info@interpr.com.au
Website: www.interpr.com.au
Unsolicited manuscripts of poetry considered for 'subsidised' publication (authors must contribute to costs).

irrePRESSible Press

4 Sunnybar Parade
Queanbeyan NSW 2620
Phone: (02) 6299 6875
Email: cambrus@goldweb.com.au
Website: www.irrepressible.com.au
Phone first to discuss proposal. Authors may contribute to production costs.

Jacobyte Books

41 Barham Street
Allenby Gardens SA 5009
Phone: (08) 8346 7449
Fax: (08) 8357 2110
Email: enquiries@jacobytebooks.com
Website: www.jacobytebooks.com
An electronic publishing company.

Magabala Books

PO Box 668
Broome WA 6725
Phone: (08) 9192 1991
Fax: (08) 9193 5254
Email: info@magabala.com
Website: www.magabala.com
Specialises in Australian indigenous literature.

Musgrave & Elgara Publications

6/36 Musgrave Street
Mosman NSW 2088
Phone/Fax: (02) 9969 8913
Email: joriemanefield@ozemail.com.au
Small publisher specialising in poetry.

Northern Territory University Press

Northern Territory University Press Committee
Faculty of Arts
Northern Territory University
Darwin NT 0909
Phone: (08) 8946 6801
Fax: (08) 8946 6955
Email: david.carment@ntu.edu.au
Preference given to books on North Australia and Southeast Asia.

Spinifex Press

PO Box 212
North Melbourne Vic 3051
Phone: (03) 9329 6088
Fax: (03) 9329 9238
Email: women@spinifexpress.com.au
Website: www.spinifexpress.com.au
Women's publishing house. Publishes fiction, non-fiction and poetry (exclusively women poets).

Thorny Devil Press

PO Box 878
Newcastle NSW 2300
Email: rt@artpoem.com
Contact: Richard Tipping

Publishes art multiples (three-dimensional editions), concrete visual poetry and other forms of word art.

University of Queensland Press

PO Box 6042
St Lucia Qld 4067
Phone: (07) 3365 7244
Fax: (07) 3365 1988
Website: www.uqp.uq.edu.au
Publishes a broad range of general interest and literary titles, including poetry.

Valvana Publishing House

118 Hale Road
Wembley Downs WA 6019
Phone: (08) 9446 8852
Publishes poetry, short stories, plays, biography, novels and music.

Wakefield Press

PO Box 2266
Kent Town SA 5071
Phone: (08) 8362 8800
Fax: (08) 8362 7592
Email: info@wakefieldpress.com.au
Website: www.wakefieldpress.com.au
Specialises in non-fiction. Also publishes a small amount of poetry.

NEW ZEALAND

Antediluvian Press

9 Daphne Harden Lane
Albany
Auckland
Phone: (09) 413 8618
Email: s.bagby@xtra.co.nz

Auckland University Press

Private Bag 92–019
Auckland 1001
Phone: (09) 373 7528
Fax: (09) 373 7465
Email: aup@auckland.ac.nz
Website: www.auckland.ac.nz/aup

Bronze Publishing

82 Parsons Street
Wanganui
Phone: (06) 345 0746
Email: joan.morrell@clear.net.nz

Hazard Press

PO Box 2151
Christchurch
Phone: (03) 377 0370
Fax: (03) 377 0390
Email: info@hazard.co.nz
Website: www.hazard.co.nz

Headworx Publishers

26 Grant Road
Thorndon
Wellington
Phone/Fax: (04) 473 5952
Email: mpirie@xtra.co.nz
Website: headworx.eyesis.co.nz

Hildegaard Productions

75 Brunner Street
Bishopdale
Nelson
Phone/Fax: (03) 548 1459

Lancaster Publishing

PO Box 78–104
Grey Lynn
Auckland
Email: lancaster@india.com

Pemmican Press

17 Makara Road
Karori
Wellington
Phone: (04) 476 5344
Fax: (04) 476 5345
Email: chris.orsman@paradise.net.nz

Pohutukawa Press

PO Box 34-293
Birkenhead
Auckland 1310
Phone/Fax: (09) 483 3171

Rainbow Books

554 Kereone Road
Morrinsville
Phone/Fax: (07) 887 3733

Rimu Publishing

49 Casey Avenue
Fairfield
Hamilton
Phone/Fax: (07) 855 5536

Sharp Axe Publishing

240 Rahu Road
RD 4
Paeroa
Phone: (07) 862 8843
Fax: (07) 862 8986
Publishes rural poetry.

Steele Roberts

PO Box 9321
Wellington
Phone: (04) 499 0044
Fax: (04) 499 0056
Email: books@i4free.co.nz
Website: www.publish.net.nz/

Street Women Press

23 Perrin Place
Palmerston North 5301
Phone: (06) 356 3462
Email: paula@streetwomen.co.nz
Website: www.streetwomen.co.nz

Te Taa Haeretahi

76 Ranui Crescent
Khandallah
Wellington 4
Phone: (04) 479 3731
Email: Llyn@actrix.gen.nz

Victoria University Press

PO Box 600
Wellington
Phone: (04) 496 6580
Fax: (04) 496 6581
Email: victoria-press@vuw.ac.nz
Website: www.vup.vuw.ac.nz
Contact: Fergus Barrowman

PUBLICITY QUESTIONNAIRE (ALLEN & UNWIN)

TRADE/ACADEMIC

E-mail version: Please insert your answers into this document and return it by e-mail to:

Hard copy version: Please complete the contact details below, and return it to us via email. If there is more than one author/editor for the book, please complete a separate page one (personal author/editor details) and return with the rest of this document.

1. **Book Title:**
2. **Author/Editor details:**
Mr/Mrs/Ms: Date of Birth:
Dr/Professor etc   (Required for cataloguing with National Library)

Home Address:
Place of Birth: (state and country)

Office Address:
Are you an Australian: citizen/resident?

Telephone No. Home: Office:

Fax No.   Home: Office:

Email:

ABN No. (if available) _____
If you wish us *not* to deduct 48.5% tax from royalty payments. See attached information sheet.

3. **Can address/phone details be released to journalists etc?**
Home: Yes / No
Office: Yes / No

4. **Promotional photographs**
Please supply photos (1 black & white, 1 colour. Please supply photo prints *and negatives*)

5. **To help us create marketing copy for your book:**
   a) Please supply a professional and academic CV, including a brief biographical note (110–150 words) and a record of your professional and academic appointments, previous publications and relevant consultancies and community service.
   b) Please summarise the *essence* of your book in 50–75 words.
   c) What do you see as the essence and major *themes* of the book?

Publicity Questionnaire

    d) List the *features* of the book you would like us to stress in our promotion, eg new research, an original theory, unusual organisation of the material. These should be outstanding selling points which will assist our marketing people in placing the book in its markets.
    e) Briefly describe your special qualifications for writing on this subject, all modesty aside.
    f) Now, please have a go at drafting a back cover blurb of 200 words for your book, including its main purpose, a broad description of the scope and contents, its distinctive features and who will benefit from it.
    g) Can you suggest any relevant 'known names' from whom we might obtain a public endorsement for your book to be used in our publicity on the cover of the book? Please explain the reasons for any names you propose.

6. **To help us reach the Australian and New Zealand market for your book:**
    a) For whom is your book written? Please give a detailed profile of the likely readership.
    b) Do you have any individual contacts in the Australian/New Zealand press, on radio or television with whom you have had recent personal dealings and who might be interested in featuring your book? Please give names and details, together with reasons why you feel they might be able to make use of this particular book.
    c) Are there any organisations, associations, societies or other groups within Australia/New Zealand who might either buy your book in quantity, or be prepared to help in its promotion? Please give full names and addresses of any active personal contacts who might be approached.
    d) Please indicate whether any of these organisations, associations or companies have newsletters which might provide special sales opportunities or through which your book could be advertised or reviewed.
    e) Do you know of any websites that might be useful in the promotion of your book?
    f) Are there any special events in Australia/New Zealand (eg conferences, anniversaries) at which your book could be promoted and which are taking place near the time of publication?
    g) Please list any media contacts within Australia/New Zealand to whom review copies might usefully be sent, with full address and the name of the current editor if known to you personally.
    h) Are there any local or other bookshops with which you have special connections or to whom your book will be particularly relevant?
    i) Are there any localities within Australia/New Zealand where either you are well known or your book will be of special interest? Please explain why.
    j) Are there any books available that could be said to compete with your own? This information is of particular help selling to bookshops and other academics, so please give title, author, publisher and date of publication (if known), plus full details of how your book improves on or differs from each title listed.
    k) *Book Awards*: Allen & Unwin are frequently invited to enter our authors and/or their works into various book and writer's awards. These range from the small, sponsored regional awards, tailored to, say, authors who were born in a particular state, through to the more obvious well-known awards. Often we are required to seek an author's permission prior to entering their book, and as the closing date often makes this a difficult task to complete, we would ask for your agreement in principle to our entering your book for such awards as appropriate. We would of course inform you immediately if your book were to be shortlisted for such awards.

The Writer's Guide

Comments: _____

☐ Tick here if you would like us to send you some flyers for you to promote the book to friends and colleagues.

7. **To help us reach the international market for your book:**

Please provide any information which may help with the marketing and publicity of your book in our international markets. This includes any particular relevance the book would have in those markets, and any particular contacts you have with insitutions, associations, leading academics etc. Use the questions for the ANZ market above to prompt your ideas.

North America (US and Canada)
the UK and Europe
South East Asia
North East Asia
South Africa
Other

8. **Please indicate the most appropriate levels at which your book will be used in universities, colleges, institutes, schools etc.**

☐ Postgraduates

☐ 1st/2nd/3rd year undergraduates

☐ Secondary school students

9. **Primary market**
If the book is a textbook, please describe as precisely as possible those courses for which your book is specifically designed or on which it is most likely to be prescribed as essential reading.

10. **Secondary market**
Please list those courses on which your book might also be recommended as additional reading.

RECOMMENDED RATES FOR WRITERS

The ASA publishes recommended minimum rates for writers and illustrators working in the Australian market. These rates recognise the professional standards, time and effort that go into writing and book illustration. Members are encouraged to negotiate fees that are higher than the minimum.

National Freelance Rates are the approved minimum payments for freelance and casual writers, photographers, artists, book editors and proofreaders. These rates are set by the Australian Journalists Association section of the Media, Entertainment and Arts Alliance.

Society of Book Illustrators Rates are the minimum flat fee payments for roughs, black and white book illustration and colour book illustration. We recommend you sign a formal agreement or contract before commencing work. These rates include a loading for 'one off' or single illustrations.

Prose Anthology Rates are the Australian Society of Authors' minimum rates for publishing both previously published and original material in an anthology.

Poetry Anthology Rates are the Australian Society of Authors' minimum rates for publishing poems in anthologies and for first publication in magazines and journals. The ASA's non-exclusive licence agreement should be used for poetry anthologies.

Teaching, Reading, Speaking, Judging are the Australian Society of Authors' minimum rates for writers and illustrators for speaking and teaching at literary festivals, residencies and in tertiary institutions and schools; reading; and judging (literary prizes etc).

National Freelance Rates 2001
Australian Journalists Association Section
Approved minimums for freelance and casual writers:

Freelance Daily Rate
$617.00 Per day
$414.00 Per half day (2/3 day rate)
$124.00 Per hour
$656.00 1000 words or less 66c per word thereafter

Book Editors and Proofreaders
$617.00 Per day
$414.00 Per half day (2/3 day rate)
$123.00 Per hour

Expenses

Freelancers are entitled to claim reasonable out of pocket expenses on top of the minimum freelance rates quoted here. These expenses could include: travel costs, telephone, car mileage, fax costs etc.

Holiday Pay

Casuals employed by Metro Dailies for 10 days or more in any year must be paid pro rata holiday leave each November/December. If you have not received this payment, please contact the Alliance. Casuals employed in other areas receive a daily allowance on top of the minimum rate to compensate for holiday pay.

Superannuation

Freelancers who earn over $450 in any one month from the one commissioner and casuals employed by most employers for 20 shifts or more within a 13 week period qualify to have the equivalent of 8% of their earnings paid into a superannuation fund—free of charge—once you have asked for it. If you are not a member of JUST or an approved company fund, please contact the Alliance or JUST Ph: 1300 362 672.

Poetry Anthology Rates 2000

These rates should be used in conjunction with the ASA non-exclusive licence agreement to print poetry in anthologies. These are minimum rates. Some publishers pay considerably more and poets are advised to encourage publishers to pay above the minimum.

Books and Anthologies

Minimum $30 per poem in any publication, with one exception, as follows: in short print run, 100% copyright anthologies, where the division pro rata of 12% of the recommended retail price cannot ensure payment of $30 per poem, this rule may be varied. In requesting permissions, the publisher should state that the pro-rata principle of payment is being preferred to the per poem minimum in a case where it is not possible to satisfy both principles at the same time.

Publishers should endeavour to remunerate according to the size of the poet's whole contribution and not leave a poet with a negligible payment. In some cases, a minimum of $30 per poet may be the only adjustment needed. If in doubt about payment, contact the ASA.

The rate is 90 cents per line per 1000 copies printed. The $30 minimum applies for the use of any poem. Rates are based on a minimum print run of 1000, then in stages of 500 copies. Rates are rounded to the nearest dollar amount.

Minimum rates for poetry in books and anthologies

		No. of lines					
Print run	*Per line*	*10*	*15*	*20*	*30*	*40*	*50*
1000	$0.90	$30	$30	$30	$30	$36	$45
1500	$1.35	$30	$30	$30	$41	$54	$68
2000	$1.80	$30	$30	$36	$54	$72	$90
2500	$2.25	$30	$34	$45	$68	$90	$113
3000	$2.70	$30	$41	$54	$81	$108	$135
3500	$3.15	$32	$47	$63	$95	$126	$158
4000	$3.60	$36	$54	$72	$108	$144	$180

Recommended rates for writers

For anthologies in which all contributions are subject to the authors' copyright, a payment of not less than 12% of the recommended retail price, divided pro rata amongst the contributors is also acceptable.

Where a condition of publication in an anthology is that the poem not have been previously published, a first publication rate equal to magazine rates below (ie $1.80 per line) should be offered.

Magazines and Journals

For first publication in magazines and journals, $1.80 per line (rounded out).

Up to 19 lines	$30.00
20–24 lines	$40.00
25–29 lines	$50.00
30–34 lines	$60.00
35–39 lines	$65.00
40–44 lines	$75.00
45–49 lines	$85.00
50–54 lines	$95.00
55–59 lines	$105.00
60–64 lines	$110.00
65–69 lines	$120.00
70–74 lines	$130.00

The Australian Society of Authors' Poetry Rates are revised annually.

Prose Anthology Rates

The Society's recommendations for payment for prose anthologies are based on reasonable royalties, bearing in mind that an editorial fee is usually paid as well. The Society is pleased to discuss special cases with any publisher contemplating an anthology and will inform ASA members when a variation of the following formula seems justified. No such decision is binding and members are at all times urged to negotiate above the minimum rates.

Minimum Rates for Previously Published Material
Price per 1000 words or part thereof on first 5000 or part thereof

Where the RRP is less than $25	$100
Where the RRP is $25–$39	$156
Where the RRP is $40–$55	$200

Plus, per 1000 words on each subsequent 5000 copies

Where the RRP is less than $25	$125
Where the RRP is $25–$39	$200
Where the RRP is $40–$55	$250

Additional payments above the first 5000 copies can be made on a pro rata basis for each additional 1000 copies.

Minimum Rates for Original Material

The table above applies to work which has already been published.

Where material for an anthology is specifically commissioned or previously unpublished, a minimum rate of $250 per 1000 words or part thereof should be paid in addition to the minimum rate for previously published material.

These rates apply to all kinds of anthologised prose.

The Writer's Guide

Society of Book Illustrators Rates 2001
These are the recommended minimum rates and represent a recognition of professional standards, time and effort that go into book illustration.
ASA (SOBI) members are encouraged to negotiate for rates higher than the minimum suggested.

- These rates cover flat fee payments.
- Another fee should be negotiated if further use of the work is required.
- The artwork and copyright of the work remain the property of the artist unless assigned and agreed to in writing.
- It is recommended that a formal Agreement or Contract is signed by all parties before any work is commenced.

The following rates are based on A4 book projects. For 'one-off' or single illustrations, please add 20%.

ROUGHS
depending on detail required, research involved and conceptual input required.
$ 45   Black & White
$ 65   Colour

BLACK AND WHITE BOOK ILLUSTRATION
$160   Quarter Page or Chapter Head
$245   Half Page
$320   Full Page
$400   Double Page Spread

COLOUR BOOK ILLUSTRATION
$245   Quarter Page or Chapter Head
$320   Half Page
$555   Full Page
$665   Double Page Spread
$945   Cover

Teaching, Reading, Speaking, Judging
Note: These are recommended minimum rates only. More experienced writers and illustrators will command higher fees. Add 10% if the speaker is registered for GST.

Fees for Speaking and Teaching
Events and Appearances
(Literary Festivals, Residencies, Tertiary Institutions, etc)
$750   Whole Day (max. 360 minutes)
$400   Half Day (max. 180 minutes)
$200   Per session (max. 60 minutes)
$3000   Weekly rate (max. 5 days — average of up to 180 minutes per day)

Schools (Primary and Secondary)
A group should comprise no more than 60 students per session.
$450   Whole School Day (max. 180 minutes — up to 4 x 45 minute sessions)
$300   Half School Day (max. 90 minutes — up to 2 x 45 minute sessions)
$200   Per School Session (max. 60 minute — up to 1 x 60 minute session)
$2000   Weekly School Rate (max. 5 days — average of up to 180 minutes per day)

Fees for Reading
$175   Session (max. 30 minutes)

Fees for Judging
$400   Whole day (max. 360 minutes)
$250   Half Day (max. 180 minutes)

Travel
Travel costs should be paid, when appropriate, in addition to the above fees.
$110   per day Accommodation (overnight)
$ 45   per day Meals
up to 50c per km Subsidy for use of own car
2–6 hours @ $20 per hour Allowance for travel time
$240 for more than 6 hours' travel time

INDEX

A Decent Proposal 243
A Fortunate Life 30
ABC Books 285
ABC Classic FM 185
ABC Radio 184–5
ABC Radio Drama 184–5, 334
ABC Radio National 184
Aboriginal and Torres Strait Islander
   Unit of Arts 333
   writers 222
Abrams, M. H. 79
Academy of Photogenic Arts 22, 334
Accessible Arts 334
ACT Write 316
ACT Writers' Centre 316, 331
adaptions 256
Addison, Joseph 35
Adelaide Review 316
Adelaide Writers' Week 294
Adelaide, Debra 201
Adele Shelton Smith Award 225
Adobe Acrobat Reader 127
Adobe Pagemill 127
Aduckiewicz, Tony 129
adult fiction 38–47
advances 152–3, 207
Aedon 288
Affordable Assessments 243
Age Book of the Year, *The* 225
agents 149, 162–7, 239–42

AIATSIS Aboriginal Studies Press 285, 353
Airplay 184
AKKA Literary Services 243
Alexander Turnbull Library 179
ALiTrA Journal 110
Allen & Unwin 38, 63, 164, 221, 222, 285
Allsorts 198
All Write 271
ALS Guide to Australian Writers: A Bibliography, 1963–1995 80
Altair 316
Altair–Australia Literary Agency 239
Amazon.com 13
Ambitious Friends 25, 26, 316
America On Line (AOL) Australia 76
Anderson, Don 200
Angel in God's Office — My Wartime Diaries 24
Angels of Russia 125
Angus & Robertson 272
   Bookworld Prize for Fiction 123
Antediluvian Press 356
anthology(ies) 143, 256
   science fiction 124
Anthony Williams Management 239
Antipodean 110, 316
Antithesis 317

Index

AOL (America On Line) Australia 76
APM Training Institute 22, 334
Apple Macintosh 70
Archibald, J. F. 136
Arnold, Matthew 35
Around the Bookshops 282
Art of Self-Promotion: Self-Promotion by Writers, The 180, 193
Article Appraisal Service 243
articles 118–20, 256
　feature 33–4
Arts ACT 300
Arts and Facts: the Arts and Tax 230
Arts Law Centre 150, 162, 230, 334
Arts NT
　Alice Springs 334
　Darwin 334
Arts Queensland 333
Arts South Australia 333
Arts Tasmania 333
Arts Victoria 333
Arts WA 333
ArtsLink 335
artwork 143
　camera-ready 176
　finished 120
Asialink 311, 335
　Literature Residency 224
assessment 243–54
assessor (manuscript) 122
Association of Australian Writing Programs (AAWP) 58, 99, 309, 335
Association of New Zealand Literature 329, 349
Association for the Study of Australian Literature (ASAL) 294
Association of Writers at Work Inc. 335
attachment 77
Auckland University Press 356

Auckland Writers and Readers Festival 300
Aurealis 317
AUSIT (Australian Institute of Interpreters and Translators) 109
　National Newsletter 317
Australasian Drama Studies 317
Australasian Performing Right Association (APRA) 349
Australasian rights 137, 146
Australia Council for the Arts 129, 168, 186, 218–19, 224, 225, 230, 333
　Literature Fund 218
Australian Author 168, 176, 200, 201, 317
Australian Book Fair 214, 294
Australian Book Publishers Association 212
Australian Book Publishers Association Directory of Members 116
Australian Book Review, The 198, 200, 317
Australian Books in Print 116
Australian Bookseller and Publisher 15, 317
Australian Booksellers Association 178, 335
Australian Booksellers Association of Members/Book Distributors in Australia 178
Australian Broadcasting Corporation (ABC) 181, 184
Australian Bush Poets Association 41, 335
Australian Business Number (ABN) 226
Australian Centre for Independent Journalism 335
Australian College of Journalism 22, 105, 335
Australian Copyright Council 156, 157, 159, 336

367

Australian Film Commission (AFC) 182, 223, 336
Australian Film Institute 336
Australian Film Television and Radio School (AFTRS) 48, 336–7
Australian Haiku Anthology 317
Australian Haiku Society 317
Australian Horror Writers 311
Australian Institute of Interpreters and Translators (AUSIT) 109, 316, 337
  National Newsletter 317
Australian Interactive Multimedia Industry Association (AIMIA) 337
Australian Libraries Gateway 87
Australian Literacy Educators' Association 294
Australian Literary Awards and Fellowships 224
Australian Literary Management 165, 239, 321
Australian Literary Studies 317
Australian Literary Translators Association (ALiTrA) 109, 337
Australian literature 213
Australian Media Guide 193
Australian Multicultural Book Review 318
Australian National Playwrights' Centre (ANPC) 50, 183, 337
  National Young Playwrights' Weekend 280
  Script Assessment and Dramaturgy 251
Australian Performing Right Association (APRA) 338
Australian Poetry Catalogue, The 2000 40, 353
Australian Poets' and Writers' Reflections 318
Australian Public Intellectual Network 321

Australian Publishers Association 129, 338
Australian Publishers Bookshow 12, 294
Australian Science Communicators 338
Australian Script Centre 50, 338
Australian Short Stories 118
Australian Society of Certified Practising Accountants 236
Australian Society for Technical Communicators (ASTC) 338–9
Australian Society of Authors 50, 78, 98, 99, 106, 109, 146, 150, 151, 157, 167, 196, 205, 207, 239, 317, 339
Australian Society of Indexers (AusSI) 339
Australian Society of Speculative Fiction Writers 339
Australian Storytelling Guild 339
Australian Studies Centre 32
Australian Taxation Office 226, 230
Australian Theatre for Young People 280
Australian Writer, The 69
Australian Writer's Marketplace, The 116, 117, 198
Australian Writers' Guild (AWG) 48, 50, 98, 99, 154, 155, 181, 182, 225, 328, 339–40
  Assessment Service 251
autobiography 29–31, 256
Autumn Writing Festival 295
Awgie Awards 225
A–Z of Authorship: A Professional Guide 160

backlists 213–14
Bacon, Francis 35
Banjo Award 32, 168
Banknotes 318
Barbalet, Margaret 100

Index

Barbara Mobbs Literary Agency 239
Bardfly Magazine 318
Barkly Regional Community Arts Officer 340
Barnard, Loretta 249
Barrowman, Fergus 357
Bates, Di 247
Baxter, James K. 219
Bean, Glenys 241
Beat Magazine 36
Beer, Diane 247
Belvoir Street Theatre 186
Benchmark Publications Management 285
Bennie, Angela 12
Berne Convention 153
Bertelsmann 11
Between Us 244
Biderman, Abraham H. 168
Big Pond 76
bildungsroman 43
biography 37–8, 256, 353
Blackwell, Sue 129
Blaine, Georgia 123
Blair, Anthony 239
Blanch, Rhonda 241
blank verse 39
Blast 318
Blast Off 271
Blixen, Karen 3
Bloomfield, Lyn 168
Blue Crow Press 322
Blue Dog 318
Blue Pencil 132
blurb 175
Bone People, The 220
Book Doctor 244
Book Publishers Association of New Zealand (BPANZ) Inc. 350
book publishing industry 128–30
Bookbeat 271
Booker Prize 7, 125, 220
Bookman Media Guide 193

bookmarks (websites) 87
book(s)
　costing 174–5
　cover 175
　design 133–4
　illustrators 144–5
　launch(es) 195, 257
　market (local) 13
　multi-volume 173
　parts of 169–73
　production 134
　publisher 147–62
　sales 12
Books and Beyond: the Christchurch Book Festival 300
Books in Print (US) 116
Books North (North Queensland Children's Literature Festival) 280
Booksellers New Zealand 350
Bookshops 177–8
B. R. Whiting Library (Rome) 224
Booranga Writers' Centre 224, 320, 331
Booroondara Writers Festival 295
Boyd, Martin a'Beckett 45
Brandl and Schlesinger 13, 130, 353
Breaksea Productions 290
Brennan, Paul 168, 176
Brett, Lily 68
Briggs, Jean 250
Brisbane Writers' Festival 295
broadband 76
broadcasting 257
Broinowski, Alison 108, 110
Bronze Publishing 356
Brooks, Kirsty 244
Brown's Mart Community Arts 340
Bryson, Fran 239
Bryson Agency 239
Buckham, Richard 185
Bulletin, The 136
Bundaberg Poets Society 324

369

Burton, Ron 6
Bush Press Communications Ltd 290
Business Activity Statement 227
Butler, Richard 248
Byrne, Jennifer 11
Byron Bay Writers' Festival 295

Cabot, Sandra 168
Cactus Publishing 353
Caldwell, Grant 245
Cambridge Grammar of the English Language 80
Cambridge University 224
Cameron Creswell Agency 239
Cameron, Lindy 125
Canberra Centre for Writing 340
Cann, John 240
Cano, Marisa 26
Cape Catley 290
Capote, Truman 7
Carclew Youth Arts Centre 280
Carnivale Literary Festival 295
CD-ROM 75, 80, 173, 180
Central West Writers' Centre 318, 331
   Newsletter 318
Centre for Science Communication 340
Challenge 272
Chanceart Publications 318
chapter
   outline 140
   sample 140
children and youth 56–7
Children's Book Council (of Australia) 55, 99, 324, 340–1
children's book(s) 210, 257
   illustration 56, 144–5
   markets 142–4
   publishers 142–5
Children's Book Week 280
Children's Literature Foundation of New Zealand 55, 350

Child's Book of True Crime, The 207
Chimaera Publications 317, 341
Chisholm Institute 324
Christchurch Arts Festival 300
Christchurch City Libraries 350
Christine Nagel Literary Service 240, 244
CiP (Cataloguing-in-Publication) 169, 170, 171, 174
City Hub, The 36
Claris Home Page 127
Cleary, Jon 197
Clouston, Brian 15
Cohn, Laurel 244
Cokley, John 241, 249
Collins Cobuild English Dictionary, The 79
Collins, Paul 124
Collins, Tom 136
Collison, Kerry 249
Colloquy 318
comedy 258
Comet 272
Commonwealth Writers' Prize 220, 221
community
   radio 185–6
   writing 25–6, 258
Community Broadcasting Association of Australia (CBAA) 186, 341
Community Radio Satellite (ComRadSat) 186
competition guidelines 121, 258
computer 68–71
   Apple Macintosh 70
   courses 74–5
   printers 71–2
   references 87
   software 72–4
Condon, Matt 200
Connect.com 76
Connolly, Margaret 240
Conscious Brain, The 93

content(s) 92–3, 140, 170
contract(s) 89, 92, 134, 149–150, 258
Cook, Brian 247
Coppertales 318
copy editing 72, 94
copyright 151, 152, 153–6, 159, 160, 161, 162, 170
Copyright Act 155, 158, 159, 179
Copyright Agency Limited (CAL) 155, 212, 341
Copyright Licensing Limited (NZ) 155, 212–13, 350
CopyRight Publishing 354
Copywriter's Companion, The 217
copywriters 217
copywriting 6–7, 21–2, 258
Cordite Poetry Review 319
Council of Australian Societies of Editors 341
Countdown 271
courses and workshops 104–6
Courtenay, Bryce 164, 200, 206
cover sheet 137, 139
covering letter 135–8, 165
    for a full length manuscript 138
    for a short work 137
    to agent 166
Creative Crop 244
Creative New Zealand (Arts Council of New Zealand Toi Aotearoa) 31, 209, 211, 219–20, 223, 334
creative non-fiction 32
creative writing 6–7
Creswell, Rosemary 239
Crime Writers' Association of Australia 341
Crime Factory 319
crime writing 258
Cunnane, Mary 241
Cunningham, Sophie 63, 164, 222
Currency Press 13
Curtis Brown (Australia) 240
Cusack, Dymphna 206

Darling, Jenny 165, 240
Darville, Helen 160
David Unaipon Award 222
Davidson, Frank Dalby 43
Davies, Kerry 246
Day of my Delight 45
Day, Marele 64, 88, 180, 193
dB Young Writers' Page 272
deadline(s) 118
Deadpan Press 354
defamation 92, 152
    and obscenity 162
    defamatory material 160
    defamatory statements 92, 132
Dell'oso, Anna Maria 200
Demidenko, Helen 221
Dendy Awards for Australian Short Films 296
Department of Communications, Information Technology and the Arts 208, 209, 211, 333
depreciation 228, 229
design (of a book) 133–4
    and layout 174
desktop-publishing (DTP) 10, 127, 176
    programs 73–4
Dessaix, Robert 32
Detrusa Promotions
    Literary Agency 240
    Manuscript Assessment Service 244
Di Mase, Jacinta 240
Dialogue 259
diary(ies) 23–4
Dickens, Charles 7
dictionary(ies) 259
Dictionary of New Zealand English: New Zealand Words and their Origins, The 79
digital subscriber line (DSL) 76
Dillard, Annie 24
Dinesen, Isak 3
Dingli, Rosanne 248

371

Dinny O'Hearn/SBS Prize for
    Literary Translation 111
*Directory of NZ Book Publishers
    and Distributors, The* 178
Disher, Garry 90
distribution (of books) 125,
    134–5, 177–8
distributor
    book 178
    independent 178
Ditmar Awards 325
Divan 319
Diversity Management 240
Dolly 272
Down South Writers' Festival 296
Dowse, Sara 100
drafting and editing 88–95
dramatis personae 49
Dramatica 49
dramaturgy 183
Dreamtime Alice 32
Drewe, Robert 43
Driftwood Manuscripts 244
Duffy and Snellgrove 130, 354
Dunedin College of Education 223
Dykes, Barbara 80

e-cash 127
edit or die 245
editing 72–3, 88–95, 169, 259
    copy 90, 94
    courses 94
    for content 92–3
    on computer 72–3
    self- 89–90
    structural 90–1
    style 91–2
Editline 252
editor(s) 89, 135, 260
    acquisitions 131
    commissioning 131
    freelance 131
    in-house 131
    magazine 145–7

magazine and journal 119
    managing 131
    professional 132, 133
    publisher's 89, 131–3
    publishing 135
editorial services 95–6
Educational Lending Right 172
    Scheme 211, 346
educational publishers 143–4
Eidolon 319
Eidolon Publications 319
electronic rights 152, 157–8, 260
Electronic/Digital Rights: A Handbook for Authors 157
Eliot, T. S. xv, 39
Ellis, Bob 32, 133
Ellis, Danielle 244
Else, Chris and Barbara 242
email 24, 76–7
Embryo Films 49, 251, 341
Emery, John 227
employment opportunities 216–17
EMPOWA 319
Encore 181
Endacott, Sarah 245
engagé 319
Enisa Hasic 245
envelopes 82
epic 39
Era Publications 286
erotic fiction 260
essay(s) 35–6, 260
Evasion 328
Evening Post, The 198
EveryWrite 245
exercise 83
expenses 227–9
Explore 272
Express Media 349

Facey, Albert 30
Falconer, Delia 44, 64, 91, 192
family history 9, 27–9, 260
Famous Reporter 319

Fantasy 267
Fast Books 175
FAW Manuscript Assessment Service 245
FEAST 296
feature articles 33–4, 260
Fellowship of Australian Writers (FAW) 56, 96, 99, 225, 327, 328, 341–2
fiction (novels and novellas) 43–7, 261
   adult 38–47
Field, Peter 11, 129
film and television production 180–2
Film Victoria 223, 342
Fine Line 150, 193
Fitzpatrick, Adrianne 250
FitzSimons, Peter 207
Five Bells 319
Five Islands Press 13, 130
Five Mile Press, The 286, 354
Flannery, Nelly 241
Flickerfest International Short Film Festival 296
Flood, Sean 199
font 133
food writing 261
formatting 139–40
Fortunate Life, A 30
fountain pen 81
four W 319
Fox, Mem 53
Fox Studios 49
Framemaker 72
Fraser, Morag 30, 36
Fraser, William 200
freelance writing 261
Freeman, Jane 42, 91, 192,
FreeXpresSion 320
Fremantle Arts Centre Press 286, 354
Fresh 328
From Strength to Strength 31
functional writing 6–7, 19–23

Furphy, Joseph 136
Futility and Other Animals 44

Galligan, Amanda 134, 206, 220, 222
Gangan Publishing 354
Gangway 320
Gardiner, Robin 241
Garner, Helen 7, 130
Gee, Margaret 193
Geelong Children's Book Festival 280
Gibbs, Julie 122, 123
Giffin, Michael 247
Gifkins, Michael 241
Ginninderra Press 354
Gleeson, Libby 205
Gleitzman, Morris 55
Glenys Bean Literary Agency 241
Glistening Waters Festival of Storytelling 300
Global Wave 272
Glossary of Literary Terms, A 79
Going Down Swinging 320
Going West Literary Fest 301
Gold, Alan 58, 125, 131
Golden Press (Division of HarperCollins) 286
Golden Relic 125
Golvan Arts Management 240
Golvan, Debbie 240
Good Reading Magazine 198, 320
Goodbye Jerusalem 32, 133
Goodman, Liz 246
Goods and Services Tax (GST) 226, 227
Goulburn Valley Writers Group 326
grammar 261
Grand Days 221
Gray, Robert 38
Greater Glider Productions 286
green office 80–3
Greensmith Books 290

Greer, Germaine 37
Gregory's 216
Grenville, Kate 64
Griggs, Tim 124
GrinSpin 320
Grove Atlantic 12
grunge novel 45
guidelines
   funding 218
   publishers' 143, 145, 148
Guidelines for Publishing in Periodicals 119

half-title page 170
Haigh, Gideon 130
haiku 13, 325
Hall, James 191
Hall, Rodney 46
Halliday, Karen 168
Halstead Press 286
Hamish Hamilton 11
Hand that Signed the Paper, The 221
HarperCollins Publishers 12, 122, 125, 129, 207, 287
   HarperCollins NZ 290
Hathorn, Libby 54, 142
Hazard Press 356
Hazlitt, William 35
Headworx Publishers 356
Heat 108, 320
Heberley, Heather 31
Hecate 320
Hecate Australian Women's Book Review 320
Heiss, Anita 168
Heist 320
Hemming, Suzanne 249
Henderson, Sara 30
Henning Christopher 221
Hetherington, Paul 60
Hewitt, Jackie 240
Heyward, Michael 12, 130
High Five News 272

Highton, Lisa 129
Hildegaard Productions 356
Hill, Jane 130
Hill, Keith 64, 148
HLA Management 240
Hodder Headline Australia 103, 129, 287
Holly Smith Manuscript Appraisal Service 246
Hooper, Chloe 207
Hope, A. D. 197
Horin, Adele 64
horror 267
hotlink 59
Hughes, Annette 239
Hugo Award 325
Huia Publishers 291
Hulme, Keri 8, 220
Hunter Writer 321
Hunter Writers' Centre 321, 331
Hyland House Publishing 287, 354
hyperfiction 58

IAD Press/Jukurrpa Books 287, 355
IBM 70
ICI Young Playwrights Award 268
Ideation 321
Idiom 23 321
illustrators (children's books) 144–5
Illustrators Association of Australia 145, 342
Imago 134, 206, 220, 222
imprint page 142, 170, 172
income
   averaging 229
   for screenwriters 215
   from books 205–15
   from stage productions 215
   sources of 205–30
index(ing) 262
Indigenous writing 262
Indra Publishing 13

Inglis, Fiona 240
Inscape 272
Insearch Language Centre 225, 342
Institute of Chartered Accountants 230
Interactive Press 355
Interactive Publications 246
International Board on Books for Young People (IBBY Australia) 281, 342
International Literary Market Place 167
International PEN Centre 110, 111, 345
international publishers 124–5
internet 13, 75–8, 262
  publishing 125–8
  writing 57–9
Internet Collaboration 49
Internet Service Provider (ISP) 76
Interplay International Festival of Young Playwrights 225, 281
interview(s) 27
  background 84
  preparing for 194–5
  subject 84
  techniques 84–6
  tips 85
  tools 85
  types 84
irrePRESSible Press 287, 355
ISBN (International Standard Book Number) 126, 169, 170, 172–3,
  Agency 172, 342
Island Magazine 321
ISSN (International Standard Serial Number) 173

JAAM 329
Jacket Magazine 58, 321
Jacobyte Books 355
Jaivin, Linda 130

Jane Parkin Editorial and Assessment Services 252
JAS Review of Books 321
Jeltje 52
Jenny Darling and Associates 240
Jetsetter 273
Jill Blewett Playwrights' Award 225
John Reed Books 128
Johnson, Margaret 244
Johnston, Dorothy 100
Jolley, Elizabeth 5
Jones, Evan Lloyd 14
Journal of Australian Studies 321
Journal of New Zealand Literature 198
journalism 7, 9, 32–5, 262
journalists 6
journals 23–4, 316–30
Journals Directory 41, 116, 117, 198, 271
Joussour Poetry Magazine 321
Joyce, James 43
Judah Waten Story Writing Competition 56
June Cann Management 240
Jungowska, Maria 253
Junior Educational Publications 291

K Zone Magazine 273
Kalimat 322
Katharine Susannah Prichard Writers' Centre 342
Katharsis 322
Keesing Studio (Paris) 224
Keneally, Thomas 7, 21
Kennedy, Margaret 241
Kent, Jacqueline 133
Kerry Davies Publishing Services 246
Kevin Palmer Management 240
'kill' fee 120
Kirby, Liat 247
Kite 329

Koala Books 287
Koch, Christopher 221
Kotuku Publishing Ltd 291
KT Publishing 323

Ladybird Books 11
Lamb, Charles 35
Lancaster Publishing 356
Landfall 198, 219, 329
laptop computer 70
Lay, Graeme 253
layout 133, 174
Le Roy, Patricia 125
Learning Media: Te Pou Taki Korero 291
Learning Wheel 246
legal deposit 178–9
Legal Deposit Libraries 303–6
letter(s) 24, 263
libraries 87, 88
    Legal Deposit 303–6
Library and Information Association of NZ Aotearoa (LIANZA) 350
licence
    fees 213
    schemes 212
    copyright 157
Life Stories Manuscript Development Services 246
lighting and ventilation 83
limerick 39
Lindsay, Norman 168
LiNQ 322
Linstead, Hilary 240
Listener, The 198
Listening Room, The 185
literary
    agent(s) 122–3, 149, 150, 162–7, 263
    competitions 120–2
    journals 316–30
    magazines 316–30
    prizes, grants, awards 165, 217–26, 263
    website 307–15
Literary Market Place 116, 239
Literature and Aesthetics 322
literature, Australian 213
Literature Fund (Australia Council) 218, 219
Little Hare Books 288
Liver Cleansing Diet, The 168
Liverpool Migrant Resource Centre 316
Llewellyn, Kate 24
Loane, Sally 11, 205
Lodge, David 162
Lohrey, Amanda 132, 133, 206, 220, 222
Longacre Press 291
longhand 65
Loos, Paul Vander 102
Lord, Gabrielle 88
Lothian Books 288
Lowdown 273
Lumby, Catharine 31
Lynk Manuscript Assessment Service 247
lyrics, song 162

Mabo: a symbol of sharing 199
MacColl, Mary-Rose 95, 105
Macleay College 22, 94, 343
Macmillan Education Australia 288
Macquarie Aboriginal Words 79
Macquarie Australian Dictionary 79
Macquarie Book of Slang in the 90s, The 79
Macquarie Thesaurus, The 79
Magabala Books 13, 288, 355
magazine editor 145–6
magazines and journals 316–30
Magpies Magazine (New Zealand) 55, 282
Mailer, Norman 7
Mallinson Rendel Publishers 291

Index

Maloney, Shane 130
Malouf, David 213
Mansfield, Katherine 5, 6, 35
manuscript(s) 135, 148
   assessment 122, 263
   binding and pagination 140
   book-length 122–5
   synopsis and contents 140
   typing and formatting 139
   unsolicited 13, 42, 122, 165
Manuscript Appraisal Agency 247
Manuscript Assessment Service 97, 247
Mappin, Alf 14
Margaret Connolly & Associates 240
Margaret Kennedy Agency 241
Marigold Enterprises 253
Market Media 247
marketing 128
   guides 117, 193, 263
   of books 134–5
markets
   book 152
   niche 168
Marrwarngang Award 222
Martin, David 197
Masson, Pippa 240
Matthews, Brian 35
Mattoid 130, 322
McDonald, Roger 32
McGauran, Peter 211
McKenna, Neva Clarke 24
McNeill, Pearlie 251
McPhee Gribble 11, 129
McPhee, Hilary 129
McVeity, Jen 193
Meanjin 322
Media Entertainment and Arts Alliance 119, 343
media guides 264
Media Network and Personnel 217, 343
Media Resource Centre 343
Melbourne Fringe 296

Melbourne Poets Union 41, 343
Melbourne Queer Film and Video festival 296
Melbourne Writers' Festival 297
Melbourne Writers' Theatre 251, 343
memoir(s) 31–2, 264
mentorship(s) 106–7
Metaphysical Review, The 322
Methold, Ken 160, 161
Metro Screen 343
microfiche 173
microfilm 173
Micropress Oz 322
Microsoft Frontpage 127
Microsoft Word 72, 127
Midlink Magazine 274
Midnight in Sicily 205
Mildura Wentworth Arts Festival 297
Miles Franklin Award 32, 221
Miller, Patti 30, 37, 246
Mimosa Publications 288
Mobbs, Barbara 239
modem 70, 75–6
Modjeska, Drusilla 43
Montana Medal Prize 31, 223
Montana New Zealand Book Awards 31, 223
Montana Poetry Day 301
Montsalvat National Poetry Festival 297
Moorhouse, Frank 44, 177, 221
moral rights 158–9, 171
Moral Rights 159
More Than Enough: A Memoir 233
Morgan, Robin 160
Moulthrop, Stuart 59
Muller, Laurie 221
multicultural writers 264
multimedia 59–60
   writing 264
multiple submissions 141
Murdoch Books 288
Murdoch, Claire 100, 199

Murison, Barbara 253
Murray-Smith, Stephen 43
Muse 322
Musgrave and Elgara Publications 355
MYOB (Mind Your Own Business) 228

Nagel, Christine 240, 244
National Accreditation Authority for Translators and Interpreters (NAATI) 109, 343–4
National Biography Award 31, 38, 222
National Book Council 60
  Banjo Award 32, 168
National Institute of Dramatic Art 50, 344
  Playwrights' Studio 251
National Library Act 1965 179
National Library of Australia 171, 173, 179, 344
National Library of New Zealand 173, 350
National Library Fellowship 31
National Library Society 350
National Playwrights Conference 183, 297
National Student Film and Video Festival 297
National Young Writers Festival 281
Navigations 322
Nelson Price Milburn 291
Nets NZ 292
New England Review 323
New England Writers' Centre 323, 331
  Newsletter 323
New House Publishers 292
New Writer 323
New York Times 10
New Zealand Association of Literary Agents 241

New Zealand Author, The 151
New Zealand Authors' Fund 209–11, 350
New Zealand Book Council 224, 350
New Zealand Book Editors Association 96
New Zealand Books 198, 199, 329
New Zealand Books in Print 116, 224, 329
New Zealand Children's Book Foundation 55, 351
New Zealand Children's Books in Print 282
New Zealand Children's Illustrators and Authors 145, 351
New Zealand Copyright Council 351
New Zealand Film Commission 182, 351
New Zealand Guild of Storytellers 351
New Zealand History Research Trust Fund 224, 351
New Zealand ISSN Centre 351
New Zealand Poetry Society 351
New Zealand Post Children's Book Awards 223
New Zealand Post Children's Book Festival 283
New Zealand Post Writers and Readers Week 301
New Zealand Reading Association 351
New Zealand Society of Authors 99, 146, 149, 150–1, 167, 351
New Zealand Standard Book Numbering Agency 352
New Zealand Writers Guild 48, 63, 99, 154, 181, 352
Newcastle Poetry Prize 222
News Corporation 12
newsletter(s) 9, 22–3
newspapers 87, 173, 264
Newswrite 323

Next Wave Festival 297
Ng, Lillian 123
Night Letters 32
Nightingale Press 288
Nimrod Literary Consultancy 247
Niski, Marcus 69
Non-Fiction Manuscript Development Service 248
non-fiction writing 23–38
Norman Bilbrough Manuscript Assessments 253
Northern Rivers Writers' Centre 328, 332
Northern Territory University Press
notebook 34–5
novel 43–7
novella 43–7
NRS Training School 345
NSW Film and Television Office 182, 223, 344
NSW Ministry for the Arts 110, 334
NSW Writers' Centre 12, 13, 38, 94, 98, 128, 230, 323, 332
NT Writers' Centre 328, 332
    Manuscript Appraisal Service 248
NT Remote Writers Group 344

obscenity 162
Odgers, Sally 243
Omnibus Books 289
One Talk 274
Online Originals 125
options 214
Orb Speculative Fiction 323
Orbit 271
outline (script) 48
Over the Fence Comedy Film Festival 297
Overland 323
Overland Express 323

OWNWrite (Writers' Group of Older Women's Network) 345
Oxford Australian Writers' Dictionary, The 79
Oxford Book of Australian Essays, The 36
OzAuthors 78
Ozemail 76

Pacific Film and Television 223, 345
page
    contents 170
    half-title 170
    imprint 170
    proofs 134, 191
    title 170
pagination 140
Painter, Gilian 150, 151
Palfreyman, Jane 43, 214
Palmer, Kevin 240
Palmer, Nettie 4
Pan Macmillan 11, 38, 289
paper 81
    recycled 81
Papers: Explorations into Children's Literature 323
papertiger 323
Papyrus Publishing 318
Parliamentary Library NZ 179
Parliamentary Library Qld 286
Parliamentary Library SA 286
Partners in Crime 345
Pascoe, Bruce 118
payment 119, 127–8, 215–16, 265
PCs 70
Pearson 11
    Australia 142
    Education NZ 292
Pemmican Press 357
Pen and Ink Services 252
PEN 345
Pendulum Magazine 323

Penguin Books Australia 11, 103, 123, 124, 129, 289, 292
performance
　poetry 52
　skills 107–8
　writing 47–52
periodicals 117–20
permission fees 152, 156, 160–2, 175
Perth Writers' Festival 298
Phillips, Glen 125, 169
Phippard, Bill 248
Phoebe Publishing 326
photographs
　copyright in 154
　of author 194
Picador 11
Picador Book of the Beach, The 43
Picaro Press 327
pictorial material 120
picture book (children's) 54
Pilgrim at Tinker Creek 24
pitch 135
PixelPapers 324
plagiarism 160, 161
Playbox Theatre Centre 345
Playbox/Asialink Annual Asian-Australian Playwrighting Competition 225
Playhouse 187
Playlab 50, 183, 184, 345
　Script Development Network 251
Playmarket 50, 184, 352
　Script Advisory Service 254
Playworks 50, 183, 346
　Dramaturgy Program 252
Playwrights Association of NZ (PANZ) 352
ПО 9
playwrights, opportunities for 182–4
playwriting 265
　awards 225–6
Poetrix 324

poetry 38–41, 265
　outlets 40
　publishers 353–7
　sprint 52
Poetry New Zealand 198
Poets' Narrator 324
Poets Union 41, 99, 319, 346, 353
Pohutukawa Press 357
Porter, Cole 162
Porter, Dorothy 41, 67
Portrait of the Artist as a Young Man, A 43
postage 82
　return 141
Potter, Christopher 12
Power of One, The 206
Pozzo, Cleo 240, 244
Practical Handbook for Arts Participation in Community Radio, A 186
preliminary pages 133
pre-press 134
pre-publication offer 176
Premier's Literary Awards
　NSW 225
　Qld 225
　Victorian 111, 205
Premier's Translation Prize 110
presenting your work 135–42
Press, The 198
printers 176
printer(s) (computer) 71–2
Professional Editing Services 248
Professional Historians Association of NZ/Aotearoa (PHANZA) 352
Project Gutenberg 13
Prolific Productions 49, 346
promotion
　(of books) 189–201
public domain 156
Public Lending Right (PLR) 172, 265
　Scheme 208–9, 346
public relations material 21

Index

publication stages of 130–5
publicist 180
   working with a 191–2
publicity (of books) 134–5, 191–201
publicity and promotion 179–80
publicity department 135
Publicity Questionnaire (Allen & Unwin) 358–60
Publish It! A Guide for Self-publishers 169
publisher(s) 265
   children's 142–4
   commercial 116, 122, 123
   educational 143–4
   finding the right 123–8
   international 124
publishing 265
   Australian industry 14
   book 128–30
   internet 125–8
Puffin 11
Pulitzer Prize 24
punctuation 261
Purchase, Shirley 79

Quark Xpress 74
Queensland Multicultural Writers' and Arts Friendship Society 346
Queensland New Filmmakers Awards 298
Queensland Theatre Company Writing Program 252
Queensland Writers' Centre 217, 299, 324, 332
   Manuscript Appraisal Service 248
   Newsletter 324
quotations 162

racist language 93
radio
   community 185–6

drama 50–1
   markets 184–7
   New Zealand 282
Radio Drama Mentorship Scheme 186
Radio New Zealand 282, 352
Radio NZ Drama 186, 282
Raftos, Rick 241
Rainbow Books 357
Random House 10, 11, 43, 133, 142, 289, 292
'rap' music 52
rates of payment 119
ratings 48
reader, ideal 8
Reader's Digest (Australia) 216
Readers' World 324
Reading Forum 283
reading(s) 41
   groups 103–4
   habits 66–7
Reading Room, The 132
Reading Time 324
recommended retail price (RRP) 152–3, 175
records, keeping 141
Red Lamp 324
Redemption Blues 125
Redoubt 125, 169, 324
redrafting 94–5
reference work(s) 266–7
Regional Writers' Network 102–3
Registration Number 226
Reid, Barrett 3
Reiter, David 246
rejection 15
   slips 115
   surviving 187
reminder letter 146–7, 148
report(s) 19–21
   annual 20
   writing 267
reportage 32–5
research 28
   genealogical 27

researching 86–8
    your market 115–16
residencies 223–5
résumé 123, 126, 165
reverse title page 170
review copies 180
review(s) 36, 196–201, 267
    bad 199–201
    of self-published works 198–9
RGM Associates 241
Richard Butler Script Consultancy 248
Richards Literary Agency 242
Richards Wallace, Nikki 242
Richards, Ray 242
Rick Raftos Management 241
rights 151–2
    Australasian 137, 146
    moral 158–9, 171
Rimu Publishing 357
Rintoul, Susan 248
Robb, Peter 205
Robert Burns Fellowship 223
Rochester, A. J. 39
Rogers, Anna 252
Roland Harvey Books 289
romance 267
Romance Writers of Australia (RWA) 346
    Australian Chapter of Romance Writers of America 335
Rosanne Dingli Manuscript Assessment Service 248
Rose, Dr Stephen 93
Round Table Writing: A Workbook for Writers Groups 102
royalties 126, 128, 134, 151, 152–3, 163, 205, 206–7, 208, 215, 227, 267
Rushby, Alison 243

SA Writers' Centre 325, 332
    Assessment Service 249

'sale or return' 177, 214
Salusinszky, Imre 36
sample chapters 140
Sandy Wagner Creative Agents 241
Sargeson, Frank 64, 233
Saturday Dominion, The 198
Saturday Night Drama 184, 185
Savage, Georgia 205
Sayer, Mandy 32
Schindler's List 7, 21, 32
Scholastic Australia 289
Scholastic New Zealand Ltd 292
School Journal 283
Schultz, Julianne 32
science fiction 124, 267
Science Fiction: A Review of Speculative Literature 324
Scope Manuscript Services 253
Scott, Rosie 106
Screen Production Academy 346
ScreenWest (Western Australia Film and Television Office) 223, 346
Screenwriter 2000 49
screenwriting 47–50, 267–9
    software 49
script 47, 48, 180–2
    assessment 97, 182, 183, 184
    development 182, 183, 184
    registration service (AWG) 154, 155
Script Clinic 182
scriptwriting 47, 269
Seams of Light: Best Antipodean Essays 36
search engine(s) 77, 315
self-editing 89–93
self-published authors 177
self-publishers 177, 178
self-publishing 93, 115, 167–80, 269
serial publications 173
sex 269
sexist and racist language 92–3
SF Commentary 324

Index

Sharp Axe Publishing 357
Shaw, Patricia 5, 207
Shearers' Motel 32
Shootout, The 299
Shopfront Theatre 281
short story(ies) 42–3, 269
Shorter Oxford Dictionary, The 79
Shortland Publications Ltd 292
Shortz (short story magazine) 325
Sid Harta Publishers Manuscript Appraisal Service 249
SideWaLk 325
Signet 11
Silver Sister 123
Simon & Schuster Australia 289
Simons, Moya 65
Simple Interface 49
Sisters 43
Sisters in Crime 346
Skinner, Rachel 241
slang 269
Small Press Guide 116
Smart, Richard 132
Smith, Holly 246
Society of Book Illustrators 56, 145, 347
Society of Business Communicators 347
Society of Children's Book Writers and Illustrators (SCBWI) 56, 347
Society of Editors 249, 347–8
Society of Literature and Aesthetics 322
Society of Women Writers 42, 99, 307, 348
software 126
Somerset College Celebration of Literature 281, 298
Sonny 177
South Australian Festival Awards 225
South Australian Film Corporation 223, 348

South Coast Writers' Centre 325, 332
  News Sheet 325
Southerly 52, 325
Southern Ocean Review 329
Southern Review 325
Southern Street 206
Southern Write 227, 325
spelling 261
Spelling Made Easy 80
Spender, Dale 93
Spinifex Press 13, 355
Sport 198, 329
St John, Madeleine 221
Steam Engine Time 325
Steele Roberts 357
Stephens, Tony 197
Stephenson, Jim 246
Stephenson, Robert 239
Stone Press 293
Stoneprint Press 293
storytelling 52, 269
  guilds 108
Stott's Correspondence College 348
Stratford, Stephen 253
Street Women Press 357
Strictly Literary 241, 249
structure 90
Studio 325
Style Manual for Authors, Editors and Printers 80
Stylus Poetry Journal 325
submission(s)
  guidelines 118, 124
  multiple 141
subscription publishing 176
Subverse: Queensland Poetry Festival 298
Such is Life 136
Sunday Star-Times Bruce Mason Playwright's Award 223, 226
Sunday Star-Times, The 198
Support for the Arts Handbook (Australia Council) 219

383

Suzanne Hemming Editorial Services 249
Swag of Yarns 326
Swallowing Clouds 123
Swyntax 326
Sydney Gay and Lesbian Mardi Gras 298
Sydney Writers' Festival 298
synopsis 140

Tabakoff, Jenny 68
Tabernaberri, Elisa xvi, 25, 26
Takahe Magazine 198, 329
Talbot, Norman 247
Talespinner 55, 283
Tamba 326
Taranaki Arts Festival 301
Tasmanian Poetry Festival 298
Tasmanian Writers' Centre 326, 332
    Manuscript Assessment Service 250
    Newsletter 326
Tasmanian Writers' Festival 299
Tauranga Arts Festival 301
tax 269
    deductions 226–30
    records 227–8
Tax and Writers 230
Te Taa Haeretahi 357
Teague, Loren 252
technical writing 6–7
teenage market 269
television writing 181
Text 58, 326
text box 174
Text Publishing 12, 130, 131
TFS (Total Fiction Services)
    Literary Agency 242
    Assessment Service 253
thesaurus(es) 259
Thomas, Constance 80
Thompson, Hunter S. 7
Thorny Devil Press 355

Thorpe, D. W. 169, 172, 224
Tikos, Bill 240
Tirra Lirra 326
title
    of article or short story 119
    page 137–9, 170
Too Good to Miss 283
Touchdown 271
trade publishers 142
translation 108–11
Transworld Publishers (Australia) 11, 103
Tranter, John 58, 125
Tranter, Lyn 239
travel writing 6, 34–5, 269
treatment(s) 48
Tropfest 299
Turbine 329
TV New Zealand 181
24 Hours 184
2BBB 185
2MCE 185
2NUR 185
2RES 186
2SER 185, 186
typewriters 65
typing and formatting 139–40
Tyrone Guthrie Centre 224

Ulitarra 108
Ulrich's Periodicals Guide 116
Universal Copyright Convention 153
University
    of Auckland 223
    of Canberra 324
    of Canterbury 223
    of Central Queensland 321
    Charles Sturt 22, 319, 327
    Deakin 322, 323, 326
    Griffith 326
    James Cook 322
    of Melbourne 317, 319, 211, 326

Monash 318
New England 323
NSW 326
of Otago 223, 329
of Queensland Press 221, 290, 317, 320, 348, 356
of Southern Queensland 318
of Sydney 322, 325
of Technology (Curtin) 321
of Technology (Queensland) 319
of Technology (Sydney) 225, 348
of Waikato 223
of Western Australia 223, 290, 324, 327
Unsweetened 326

Valley Micropress 329
Valvana Publishing House 356
vanity
   publishers 168, 176
   publishing 121, 167–8, 175, 176
Varuna Writers' Centre 224, 326, 332
   Newsletter 326
Verandah 326
Vernacular 326
Vesterberg, Bernt 243
Victoria University Press 357
Victorian Federation of Community Writing Groups 348
Victorian Premier's Literary Awards 111, 205
Victorian Writers' Centre 328, 332
   Assessment Service 250
*Viewpoin*t 55, 326
Viking 11
Vintage 103
Vision Science Fiction, Fantasy and Horror Group 349
Vogel Award (*The Australian/Vogel Literary Award*) 45, 221
Voices 133
Voices on the Coast Youth Literature Festival 282
Voiceworks 56, 274

WA Gay and Lesbian Film Festival 299
WA State Literature Centre 327, 332
   Newsletter 327
Wagga Wagga Writers Writers Newsletter 327
Wagner, Sandy 241
Wagtail 327
Waiatarua Publishing 293
Waikato Children's Literature Association 352
waiver 159
Wakabayashi, Judy 110
Wakefield Press 356
Waldren, Murray 90, 221
Wallace, Christine 35
Wallace-Crabbe, Chris 35
Walleah Press 319
Waltzing Matilda Bush Poetry Championship 299
Wannabee Publsihing 250
Warburton Film Festival 299
Waterlily: Blue Mountains Journal 22
Weather Permitting 28
Webby, Elizabeth 233
website
   Aboriginal 307
   Australian arts 307
   Australian studies 307
   author sites 307–8
   bookshops 308
   children and young writers 308
   competitions 309
   copyright 309

dictionaries and thesauruses 309
editing 309
encyclopaedias 310
folklore and mythology 310
genealogy 310
grammar 310
illustrators 310
libraries 310
literary 307–15
marketplaces 310
online books 311
poetry 311
publishers 311
quotations 312
review sites 312
science fiction and fantasy 312
screenwriters and playwrights 312
search engines 315
Shakespeare 313
songwriting 313
style manuals 313
women writers 313
writing and illustrating books for children and young adults 313
writing groups 313
writing resources 313
your own 127, 195–6
Weekend Australian, The 90, 198
Weekend New Zealand Herald, The 198
Weekly Book Newsletter 113, 327
Well Read 55, 283
Wellington Children's Book Association 55, 352
Wendy Pye Ltd 293
Westerly 327
Western Australian Screen Awards 299
Western Word 327
Whitakers (UK) 116
White Gloves National Film Festival 200

Whitehorse Manningham Regional Library Corporation 56
Whitford, Meredith 244
Whitton, Rhonda 243, 248
Who's Who of Australian Writers 80
Wilding, Michael 42, 67, 118, 187
Williams, Anthony 239
Williams, Christopher 49
Wilton, Deborah 63
Windows XP 76
Winedark Sea 327
Witch Words 250
Wolfe, Tom 7
Women in Film and Television 349
Women in Publishing 349
Women's Book Weekend 301
women's writing 269
Woolf, Virginia 35
Woolfe, Sue 43, 64, 221
Woolley, Pat 327
Woorilla 327
word count 54, 119
Word Festival Canberra 300
Word of Mouth Writers Festival 300
word processor 65, 70
word-processing programs 72
Workaway Guide, The 168
Working Press 290
Working Title 250
workshops 104–6
World of My Past, The 168
World Book Day Aotearoa 301
World Wide Web 75, 76, 77–8, 87
Wright, Viki 246
Wright Write 253
Write Edit Print: Style Manual for Aotearoa New Zealand 80
Write Now 330
Write On 63, 164, 165, 222, 328
Write Stuff 328
Write Turn 328
Write Up 63, 64, 148

Writer Writer 328
writer-illustrators 143
Writer's Bookcase 349
Writer's Friend 328
writer's library 78–80
Writer's Voice 328
Writers and Copyright 156
Writers and Tax 230
writers'
   expenses 227–9
   groups 100–3, 270
   income 226–7
   rates 266, 361–5
Writers' and Artists' Yearbook 116, 167, 239
Writers' Centre(s) 97–8, 331–2
Writers' Cottage, The 349
writing
   as a career 203–330
   as therapy 26
   courses 270
   for children 52–5, 257
   for the stage 47–50

   functional 19–23
   habits 64
   television and film 47–50
Writing for Success 328
Writing Matters 251
Writing Your Life: A Journey of Discovery 30, 37
WriteSpot Publishers International 250
Wyndham, Susan 12
Wynne Tara 240

Yaddo Artists' Colony (NY) 224
youth
   festivals, workshops and organisations 280–2, 283–4
   publications 271–4, 282–3
   writing awards and competitions 274–80
Youngstreet Poets 349
Yuanxiang (*Otherland*) 328

zines 57–8